Tunnelling Commander
on the Western Front

Tunnelling Commander on the Western Front

Major Alexander Sanderson DSO, MC & Bar in Two World Wars

Myles Sanderson

FRONTLINE BOOKS

First published in Great Britain in 2024 by
Frontline Books
An imprint of Pen & Sword Books Limited
Yorkshire – Philadelphia

Copyright © Myles Sanderson 2024

ISBN 978 1 39908 887 9

The right of Myles Sanderson to be identified as
Author of this Work has been asserted by him in accordance
with the Copyright, Designs and Patents Act 1988.

A CIP catalogue record for this book is
available from the British Library

All rights reserved. No part of this book may be reproduced or
transmitted in any form or by any means, electronic or mechanical
including photocopying, recording or by any information storage and
retrieval system, without permission from the Publisher in writing.

Typeset by Mac Style
Printed in the UK by CPI Group (UK) Ltd, Croydon, CR0 4YY.

Pen & Sword Books Limited incorporates the imprints of After the Battle, Atlas, Archaeology, Aviation, Discovery, Family History, Fiction, History, Maritime, Military, Military Classics, Politics, Select, Transport, True Crime, Air World, Frontline Publishing, Leo Cooper, Remember When, Seaforth Publishing, The Praetorian Press, Wharncliffe Local History, Wharncliffe Transport, Wharncliffe True Crime and White Owl.

For a complete list of Pen & Sword titles please contact

PEN & SWORD BOOKS LIMITED
47 Church Street, Barnsley, South Yorkshire, S70 2AS, England
E-mail: enquiries@pen-and-sword.co.uk
Website: www.pen-and-sword.co.uk
or
PEN AND SWORD BOOKS
1950 Lawrence Road, Havertown, PA 19083, USA
E-mail: uspen-and-sword@casematepublishers.com
Website: www.penandswordbooks.com

Contents

The Colonel and the Tunneller   vii
Introduction and Acknowledgements   ix
Abbreviations   xiii

Part One: 1756–1890   1

Chapter 1   Engineers, Surveyors and Tunnellers   3

Part Two: 1891–1914   9

Chapter 2   A New life in West Australia   11

Chapter 3   Success and Tragedy   26

Chapter 4   Student to Mining Engineer   30

Part Three: The First World War, 1915–1918   41

Chapter 5   Enlistment in the Mining Corps   43

Chapter 6   Arrival: Mining Corps   53

Chapter 7   Into, and Under, the Front Lines   62

Chapter 8   Battle of Fromelles   72

Chapter 9   Sanderson Takes Command   112

Chapter 10   3rd Australian Tunnelling Company under Hill 70   120

Chapter 11   Underground War Intensifies   129

Chapter 12   Battle of Arras   141

Chapter 13   Allied Mining Raid on Hill 70   151

Chapter 14	Canadian Assault on Hill 70	161
Chapter 15	Hythe Tunnel Fortress, Hill 70	171
Chapter 16	The *Kaiserschlacht*	185
Chapter 17	The Battle of Lys	192
Chapter 18	The Allied Counter-Offensive	200
Chapter 19	Defusing Traps and Mines	209
Chapter 20	The Armistice and Repatriation	213

Part Four: Post First World War and the Second World War — 219

Chapter 21	To England and Marriage	221

Commonwealth Engineer Units' Honour Rolls	231
Postscript	243
Australian War Museum Exhibits	245
Author's Note	246
Notes	247
Bibliography and Sources	263
Index	266

The Colonel and the Tunneller

1. The Colonel and the Tunneller
   Were strolling up the line,
   They cursed like anything to see
   A bursting five point nine;
   'These damned things should be stopped,' they said,
   And then it would be fine.'

2. *'Oh! Colonel dear'* the Tunneller said
   *'I really think we might
   Take shelter here, a tunnel deep
   Leads downward on your right,
   With forty feet of head cover.'*
   The Colonel answered: *'Quite.'*

3. And then he talked of Aeroplanes,
   And whether shrapnel stings,
   Of Gas, and Girls, of Dugouts, Duds,
   And whether bombs have wings,
   The Tunneller said nothing but
   'I hates the bloody things.'

4. *'If forty Huns with forty Guns
   Strafed you with five point nines
   Do you suppose,'* the Tunneller said,
   'They'd chase you from your lines?'
   'Lord bless you! No!' the Colonel said,
   'We'd shelter in your Mines!'

5. *'But Cherrio! My Boy,'* he said,
   *'Now that the Strafe is done,
   I think I'll push along a bit,
   We always mess at one.
   Drop in and dine with us one night.'*

But answer came there none,
And this was scarcely odd because,
The Tunneller had gone!¹

Composed in the Hythe Tunnel, Loos, by Lieutenant D'Arcy Wentworth, 3 Australian Tunnelling Company, July 1918

Introduction and Acknowledgements

My grandfather, Alexander Sanderson, was 19 years old in 1901 when Queen Victoria died. Alexander, known as 'Alex', kept a full and detailed documentation of his days as an engineering student in Western Australia (W.A.), including Charles Yelverton O'Connor's original plans for Fremantle Harbour and the Goldfield pipeline, a rare portrait photograph of C.Y. O'Connor, his own student notebook, and many technical documents and booklets relating to construction work in the early days of the colony.

The Battye Library in Perth, W.A. have preserved documentation on Alex's Kimberley explorations, kindly locating eight original photographs taken during his 1915 expedition. I am most fortunate to have a copy of the original 2-inch spool tape-recording made by Miss Molly F.L. Lukis, the First State Archivist of the Battye Library, who came to Beckenham, London in 1967 to interview Alex about his life. Included in this book are annotated transcripts of that interview, giving a further dimension and vitality to his story. (I hold the copyright to this recording.) The original transcript by the Battye Library omitted many important details of the interview which I have since re-transcribed more fully, after a sound-recording studio improved the sound.

When the Armistice finally arrived in November 1918, the fortunate survivors often found words inadequate to describe their overwhelming experiences. They felt that people at home were unreceptive to their stories or could not perceive what they had been through. In 1967, when my grandfather was persuaded by the Battye Library to give his long interview about his life, it mainly concerned his early life in Western Australia; discussions of his experiences on the Western Front were limited to his arrival in Hazebrouck in May 1916.

I am fortunate also to have the copious notes made by the Australian war historian C.E.W. Bean at Noeux-les-Mines on 23 February 1918 when he visited the 3rd Australian Tunnelling Company and took down, in shorthand, Alex's account of his company's tunnelling activities. This original report, a copy of which was given to Alex by Charles Bean, forms an important part of my family archives and this story. Alex's family archives also include an original pencil sketch drawn by Bean of the Fromelles battlefield, which he sent to Alex and requested that he modify, as well as two personal letters from Bean requesting clarification of the details of the battle.

Alex left many original photographs of his fellow officers and himself, as well as detailed correspondence from his wartime life. Surviving today are copies of the many personal letters he wrote to relatives of his soldiers who died during the war, meticulous details of each death and burial details of the Australian tunnellers in his company, as well as a variety of maps, plans, and aerial photographs. Alex retained a thick file of original instructions, mining notes and diagrams from the Controller and the Inspector of Mines. The detailed records maintained by Alex, both before and after taking command, and his preservation of those records, are the basis for much of what is written here concerning that period of his life. Recently, our family found Alex's meticulous repair ledger for bomb damage repairs to London Transport's underground stations, depots and tunnels in the Second World War, when he was based in South Kensington underground station. (My interview about this can be viewed in Series 3, Episode 2 of 'Secrets of the London Underground', on I.T.V.)

I am grateful to the Australian War Museum in Canberra for preserving his other personal notebooks, letters, photographs and files.

I have quoted extensively from the online Australian War Museum's 3rd Australian War Diaries, Appendices and Mining Notes; originals of many of these were preserved by Alex in his own archives.

As I researched my grandfather's life and discovered the long-forgotten archives stored at various locations by my family, it became evident that here was a man whose life story could not be condensed into the three short years of wartime. From his birth in New Zealand, to his family's move in 1891 to Western Australia, his training in Perth with C.Y. O'Connor (a fellow New Zealander and Western Australia's chief engineer in the late nineteenth and early twentieth centuries), his involvement with gold mining at Kalgoorlie as a land surveyor and civil engineer, to his ambitions to develop land in the Kimberley, his life was full and diverse. The First World War was to dramatically and swiftly change the direction his life. Alex enlisted and sailed for the European theatre of war with the Australian Mining Corps. He assumed command of the 3rd Australian Tunnelling Company when his good friend, and the original unit commander, Major Leslie 'Jack' Coulter, was killed in action on a raid.

Although aware of my grandfather's distinguished military career, I had few occasions to meet him. My father was posted abroad on Her Majesty's Service as a soldier and diplomat from my birth until I left for university at 18. At family occasions, Alex stood apart, quiet and observant, always smartly dressed in a suit and tie.

Aged 15, I interviewed my grandfather about his life on a small reel-to-reel tape recorder, sadly later stolen. I do recall talking to him on two other occasions. On the first, Alex described how a fellow student flicked the ink from his pen over Alex's neatly produced drawings; he rose and took the offender's inkwell, tipped the contents on top of his head and slowly rubbed the ink in. Here was a man, I thought, who does not take offence lightly. On the second occasion, I sat down next to him on a sofa in his architect son's 400-year-old family barn. He must have been 88 years old, near the end of his life. I was 18.

'See up there', he said, pointing to a metal bar spanning the width of the old barn, 'I could calculate in my head all the forces along that rod.' With the benefit of hindsight, I have many questions that I could have asked Alex on the sofa that day, especially about the Battle of Fromelles.

I must acknowledge the advice and help of the author Damien Finlayson who has offered me further insight into the history of the tunnelling companies, both from meeting on the Fromelles battlefield and through his excellent book, *Crumps and Camouflets*. Thanks are due also to the helpful authors Paul Cobb and Peter Barton. Peter gave me valuable advice and extensive German sources by email, while Andy Prada and the members of the Durand Group, who have produced several films on their explorations of tunnels, kindly welcomed me into their underground sites; in the Hulluch Tunnel they showed me a sliding tunnel door with loophole that my grandfather had designed and installed. Alex would have been surprised to learn that one day his grandson and great-grandsons would walk through the chalk Copse and Hulluch tunnels and peer inside the collapsed end of the Hythe Tunnel.

It was a pleasure to converse with Jim Henry, the son of Major James 'Lollylegs' Henry D.S.O. M.B.E., O.C. of the 1st Australian Tunnelling Company, who informed me that 'my father invited your grandfather up to Messines to witness the firing of the Hill 60 mines'. In Perth W.A. Fred Shelley, nephew of Major Edric Noel Mulligan D.S.O., Croix de Guerre MiD, the O.C. of the 2nd Australian Tunnelling Company, was most informative on the early years of the colony. Mulligan steadfastly commanded his company throughout the war but the wartime mental strain on his nerves sadly blighted his life back in Australia.

I am very grateful to the Dean and Chapter of St Paul's Cathedral for their generous permission to publish the wonderful Tunnellers' Fallen scrolls they have preserved so well and for the kindness of the vergers in giving me access to the Kitchener's Chapel. I am also grateful to the helpful Arras History Archives staff for permission to reproduce a watercolour by a German war artist.

I acknowledge especially the dedicated creators of the Australian tunnellers' descendants' website tunnellers.net (the determined and energetic historians Donna Baldey and John Reading) from whom, over two decades, I have received a wealth of source materials and information. In 2010 I met John to carry out research together in Perth and Kalgoorlie where we met fellow descendants of tunnellers. The accounts of individual sappers (Italian *Zappa:* a 'spade') quoted here are the fruit of years of research by this Queensland team, in contact with literally hundreds of descendants of tunnellers who have generously passed on their family archives and recollections. We are grateful to Maxence Druelle and Philippe Clerbout for their dedication in creating a unique memorial site; a reflective gathering place on days of commemoration for current and future generations to contemplate the endeavours and sacrifices of those who went before.

This is a story that, at its heart and historically, revolves around technology and engineering. It is by nature a patriotic story because patriotism was the spirit of the age.

When Alex arrived in France in 1916, he had never seen an aeroplane. The first aircraft from Europe would land on the continent of Australia in December 1919, two weeks before Alex embarked for 'Dear Old Australia', aboard the *Runic* from Liverpool as O.C. troops on 23 December. Alex's troopship was the very last Australian transport of the 137 ships on the 176 voyages undertaken to repatriate Australian troops. They were virtually the last A.I.F. men out of Northern Europe.[1]

Abbreviations

3 A.T.C.	3rd Australian Tunnelling Company
A.E.F.	American Expeditionary Force
A.E. & M.M. & B.C.	Australian Electrical & Mechanical Mining & Boring Company
A.I.F.	Australian Imperial Force
A.M.F.	Australian Mechanical Force
A.N.Z.A.C.	Australian and New Zealand Army Corps
A.W.M.	Australian War Museum
A.W.O.L.	Absent without leave
B.B. & C.I.R.	Bombay, Baroda and Central India Railway
Bar (to a medal)	Second Similar Medal
B.E.F.	British Expeditionary Force
B.R.D.	Bavarian Reserve Infantry Division
B.T.	British Time
Bund	German Archive File
CB/AS	Charles Bean and Alex Sanderson's 1918 interview
C.C.S.	Casualty Clearing Station
C.E.F.	Canadian Expeditionary Force
C-in-C	Commander in Chief
C.M.G.	Companion of the Order of St. Michael and St. George
C.O.	Commanding Officer
C. of M.	Controller of Mines
Coy.	Company
C.Y.	Charles Yelverton (O'Connor)
G.O.C.	General Officer Commanding
D.C.M.	Distinguished Conduct Medal
D.S.O.	Distinguished Service Medal
D.L.I.	Durham Light Infantry
F.F.F.	Forlorn, Famished and Far from home
G.I.P.R.	Great Indian Peninsula Railway
H.M.A.T.	His Majesty's Australian Transport
H.M.A.S.	His Majesty's Australian Ship

H.Q.	Headquarters
I. of M.	Inspector of Mines
L.G.	Listening Gallery
M.C.	Military Cross
M.G.	Machine Gun
M.i.D.	Mentioned in Despatches
M.M.	Military Medal
N.C.O.	Non Commissioned Officer
N.S.W.	New South Wales
O.B.E.	Order of the British Empire
O.C.	Officer Commanding
O.H.L.	German High Command (Oberste Heeresleitung)
O.P.	Observation Post
O.R.	Other Rank
P.O.W.	Prisoner of War
P.W.D.	Public Works Department
Qld.	Queensland
R.A.E.	Royal Australian Engineers
R.A.F.	Royal Air Force
R.E.	Royal Engineers
R.F.C.	Royal Flying Corps (until 1 April 1918)
R.I.B.	Reserve Infanterie Brigade (Bavarian)
R.I.R.	Reserve Infanterie Regiment
R.S.M.	Regimental Sergeant Major
S.A.S.	Special Air Service
SM	Stadtarchiv München (Munich State Archives)
S.T.O.V.L.	Short Take-off Vertical Landing
Tas.	Tasmania
V.C.	Victoria Cross Medal
Vic.	Victoria
W.A.	Western Australia

Part One
1756–1890

Chapter 1

Engineers, Surveyors and Tunnellers

Scotland, England, India, New Zealand

The Sanderson 'MacDonnell' Clan

The history of Major Alex Sanderson's forebears has its origins among the Clan MacDonnell of Glenngarry, on the west coast of Scotland. The family name is of Norwegian origin. The MacDonnell war cry was *Creagan an fhithichnx* (the raven's rock) and the family names were Alexander, Lauchlan and Sanderson.

Major Alex Sanderson's great-great-grandfather was William Sanderson, a watchmaker born in 1756. William had been taught his trade by his uncle Henry at his shop 'The Dial and Sun' in the Strand, London. After his apprenticeship, William started his own watchmaking business in Doncaster. On his death in 1805, his widow, Mary, was selected by Earl Fitzwilliam of Wentworth Woodhouse, one of the largest private residences in England, as a gentlewoman for the countess and governess to her son, Lord Milton. The Fitzwilliams' land straddled the rich Barnsley coal seam; their coal mines were safe and the villagers' living conditions were among the best in Britain.

Tunnelling proposals in Yorkshire

Mary's son Henry became the earl's estate surveyor, later carrying out surveys for canals and turnpike roads, the primary method of transport before the railways. Henry became a surveyor of early railway lines, laying out the routes from London to Brighton and Doncaster to York. He proved a precise and adept surveyor of tunnels, and his Australian great-grandson Alex would carry on this tradition on the Western Front.

In May 1830 when a railway project was proposed to extend the Sheffield and Peak Forest project to meet the Liverpool and Manchester Railway, Henry Sanderson provided a rough sketch of several possible routes. Later: 'In the Cutler's Hall in Sheffield the capital was fixed at £600,000… George and Robert Stephenson were appointed the Engineers… Henry Sanderson was selected to take the levels and prepare the Parliamentary Sections.'[1]

Henry Sanderson would have his differences with George Stephenson, believing his plans to be unsound. He was: 'concerned at the amount of tunnelling, 6½ miles, and the inclined planes proposed by Stephenson on a route with an inclination of 1 in 99, on the western side of the summit, and of 1 in 78 on the eastern.' Henry proposed an alternative route, with 2 miles less tunnelling and less steep inclinations: 'which, with mean inclinations of 1 in 135 and 1 in 100 to attain the summit level, could be wholly worked by locomotives.'[2]

Henry was 'particularly destructive in his comments on Stephenson's calculations', declaring that:

> the engineer of the wonderful Liverpool and Manchester Railway, who has had the good fortune to be suffered to spend a million of money thereon… writes nonsense…Mr Stephenson at first estimated the Hathersage tunnel at £15 per yard, yet afterwards reduced it to £10. Let us now make a simple calculation by comparison with any existing work of equal magnitude. We have no instance of so long a tunnel through similar strata. The nearest in length is the Huddersfield Canal tunnel of 2¾ miles. It required a long term of 17 years, and the sum of £130,000 for its completion. Mr Stephenson's estimate of the Hathersage tunnel is only £55,000, to be completed in a quarter of the time![3]

With such criticisms, the project for a Sheffield and Manchester Railway was eventually abandoned in 1833, 'hampered by the forbidding Pennine Ridge'.[4]

In 1847 Henry published detailed plans to renovate the entire crumbling London sewer system, whole sections of which were hundreds of years old. His proposals for a completely new sewerage system beneath the capital's streets illustrate Victorian engineers' self-confidence in robust construction. 'The material proposed is Cast Iron: the form, upright sides, with a segmental roof and concave bed: the capacity 60 square feet increasing to 75 at the lower end. The fall producing a velocity of 30 inches per second when half full: 7 million cubic feet would be discharged in 24 hours.'[5]

Henry Sanderson died suddenly in 1849 and it was not until 1860 that the great Victorian engineer Bazalgette commenced his successful rebuilding of London's sewers. Henry would have been fascinated to know that his great-grandson Alex would, almost a century later, be based under these very same London streets, overseeing repairs to the network of underground passenger tunnels, bombed by enemy flying machines.

Five of Henry's sons pursued their father's surveying career: Alexander and William surveyed for Robert Stephenson in England and India, while Charles surveyed the Great Western Railway under Isambard Kingdom Brunel. Brunel was Vice-President of the Institute of Civil Engineers while his friend (and rival), Robert Stephenson was President. The I.C.E. records fully outline Charles' life and engineering career:

> Mr Charles Sanderson was born in Sheffield in July 1824. He was the third son of Mr Henry Sanderson, Engineering Surveyor to Lord Fitzwilliam and a man of remarkable mental capacity. When Mr C. Sanderson had prepared a scheme for the drainage of London, Lord Fitzwilliam, in a letter, wrote to recommend him to one of the Commissioners for Metropolitan Drainage: 'If the author has inherited the abilities of his father, who was in my employ, I am sure that anything he suggests will be worthy of consideration.'
>
> At the early age of 16, Charles executed a map of the country 10 miles around Reading. In 1844, aged 20, engineering work was offered to him on the Great Western Railway, under the direction of Mr Brunel, in every department of engineering construction.

Only one of Henry's eight sons died in England. Alexander, Charles and William died in India, while Edmund, John and Henry Junior emigrated to Australia, where Henry Junior surveyed the Brisbane River area of Morton Bay (the previous name of Queensland).

Half a century later, in 1897, aged 16, Alex Sanderson would excel as one of the select group of engineering cadets under the direction of Western Australia's Engineer-in-Chief, gaining the highest marks in Perth's Public Works Department exams. In 1916, aged 34, having inherited Henry Sanderson's eye for technical detail and surveying skills, Alex would be appointed the technical expert of the Australian Mining Corps and sent to the Western Front. Here he would complete very accurate surveys of his company's fighting tunnels, using only an ordinary 4-inch land-surveying theodolite. Alex's precise measurements of bearings and distance, helped by his sappers' directional listening skills, would enable the Australians to outmanoeuvre the enemy underground, steering them towards galleries where they could be blown up and destroyed.

Alexander Sanderson

Henry's son, Alexander (Major Alex's grandfather), had joined the Royal Navy in 1840 aged 14 as a midshipman and remained at sea until he was 17. Alexander was involved for a decade in the surveying and construction of Portland Harbour's breakwater at Weymouth, one of Victorian Britain's greatest engineering feats. Fifty years later, in Western Australia, Alex would survey the quarry railway line that transported his huge granite blocks for the breakwater north mole of Fremantle Harbour, Perth.

Alexander married a fisherman's daughter, Susan, from Weymouth, where Alex's father William had been born in 1859. Sanderson family life changed dramatically when Alexander obtained a position as Chief Surveyor on the G.I.P.R. (Great Indian Peninsula Railway), through the influence of his brother William.

With the Government of India Act of 1858, the Raj began its British administration of India, destined to last until 1947. The Sanderson family were present in India at the beginning of the Raj, and almost to the end of the Viceroy.

In December 1858, four months after the Raj took over from the East India Company, Alexander sailed for Bombay to take up his new post. Susan departed later with her children to join her husband. Alexander's brother Charles had been appointed, also by Robert Stephenson, as the Chief Engineer of the B.B. & C.I.R. (Bombay, Baroda and Central India Railway).

At this time, Britain saw itself at the vanguard of progress, with its pre-eminence in the scientific advancement of railways, steam ships and the electric telegraph. As the first industrial nation: 'it identified itself as the banner-bearer of civilisation, destined to transform the world for the better and gifted with a powerful sense of national destiny.'[6]

However, aged only 34, Alexander was bitten by a mosquito and died of 'jungle fever' (malaria) at Asserghur Fortress in 1860. Susan and her children journeyed back to Bombay by sedan chair:

> with lighted torches by night, and carried by faithful sepoys. It was a terrifying journey with India still in a state of unrest and mutiny. For safety, Susan carried a revolver for her family's protection. She was terrified of the thing but whenever the Indians appeared to question her instructions, she would point her unloaded revolver at them, as if she was preparing to shoot.

On the ship back to England in 1861, Susan met a carpenter, veteran Sergeant Major Samuel Corrigan, who had fought in the 1854 Crimean War. In 1863, the couple departed aboard the *Captain Cook* for a new life in New Zealand, accompanied by Susan's four children, including Major Alex's father William. It was a very rough passage that involved sailing through frequent gales, a destructive hurricane and past many large icebergs. After 118 days at sea, and an epidemic that killed eleven passengers, they reached Lyttelton in South Island.

Engineers, Surveyors and Tunnellers 7

Map 1: **New Zealand at the time of Alexander Sanderson**

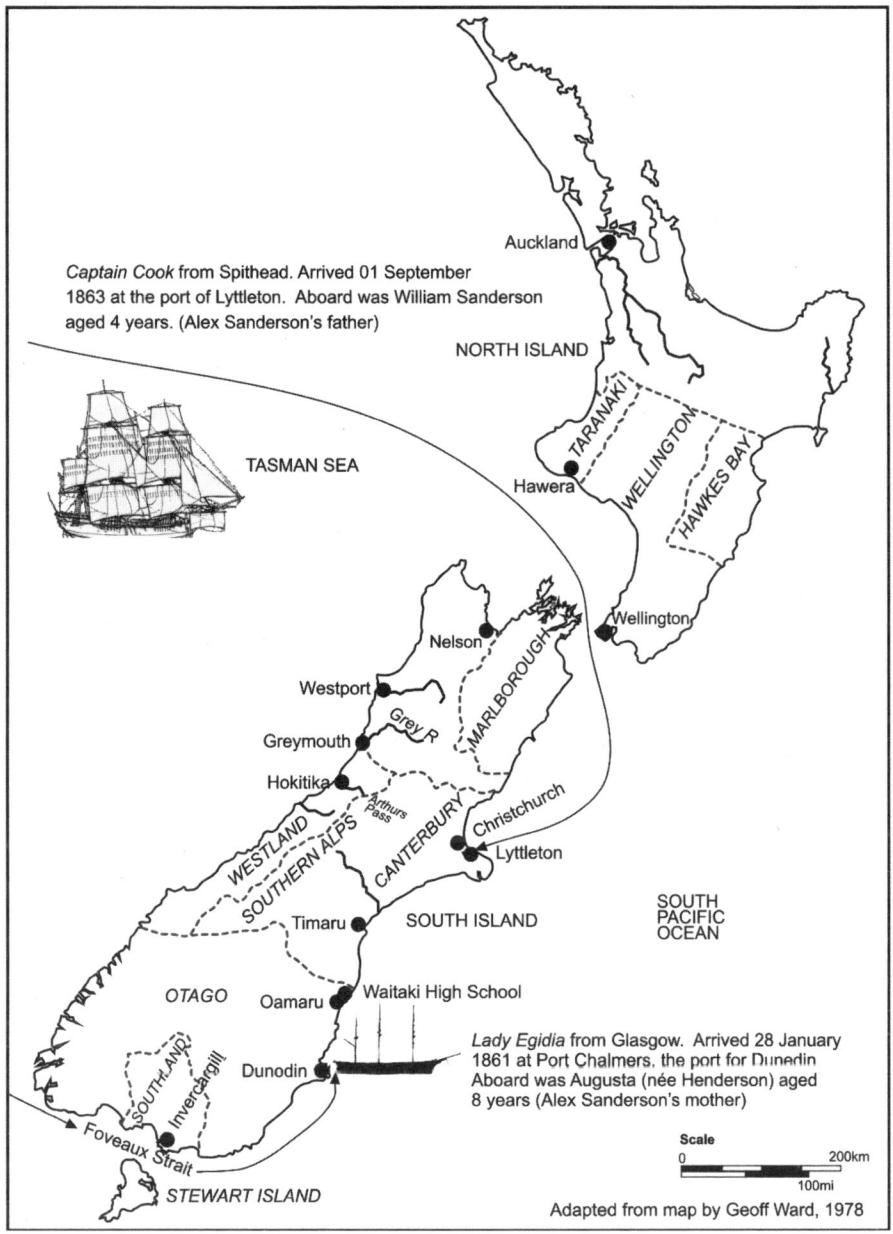

Adapted from map by Geoff Ward, 1978

Augusta Henderson

Major Alex's mother, Augusta Henderson, was born in Edinburgh in 1852. Her widowed mother could not afford to care for her youngest daughter and gave her up for adoption to a childless couple. In 1860, aged 7, Augusta and her new family set sail from the Clyde for New Zealand aboard the *Lady Egidia*. It was a horrendous 107-day voyage through stormy seas, with the tragic deaths of thirty children and two adults. Before the ship safely anchored off Port Chalmers in the Otago province of South Island, the passengers had suffered greatly from the fear of disease, the waves surging over the decks, the squalls that frequently brought down the sails and from increasing thirst and hunger.

Augusta's adoptive parents were kind and hard working, so the family thrived, although life was harsh and the weather cold. They moved to the very south of South Island, on bleak Stewart Island, where they purchased land and set up a carpentry business. Their saw millers felled the mighty Rimu coniferous trees in the pine forests, with demand for timber increasing rapidly during the gold boom of the 1860s. Later, Augusta attended a school for young ladies in Invercargill. She had beautiful handwriting and became very well-read. Her family moved to Oamaru, where many magnificent buildings had been constructed from the attractive local limestone and where an infrastructure of roads, railways and a harbour was rapidly developing.

Marriage of Alex's parents

Alex's parents, Augusta and William, met as neighbours when they were 26 and 22, respectively, and were married in 1878. They would have seven children, with two dying young. Alexander Sanderson was born in Oamaru in 1881. Known as 'Alex' from an early age, he was educated by a private tutor from the age of 6 to 9, and later at Waitaki High School. Alex's brother William Lauchlan, later to serve in the 10th Light Horse Regiment, was born in 1890.

Alex's father William worked on the Oamaru harbour front in a sawmill supplying timber, wood and iron merchants. By 1890 he was a hardware store owner and a ship's chandler. With a worsening economy, departures from New Zealand were increasing and from 1896–1900, emigration figures exceeded immigration by 13,200.[7] Even the Sanderson family began to consider leaving New Zealand for a life in Australia.

Part Two
1891–1914

Chapter 2

A New life in West Australia

New Zealand, Australia

'They made a way in the wilderness and rivers in the desert.'
Sir John Forrest, quoting the prophet Isaiah (43:19),
when introducing the Goldfields Water Supply Bill in July 1896.[1]

Arrival in Perth

Alex's father William was not well when he and his family sailed in 1891 from Lyttleton for Albany and Perth, in Western Australia. It was thought the warm climate of the colony would improve his health and the economy was stronger in Australia, with more opportunities for advancement.

When William Sanderson and his large family arrived by boat in Albany, they were apprehensive at what the future would hold for them in their new country. Prior to the opening up of Fremantle Harbour to large ships, sea passengers arriving in Western Australia bound for Perth had to dock at Albany on the south coast. There were no cabs or porters and the family had to struggle with their heavy bags from the port into the town. They would not, however, have had to take the tiring three-day coach journey to Perth. On 1 June 1889 the private Great Southern Railway had opened a railway line from Albany station which connected to the government railway line, only 50 miles east of Perth.[2]

When Alex arrived in Perth it was a small city of only 8,447 inhabitants and was very much a 'frontier' colony. Alex's future 'Chief' Charles Yelverton O'Connor arrived from New Zealand in the middle of the same year when the population of the whole of Western Australia was still only 49,782 souls.[3] By Australia's federation twenty years later in 1901, Perth's population had grown threefold. In the meantime, William Sanderson was appointed as a manager and his son Alex started at Perth High School, aged 9.

Alex's destiny was to study engineering as one of the few cadets of the brilliant Engineer-in-Chief C.Y. O'Connor, who had acquired his professional skills and working experience in South Island, New Zealand.

12 Tunnelling Commander on the Western Front

Map 2: **A General View of Western Australia**

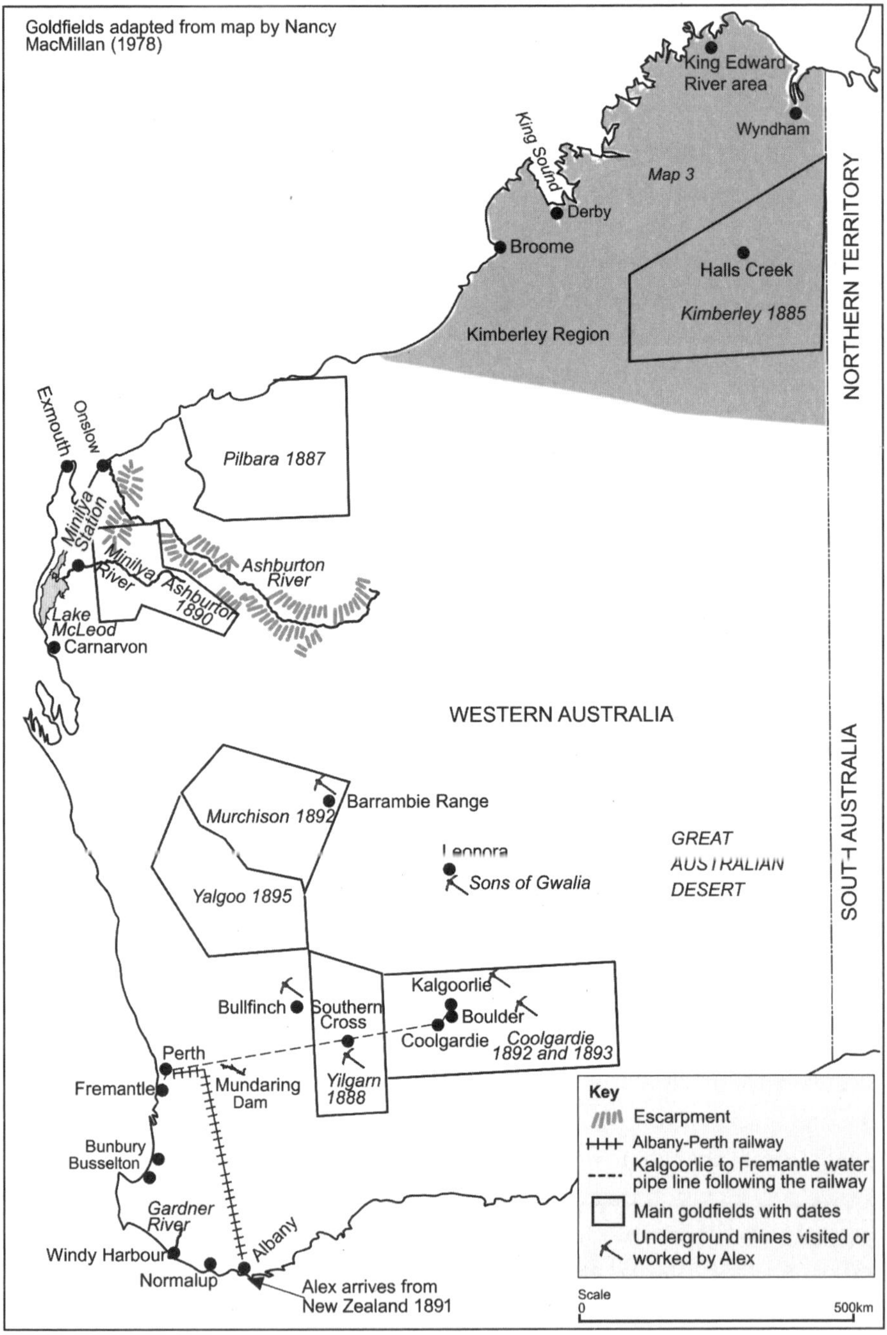

Gold discoveries in West Australia

By serendipity, the arrival in 1891 of the O'Connor and Sanderson families would coincide with the discovery of large deposits of the precious yellow metal which would transform the vast colony, ensure its future prosperity and growth, and influence the futures of these two talented and versatile individuals: the Engineer-in-Chief and his cadet Alex Sanderson.

Gold fever had already seized the other colonies. The first finds in Western Australia attracted hardy, experienced prospectors from across the continent. In the isolated Kimberley region, to the far northwest, visits by the government geologist (1883–4) had indicated the likelihood of gold deposits on the Lennard River. When the first prospectors arrived and found ten ounces of gold in 1885, it set off the Kimberley gold rush; the first in Western Australia. By the end of 1886, 2,000 hardy, experienced miners had arrived from Australia's eastern colonies and passed through the new ports of Derby or Wyndham, a six-pub town with gold-scales on bar counters to weigh gold dust or nuggets which paid for the imported beers and spirits, or champagne if a rich find was being celebrated. After the initial discoveries in Halls Creek, however, the disappointing yields and an export duty of 2s 6d per ounce on gold dashed their hopes. The numbers of miners prepared to endure the harsh conditions diminished as sickness, a lack of provisions and poor returns took their toll. By the end of 1890, only one Kimberley mine remained.

Further south, prospectors struck paydirt in the Pilbara, Murchison and Yilgarn goldfields. In 1888 the first gold mining claim at Golden Valley in the Pilbara region was filed, after a boy on Mallina Station picked up a stone to throw at a crow. Noticing it was heavier than usual, the boy examined it closely and found it was a solid gold nugget. His lucky find led to explorations of the surrounding gold reefs where nuggets of 30–40 ounces were found. It was in the goldfields east of Perth, however, that the richest discoveries were made. Here, 394 mining claims were granted in 1889.[4]

In 1887 gold was discovered in the Yilgarn (the Aboriginal word for the extensive white quartz found in the low hills and sandy plains). Many mining companies were registered, and the Perth Stock Exchange was set up.[5]

The rich 'Southern Cross' goldfields, where Sanderson would later prospect, were named by Hugh Fraser and his pals after the star constellation that had guided their prospecting party south by night and had led to the discovery and registration of 'Fraser's Mine'. When the news of their finds reached Perth, prospectors flocked eastwards. Fraser floated his gold mine in 1889, but it was later closed due to his poor mining skills and mismanagement. He died penniless, his life an example of unrealised dreams.[6]

In September 1892 rich, auriferous seams were discovered by prospectors Bayley and Ford. After setting up camp at Coolgardie, they had discovered 20 ounces of gold before dinner. Arthur Bayley set off to Southern Cross, leading two horses laden with gold. Awaiting the opening of the bank, he unwisely let slip to Cohn, a mine manager, that there were 554 ounces of gold stored in his packs. Early the next day rival prospecting teams, including Cohn's, headed for Coolgardie. Within three years the 'Old Camp' would grow to a town of 6,000 people. In another three years Coolgardie counted 15,000 inhabitants involved in, or supporting, goldmining, with 25,000 others living in the bush around the town.[7]

These exciting finds unleashed W.A.'s largest gold rush while the rest of Australia was in a severe economic depression.

When 'Paddy' Hannan's party struck rich pickings in 1893 at Kalgoorlie in the Eastern Goldfields, the floodgates opened. Thousands were seized with 'gold fever' and headed east by camel, on foot or on bicycles to try to make their fortunes, unprepared for the risk of heat stroke, dehydration or disease. Many died of thirst. Fremantle was the focal point of departure for these prospectors, converging from across Australia and the world. Ignoring the lack of roads or railways to transport them the 360 miles towards Coolgardie, all went east, keen to make their fortunes in the arid, waterless goldfields.[8]

The inaccessibility of the new goldfields and the shortage of water for the growing population of prospectors and their camp followers were urgent and expensive challenges that the government and the P.W.D. (Public Works Department) needed to resolve without delay. Water in Victoria and the New South Wales' goldfields had been easier for gold prospectors to access, and the bush tucker eaten there was not to be found in the sparse, rugged W.A. deserts.

Sir John Forrest and C.Y. O'Connor

In the expanding crown colony of Western Australia, changes were afoot. A new constitution and government had been formed in 1890 and a capable, respected leader was elected as Colonial Treasurer (Premier) and then knighted in May 1891. This was John Forrest, a 43-year-old former Surveyor General and a renowned explorer, with three successful expeditions to his credit (1869–74). In 1870 Forrest had made the first west-to-east crossing of Western Australia with a five-month trek from Perth to Adelaide.

In 1883 Forrest had organised the first large-scale survey of the Kimberley, before returning in 1886 to view the recently discovered Kimberley goldfield and select a site for the port of Wyndham. Described as a 'man of forthright rectitude, robust common sense and homely hard-headedness',[9] Sir John later became Minister of Defence in the federal government.

Like O'Connor, Forrest was an optimistic, far-sighted planner who saw that a rapidly growing colony required significant investment to fund any extensive programme of public works. At the time, Western Australia was the only Australian colony able to obtain finance in London. In 1896 Forrest introduced the Coolgardie Goldfields Water Supply Loan Bill to raise a loan of £2.5 million in London, declaring: 'Now is our chance…we have cheap money, good credit, and what is more the eyes of the world are upon us.' The public debt of W.A. rose from £1.4 million to £12.2 million in the decade he was Premier. Forrest understood that foreign borrowing could be repaid through the prosperity created in the rich goldfields and by the expansion of rural agriculture. His political rise and the goldfield expansions complemented each other, with the gold providing the wealth to pay the interest on the foreign loans for the capital projects he carried out.[10]

Forrest knew that he had to find an exceptional Engineer-in-Chief to achieve his ambitious development plans for Western Australia. Hearing of O'Connor's reputation in New Zealand, Forrest had telegraphed him with the offer of the post, describing the very wide scope of the extensive work to be undertaken as: 'Railways, harbours, everything.' Forrest omitted to mention at this stage that the duties of the post would include the additional onerous role of General Manager of the Railways.[11] This heavy responsibility would be for a vast colony, a third of the size of the whole Australian continent.

NEW ZEALAND

O'Connor had spent eighteen years managing engineering projects in New Zealand, including a section of the challenging road linking the east coast to the west coast of South Island through the remote 'Arthur's Pass', 7,500 feet above sea level, as well as the harbour breakwaters at the mouth of two major rivers on South Island's remote and beautiful west coast.[12] This was valuable marine experience for his successful planning of the two moles of Fremantle Harbour. In 1880 O'Connor had been admitted into the Institute of Civil Engineers (I.C.E.) and his wide responsibilities included the design and construction of railways, roads and bridges, as well as the reservoirs and aqueducts carrying water to the New Zealand goldfields, the latter providing invaluable knowledge for his later Coolgardie water pipeline.[13] Meraub Tauman's book *The Chief* describes O'Connor as thorough, imaginative and 'a natural leader of men, confident of his own capacity'.[14]

O'Connor's final New Zealand survey and consultancy in 1891 was as a marine engineer for Timaru Harbour, sited at the Gisborne river basin; a difficult construction due to its continually shifting sands and shingles. The original harbour had been designed in 1880 by the eminent British harbour engineer Sir John Goode, formerly the resident engineer of Portland Harbour at Weymouth, completed in 1868. In 1891 O'Connor criticised the alteration to Goode's original Timaru Harbour design, with the change to its location made by locals. O'Connor's view was that Timaru Harbour could be kept open and not silt up provided a thorough marine survey was carried out, and if continuous pump dredging was undertaken, together with regular, systematic recordings of the movement of the sea-bed shingle-bank.[15]

Battye Library interview

The following interview with Miss M.F.L. Lukis of the Battye Library, Perth was recorded when Alex Sanderson was 85 years old. His powers of recall regarding O'Connor's views on Timaru and Bunbury harbours were quite remarkable, given his advanced years.

Interviewer: *O'Connor was generally liked by the people who worked for him then?*

AS: *Well, yes, mostly, I think, mostly. Some people, you know, are pleased to take up a story, if someone starts it. I remember the story coming over about the silting up of Timaru Harbour and O'Connor said to me, when I was discussing the amount of silting at Bunbury:*
  'Well, that's worse than Timaru.'
  He just said to himself, 'That's worse than Timaru!'
  Well, afterwards, at Timaru, they found that they could keep the harbour clear with one single dredger. But they had to keep that dredger going. I don't think they'd even had to do that continuously in Bunbury. Anything like that, O'Connor worried about, it worried him.[16]

Although O'Connor had appeared 'abrupt in his manner and austere' to a previous young New Zealand cadet in 1874, working in his residential office on the west coast of South Island, his 'kindly and considerate nature and his unfailing acknowledgement of service performed' was the basis for a solid relationship in Perth with his cadets. Tauman notes that O'Connor 'was especially considerate of young engineering cadets. In Western Australia, Alexander Sanderson spoke of his interest, encouragement and acknowledgement of good work.'[17]

O'Connor had become increasingly disillusioned and frustrated with his position as Undersecretary for Public Works in New Zealand, a post he had held for seven years. Tony Evans writes that: 'The tasks that O'Connor faced as Under Secretary were of the order of Hercules. The pressures upon him… would have daunted a lesser man…he felt that he was not being treated fairly, and it was not long before he began to consider opportunities for engineers overseas.'[18] Leaving family and friends was an emotional wrench for his wife and children. However, in May 1891 he left his adopted country to take up his new Australian appointment in Perth, W.A. at a salary of £1,200 per annum.[19]

When O'Connor arrived in Perth the rail network was still very small (188 miles of government lines)[20] and the existing construction and rolling stock were of a poor standard, leading to frequent accidents.[21] The great legacies of O'Connor as Engineer-in-Chief of Western Australia were Fremantle Harbour, the Eastern Railway and the Coolgardie Water Supply Pipeline. Western Australia's population was growing rapidly after the gold discoveries. The rapid expansion created an urgent need for a working port and a well-engineered pipeline to pump plentiful supplies of water to the parched eastern goldfields. The construction of the Eastern Railway itself required good water for the running of the locomotives. Alex Sanderson's teenage years from 1891 until 1899 were particularly arid years for Western Australia, with the years 1894–7 being the driest.

Tragedy in the Sanderson family

In 1893, when Alex was 11 years old, Perth suffered a smallpox epidemic. Disease spread fast through the then small city. This same year Alex Sanderson's family life was shaken to the core with the early death from diphtheria of his father, William, aged 34, just weeks after Alex's well-loved 2-year-old brother Murcheson had succumbed to the same disease. Now Alex and his five other siblings, aged from 3 to 14, would be raised by their strong mother, Augusta. The older children would rally round to help with the younger ones. In 1897 there was an outbreak of typhoid in the city, resulting in 223 deaths, most probably due to residents using backyard wells at a time of reduced pipe water supplies.[22] Alex's brother Victor would die in 1889, aged just 6. The Sandersons owned a home in Claremont. Augusta never re-married and her sons left school at the earliest opportunity to support the family.

AS: *Oh, Perth was a great place in those days! The Honourable Miss Candy lived further up the road and used to drive in a lovely dog cart. She later became the*

Duchess of Newcastle. I knew her well and used to stay with the duke and her on leave from France.

(Alex's friend The Honourable Miss Kathleen Candy (1872–1955) married the 7th Duke of Newcastle in 1889. The Duchess of Newcastle became a noted show judge and dog breeder, even purchasing one of Tsar Nicholas II's Borzoi dogs when entered for Crufts.)

AS: *When I was going to Perth High School, we lived in St George's Terrace, just down the slope from the old barracks. We had a house which was afterwards the German Club. Henry Lefroy lived on the corner. Across the road lived John and Alexander Forrest.*

Henry Lefroy was an explorer and pastoralist. In 1879 John Forrest's younger brother Alexander, a very capable surveyor and bushman, undertook a six-month exploration of the northwest Kimberley district, naming the King Leopard Ranges, and the Margaret and Ord rivers. Alexander Forrest identified promising well-watered pastoral country on the Fitzroy and Ord rivers, afterwards followed up by Alex Sanderson. Both Forrest brothers were land agents who invested heavily in Kimberley station properties, with Alexander investing heavily in the goldfields, to varying success.

At the close of the nineteenth century, Perth was still a small city. No doubt for Alex Sanderson, having these famous explorers and politicians as close neighbours and being welcomed into their homes was a distinct social advantage; the Forrests had well-connected relatives in business and politics. Hearing the Forrests' adventures first-hand would have inspired the young Alex Sanderson to later undertake his own expeditions to the Kimberley when seeking pastoral land near the Ord River and exploring the Cambridge Gulf for a suitable cattle port. The two influential Forrest brothers living across the street would certainly have helped their young neighbour to obtain his cadetship with the Engineer-in-Chief and have supported his career in the Public Works Department. On the death of Alexander Forrest in 1903, a statue of him was erected at the crossing of Barrack Street and St George's Terrace.[23] It is perhaps through the Forrest brothers, or their acquaintances, that Alex Sanderson was invited to join the Grand Lodge of the W.A. Freemasons, founded in 1900.

Cadetship with the Engineer-in-Chief

Alex Sanderson was evidently a bright pupil, leaving Perth High School on 1 April 1897, aged only 15 years and 4 months, to enrol on a four-year cadetship in the Engineering Division of the P.W.D. of the W.A. Government, now numbering 874 staff. The system of admitting cadets was introduced in 1894 and formalised by regulations signed by the Engineer-in-Chief only three months before Alex Sanderson joined. Cadets were taken on between the ages of 16 and 21, provided they passed the qualifying examination. Three and a half years of their four-year cadetships were undertaken in the field on surveys and works, under the supervision of department engineers. From 1897–1901, Alex Sanderson studied hard and gained wide-ranging skills in surveying; the design and construction of railways, roads, tunnels, timber and steel bridges; water supply; sewerage and drainage; mechanical and electrical engineering; as well in as drawing office work (designing, drawing specification and estimating). In the first year the cadets received no salary, but in the following year were paid £50, rising to £70 and then £90 in the final year. Out of their salaries the cadets were expected to purchase their own survey equipment, by monthly salary deductions, until they had paid off and owned their instruments.[24]

AS: After I left Perth High School I went and joined C.Y. O'Connor as an engineering cadet. I was almost 16. Quite a number of us sat for the examination and I was fortunate enough to come out top. In those days it was just mathematics and mechanics and a certain amount of chemistry etc. but it was just an entrance exam. Later on we had an exam each year in which I always came out on top. C.Y. was very pleased. Anyway, I got experience, I worked on the Coolgardie Water Supply, Mundaring Dam and Fremantle Harbour.[25]

Under Forrest's premiership, Perth became W.A.'s main rail terminus. By 1900, when Alex Sanderson was 17, the widening of the Swan River was completed and the new port of Fremantle welcomed international mail and passenger steamers. The port, in whose construction Alex was directly involved, greatly increased Western Australia's communications and prestige a year before Australia's Federation in 1901.

In many respects, O'Connor replaced the father Alex had the misfortune to lose to diphtheria at an early age. Their New Zealand backgrounds had been noted by unkind critics and in 1893 were commented upon unfairly for political ends when the elected member for Perth rebuked the Engineer-in-Chief in the Perth Assembly for his: 'undue preference given to persons hailing from New Zealand.'[26]

The 'Chief' was a crucial influence on his young cadet's intellectual, technical and personal development. Sanderson had much to be grateful for in his apprenticeship to the gifted Irish engineer. Alex's four-year cadetship could not have been organised by a more capable teacher. The wide-ranging training which O'Connor offered his P.W.D. cadets reflected his own exceptional skills and talents. He had a genius for analysing engineering problems, organised detailed research, grasped all the technical challenges involved and identified the skills, tools and materials required to complete a project in hand. The solutions O'Connor proposed were usually ingenious, practical and economic in the long term, yet often simple in their conception.

Fremantle Harbour

Fremantle was 12 miles from Perth and 300 miles from the port of Albany, where the mail station had been located since 1852. To develop, Fremantle Harbour needed to meet international standards. Previously, cargo was offloaded onto an unsheltered mile-long jetty (closed in bad weather), then taken by road through Fremantle, loaded onto barges and carried up the Swan River to Perth.

Fremantle's inner harbour in the mouth of the Swan River had been started in 1892 with the construction of two moles and with the blasting and dredging of the rocky bar which blocked the entrance channel to the Swan River.

Dreaming track

The *West Australian* newspaper has written that some local inhabitants disapproved strongly of these harbour works. A descendent of the Nyoongar tribe, Noel Naanup has described his Aboriginal ancestors' views on O'Connor's projects in stories passed down through Noel's uncle:

> 'To my people he was a curse. So they put a curse on him, they sung him. All the tribes of the Bibbulmun nation were focussing on the same thing, the wrong he had done.'

The ancient stories were that O'Connor had ruined the ancient dreaming track by blasting the Swan River to create a harbour and through his role in piping water from Mundaring Weir. Much of the early history of the area, the birthplace of European settlement in Fremantle, had tragic consequences for Aborigines and their culture.

'The water covers the ancient dreaming track. In the old times the land stretched out there,' Noel said, pointing out towards Rottnest, Carnac and Garden islands. To the old people the islands…the whole area was Derbal Nara, or like the palm of the hand.

'They buried their people along the river bank. Now they are trapped under water.' Happily, in the Dreamtime story, the seagull sits on the water above the grave site, picks up the spirit of the people and carries it back to land.[27]

The harbour was formally inaugurated by the governor's wife tipping the first truck of Rocky Bay limestone. At this time, the Works & Buildings department counted only nine staff and O'Connor received permission to recruit engineers and support staff.[28]

The North and South moles would shelter the approach to the Swan River for ships entering the harbour basin entrance through a dredged channel, with adequate room in the inner harbour for them to swing around. O'Connor envisaged using the excavated rock from the dredged channel for the harbour moles.[29] A quarry site at nearby Rocky Bay was surveyed and opened, with rails laid for the breakwater of the North Mole at Rous Head. The Rocky Bay limestone excavated later proved to be too easily broken. It did not meet O'Connor's criteria of 2.64 specific gravity and had to be discontinued in favour of tougher stone from a new quarry at Boy.

For the next three years O'Connor would personally supervise the harbour construction, attending to every minor detail. Forrest had declared that Fremantle would become 'the Brindisi of Australia', with a transcontinental line to Adelaide and described O'Connor as 'an able and energetic, brave and self-reliant man'.[30]

By 1894 the protection offered by the North Mole enabled dredging and the for the construction of the South Mole to begin.[31] It was a punishing workload for any man, and, considering his heavy other duties as Engineer-in-Chief of a colony a third of the size of the continent, as well as acting General Manager of the government railways for five years until December 1896, O'Connor was under enormous pressure.[32] This was at a time when the P.W.D's funding was inadequate and it lacked experienced engineers to assist him. The harbour construction and the gold discoveries of 1892–3 increasingly caught the eye of professional surveyors and engineers, as well as skilled workmen keen to find work in the expanding colony. Another 384 more experienced staff were recruited in 1895–6 to meet the demands of the increased capital works.[33] With a bridge built over the Swan River, and the North Mole completed in early 1896, a railway line was organised to carry stone from Rocky Bay to the South Mole.

In 1897 Queen Victoria celebrated sixty years on the throne. In May of that year, a month after Alex joined the department, the (unfinished) Fremantle Harbour was officially opened by Lady Forrest when she steered the steamer *Sultan* through the channel. Other vessels then sailed into the harbour, no longer berthing at the ocean jetty.[34] Now there could flow through Fremantle's inner harbour all the machinery, equipment and materials needed for O'Connor's next great engineering feat: the 325-mile water pipeline to the Eastern Goldfields, as well as the equipment required for the new railways and for the underground mining developing there. Three years later, in 1900, London would finally agree that Fremantle could now replace Albany as the port of call for postal mail carriers.[35]

Alex was now nearly 19 years old and had been working for O'Connor for three years. As new money became available, the North Mole of the harbour was extended from almost 3,000 feet to 4,800 feet. Alex Sanderson described his part in the construction of the harbour:

AS: *I worked quite a lot on Fremantle Harbour. The harbour moles were built of limestone so I was given the job of opening up a quarry at Darlington for granite and all night we had trains running down to Fremantle from Greenmount. They could only run at nighttime because it would [not] interfere with the traffic so much, but we mined and quarried sufficient granite there to cover the whole of the North Mole and I believe afterwards, after I left, they covered the South Mole. Oh, yes! My granite will be there today, oh yes that will never wash away. It was very, very good parts of solid granite.*[36]

Railways

O'Connor turned a badly surveyed, underfunded and inefficient railway system into an efficiently operating rail network with suitable locomotives and wagons, served by improved workshops for maintenance and repair. His progress was achieved in the face of parliamentary opposition to the necessary capital outlay. The astute O'Connor realised that the current world trade and the prices of raw materials favoured speedy development, thus saving heavy interest on loans.[37] He considered that an adequate water supply for the steam locomotives could only be achieved with a goldfields pipeline running alongside the length of the railway line. In June 1894 the railway to Southern Cross was completed, bringing cheaper water at 4 pence a gallon. In summer the steam trains required truckloads of water.[38] No railway line yet reached Coolgardie or Kalgoorlie (an Aboriginal word for 'place of the silky pears'), 139 miles beyond Southern Cross.

Goldfields Water Pipeline Scheme

The water existing in tanks, in boreholes and the wells in the Yilgarn was already scarce before the 1889 gold rush to Southern Cross and the rush after 1892, heading towards Coolgardie. Water had to be carted for miles, being later pulled by camels, and was sold at exorbitant prices. In 1893 O'Connor was tasked with finding a solution and set up the Goldfields Water Supply in an attempt to find and store water in a river-less region whose geology was unknown.[39] Water tanks were excavated along the tracks east from 'the Cross' to Coolgardie. All the while foreign investors were putting money into the W.A. mines.

A letter in the *West Australian* of March 1894 had suggested a pipeline with pumping stations be built alongside the then incomplete Coolgardie railway line, with the sale of water financing the construction.[40] By 1895 John Forrest was considering a plan to ensure a permanent flow of water to the goldfields, although he was at first sceptical, describing such a scheme as 'mad and impractical'.[41] Charles Harper and H. Venn had suggested that they were the first to propose such a pumping scheme. However, O'Connor had been gathering facts and possible solutions for a permanent supply of water for the Yilgarn railway and Coolgardie when Forrest consulted him about the possibility of a pipeline to the goldfields. O'Connor estimated it would take three years to complete.[42]

AS: *I noticed in the papers there had been some talk as to who originated the Coolgardie Water Scheme: that scheme was originated entirely by C.Y. O'Connor. He got T.C. Hodgson over here, who was afterwards his Resident Engineer on the scheme, to go into various things but the whole thing was entirely conceived by O'Connor.*

Interviewer: Mr Harper thought that he dropped the suggestion?

AS: *There was no suggestion, I am absolutely certain of that. Nat Harper told me one night, one evening: 'I was the first one to propose the Coolgardie water scheme, the pipeline.'*

I said: 'You were NOT the first one!'

I said a lot of work had been done before anyone outside knew anything about the scheme. It was originated in C.Y. O'Connor's mind and there was quite a lot of work done. In fact, surveys had been started on the Helena catchment area and, when I first joined as his cadet, he'd had people out surveying the catchment area. I joined him at the beginning of 1897.[43]

In *The Chief*, Meraub Tauman described how, by October 1895:

All the essentials of O'Connor's pumping scheme were stated: plans were drawn... The scheme O'Connor designed was arresting in its dramatic simplicity. Water would be stored at a suitable site on the higher rainfall western escarpment. From a storage reservoir it would be lifted 1,000 feet over the Darling Range and then pumped inland across the plateau to Coolgardie some 328 miles eastwards. With pitiably limited resources but with full cooperation...of his staff...O'Connor steadily assembled data relevant to his plan.[44]

Tony Evans described how: 'The enormity, thoroughness and accuracy of this investigation was one of the lasting achievements of C.Y. O'Connor – ably assisted by his staff.'[45]

By 1896–7, a survey map, in longitudinal sections, was prepared of the 325-mile route of the planned water pipeline, following the contours of the uphill terrain from Mundaring Dam to Mount Charlotte in Kalgoorlie.[46] In 1895 the Melbourne firm of engineers Mephan Ferguson had sent details of the 'costs and performances of spiral riveted pipes of 24 and 30 inches in diameter'.[47]

In January 1896 the shortage of water had reached a crisis point. Forrest received a telegram stating that 'Many teams cannot get away for want of water, horses starving, carriers indignant; look out for starvation. If you cannot make better arrangements…the goldfields must starve.'[48]

The railway department reacted at once to the crisis and started daily trains to the Coolgardie goldfields carrying 15,000 gallons of water.[49] There was always short-sighted opposition to the remarkable Coolgardie Water Supply Scheme, with unwarranted accusations of financial extravagance levelled at the Engineer-in-Chief. The manager of Fraser's Mine, where Alex would later briefly work, stated: 'The proposal to spend several millions on the fanciful project of a departmental engineer is simply outrageous nonsense. It is a scheme of madness.'[50]

However, the manager of the Oroya Gold Mine, where Alex would also later work, was very positive on the social benefits a freshwater pipeline would bring for the working miners' health and living conditions, over and above the working requirements of the mines.[51]

There was judged to be no alternative to the project and in September 1896, a bill approving it was passed. It would be the subject of acrimonious disputes for the next six years.[52]

It was not until October 1898 that the Construction Bill was approved by parliament, the same month that the contracts for the steel water main pipes were signed. The necessary tenders and the placing of the orders for the machinery and materials would take longer, with the colony suffering from an economic depression which delayed the pipeline's construction until 1899.[53]

In March 1899 a Mining and Industrial Exhibition was held in the goldfields. As one of the surveyors of the railway line, 17-year-old Alex Sanderson would have been aboard the special train that travelled from Perth to Coolgardie, where the exhibition was held for three months. Colourful, entertaining camel races were staged by the Afghan residents and Alex would himself ride camels on his adventurous treks through the outback.[54]

Alex Sanderson was closely involved in the meticulous planning for O'Connor's legendary pipeline project. The Engineer-in-Chief had realised that the success of the 325-mile pipeline depended on the correct water pipes being chosen;

ones that would minimise leakages. The Chief had an office in his home where he found he could get more done than in Perth, and Alex worked here while carrying out the research for O'Connor.[55]

A.G. Evans describes the work done by O'Connor's assistants: 'The first file, comprising papers relating to the selection of the pipes that would carry water the 350 miles, includes evidence from around the world of the relative merits of wrought iron, cast iron and steel; and tables of comparative costs of pumping 5 million, 10 million and 100 million gallons of water per day.'[56]

AS: *I used to do calculations for C.Y. O'Connor. He picked me out as the right person to get all these statistics for him in the various journals which had been issued by various people. He gave me a table in his room so that, at any time, if I wanted to talk to him about it, I could. I was getting all this information. I think I made absolutely thorough research, as far as you could get from these publications, of the leakage from water mains, from about 2 feet to 3 feet diameters. Well, at that time, the first main proposed was a 2-feet main. We afterwards – after going into it further – decided on a 30-inch main. I had all these statistics of the various types of mains. O'Connor took all that information with him when he went to London to see the consulting engineers in London about this scheme.*[57]

O'Connor left for London in January 1897, armed with Alex's statistics, and returned eight months later, in September.

As well as the actual size of the pipes, the other crucial factor was their jointing. O'Connor's far-sightedness favoured the locking-bar pipe, designed by Mephan Ferguson of Melbourne, whose patented pipe reduced water leakage: the pumped water flowed more easily through the pipes' rivet-less interiors. The crucial choice of pipe type would ensure the success of the Goldfields Pipeline.[58]

O'Connor's recommendations were finally accepted in October 1898, with commercial agreements signed for the supply of 30,000 steel locking-bar pipes, 30 inches in diameter and 28 feet in length (the railway wagons were 30 feet long). Due to the delay in placing orders for the required 70,000 tons of steel plate, the W.A. government were forced to look to America and Germany. The British, who had raised the funds, would supply only the joint rings and locking bars.[59]

(After the First World War, Alex Sanderson would later establish his own pipe company in London at Rotherhithe, the location of Marc Brunel's tunnel under the Thames, the first tunnel ever constructed under a navigable river. Sanderson's factory would produce patented reinforced concrete pipes, a product unavailable in nineteenth-century Australia. Unfortunately, Sanderson's factory would be forced to close due to his major competitors' unfair cartel.)

Chapter 3

Success and Tragedy

Australia

O'Connor's tribulations

O'Connor was later criticised for his recommendation to purchase an expensive patented caulking machine which would speed up the sealing and thus the laying of the pipes. The inventor of the caulking machine himself offered to take over the pipeline project from the P.W.D., vowing to complete it all by September 1902, and at a lower price. O'Connor's decision to recommend this private contractor would later have profound repercussions, laying him open to criticism in parliament and the press. A proud and sensitive man, O'Connor was disturbed by the accusations and it affected his mental state. Already stressed by overwork, he took it to heart.[1]

With the resignation of Premier Sir John Forrest to pursue federal politics, O'Connor had lost his biggest ally at a time when he desperately needed this personal and governmental help. The P.W.D., with four governments following in quick succession, was unable to offer him the professional support he so needed.[2]

The final instalment of the Coolgardie Water Supply Loan was sought in London in September 1901.[3] On 26 January 1902, an article in Perth's *Sunday Times* attacked a private contract, arranged to speed up the completion of the pipeline, as: 'a scheme that smacks of nauseous suspicion, if not of corruption, from start to finish.' Personal invective was directed at O'Connor: 'that man whose whole career in the service of the state is fraught with sinister conundrums and peccant marvels.'

A further vicious and personal *Sunday Times* attack on the Engineer-in-Chief's character appeared on 9 February:

> This shire engineer from New Zealand has absolutely flourished on 'palm grease' since the first day… If he is not immensely rich there is some mystery somewhere…this man has exhibited such gross blundering…in his management of great public works…he has robbed the taxpayer of this state out of millions…with reckless audacity, incompetence…this crocodile imposter…his reckless extravagant juggling with the public funds.[4]

O'Connor's daughter Bridget met her father on his return from Adelaide by ship: 'He asked how things were concerning the Coolgardie Water Scheme and the papers...He was unusually depressed.'[5]

While O'Connor had confidence in his own abilities, he felt he was personally answerable for all the project's problems. He was anxious and worried that his pumping scheme would be delayed by politics and incomplete by the end of 1902. The questioning of his personal integrity and the misrepresentations were particularly wounding for this sensitive man.[6] In March 1902, wearied by lack of sleep and suffering from optic neuralgia, with his doctor away, O'Connor's depression deepened. His physical health was further worsened due to cirrhosis of the liver. His daughter Bridget was unavailable to accompany him on his usual early morning beach exercise, and on the morning of Monday, 10 March, he left a note on his desk:

> The position has become impossible. Anxious important work to do and three commissions of enquiry to attend to... We may not have done as well as possible in the past but we will necessarily be too hampered to do well in the imminent future. I feel that my brain is suffering and I am in great fear of what effect all this worry may have upon me - I have lost control of my thoughts... The Coolgardie scheme is all right and I could finish it if I get a chance and protection from misrepresentation but there's no hope for that now and it is better that it should be given to some entirely new man to do who would be untrammelled by prior responsibility.

O'Connor's last instructions for the Coolgardie Water Scheme were to 'Put the wing walls to Helena Weir at once'.[7]

In 1900, O'Connor had approved the commencement of the concrete pour for the wall of the Mundaring Dam. This was achieved by a constant stream of labourers wheeling wet cement in barrows down the sharp incline of the embankment. By 1902 the weir was almost finished. Meanwhile, work had continued apace on the trench laying of the water pipes which O'Connor had decided should be joined with locking bars, rather than the usual rivets. The trench protection minimised the expansion and contraction of the 28-feet-long pipes in the extreme West Australian climate. Where the pipeline crossed gullies or salt lakes, the pipes were laid above ground on wooden trestles, protected by galvanised iron shelters packed with sawdust insulation.[8]

Alex Sanderson and O'Connor worked together until the latter's death on that fateful Monday morning in March 1902. O'Connor always extended his encouragement to his young cadets; Sanderson always kept in his trunk an original photograph portrait of O'Connor (see plates).

Alex fondly remembered the personal support offered by his mentor:

AS: *He treated me very, very well and took an interest in me and I'll never forget that.*[9]

In Ireland, O'Connor had been articled at 17 to a railway engineer who was 'particularly kind and encouraging to assistants, anxious to recognise ability whenever he found it'. Just as the Commissioner for Public Works in Ireland had signed the young O'Connor's letter of professional recommendation for a post in New Zealand,[10] O'Connor had signed his cadet Alex's engineering graduation certificate on 26 February 1902, just twelve days before he killed himself, the balance of his mind disturbed. Fremantle Harbour was still unfinished on his death.

Alex noted in his Battye Library interview that: 'he'd escaped me in the afternoon' to describe how he had missed his planned meeting with the Engineer-in-Chief on the previous day, 9 March. He knew O'Connor was upset. They were evidently close.[11]

After 07:00 on 10 March, O'Connor's horse carried him beyond Fremantle town, along South Beach to Robbs Jetty, where he dismounted and released his horse. Wading into the Cockburn Sound into 2 feet of water, he removed his dentures and placed them carefully in his pocket, before removing the pistol belonging to his son Frank. He put the muzzle in his mouth, turned to face the dunes and shot himself.[12]

Interviewer: *Were you near O'Connor towards the end of his life, when things were getting him down?*

AS: *I saw him almost daily at that stage.*

Interviewer: *And you could see that his state was....*

AS: *Oh yes, he was.*

Interviewer: *... upset, obviously?*

AS: *Yes, he was worrying, you see, I could always tell when he was worried about things like that. I'll never forget – he'd escaped me in the afternoon* [the day before] *and he spotted me down... He was an engineer, even in the way he committed suicide. He was greatly worried that people...there were letters in the paper and all that sort of thing, you know, and people saying: 'The Mundaring Dam will never fill and they'll never get water in.'*

We'd had a particularly dry season – two particularly dry seasons. Later on, in fact, not many months after he died, the dam was overflowing. He left a note on his desk, to build the wing wall, not to neglect building the wing wall to the dam, meaning that he realised, he was sure, it would overflow. Instead of which it had been getting very little water coming into the dam at that time. It overflowed within a year afterwards and it has overflowed ever since, every year. In fact, shortly after that it was overflowing so much that they started surveys there to take the water that overflowed for the Perth water supply. When this awful accident happened to O'Connor, C.S.R. Palmer came in and took his place afterwards.

O'Connor didn't leave a lot of money, he had a big family and Palmer knew this. After O'Connor's death, I stayed on in the Public Works as I had to finish my cadetship.[13]

C.S.R. Palmer would countersign Alex's graduation certificate on 6 March, four days before O'Connor's death. Over 100 years later, O'Connor's 350-mile goldfield pipeline was named a 'World Engineering Landmark' by the American Society of Civil Engineers, to rank alongside the Golden Gate Bridge, the Panama Canal and the Eiffel Tower. When constructed, it was the first major pipeline built of steel and the longest freshwater pipe in the world.

Both Alex Sanderson and his mentor were imaginative and highly skilled professionals, very much 'ahead of their times' and good listeners. They were hard-working and resilient surveyors and engineers, with an expertise across a broad spectrum of civil engineering. Both were individuals with high integrity and were able, considerate managers of men. Alex was very well-organised, with an engineer's meticulous eye for detail; it later irritated him if people did not follow the correct procedures.

Interviewer: *After O'Connor's death did you stay on in the Public Works?*

AS: *Yes, I had to finish my cadetship. I stayed on but I was largely* [occupied] *on the construction of the Southern Cross to Coolgardie and Kalgoorlie railway, where I spent some time with Charlie Babington and R.J. Anketell, the two engineers I was working under.*[14]

In 1895 Richard Anketell was appointed as Resident Engineer of the Southern Cross to Coolgardie railway works. After completing this section of the railways, he surveyed the 'Pipe Tracks' for the Goldfields Pipeline. The young Alex Sanderson would accompany Anketell on these surveys.

Chapter 4

Student to Mining Engineer

Australia, New Zealand

Graduation as an engineer surveyor

On 26 February 1902 Alex passed the Engineering Examination for entrance as an Assistant Engineer in the W.A. Public Works Department (based on the standard of the Institute of Mechanical and Civil Engineers). His Passing Out certificate recorded that Alex had completed:

* 27 months in the Drawing Office
* 5 months on surveys for railways
* 17 months for other engineering projects
* 2 months on construction of railways
* 5 months on other construction projects

AS: *As a matter of fact, before I actually started mining, it was during one of those holidays that I met Herbert C. Hoover, the future U.S. President, then a mining engineer. I joined Bewick Moreing and I was sent by Hoover to the Philippines where they had some dredgers working in Luzon Harbour. When I got back to Australia from Manila, I was mining for some time in Kalgoorlie. I used to meet miners and newspaper people like 'Smiler' Hales on the 'Coolgardie Miner'. I remember Vosper with his long hair, a very good speaker too.*[1]

Vosper, the editor of the *Coolgardie Miner* newspaper, was 'a political firebrand' and a staunch republican. He set up the *Sunday Times* of Perth, a newspaper which had published several personal attacks on C.Y. O'Connor and his part in the Goldfields Pipeline. Vosper may have been Premier one day, had he not died aged 31, a year before O'Connor committed suicide.[2]

With Herbert C. Hoover

Alex worked closely with H.C. Hoover (later the 31st American President, 1929–33), a graduate of Geology and Engineering at Stanford University, who had translated Georgius Agricola's 1556 Latin book *De Re Metallica* on the art of mining, refining and smelting metals: the most important book on mining for two centuries. Hoover was appointed by Bewick Moreing, aged only 22, as the Mining Inspector for all its Western Australian gold mines at $6,000 a year, arriving at Albany in 1897 and taking the newly laid narrow gauge railway to Perth. Like Alex, Hoover moved around at first on camels which, unlike Alex, he hated, as he did the 'red dust, black flies and white heat'. Desert conditions were tough and thirty-six of Bewick's mining engineers contracted typhoid fever due to the poor water in the goldfields.[3]

In 1903 Hoover swapped his horse and buggy for the first of three new French automobiles to travel the tracks between mines. Hoover recommended the purchase of the 'Sons of Gwalia' (Wales) gold mine at Leonora, which became the third most productive mine in W.A. He was very generous to his mine managers, importing quantities of quality Scotch whisky and French claret to reward them. Bewick would soon control 50 percent of the gold produced in the state, running big mines on the Murchison and Kalgoorlie goldfields, including the Oroya Brown Hill Mine, where Alex would later become manager. By 1904 Bewick Moreing had overextended itself in acquiring the two big Kalgoorlie-Boulder mines: the Golden Horseshoe and Great Boulder Perseverance.[4]

Alex Sanderson qualifies

From 1903 to 1904 Alex was employed as an executive engineer in the Eastern Goldfields Division of the P.W.D. He qualified as a 'Licensed Surveyor of Australia and New Zealand' and passed the first two years' exams in 'Mining, Engineering & Metallurgy' when attending lectures at the Kalgoorlie School of Mines.

Between 1904 and 1907 Alex was employed as an engineer for Smith & Timms, a railway and public works contractor in Australia and New Zealand. He was involved in the 113-mile duplication of the Eastern Goldfields Railway between Perth and Kalgoorlie, enlarging a railway tunnel of 1¼ miles. In Perth Alex oversaw the design and construction of the Claremont Water Supply (sinking a deep well bore, lined with a 10-inch diameter steel casing to 2,100 feet) as well as a steam pumping plant, a reservoir with its complete reticulation (network of mains pipes). In South Australia, Alex worked on the construction of the Adelaide Electric Tramways, and a tunnel and duct to the collecting reservoir of the city's water supply.

NEW ZEALAND

In New Zealand Alex was constantly 'on the go'. In South Island he supervised the manufacture and erection of gold-dredging plants in Otago (his birthplace), and built a section of the G.T. Railway, planning its tunnels, bridges, culverts and railway station buildings. In North Island he surveyed the headworks of the Hawera Hydro-Electric Power Scheme (driving a pipe tunnel through rock and fixing heavy steel pipes down to the power station) and designed a large reinforced concrete goods shed for the Auckland Harbour Board.

AUSTRALIA

Oroya Brown Hill Gold Mine

AS: *I took on a job at the Oroya Brown Hill Mine as Underground Manager. (I was later Underground Manager of Fraser's Gold Mine.) They were having trouble and wanted me to put in a new shaft. While I was working in Kalgoorlie, the singer Ada Crossley came and gave a concert in Kalgoorlie and I arranged to take Maudie Turner to this concert. Maudie and Minnie Turner had a hotel at Kalgoorlie and were very well known there. At that time, I was mending and re-lining the Oroya Brown Hill shaft. I couldn't get up quickly. Something had happened and they couldn't run the winding engine. I was down below. Ada Crossley had visited the mine the day before, put her name up down on the 1,700-foot level and had 'shouted'* [paid for] *some tickets. I had arranged to take this girl Maudie and I had to climb up 400 feet of ventilation shaft to get out. 400 feet! You can't imagine what it is to climb that height on a vertical ladder. When I was getting near the top, I thought that I'd fall off at every moment. I was absolutely exhausted. When I finally got to the top of an old ventilation shaft, there were big beams across, with spaces in between to let the ventilation come through. I couldn't move the beams. I hadn't the strength to move them. I had lost all my strength climbing and I was crawling about with my hands pushed above when someone just happened to see me. Otherwise I might have never got out. I didn't enjoy the Ada Crossley concert that night, I tell you!*

I worked at Oroya but I'd knocked myself out. I decided when I'd finished the job that I'd go back to New Zealand, where I still had relatives, to spend a couple of months fishing. When I got to Melbourne, however, I was offered a job by a friend of mine, Sir John Monash – John Monash in those days.[5]

Engineering with John Monash

In 1897 Monash and Anderson, his then partner, had become the Victorian agents for a Sydney company with Australian patent rights for the Monier reinforced concrete construction method. In 1898 Monash had spent a year on business in Perth where he had dined at the exclusive Weld Club with the Premier Sir John Forrest, together with Forrest's brother Alexander and C.Y. O'Connor. Monash wrote that he had met 'the genuine original 'sandgropers' (slang for gold prospectors) when he dined at home with the Forrests, one of the 'six great families' of Perth. Alex's house was across the street from that of Sir John Forrest.

Monash visited Kalgoorlie on three work trips when O'Connor was at a critical stage of his goldfields water scheme. It was then that Monash probably met and befriended the 18-year-old Alex Sanderson, who would later work with him in Melbourne on the construction of the opera singer Madame Nellie Melba's house in Collins Street. Melba was the daughter of David Mitchell, a part owner with Monash of the Monier Pipe Company, having bought the product's patent rights in Victoria. Melba later made history with the first live singing broadcast from an improvised studio in Marconi's factory, using a telephone receiver adapted as a microphone, attached to a hat stand.

In 1905 Monash had become the superintending engineer of the Reinforced Concrete & Monier Pipe Construction Company Coy. Ltd. In 1906, in a minor Australian construction boom, Monash took on four assistant engineers and, in 1907, the 25-year-old Alex Sanderson went to work with him.[6]

AS: *They were just going to build a house for the singer Madam Melba. Her father was investing some of her money for her in the big 14-story Collins House in Collins Street and they wanted an engineer who had some experience with concrete. Monash offered me this job. So, instead of going on holiday, I joined this firm. I only stayed until we'd finished Collins House. I didn't have my holiday in New Zealand for some time after that.*[7]

Alex Sanderson's CV shows that from 1907 to 1911 he was the Principal Construction Engineer for Monash's Reinforced Concrete Coy. Ltd., of 'Melbourne, Australia & New Zealand'.[8] He supervised the installation of the concrete sheet pile facings of the quays for the Sydney Harbour Board, he organised the initial construction work of the Sydney sewerage system. The earthquake in San Francisco had made construction with reinforced concrete more widespread and accepted.

Gold prospecting

AS: *Then I returned to Western Australia because some prospectors had discovered the Bullfinch Mine. Charlie Jones and his party were being financed by Dorrie Doolette,* *who was quite a well-known chap on the goldfields. They'd struck this rich deposit on the Bullfinch and I went with thousands of others. I was curious, you know, we thought it was 'boomed up' and it was going to be very, very rich. Charlie Jones took me down the main shaft and I remember taking my hat off and scooping some of this ore out into my hat. I took it up and dollied it. It was very soft. Well, the stone was very soft. I got about a tablespoon of gold. I thought to myself: 'By Jove, they've got something pretty good here!'*

I suppose Jones showed me the best place to pull it off. Then I prospected around the area myself for a few weeks but couldn't discover anything worth my taking on as a lease, so I left. When they floated the company, I bought some shares in it. The values of course didn't go down.[9]

Dorrie L. Doolette wrote a long poem on Coogardie, where he mined. In it, he describes the risks and the rewards of gold mining underground:

The Old Coolgardie Road

> To some, past all their dreaming,
> To some, the nameless grave,
> To some, for their redeeming
> Your countless gold you gave.
>
> by D.L. Doolette[10]

Jones had evidently 'gilded the lily'. One of the techniques adopted by some unscrupulous miners to attract investor's capital was to load a shotgun with small pieces of gold and fire them into the mine wall.

Charles Jones ('Champagne Charlie') was financed by Dorrie Doolette, the son of Sir George Doolette who sat on the boards of many Western Australian mining companies, including Oroya Brown Hill where Alex had been Underground Manager in 1903. Jones had initially explored the Yilgarn Goldfield from Southern Cross down to Parkers Range, but a lack of water forced him to abandon his search for gold here. He headed south, in Golden Valley, following the ironstone formation before finally striking gold at the Bullfinch. Hundreds of prospectors had passed this way but none except Jones had stopped to examine the rocky outcrop. Realising the importance of his find and telling no one, he hurried back to Southern Cross to register his 'new find' with the Mining Registrar. Having summoned his sponsors by telegraph, they took samples before pegging out three 24-acre mining leases in December 1909 at £8 10s each. Bullfinch's first 57 tons yielded a rich 5 ounces of gold per ton.[11]

Hundreds like Alex Sanderson turned up to invest. Perth's *Sunday Times* in October 1910 described Bullfinch as 'THE STATE'S GREATEST GOLD FIND'. Dorrie, who had gone bankrupt in 1897, saw his fortunes restored when Bullfinch Proprietary (W.A.) was floated on the London Stock Exchange. He developed the Bullfinch string of mines: Chaffinch, Blackfinch, Redfinch, Yellowfinch, Greenfinch etc, near Southern Cross. Doolette had the Midas touch and became fabulously rich. He was a free spender and money had no meaning for him; at a banquet in London every guest was given a bullfinch replica, cast in gold from the Bullfinch Mine.[12]

Later Sir George was most generous to the Australian tunnellers on the Western Front, donating many books to the tunnelling companies' comfort fund in France. The Australians even named a corps battle H.Q. 'The Bullfinch dugout'. Dorrie was to die in poverty in Perth in 1925.

Managing gold mines

In 1911 Alex returned to mining with his appointment as General Manager and Engineer of the Barrambic Ranges Gold Mining Company, working their mine of quartz reef in hard greenstone schist rock from the surface down to 500 feet. Alex supervised the mechanical and chemical treatment of ores for the extraction of gold. He sat on the Board of Examiners for the Licensed Surveyors and the Mine Manager's Certificate, on behalf of the Chamber of Mines.

In 1912 Alex was Underground Manager of the Associated Northern Gold Mine in Kalgoorlie, and for four months acted as the Superintendent and Chief Engineer. He was mining in both hard and soft rock, gaining experience of working with a range of rock drills, air compressors and winding engines, as well as electric power and lighting plants. His wide responsibilities included mine ventilation and drainage, pumping, and the timbering of shafts, drives and stopes (a step-like excavation area produced during the extraction of ore-bearing rock). He became an expert in the handling of explosives of various kinds, blasting with time fuses and with electric instantaneous and delayed-action detonators. In late 1915 Sanderson's extensive mining experience, qualifications and ability singled him out for the specialist role as a technical expert in the newly formed Mining Corps. His engineering and mining skills and detailed knowledge of the underground machinery and explosives would prove invaluable during his later command of a tunnelling company on the Western Front.

Map 3: **Alexander Sanderson's exploration of the Kimberley, W. A.**

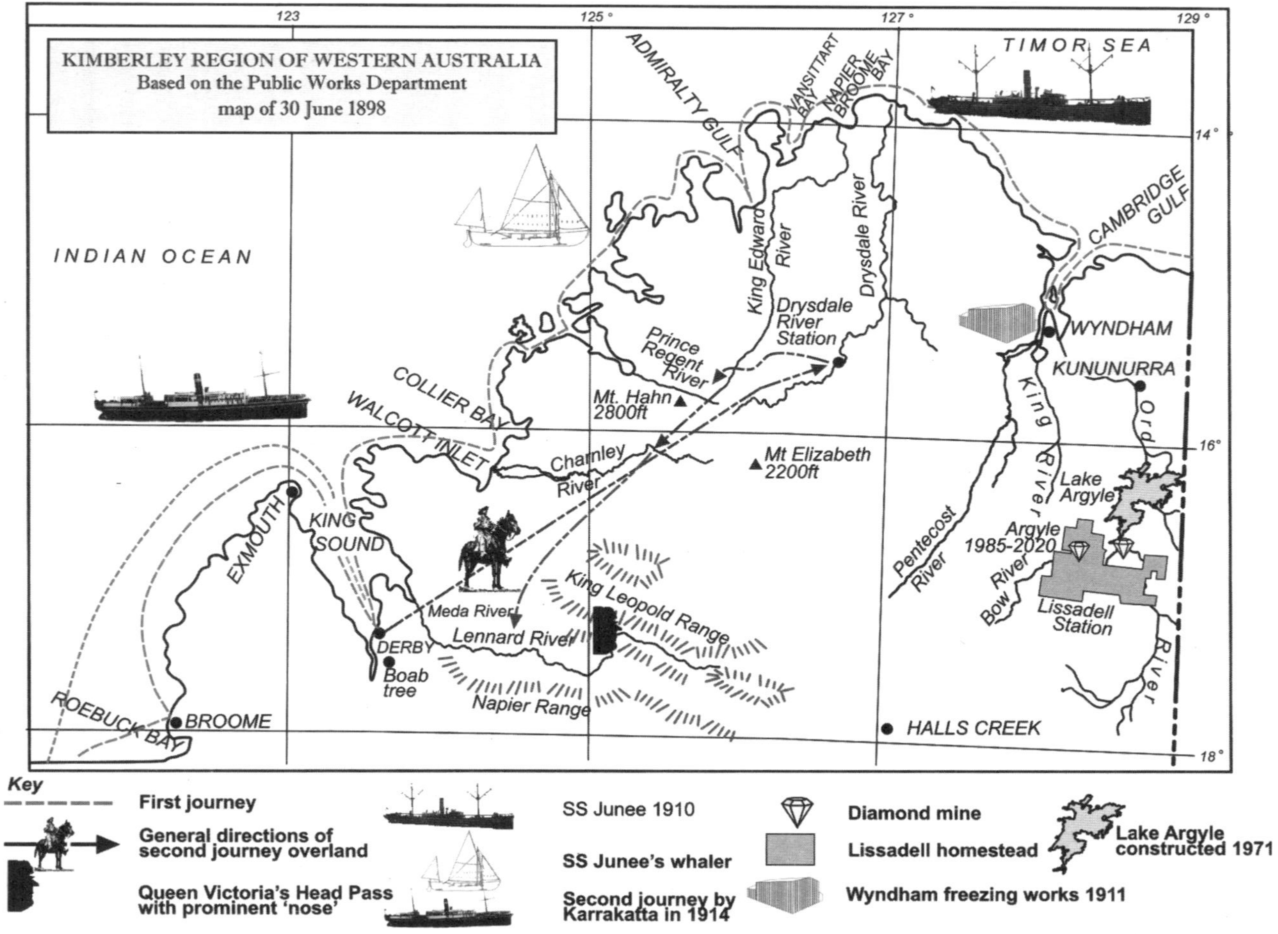

Government work in southwest Australia

Interviewer: *When did you re-join the government and go up to Wyndham? Was that just a contract?*

AS: *That was a contract, except that the Lands and Surveys people got me to go down and explore country around Nornalup Inlet, in the South of Western Australia, between Albany and Busselton. I did a few months' work down there, surveying and cutting up some areas of blocks for small farms on the Gardner River. Then when I got back to Perth, an engineer called Castilla asked me to go up and examine the country northeast of Wyndham for his firm, to see if I couldn't get a deep water site for the freezing works they were proposing.* (See colour plate Kimberley map)

So I went up and explored that area. I took such a fancy to that country and liked the chaps I had with me. I'd met some fellers from the Malden River Station and they told me all about country they'd seen further west on the Charnley and the Lennard rivers. I said that I might like to come back and explore that country. I saw two of the finest deep-water harbours in the world: Admiralty Gulf and Vansittart Bay.

When I was exploring for the port, they gave me Captain Airey's government steamer; we had to take soundings and all that sort of thing. I also had pack horses and that's where I met Wally Smith, the chap who afterwards went with me on the trip which I made on my own account, when I wanted to take up some country. I was up there some time, for six or seven months. At the same time, I also did some other work for a timber company.

I sent a written report to the Chief of the Lands Department and the Agricultural Department, who were dealing with it then, mostly on the fact that I did find where they could have a good deep-water harbour – and good country behind it. I was told afterwards, when I returned, that the political influence to bring it right into Wyndham overshot everything else. From the stations on the Ord etc., it would not be as far as to take the cattle, as they now have to take them to Wyndham. From East Kimberley they could have got to this port at the entrance to Cambridge Gulf quite easily, but it would have been further to take the cattle from the western side. It's a long way; you have to come practically down to Hall's Creek to get there.

Horseback expedition out of Derby

AS: *When the opportunity came after I'd been up north, just when the war was starting, I'd had to spend a lot of capital arranging for horses and equipment to meet me at Derby. I'd met a lot of pastoralists, Charlie Ross and others. It was then I decided that someday I would take up land, go in for breeding sheep and get a station somewhere. I had a fair amount of money in those days. I'd been lucky in shares: mining shares and that sort of thing. While I was doing some work in Sydney I'd been introduced to a*

Mr French, General Manager of the Bank of New South Wales. He'd kindly invited me up to his house. I had a fair amount of money and I used to discuss financial things and my position with him. We'd got very friendly and I spent a good deal of my time with him. Well, after he knew what I had spent, what it had cost me – which was a few thousand pounds – he had actually arranged before I went away, if I liked this country, to give me quite an additional lump sum advance, in addition to the money I had with him. It was all fixed up that if I took up country up there and decided to start it going and put cattle on it, he was going treat me quite liberally as my banker.

When I did go back to the Kimberley, I went up on the 'Karrakatta': Johnny Rees was Master then. I got off at Derby. I'd arranged for these fellers to meet me with horses and we rode up right up through that country. There was Tom Laurie, who'd had good mining experience and knew the Aborigine people. The other two fellers were Louis Martin, who'd been my foreman in the survey work down south, and Wally Smith, who was well known; he'd been a stockman up north for years. He could talk the language. These fellers met me at Derby and we rode right up to the Drysdale Mission. Then I came back and further explored the country near the King Edward and Prince Regent rivers, and a little further south of that, on the Lennard and Charnley rivers. There were two rivers there that I didn't know the names of, so before I went away, I went to see Fred Brockman, the Surveyor General. He'd been up over that country with his exploring party and gave me a whole lot of information about it. I found some magnificent country and I decided what I was going to apply for. I mapped it out. I could show you on the map. It was a big area just north of the Lennard River and just on the headwaters of the King Edward and Prince Regent rivers.[13]

In his old age Alex told his family that he had shared his tent with a pet tarantula spider while camping in the outback. It did not bother him that during the night it used to come down and take a little of his blood.

An incident told by Alex to Charles Bean in 1918 described how:

CB/AS: *When up in the Kimberley, Sanderson had an interesting experience, on two occasions, when spears were thrown at him. Once, when he was riding his horse up a gulley, a spear suddenly whizzed past his shoulder into the ground. He flung himself over the far side of his horse, and as he did so he saw what he thought was a boomerang coming wobbling through the air towards him. It turned out to be the rotary motion of a spear shaft which whizzed past, just clear of the saddle where he had been sitting.*[14]

It is probable that Sanderson's exploring party was not welcome in Aboriginal territory. Nor were the steel telegraph poles, which some climbed to remove the porcelain insulators to chip and shape as effective spearheads, bound on with kangaroo sinews. Throughout the nineteenth century the indigenous people of the Kimberley suffered greatly, as they did in other regions of Australia, when settlers and cattle ranchers invaded their traditional lands, treating them harshly and, on occasions, with extreme violence. Aboriginal warriors resisted the seizing of their tribal areas, spearing young cattle and fighting back. Many Aboriginal people were killed or chained and sent south by boat to prison on Rottnest Island, off the Perth coast.[15]

Members of Alex Sanderson's party witnessed indigenous people guarded by settlers armed with rifles; one of the nine photographs included in the Battye Library expedition collection shows such a group, probably in their employment.

AS: *We didn't have Aborigines with us so very much on these trips, but I had fellows that had experience with them, you know. The Aborigines, in that part of the country, their areas were very small, and they wouldn't go very far. I had some trouble with them on one occasion, when a witch doctor wanted to perform an operation on one of them, an Aborigine boy with us, because he'd got out in the other country, where I shouldn't have taken him really. He'd got into another tribe.*

War breaks out in Europe

AS: *That was early in 1914. I got back at the end of July 1914 and I was making arrangements to put in my application for this country, when the war came along – the 4th of August.*

I came back when the war was just starting and all plans were altered. I went and told Mr French that I was giving all this up because I thought I ought to go to the war. He said:

'Well, the war can't last more than four or six months. Financial conditions will stop the war.'

I didn't think he was right. I said, as far as I could see, the war might go on for five or six years. 'No, No!' He wouldn't have it at all! He tried all he could to dissuade me and he said I was very, very foolish: 'You are foolish not to go on. You'll waste a lot of time now going to war, and you'll be coming back in six months. Why do that?'

Interviewer: *You knew more about it than he did as it turned out!*

AS: *I decided to see the world. I suppose I'd always been patriotic and I thought I ought to go to the war and there it was. I said, 'I shall leave this until I come back.'* [laughs]. *Well, I firmly intended to and I would have gone back there, if I hadn't got married. But I decided I could never take my wife out there, to a place like that, it was no good. I did inquire later…*

Interviewer: *… whether that country had been taken up yet?*

AS: *Yes, I wrote to the government about it and asked if it was still open and they sent me a plan showing that much of it had been reserved for some reason.*

Interviewer: *... for Aborigine missions or reserves?*

AS: *It was all reserved. I sent the government a written report when I came back from that trip. They didn't entirely say that I couldn't, so I went to see Sir William Vestey, thinking he might come into it with me. 'Oh', Sir William said, 'No! You can't do anything out there. The Aborigines would spear all your cattle!'*[16]

Vestey advised Sanderson against taking on the Kimberley Lissadell Station and later bought the Ord River cattle station himself for £250,000.[17]

Camels

Interviewer: *Did you ever have trouble with camels, did you ever work with camels on the goldfields?*

AS: *Yes I did. I had a lot of experience with camels. I went on a surveying expedition up across the Ashburton [desert] where there is now the big iron mine – the idea being that the land was thought to be all artesian and the government were proposing to put some bores down. When the government didn't, I went across that country and recommended certain bores. One was on Minilya Station, Don Macleod's sheep station. Don said: 'Well, if the government won't do it, you can arrange for a boring contractor to come, I'll put it down at my own expense', which he did do. He got water, a good supply of water, so my efforts weren't wasted.*

I had camels with me and we had quite a good time with the camels until they got onto some gastronomic poison and we lost all except two. We didn't have Afghan drivers. They were fellers that had been brought up on Sir Thomas Elder's breeding station for camels in South Australia. They had learnt a lot about the camels and they were very good. We hobbled them out at night-time. There's good feed all through that country. My riding camel used to get a belly full of grass and then she'd come every night and sniff around until she found me. She wanted to get close to me and then she would dump down. Many a time in the morning, when I was waking up, I would pull her leg out and put my head on it and she'd keep it out there. She'd feel and see my head on it. She wouldn't pull her leg away, although it strained her leg pulling it out. She was a lovely camel.[18]

Alex understood that camels are intelligent but temperamental animals who can kick and bite, unless handled with firmness and consideration to which they respond with gentle familiarity and humour. Trekking in Australia began at first light to avoid the hottest part of the day. During the midday billy tea stop, the animals were grazed out; sitting in the shade and sleeping. In dust storms the camels closed their eyelids and nostrils, filtering the air.[19]

Part Three

The First World War, 1915–1918

Chapter 5

Enlistment in the Mining Corps

Europe, Australia, Egypt, New Zealand

> Death closes all: but something ere the end,
> Some work of noble note, may yet be done,
> Not unbecoming men that strove with Gods.
> The lights begin to twinkle from the rocks:
> The long day wanes: the slow moon climbs: the deep
> Moans round with many voices. Come, my friends,
> 'T is not too late to seek a newer world.
> Push off, and sitting well in order smite
> The sounding furrows; for my purpose holds
> To sail beyond the sunset, and the baths
> Of all the western stars, until I die.
> *Ulysses* by Alfred Lord Tennyson[1]

EUROPE

War breaks out

The catalyst for the First World War was the assassination in Sarajevo on 18 June 1914 of the Archduke Francis Ferdinand, the heir to the Hapsburg throne, and his wife, by a fanatical Bosnian Serb nationalist. (Eighty years later, Alex's son Lieutenant Colonel John Sanderson, aged 74, fluent in the Balkan languages, would fly into war-torn Sarajevo in a Chinook helicopter on a secret mission with an S.A.S. team to identify Serb guns shelling the city.)

The nations of Europe were tied by a complicated network of alliances. Austria declared war on Serbia and bombed Belgrade. Tzar Nicholas II ordered a partial mobilisation of the Russian Army. Germany viewed this as a declaration of war. Their leaders believed, with their country encircled by nations in hostile alliances, that war was unavoidable and 'the sooner the better'. Germany was jealous of the British Empire's rich colonies. It had never accepted the ceding of Alsace Lorraine to France and it felt that now was the time to strike while it had the advantage in military equipment and power.

After declaring war on Russia on 1 August, and on France on 3 August, Germany invaded neutral Belgium, putting into operation Count Von Schlieffen's long-devised plan to invade France across the plains of northern Europe. Britain, allied to Belgium by an 1839 treaty, declared war on Germany on 4 August. The invading German infantry shouted: 'Nach Paris' [To Paris], as they fitted the dark cloth on their brightly pointed helmets. The reply of the defending French *Poilus* [Hairy Ones] was: 'À Berlin' [To Berlin]. Becoming conspicuous targets, they would soon change their bright red trousers and kepis for *Le Bleu Horizon* and *Le Casque Adrian*.

Winston Churchill, who later wore an Adrian helmet himself in the trenches, wrote: 'Germany clanked obstinately, recklessly, awkwardly towards the crater and dragged us all in with her.'[2]

AUSTRALIA

As part of the British Empire, Australia was now automatically at war too. As John Monash explained: 'The purpose of the war is to help the Empire to crush a peril which may mean the end of Australia as a free country.'[3]

Formation of a mining corps

Lieutenant Colonel T.W. Edgeworth David, C.M.G., D.S.O., a graduate in Geology of New College Oxford, first pushed the concept of forming a mining corps, although David later credited a W.A. miner and infantry officer, Lieutenant I. Thomson, with having the original idea. David initially envisaged raising a mining battalion for Gallipoli and studied the Anzac campaign from a strategic and geological point of view, before proposing a plan to Senator George F. Pearce for the Western Front in France. Discussions with Pearce led to the first steps being taken to raise an Australian mining battalion.[4]

On 9 September 1915, Pearce sent a cable to the Secretary of State for the Colonies:

> In view of Commonwealth's exceptional resources in expert mining engineers and machinery, this government [is] prepared to organise at once and despatch at [an] early date a Mining Corps numbering up to 1,000 for service in the Dardanelles or elsewhere…to consist of miners skilled in the handling of mining machinery and plant for rapid tunnelling,

whether with or without explosives, experienced mining engineers and geologists and fully equipped with all the necessary machinery.

The reply came rapidly: 'Army Council greatly appreciate and gladly accept offer of mining corps…it would be most valuable in [the] form of tunnelling companies. These are being organised here on basis of two hundred experienced face men to one hundred less skilled assistants.'[5]

No one apart from Pearce was aware that the London War Office cables had requested tunnelling companies, not a battalion, the Australian Defence Department perhaps reckoning that it was better the Mining Corps learned about that once in France. In September 1915, Pearce set up a mining battalion-size unit, with initial recruiting starting in November and the age limit extended to 50. Immediately, fifty men in Broken Hill volunteered. The battalion headquarters were to be raised in Victoria, with No.1 Company raised in New South Wales, No.2 Company in Victoria and South Australia (including Broken Hill) and No.3 Company in Queensland and South Australia.[6]

Edgeworth David threw himself into recruiting miners and surveyors for the corps by appeals made in patriotic personal speeches (one during the entr'acte at the Tivoli Theatre, Sydney). Among his recruits were many of his former university students, mostly engineers. David was enthusiastic to play his part in Europe, in spite of his age, seeing it as 'absolutely the chance of a lifetime to get across to the other side'. Many of the miners enlisting were born in Great Britain and saw enlistment in the corps as a rare chance to see their relatives again. Indeed, Edgeworth David himself was a graduate of New College, Oxford.[7]

Recruiting for the West Australian Miners' Corps contingent began on 1 December 1915. Miners signing on were strong, self-reliant individuals, hardened by harsh desert conditions. William Powell, 32 years old, was a typical recruit. After unsuccessfully gold-prospecting, he had tried farming cheap virgin land. After a drought devastated his crop, Powell laboured laying the trans-Australia Railway line across the Nullarbor Plain, before finally enlisting in Kalgoorlie.[8]

Charles Bean interview

In his conversations with C.E.W. Bean at Noeux-les-Mines, France in 1918, Alex Sanderson would give a full description of the corps' recruitment in Australia and of his company's tunnelling activities on the Western Front.

Bean had reported as an official war correspondent in Gallipoli, where he was wounded in the leg, and in France, where he was 'embedded' with the Anzacs. Bean was determined to record, in as much detail as possible, a comprehensive account of the operations undertaken by the A.I.F., noting the individual histories and wartime actions of hundreds of Australian combatants.

Letter from The Official War Historian Charles E.W. Bean to Major Alex Sanderson

> 9 March 1918
> My dear Sanderson
> I have worked out an account, as far as I can remember it, of what you told me of the doings of your company... I shall be obliged if you will be so good as to run through it and correct anything that is wrong or add any particulars that strike you as interesting or important. You may feel diffident of there appearing so much about yourself but if you could give us some personal notes about the late CO or any other officers also, they would be equally valued. I simply put down all that I can get. Will you let me have this copy back when you have annotated it.
> Yours Sincerely, C.E.W. Bean.[9]

Bean noted (in shorthand) during his interview with Sanderson that:

The Mining Corps when raised in Australia was really Territorial, and the 3rd Company came from Western Australia, Tasmania, and Queensland. The officers were chosen by boards of mining experts in the various states, and there was a good deal of competition. In consequence exceedingly capable men, such as Mine Managers, or men in similar positions, were chosen. In addition to the Company's officers, there were attached to Headquarters about five experts. Major Edgeworth David was of course the leading expert, and Captain Sanderson was one of them.[10]

Major General McNicoll wrote that the tunnelling officers should be experienced mining engineers or surveyors with underground experience, with N.C.O.s and sappers being 'experienced in underground work as foremen, shift bosses, facemen, tunnellers, carpenters and blacksmiths'.[11]

On 11 December 1915, Alex Sanderson enlisted and was appointed a Second Lieutenant.

Enlistment

AS: *After I had enlisted in the A.I.F.* [Australian Imperial Force] *as an Australian engineer, I was appointed, temporarily, as an instructor with the commissioned rank* *of Lieutenant at Moore Park, Sydney where was located the Military Engineers' Training School. On 16 February, on the recommendation of the Kalgoorlie Chamber of Mines, I was promoted to Captain and posted to the Technical Staff of the Australian Mining Corps, to advise on military mining operations and the machinery and plant which should be taken with the corps to France.*[12]

Alex's older brother, William Lauchlan, a surveyor and drainage engineer, had enlisted in October 1914. Sergeant Sanderson had embarked from Australia in February 1915 with the 10th Light Horse, and left Egypt for Gallipoli in May 1915. 'Lauch' was one of the few lucky survivors of the legendary Nek Charge. After promotion to Second Lieutenant, he sustained a gunshot wound to his back in August 1915 and was evacuated to hospital in Malta. After recovering in England, he was re-assigned to the 4th Divisional Artillery in the Middle East.

Alex declared himself a single 'Civil & Mining Engineer and Licensed Surveyor', and on 1 February 1916 completed the 'Attestation Paper of Persons Enlisted for Service Abroad'. The following day he was taken on the strength of Mining Corps Headquarters. On 14 February, Alex underwent a medical examination at Casula, N.S.W. and was judged 'fit for active service'. He signed his papers, stating that he had been in the Engineer Officers Training Corps for two months. He was then '34 years old, 5ft 9in tall and 169 lbs, with a fair complexion, grey eyes and light brown hair'. Alex gave his address as the family home ('The Gables', Stirling Road, Claremont, W.A.) and he named his mother, Mrs Augusta Sanderson, as his 'Next of Kin'.

Training camps

Initial training of No.3 Company was at the Helena Vale Camp at Blackboy Hill. On 18 December 1915, a single officer and 274 O.R.s (Other Ranks) embarked from Fremantle W.A. for Sydney aboard the troopship SS *Indara*. Disembarking on Boxing Day, they marched into Casula camp near Liverpool, where Mining Corps units of the Australian Corps of Engineers from across Australia were gathering to undergo intensive training in specialist mining and military drill. On their shoulders they displayed a purple 'T' (for 'Tunneller') patch. When joined by the 4th Section of Tasmanian Miners, the corps' strength comprised 15 officers and 349 O.R.s, under the command of Second Lieutenant Leslie J. Coulter.

On 19 February 1916, the Domain parade ground in Sydney was lined on all four sides by families and friends, held back by police and garrison troops, as they cheered and applauded the civic parade of the departing miners. Parading

Map 4: The Australian Mining Corps journey to Europe

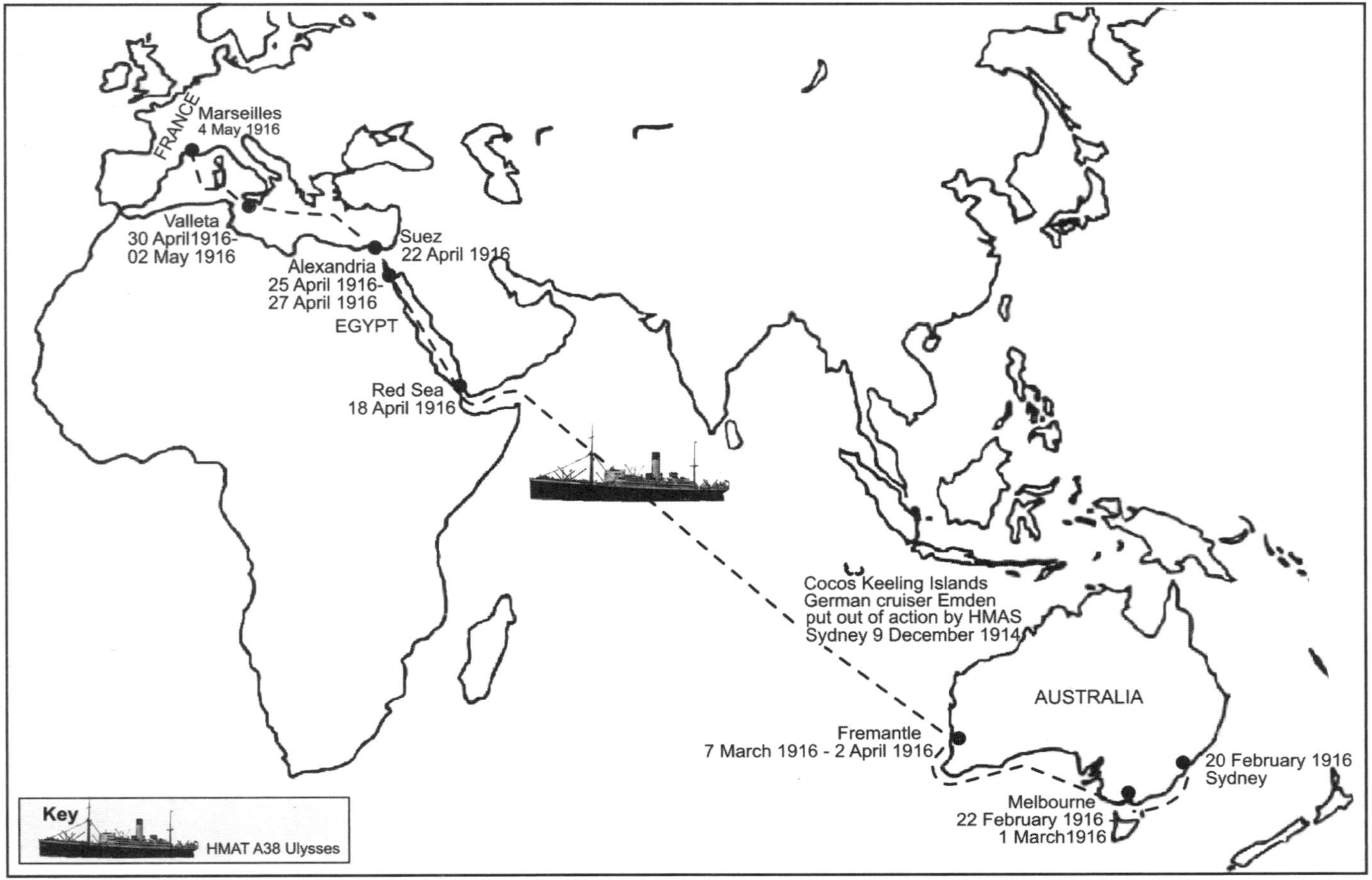

with the infantry were the band of the Light Horse Regiment and rank upon rank of the Miners' Battalion.

On 20 February 1,248 men of the Miners' Corps boarded A-38 *Ulysses* (transport ships were named after Greek mythological figures) at Quay No.1, Woolloomooloo, Sydney and sailed for Melbourne, arriving two days later. The *Ulysses*, with a beam of 68 feet, a length of 563 feet and a cruising speed of 13–14 knots, was a 1913 ship built in Belfast.

The corps camped in Broadmeadows for a week while cargo was loaded, including useful cold weather gear of 1,000 sheepskin vests and 400 mittens. On 1 March, after an inspection by the Governor General and the C-in-C of the Commonwealth military forces, they departed west across the Great Australian Bight, arriving in Fremantle a week later, where a further fifty-three members were taken on board.

The *Ulysses* holed

On 8 March, the Mayor of Kalgoorlie ceremoniously presented the corps with a flag and at 18:00 that evening, the *Ulysses* departed from Victoria Quay of Fremantle Harbour, bound for Europe. However, as the troopship cleared the mouth of the Swan River, the Captain was forced off course to avoid an incoming ship and ran his ship over uncharted rocks on the seabed. With the forward hold filling with 2 metres of seawater, the pumps were manned. The rock's impact had caused rivets to fracture and hull plates to part. The Captain managed to refloat the ship but as the *Ulysses* was taken in tow by a tug, the rope wrapped itself around the propeller and divers were required to go down to free it.[13]

Interviewer: *Tell me about the Mining Contingent that you took away.*

AS: *Yes, well, we had some rather interesting experiences. We left Melbourne in the John Hart liner, the big* Ulysses, *a 14,500-ton ship. We had the whole contingent aboard and called in at Fremantle to pick up the West Australian part camped near Midland Junction and waited for the boat to come in. When leaving Fremantle Harbour we ran onto a reef. She was drawing so much water, a lot more water than the mail ships and other ships take, and the Captain got the ship too far out towards Garden Island, too far south. He ran against a reef, stripping the plates for about 40 feet. Well, we started pumping. We came back in by pumping. Fortunately, the reef only damaged the outside plates of the ship at one place, where the ship just grazed along a rock and put a gap on the outside plates. But the inner bilge plates, the second lot of plates forming the bilge of the ship, were not punctured.*

We came in into Fremantle Harbour alongside the quay. I'd never before been down in a diving suit but I went down in a diving suit in Fremantle Harbour and examined this great rent in the side of the ship. They sent cables and telegrams to Melbourne, to the Defence Department who said they couldn't get another ship and they'd be perhaps three months and that we'd be locked up in Fremantle. Well, I'd been the technical advisor for the Mining Corps. I was called in, having engineering knowledge and I suggested that we put 250 tons of reinforced concrete into the bilge. The Captain didn't like the scheme, he was a bit nervous. He was a chap who didn't impress me at all. [Alex speaks with disdain.] *He was rather scared to go across. At that time, the* Emden *was scouting about, it had been sinking ships. Some other German ship too, had been scouting about in the Indian Ocean.*

[Note: In fact, SMS *Emden* had been destroyed by H.M.A.T. *Sydney* in November 1914, fifteen months before Alex's departure aboard the *Ulysses*.]

Anyway, my report got across to Melbourne and they decided to let us try to put this 250 tons in. We unloaded the Ulysses *and turned her over as much as we could in the harbour and we pumped the water out at the tide. We covered her with tarpaulins and timber on the outside, and put the concrete into the ship. Then we gave it about three weeks to harden. We were all in the Midland Camp.*[14]

While they waited, Captain Sanderson, a former freemason of the city and well connected, invited his fellow officers, smartly dressed in their new uniforms, to dine at the influential Weld Club, many of whose members Alex knew well. The *Sunday Times* noted on 26 March: 'The Mining officers are the "swankiest of the swankiest" and, judging from appearances, have made a deep impression on many of the local girls.'[15]

Departure from Australia

Finally, on 4 March, the whole force paraded at Fremantle with their band, before setting off again from Victoria Quay at 09:30. The Mining Corps on board the *Ulysses* now comprised 1,303 men, a Headquarters' staff of 40; No.1 Company – 390; No.2 Company – 380; No.3 Company – 392; and 101 members of the 1st Mining Reinforcements (in Australian slang known as 'Deep Thinkers').[16]

AS: *We started off, loaded up again, and went off from Fremantle. When we got to the Suez Canal, she was drawing water, a good deal of water was coming in, but the pumps could easily keep it under control. But we ran aground in the Suez Canal, and this Captain, I can't think of that feller's name…*

Interviewer [interjects, laughing]: *Perhaps it's just as well!*

AS: *Well, they gave us a new ship and we transferred all the cargo and everything.*¹⁷

EGYPT

When the *Ulysses* arrived at Alexandria on 25 April 1916, seventy-five days after leaving Sydney, the troops and the 200 tons of Mining Corps stores and equipment were trans-shipped to the 'rather decrepit' Cunard liner H.M.A.T. 81 *Ansonia* (later torpedoed and sunk by a U boat in 1918).¹⁸ The following day the Mining Corps were route-marched through to their new ship, departing for Malta with a Royal Navy escort at 06:00 on 27 April.¹⁹

On board, some of the sappers had invented a refrain, their own version of the popular 'marching' song, 'It's a Long Way to Tipperary':

It's a Long Way to West Australia

It's a long way to West Australia
It's a long way to go
It's a long way to West Australia
To the sweetest girl I know
Goodbye, Midland Junction
Farewell, Perth so fair
It's a long, long way to West Australia
But my heart's right there

When upon the ocean wide, he suffered 'mal de mer'
And longed for Blackboy Camp again and squad drill on the square
He longed again to peel the spuds that made the good old stew
And he wished the boat would sink with all its bally crew

AS: *The Captain got the wind up, and when we got into Alexandria, he wouldn't go any further. He said: 'No!', he was not going to take this ship. He was a very windy sort of chap. We were all very annoyed about him but he communicated with the Admiralty and he wouldn't take the ship out. Perhaps just as well he didn't, because we'd hardly left in our new ship, we had just got outside Alexandria, when a submarine, two submarines, had a go at us, right in daylight. We were zig-zagging all the time. We saw the submarines; we were firing at them with our rifles. The torpedoes they fired at us just missed the ship. One came almost parallel with the ship, right alongside and just missed it by a few yards.*

Interviewer: *…and the other ship, the* Ulysses, *probably couldn't have negotiated like that?*

AS: *Well, I don't know, I think she could have, but the Captain didn't think so!* [laughing] *But anyway, he was too windy. We got through. We were just going into Valetta Harbour in Malta, when we saw a Royal Navy ship blown up by a torpedo from a submarine.*[20]

[Note: 'While approaching the harbour entrance, the *Ausonia* passed an Allied minelaying ship and managed to disturb several mines which, fortunately, failed to explode. Once they had floated to the surface they were fired on and destroyed.'][21]

The Mining Corps arrived in Valetta, Malta on 30 April 1916. On 1 May, they marched past Lord Methuen, the Governor General of Malta, who took the parade salute. After a short stay, the ship continued to France, finally docking at Marseille at 06:00 on 5 May.[22]

Chapter 6

Arrival: Mining Corps

France and Australia

The Australian Mining Corps, consisting of a Headquarters staff and three companies, all disembarked. Shortly before midnight, the majority of the Mining Corps entrained that same evening for Hazebrouck, a strategic town and rail junction 150 miles north of Paris and 16 miles west of Armentières, on a journey that took three days.

AS: *We loaded up. We had 200 tons of machinery and all sorts of drilling machines, electric generators and various things. I was the one that had been responsible for the listing of and buying of all this stuff. The Western Australian Government Defence Ministry – it was a Labour government at the time – and Senator Pearce whom I'd known well in Western Australia when he was the Minister for Defence, shook me up about ordering. They gave me 'carte blanche' to make out a list. I made a very complete list of what I thought would keep the 2,000 men employed well, and able to work at a big speed.*

Interviewer: *Was this machinery that was used for mining in Australia? The type of things that you bought up from Australia, were they mainly mining?*

AS: *No, not this particular type, but this was what I knew. I'd read up and got a good idea of what they were doing on the front, you see. My whole idea was to do it mechanically instead of by hand.*

Interviewer: *And they hadn't thought of this in England?*

AS: *They had NOT thought of it at all. No, no machinery except by hand: hand pumps, hand compressors and all that sort of thing, not worked by power.*[1]

Five officers, including Captain Morse and Captain Sanderson, together with 88 O.R.s, remained at Marseille to unload the plant and machinery from the *Ansonia* and load the crated equipment into forty-seven railway trucks and carriages.[2] There were thirteen electrical generating sets, underground ventilation and pumping equipment (nineteen water pumps), as well as forty portable drilling

Map 5: **France and Belgium at the time of 3rd Australian Tunnelling Company**

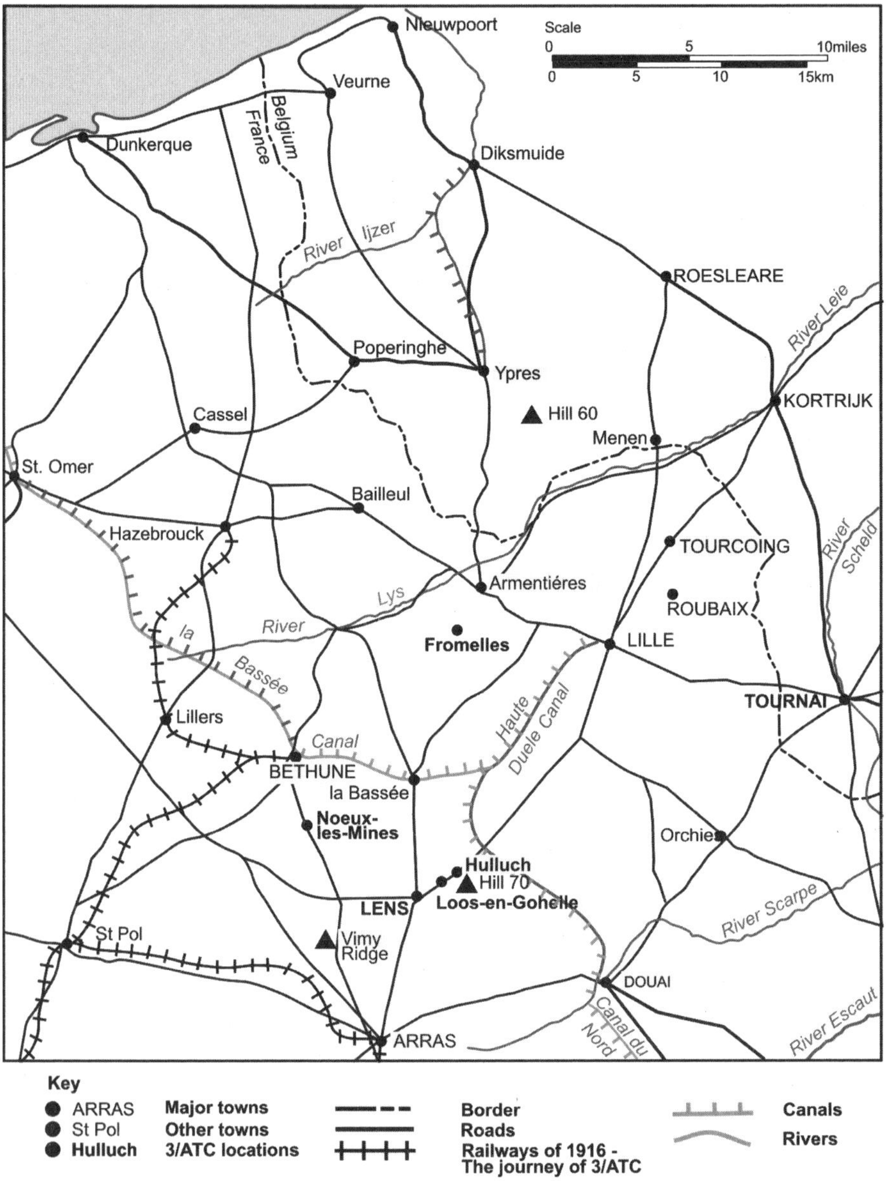

Key
- ● ARRAS — Major towns
- ● St Pol — Other towns
- ● Hulluch — 3/ATC locations
- ▬ ▬ ▬ Border
- ▬▬▬ Roads
- ┼┼┼┼ Railways of 1916 – The journey of 3/ATC
- Canals
- Rivers

machines. A Studebaker car was unloaded, donated by businesses in the five main Australian cities, with its five tyres provided by the Goodyear Tyre Company.³

AS: *Mr Sullivan, whom I knew very well, was the President of the Chamber of Mines. He gave us a motor car, an American motor car. It was given to the O.C. of the Australian Mining Corps as a present by the institution. We landed it and I hadn't seen* *it out of the case before. It was the first I saw of it. Painted on the bonnet was 'O.C. Australian Mining Corps'* [laughs] – *across the bonnet in big letters!* [laughing] *Of course, we rushed to get a painter with a pot of paint and a brush to paint that out. It was quite ridiculous, you know, the silly things that are sometimes done.*[4]

With all the equipment safely stored aboard the train, Sanderson and his colleagues left Marseille on 11 May for the long rail journey to Hazebrouck, via Lyons, Abbeville, the outskirts of Paris via Versailles, Boulogne, Calais and St Omer.[5]

Interviewer: *And when and where did you first work on the minefields?*

AS: *We were told to go to Hazebrouck in France; the train was to take us and drop us off there. People came down, the Inspector of Mines and various people from G.H.Q., and they looked at all this stuff – the 200 tons of stuff – and they said to me: 'What are you thinking? You can't get this up to the front line! You can't make use of this!'*

They all looked down their noses and they all went away. [Laughs] *But we showed them we COULD make use of the equipment and we showed them we could go THREE times as fast as they could. Then they got me to come across to England and give the Quarter Master General information and buy the same sort of plant for the other British companies.*[6]

Arrival and splitting up

C.E.W. Bean's interview with Major Sanderson explained that:

CB/AS: *When the Australian Mining Corps came to France it bought with it a quantity of electrical machinery for the lighting of galleries, boring of shafts etc. This drew on it…the notice of the other Mining Corps in France, who were rather inclined to laugh at it for its machinery and technical gear which was considered impractical and rather absurd for the active mining operations on the front. In fact, the company began to be rather ashamed of the equipment which it had bought. It was dumped at Hazebrouck, and the company trusted that it would be forgotten there.*

Shortly afterwards, however, the miners at the front began to strike water, and to put in tunnels of considerable length, when electrical lighting was perfectly feasible. The tunnelling companies then began to understand the situation, and the possibility of mine lighting and that their gear was not at all useless after all, but that actually, they were the only adequately equipped mining corps on the whole of the British front. The Corps was then about to be split up into three separate tunnelling companies. G.H.Q., finding how useful the machinery and equipment was, especially asked that the small mechanical and electrical engineering sections which were attached to each company should be combined into a separate Australian Unit. The A.I.F. agreed and the A.E. & M.M. & B.C. (Australian Electrical and Mechanical Mining & Boring Company), better known as the 'Alphabet' Company, was formed under Major Morse. For a long time, this company was the only one of its sort in France, and did the whole of the electrical lighting and working of power plants for all the underground operations along the whole British front. So much so that the 3rd Australian Tunnelling Company found that, when first they wanted their own galleries lit with electrical light, they could not get the services of the Australian Alphabet Company, which was too busy elsewhere. No less that thirteen British companies were being supplied by it. The Alphabet Company has in 1918 more than duplicated all its original gear and machinery.[7]

In May 1916 many of the British mining systems – especially in the clay of Flanders – were badly equipped and waterlogged, with bad lighting and ventilation. Damian Finlayson noted in his tunnelling book *Crumps and Camouflets* that General Harvey, the Inspector of Mines, recognised the potential of the equipment. On 20 May, within eight days of its arrival at Hazebrouck, he had a 9-kilowatt electric generator and a Wombat boring machine installed at the Second Army Mine School near Ypres. Two months later, the First Army School at Houchin, 2 miles west of Noeux-les-Mines, had the same equipment, training tunnellers in the use of the 'Wombat' to drill ventilation holes in underground dugouts and chambers. Major Morse, O.C. of the Alphabet Company, acquired the Studebaker car. Within four months it was in an unrepairable condition, ruined by French cobblestones.[8]

During the first week in October 1916, the A.E. & M.M. & B.C. unit was officially formed. With a strength of only 300 men, it worked with all five armies of the British Expeditionary Force (B.E.F.) along the entire Western Front, providing lighting and ventilation to dugouts and tunnels, as well as geological boring equipment for water supplies.[9]

The Mining Corps men were predominately volunteers from the mining industry across Australia who were accepted up to the age of 49, in recognition of the wide mining experience and knowledge they could pass on to the younger men. Several ignored a few birthdays on enlistment. Sapper William Watson, a 54-year-old married brickmaker from Perth, had declared himself to be '49 years'. Watson had his first heart attack in Sydney soon after enlistment, running to put out a bush fire in the camp. He never made it to the front line; in June 1916 he was repatriated as 'unfit for general service'.[10]

The Australian Mining Corps was always composed of volunteers while British soldiers had been volunteers until March 1916, when conscription was imposed by the Military Services Act on all single men between the ages of 18 and 41. In May 1916, a second Act of Parliament extended conscription to British married men as well.

AUSTRALIA

Back in Australia, on 1 May, and enlisting in the tunnelling reinforcements, was Sapper James Joseph Hallinan, 21, from Sydney who had completed a carpenter's apprenticeship and declared service with the Signallers' Militia. Interviewed in 1987, aged 93, James would describe how he came to join the Miners' Corps:

> When I enlisted at West Maitland, I was examined by a doctor. When we'd signed the papers to serve our 'God, King and Country' and the rest of it, we were transferred to the Newcastle Showground where there was thousands of soldiers... Our first accommodation was on the bare seats in the grandstand.
>
> 'Alright,' the officers would call out, 'we want volunteers for the infantry. Are there any volunteers for The Light Horse? Any volunteers for the artillery?'
>
> You'd automatically fall out if you wanted to. We were called up for 'Home Service' and they couldn't send us overseas. We could 'volunteer', on their invitation.
>
> A Captain Richards addressed the crowd: 'Are there any miners here? Hands up the miners! Anybody work in the mines?'
>
> Lots of my mates put up their hands.
>
> 'Righto! Fall out!'
>
> One fellow said: 'Come on, Jim!'
>
> 'No!', I said. 'I want to join the Signalling Corps.'
>
> 'The Signalling Corps is not taking any more recruits,' said the officer.
>
> The Captain came over and said: 'Are you a miner?'
>
> Two mates said: 'Oh, he worked with us. He used to go down sometimes, but he was mainly up around about the pit top.'
>
> 'Come on!' Captain Richards says, 'We want men like you. We don't want facemen over there. We want men of all trades in the Miners' Corps.'
>
> Then they transferred us as reinforcements to Seymour Training Camp in Victoria, 60 miles south of Melbourne. We were training for the Miners' Corps, using explosives, doing shaft and trench work, filling sandbags and drilling holes. You say: 'Prepare the bull!' This was a plug of guncotton, fixed to a wire, with a detonator on the end. When they're ready, that's

lowered down and the charge is planted. The bull's explosion blows out all the loose soil and any water.

That's the sort of training we got, as miners, for Gallipoli. Then they were sending the men from Gallipoli to France and they changed the names of the 'Miners' Battalions' to 'Tunnelling Companies'. We went to the Salisbury Plain in England and were allocated to Numbers 1, 2 or 3 of Australian companies in France. When we landed in France at the end of 1916, we had a long route up to the final camp. We got the train at night, in a snowstorm. We finished up at Béthune. Eventually some lorries picked us up and took us to the final company we was attached to: the 3rd Company.[11]

FRANCE

Marching out

After their arrival in France in May 1916, Major T.W. Edgeworth David, the amiable geologist of the Technical Staff, was attached to the staff of the Engineer-in-Chief at G.H.Q. Captains Morse and Hunter were moved to the Alphabet Company and Captain Pollock went to the Second Army Mine Rescue and Listening School. Captain Sanderson was posted to No.3 A.T.C. 'for special duty'.[12]

On reaching the Western Front the tunnelling officers were informed by the C. of M. of Second Army that all B.E.F. mining operations were controlled by the Director of Mines at G.H.Q. and that the tunnelling companies would be reporting to the C. of M. within their Army area. As there was no place for a battalion headquarters, the Mining Battalion was broken up forthwith.'[13]

By the autumn of 1918 there would be three Australian geologists on the Western Front: Major T.W. Edgeworth David C.M.G. (nicknamed 'Old Prof'), Lieutenant G.A. Cook of 2 A.T.C. and Lieutenant C.S. Homan of 3 A.T.C.[14]

The timing of the arrival of an Australian Mining Corps staffed with experienced, energetic and innovative specialists, engineers and miners proved a vital addition to the allied mining effort. The British mining industry could no longer afford to lose its coal miners and the attrition rate for fighting miners was high. The arrival of the Australians coincided with a gradual strategic shift from defensive mining to the offensive firing of mines, reflecting the improved organisation, training and activities of the tunnelling companies. At this time, it was calculated that along the British sectors of the Western Front, the underground war was at its height, with a mine blown every three minutes.

CB/AS: *After the Mining Corps was split up in France into three separate companies, Captain Sanderson was asked by Major Coulter to join him in the 3rd Company. There was at first a certain estrangement between the company's officers and the experts, whom the company scarcely considered as being one of themselves. But this soon cooled down, and Sanderson became one of the most prominent fighting officers among the tunnellers. At that time, the mining on the British front was in a very elementary stage. It was the Germans who made the first start in mining on the British front: they had the British beaten before the British Army was aware of it. A number of nasty mine explosions occurred. The British had to start working at a furious rate and under great difficulties, to protect themselves. Sanderson tells me that the work which some of the British Infantry Battalions, quite inexperienced in mining, had done at this time, has never been sufficiently recognised. The work was hastily organised: our men had to push out their defensive and offensive galleries when the Germans had ceased working, and by heroic efforts the British Mining Engineers and the Infantry in the early days managed, after a time, to get more or less equal with the Germans.*[15]

All new tunnelling companies were under the command of the British Engineer-in-Chief General Fowke. Major Coulter's 3rd Australian Company, with a strength of 14 officers and 354 O.R.s, were initially allotted to XI Corps, First Army commanded by Lieutenant General Sir Richard Haking, who had been responsible for the 1915 disastrous Battle of Aubers Ridge. Haking was about to repeat this failure at Fromelles in July, with appalling results.

Each tunnelling company consisted of four sections, each divided into three squads, led by a Lieutenant and a Sergeant. 3 A.T.C.'s sections were allocated to different locations. From 13 to 16 May, Nos. 1 and 2 Sections were deployed to relieve 255th Company R.E. along the Laventie front line, which stretched between the Boar's Head salient (where the first mine attack of the war by German Pioneers had taken place in December 1915) and the Sugar Loaf salient at Fromelles. No.3 section was temporarily billeted in Le Hamel with 254th Coy. R.E., while No.4 section went to 251st Coy. R.E., both to receive instructions from experienced units.[16]

When Alex Sanderson arrived in May 1916, the German Mining Corps were changing to units similar to the British called *Pionier-Mineur-Kompagnien*, each with 6 officers and 262 O.R.s, divided into three sections. By 1918 there would fifty *Mineur-Kompagnien*. The job of the *Pionier-Kompagnien*, of which there would be 700 by the end of 1917, was to project asphyxiating gas, and operate *Flamenwerfer* and *Minenwerfer*.[17]

1916 proved a decisive year of the war, as the Allies and the Central Powers developed new strategies and offensives to try to break the deadlock on the Western Front, a place the Australians, in their battlefield lingo, would soon refer to as 'The Corpse Factory'.[18]

AUSTRALIA

First Reinforcements

On 17 May 1916, the *City of Edinburgh* troopship arrived in Marseille bringing Mining Corps reinforcements. In Australia, on 20 May, the *Sydney Morning Herald* reported on an inspection by the Sydney District Commander of the A.I.F. troops, parading before a crowd of 10,000 people. Among them were the 4th Tunnelling Company (including Queenslanders) and the 1st Reinforcements, as well as one keen enlisted animal:

> The bands of Liverpool Headquarters and the Engineers played selections of music. The Commandant took the salute, as the various units marched past in columns of companies… One company had with it a small kangaroo as a mascot. The animal was held on a ribbon, but when it drew level with the saluting base it bobbed up and down, as if anxious to do its share in the saluting lines, as its male friends were doing. The crowd roared.[19]

H.M.A.T. *Warilda* sailed from Fremantle on 1 June for the European theatre, with Mining Corps reinforcements recruited in Queensland, Victoria, South Australia and Tasmania. The previous day the *West Australian* had reported: 'The men of No.6 Tunnelling Company met with a hearty reception from the large crowd as they swung along to the music of the Blackboy Hill band. The route was bedecked with flags. At the head of the 400 tunnellers, parading in full fighting equipment, was their recently presented flag.'[20]

Aboard the *Warilda* was 22-year-old Sapper 'Bobby' Walton from N.S.W. His grandson remembers his grandfather describing how: 'He and a group of mates went down to the beach on New Year's Eve in 1915, had a few beers and all decided to join up', before enrolling that same day in Sydney. Walton described digging tunnels in France with sharpened shovels and told of an incident later in the war in a rest camp, where he had been withdrawn after a long period in the front line. A British Regimental Sergeant Major was 'yelling at the troops and putting soldiers on a charge for any minor infraction of discipline, such as "mud on uniform" or a "missing button", anything that caught his eye.' One annoyed Australian soldier took exception to this behaviour, raised his rifle and shot the R.S.M. dead. The camp was surrounded by blue-capped M.P.s, the Australian officers were recalled from leave and the men marched out of the camp the next day. Although the affair was hushed up, the lesson was learned that it was not wise to shout at tired, but armed, Australian soldiers.[21]

FRANCE

The 4th, 5th and 6th Tunnelling Reinforcement Companies, comprising 1,064 officers and O.R.s, docked at Plymouth on 18 July, the day before the Fromelles battle, and were detrained to Amesbury and Tidworth. In France they were absorbed into the existing three companies which became independent units, much to their manifest satisfaction. They had chaffed at control by battalion headquarters and put on their colour patches, a purple 'T' inside of which were attached the company numbers: 1, 2 or 3.

Mining underground on the Western Front was now assuming a major role in the tenacious and relentless war between the opposing trenches. Simon Jones, in his book on underground warfare, writes that: 'A census, taken in June 1916, disclosed the fact that 8,000- 24,000 men (including the attached infantry) were continually employed on underground work. In June 1916 mining reached its zenith along the most active sector, the British First Army front, which centred on the area Givenchy-lès-la Bassée, Hulluch and Loos up to Laventie.'[22]

By 1918 there would be 19,000 allied tunnellers on the Western Front in thirty-three 'secret' tunnelling companies mining underground: twenty-five British (170th to 185th and 251st to 258th), one Portuguese (1918 only) and seven Commonwealth; three Canadian, one New Zealand and three Australian (plus the Alphabet Company).[22] In June 1916, along the First Army front from Laventie to Vimy Ridge (north end), 79 British and 73 German mines were fired. On the whole Western Front, out of a total of 227 mines, 101 were fired by the British and 106 by the Germans – or one mine every three hours.[23]

Chapter 7

Into, and Under, the Front Lines

29 May 1916

Colvin, Ducks Bill and Mauquissait

CB/AS: *The 3rd Australian Tunnelling Company first went into the line in May 1916 to the two mining areas known as Colvin* and Ducks Bill,* near La Bassée. The Mauquissait salient was north of Colvin. A little further north of this were the workings known as Winchester* and Red Lamp. These two were considered by the British to be dangerous centres, and so the young Australian Company was not initially put into them. In the summer, however, the southernmost workings of the Winchester system were entrusted to them. 3 A.T.C. were allocated a mining sector southwest of Armentières, where the 1st and 2nd Army division line met, relieving 255 Coy. R.E. These workings were in blue clay at depths from twenty to thirty-five feet.*[1]

[*These existing mine systems were all named after the communication trenches connected to them. The allocated area was very flat land with only elevations being the Aubers Ridge.]

From 27–31 May, 3 A.T.C. were involved in purely defensive mining, protecting the infantry from hostile mines. The British 61st (2nd South Midland) Division, who were to fight at Fromelles in July, were new to the trenches and they, too, were finding their feet in this hostile theatre of war.[2]

Bean described these British infantrymen as: 'still inexperienced and of much slighter physique than the Australian.'[3]

Ammonal explosive

Having taken over the protection of the line on 29 May from 255th Coy. R.E., the Australian miners were soon in action. A German gallery was heard approaching within 8–10 feet. In response, at a depth of 26 feet, they laid a charge of 480 lbs of ammonal in Winchester tunnel, 450 feet out from the British front line. Noting that enemy activity had ceased, the Australians immediately tamped up their tunnel for 130 feet, leaving two air spaces of 10 feet, to absorb

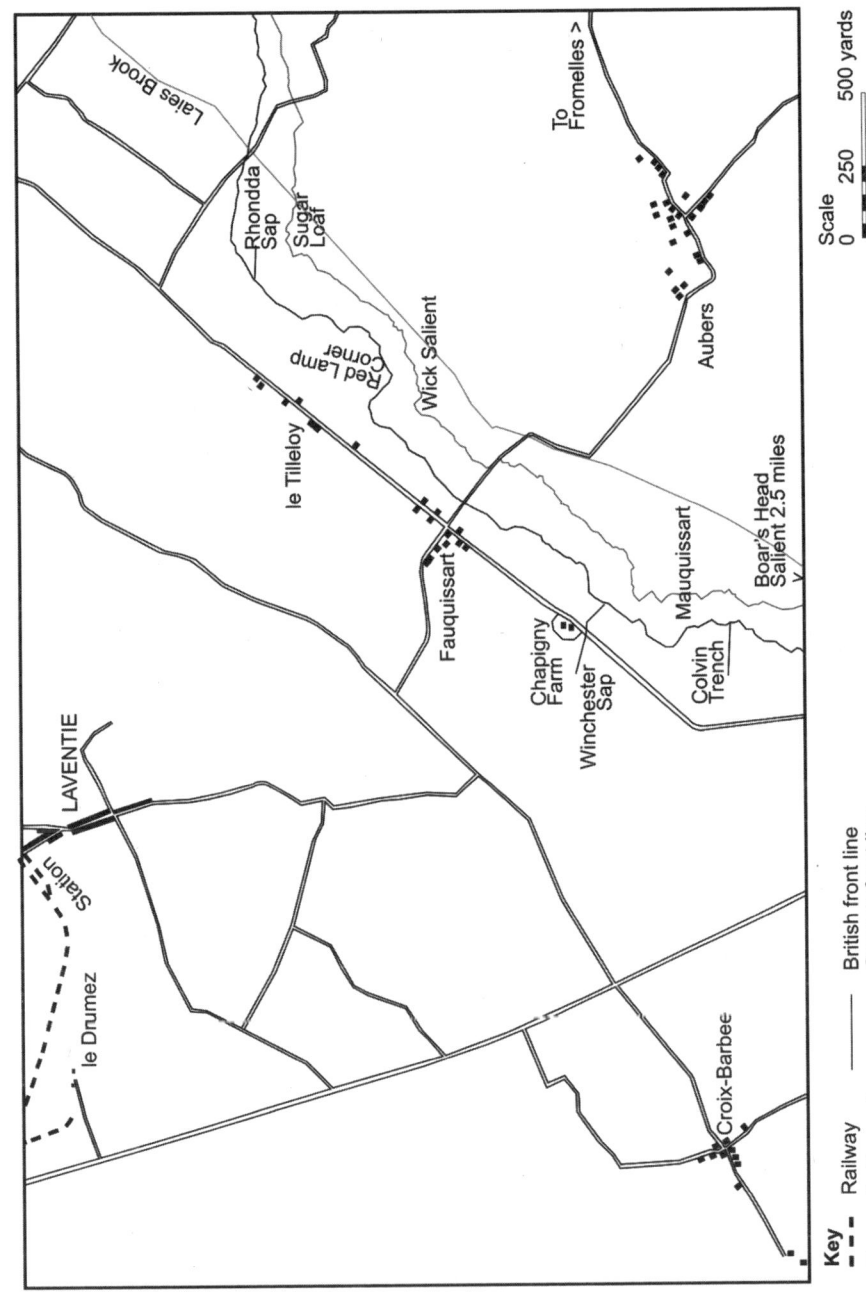

Map 6: Sections 1 and 2 of 3 A.T.C. take over the front South-West of Fromelles May 1916

an explosive back blast, before the C.O. Major Coulter ordered the ignition of their charge, aimed also to assist a British infantry attack. The 'pear' shape and direction of the resulting crater (95 x 75 feet), created by 3 A.T.C.'s explosion, indicated that the company had inflicted casualties and destroyed the German gallery. An enemy machine-gun emplacement was silenced by the blast and was believed destroyed. Large blocks of clay were lying against the German parapet.[4]

Robert Graves described his experiences of being on the receiving end of ammonal explosions when on the Somme in 1916. The Germans opposite were sending over 2-gallon cylindrical drum mortars, filled with scrap metal, and fired from a wooden cannon buried in the earth. These home-made cannisters, discharged with a time-fuse: 'contained about two pounds of an explosive called ammonal that looked like salmon paste, smelled like marzipan, and, when it went off, sounded like the Day of Judgement. The cannister could easily be heard approaching and looked harmless in the air, but its shock was as shattering as the very heaviest shell.'[5]

The tunnellers' underground mine explosions were, by contrast, static and undetected until they were set off.

Ammonal was a powder mix of 75 percent ammonium nitrate, 20 percent aluminium and 5 percent carbon, and was altogether 350 percent more powerful than gunpowder. It was hydroscopic and needed packing in waterproof covers. Ammonal's tin-lined boxes were not entirely waterproof; if left in a mine for several days, they were stored in either guncotton bags or 4-gallon petrol tins (holding 50lbs of ammonal) which were then sealed up with pitch and safe for transporting. Guncotton was used for shattering and ammonal for lifting. The charges were exploded after the insertion of detonators into holes in guncotton primers, followed by the insertion of the primers into holes in the guncotton slabs. Initiation was either by a Bickford safety fuse, joined to an instantaneous fuse for the simultaneous detonation of more than one charge, or by exploder and electric leads. Instantaneous detonating fuses were used later in the war.[6]

Silence from the enemy's direction was an ominous, worrying sign. It meant the enemy could be charging and tamping their mine, or a camouflet (*Quetschmine* in German), a controlled explosive counter charge. ('Tamping' involved piling up sandbags to seal a chamber off and prevent explosive forces and gasses blowing back up one's gallery.)

3 A.T.C.'s strength was now 14 officers and 352 O.R.s, with three attached officers and 102 O.R.s. Mining work of a defensive and offensive nature was continued; an average of 400 feet of driving per week being achieved on all gallery faces.[7]

Captain Oliver Woodward, 1st Tunnelling Company, would explain in his 'War Story' the arrangements for the underground protection of front-line trenches:

From points in the front or in support trenches, shafts, either inclined or vertical, were sunk at from 100 feet to 200 feet intervals, and from these, drives were put out towards the enemy lines. These drives were then connected by cross-cuts, which formed the main lateral gallery...located from 75 feet to 120 feet ahead of our own front line. Then at intervals of about 50 feet, listening posts were driven from this lateral gallery towards the enemy lines...at right angles to the left and right... These 'T' heads were carried toward each other to ensure that the area between should be under control of a counter mine fired from either listening post. As an added protection, bore holes 8 inches in diameter were put in and charged with a torpedo carrying from 100 to 200 pounds high explosive.[8]

Listeners

Listeners, positioned under No Man's Land, were constantly alert for the slightest sound of enemy activity. The historian Peter Barton noted that German miners often gave themselves away by the tramping sound of their hobnailed boots, the noisy installations of their mortice and tenon supports, the nailing of wooden rails to the gallery floors (the British screwed them in) or the movement of the wooden wheels of the German trucks on their timber rails.[9]

In the early stage of the war the British had used basic listening sticks. The French put their ears to water bottles to hear the vibrations of enemy work, but then developed pocket-sized 'geophones', special stethoscopes which could determine the direction and distance of enemy activity through the amplification of the sound waves transmitted from the ground at an intensity two and a half times greater than listening with the naked ear.[10] A Lieutenant in 171 Tunnelling Coy. noted that with a geophone he could hear 'the earthworms crawl (like elephants in lead boots) and ants walk'.[11]

Sound travelled further underground than through the surface air. A doctor's stethoscope was adapted so each earpiece was connected to rubber tubes and, via small nipples, to separate wooden sensors within which two mica discs enclosed a mass of mercury. The listener moved each disc to-and-fro across the surfaces of the surrounding tunnel faces until the two sounds heard 'balanced' in each ear. Two sensors were used to identify the direction of enemy sounds. One sensor alone (again with both earpieces) was used to work out distance. By taking bearings of the sound with compasses, the observations from different listeners could triangulate, and pinpoint precisely, the location of the enemy's tunnels. These notes would be speedily collected to be collated on central company reports and noted on underground plans. Later remote electronic systems were set up to carry information to a central Listening Chamber where one man could monitor up to fifty posts stretching over 3 miles.

Listeners would be sent on courses to improve their skills. Some listeners had very acute hearing. These patient, self-disciplined tunnellers needed nerves of steel to sit alone silently for hours in listening posts, dug out from advanced lateral tunnels parallel with trenches, far out under No Man's Land, straining their ears for any sounds that would betray the signs of the enemy's presence. The laterals, access inclines and shafts helped with air flow to ventilate the tunnels. Listeners were trained in Mining Schools to identify their own breathing, exploding shells above, water flowing through the chalk tunnels or the noises of their own colleagues' excavations with grafting tools.

British Mining notes of March 1916 from the Listening Schools advised the distances that various enemy activities could be heard through average chalk:

	Naked ear	With a Geophone (distances in feet)
Picking	150	300
Shovelling	70	120
Dirt Falling	35	60
Walking	50	80
Talking	12	50[12]

Some listeners were so adept they could track the course of the approaching enemy tunnellers, estimating their speed of progress in a merciless, blindfolded 'cat and mouse' pursuit. The Assistant Inspector of Mines, Major R. Stokes M.C., wrote that two or three times a day all underground work was stopped at a synchronised agreed time, within a specified area for a focussed, total listening silence.[13]

Digging tunnels in chalk had advantages over clay, as chalk was a dry and strong material. Indeed, modern archaeologists welcome the very stable conditions of the First World War chalk underground tunnels of Artois and Picardy – the modern department of Pas-de-Calais – many in pristine condition and intact a century after the war. However, clay transmitted sounds of mining less well. The disadvantages of tunnelling in chalk was that, with the flint deposits, it made an audible ringing sound when struck which could be heard at a distance. It was almost impossible to dig tunnels silently in chalk areas, which is one reason the British dug deeper where they would be less likely to be audible. Chalk was very porous and water could seep through and flood lower galleries, especially the deep tunnels.[14]

The Australian tunnellers were on the alert, moving quietly in their galleries, making signs and whispering to each other and avoiding coughing; they knew their lives depended on being as silent as the mice that warned them of gas.

Tunnellers were given a private code of two or three letters for passing the most urgent messages, which were to be learnt by heart and not revealed: B = I want bags, SD = I want explosives.

Other messages encoded were: 'I want advice, can you come? Yes. No. Carry on. I must blow shall I wait for you? I must blow at once. Hostile blow in front. Hostile blow right. Hostile blow left. No casualties. Casualties.'[15]

The 3 A.T.C. War Diary notes that to clarify underground locations:

> The drives, fighting points and listening galleries were given a nomenclature by combination of letters and numerals. For instance, the first number represented a Shaft i.e. 22. 'D' stands for deep level and refers to depths between 50 feet and 75 feet. 'DD' stands for a deep/deep level and refers to a depth over 75 feet. 'R' is right and 'L' is left, thus a drive referred to as '22 DDR1L1' reads: 'From Number 22 Shaft, deep deep level, first turning to the right and then first turning to the left.

CB/AS: *On 20 June, 3 A.T.C. began to sink a shaft at Mauquissart, between Colvin and Winchester, for a defensive tunnel system to protect a strong Machine Gun position from an underground attack. A parapet was erected and the sinking of a shaft commenced, with a collar set constructed (a structural wood frame around the top of a shaft). From these works the Australians distinctly heard Germans mining from the trenches opposite. When patrols of tunnellers were sent out into No Man's Land at night to listen from the surface, they could hear the Germans mining and alerted the infantry. The Australians were about to start counter-mining when they were relieved and sent to the Red Lamp and Winchester sections, and for special work in the Fromelles section. Before they left, the Australians, anticipating trouble underground, reported this to 257 Coy. R.E. who relieved them between 13 and 18 July. The British tunnellers were warned that the enemy was active near their second shaft site, about 200 feet away. However, as 257 Coy. could not confirm the Australians' suspicions, or discern any signs of the enemy approaching underground, they abandoned the shaft sinking. In August 1916 the Infantry garrison in this salient was blown up, with twenty-five men killed and forty wounded.*

Perhaps this is one of the reasons for Alex Sanderson's comments to Bean that the early British mining companies (numbering from 170 onwards) 'contained a fair number of experts and did some comparatively good and sound work'. The later companies (whose numbers ranged from 250–260) were 'much less efficient and were certainly children in the hands of the Germans when the Australians were first tunnelling along the front'.[16]

Red Lamp

'Red Lamp' was named after the lamp that had been hung at night on the salient's apex; if a man passed in front of the lamp he was friendly. Here the old main gallery was turned, 34 feet deep and 180 feet out, and used as a listening post, while the right-hand tunnel, 36 feet down and 377 feet in length, was turned and dug as a flank drive to protect the salient. There were three shafts here giving access to five underground galleries, where seventeen digging tunnellers were relentlessly driving forward, supported by pumpers excavating the water and alert listeners crouching patiently in their underground posts. When, on 9 June, an enemy gallery was heard rapidly approaching their workings from the direction of the German-held Wick salient, it was decided to blow them.

Mining HQ had instructed: 'If we do not blow the Germans, they will blow us. The Germans are probably employing every available man they can on this front. They are fully aware we have tunnels which can be turned into mines, and they know their exact locations.'[17]

Fauquissart, Chapigny, Winchester and Armentières

At Fauquissart, seven 3 A.T.C. men were working underground; three at the face, two on the pumps, one listening and one N.C.O. The same was also true at Chapigny. At Winchester, a drive was put in to avoid a badly broken old drive where a dangerous rush of water had been struck previously. Two teams of four men at Winchester were driving two faces forward at two shafts, while the others were pumping water out or listening intently.[18]

In the Armentières area, with its high-water table, shallow mining was impossible. Even deep mining was difficult, and it was confined to defensive systems, justified more by their effect on the morale of the troops in the firing line rather than by the degree of protection afforded.[19]

Explosive push-pipes

On 3 June, 3 A.T.C. had fired its first 'push-pipe' mine, a method of rapidly creating trenches in No Man's Land prior to an attack. The 'pipe-pushing' technique was an Australian innovation that used a Barrett hydraulic jack, positioned inside the front-line trench, to push successive joined-up sections of hollow steel pipes – each containing wiring, detonators and 6 kilograms of ammonal explosives – through a parapet wall and forward under No Man's Land at a depth of 2 metres.

On the night of 29/30 June, Major Coulter and nineteen miners attempted to blow a 50-metre-long communication trench between a British and German sap by electrically exploding a push-pipe, a procedure not yet attempted on a battlefield. The objective was to support a British infantry attack to seize and hold the Boar's Head salient, 2 miles southwest of the Sugar Loaf.[20]

The Australian blowing of the instantaneous trench was partially successful; only half its length ignited. The two Royal Sussex Pals raiding battalions managed to reach and enter the enemy trenches, but their brave attempt to capture the salient failed. The enemy lines were almost undamaged by British artillery fire and their defenders were well-prepared. The enemy had put up mocking signs asking: 'When are you coming over, Tommy?' and shouted: 'Come on, Sussex' as they fired their machine guns. Two hours later, a strong German counter-attack drove back the Pals, inflicting 1,153 casualties.[21]

Major Coulter had shown, though, that an instantaneously created communication trench could offer a measure of protection for attacking infantry and also be useful for re-supplies and the evacuation of wounded. Lieutenant General Haking acknowledged 3 A.T.C.'s push-pipe skills by including their use in his planning for the forthcoming Fromelles offensive, under the 9th Corps.[22]

The flaw in the whole push-pipe system was that the pipework wiring, prior to its blowing, was very exposed to enemy shelling, as Captain Alex Sanderson would discover on 19 July in No Man's Land opposite the Sugar Loaf salient.

Battle of the Somme, July 1916

At 07:30 on 1 July, 45 miles to the south of Fromelles, after five days of bombardment of enemy lines, a vast offensive on the Somme began which would last 143 days and inflict 57,470 British casualties on the first day.

German raid

Coulter's report of 3 July noted that on 1 July, 3 A.T.C. blew a mine off Colvin Trench in No Man's Land, forming a crater. The Germans retaliated with an intensive two-hour night-time bombardment, followed up by a hostile raiding party which entered the British front line where the Australians were working underground. The raiders blew in a shaft and a magazine store containing 1,300 lbs of guncotton and ammonal, creating a crater 40 x 19 feet. A second mobile charge destroyed a dugout and damaged another shaft.[23]

Both sides raided primarily to destroy the enemy's shafts, as sinking new shafts was very time consuming. Their destruction would deny the defenders access to their tunnels and impair their underground fighting capability more than the 'blowing in' of an underground gallery, which could be repaired. During the enemy raid, two tunnelling officers withdrew all the sappers but remained to tend to a wounded man and were themselves wounded. Lieutenant Kennedy would return to duty a year later, while Lieutenant Harry Seale, a metallurgist and mining manager, was evacuated by hospital ship to England with a dislocated hip, a facial gunshot wound and his vision affected. In November 1916, Seale would be repatriated to find his relieved wife Isabel, whom he had married just before his departure to war, welcoming him back at Fremantle Harbour.[24]

Infantry panic

On 3 July, at around 02:00, there was a scare in the front trench. Eight of the attached British infantry took fright and disappeared over the parados. The 'poor bloody infantry' faced the constant fear of the enemy shelling them by day, raiding them at night or 'lifting' (blowing them up) from underground tunnels. As the 3 A.T.C. War Diary succinctly put it: 'They got the "wind up" very badly on this particular night.' For nearly half an hour there was no one in the firing line for a distance of 100 yards. Corporal Mason of 3 A.T.C. later reported:

> I was in No.10A Shaft and heard someone outside call out: 'They are over!' I went outside with two A.I.F. men and found the fire trench blocked with infantry, crowding out and making for the communication trench. When I asked where they were going, they said: 'The Germans are over!' They didn't know where their officers were. I told them their place was back at their posts even if the Germans were over, and we induced them to return to the firing line.[25]

Captain Knyvett described what happened when a man's nerve got past breaking-point:

> He would see an imaginary enemy bearing down upon his sentry-post and fire wildly, giving alarm to the whole line. A German sentry would reply to him, more of our men would fire back, more Germans would join in, star-shells make the night as bright as day; then Fritz would 'get the wind up' thoroughly and call for artillery support, our guns would blaze in reply, and there would be many casualties. Just because one man lost his nerve and 'saw things'.[26]

Red Lamp Section

In the Red Lamp main tunnel, 233 feet out from Shaft No.2 at a depth of 36 feet, 3 A.T.C. tunnellers broke into an old British lateral drive. Coulter's weekly

Mine Report of 12 July records that: 'We have now pushed past through an old gallery at 327 feet.'[27]

In 1918 Alex Sanderson would describe this old gallery to Charles Bean:

CB/AS: *There was a story up near Fromelles of a mining gallery which had been pushed by the British Infantry across No Man's Land in the soft clay and exploded near the German lines. A crater existed near the German parapet at this point, but our officers could not believe that this was really a British working, as the difficulties of the soft clay must have been insuperable at the time. Sanderson says that during the summer of 1916, during mine workings on that front, the Australians of No.3 Company had dug into these old works, and actually found part of this old British shaft. It had been worked through the soft clay without any mining props or sets. No timber of any sort was available to help the infantry shore up the sides of the tunnel. It must have been rushed across No Man's Land, by the rough means they had in hand, in about three weeks' desperate working. When their rough calculations led them to believe that they were beneath the German lines, they had blown the mine. Their calculations had not been quite accurate. The tunnel was a trifle out of the straight, and the crater about 15 yards from the German parapet. Sanderson says that it is quite possible that some Germans were overwhelmed by the debris in the German trenches. The sides of the tunnel must have been bulging, almost to the point of breaking in, by the time it was ready to blow. It must have required great pluck for the British infantry to have pushed out blindly into the German section in this way. This mine was on the site of the Red Lamp Section. Perhaps the British Infantry were assisted by a few miners.*[28]

As the Australian tunnellers broke into the old British Red Lamp gallery, there would have been a change in air flow and pressure in the Australian tunnel.

Chapter 8

Battle of Fromelles

19 July 1916

'If the historian cannot write that drama in its full truth, with the interplay of good and evil, wisdom and folly, of all parties working to its complex conclusion, then so much less the historian he.'[1]

Alex Sanderson was a '19 July man'; one of the few to survive a battle that resulted in the greatest number of Australian casualties of the war in a single day: 6,533 killed and wounded.

Background to the attack

On 14 February 1916, generals Joffre and Haig had met at Chantilly to discuss plans for a coordinated breakthrough on the Western Front. For political reasons, and against his better judgement, Haig agreed to a joint 30-mile offensive in Picardy, on the Somme, with twenty-five British and thirty-nine French divisions.

A week later, however, on 21 February, General Erich von Falkenhayn launched his deadly 12-mile front offensive on the strategic town of Verdun to break through the French Army's salient and force the French government to negotiate a truce. His aim was not, as he later claimed, to 'bleed the French Army to death'. This excuse, the historian Sir Hew Strachen explained, 'was a way for Falkenhayn to rationalise the failure to achieve a breakthrough'.

A few dozen stubborn French *Poilus* had delayed the first wave of German infantry and Verdun itself had been held. Fort Douaumont was captured on the fourth day but was later retaken, along with Fort Vaux, by General Nivelle, who, on 8 April issued his famous command: 'Ils ne passeront pas!' (They shall not pass!).

La voie sacrée ('the sacred way'), the lifeblood of the sacrificial French resistance, brought an endless flow of men, ammunition and weaponry up the narrow road to supply Verdun, with one vehicle passing every fourteen seconds. Forty divisions of the French Army would be rotated through the 'Mill on the River Meuse'. By the end of the Verdun offensive in December 1916, 162,440 French soldiers, as well as 143,000 Germans, would be killed. The French had now suffered 2 million casualties since the war began.[2]

Haig was preparing for a mid-August attack but, on 26 May, Joffre insisted that their Somme offensive must start on 1 July. With French troops diverted to shore up Verdun, by the start of the Somme battle only five of Joffre's divisions – not the forty planned – remained on an 8-mile front to support a British front of double that length.

Aubers Ridge, 1915

In May 1915, in the Battle of Aubers Ridge, the British 1st Division had attacked and failed over the very same ground the English and Australian divisions would be ordered to cross on 19 July 1916, along a 4,000-yard front at Fromelles, and against the same well-prepared enemy.[3] The Aubers Ridge attack was a disaster for the British, with no ground or tactical advantage gained at the expense of a casualty rate ten times the enemy's. The shortage of shells in France precipitated a major political storm in England, with Lord Kitchener ceding control of the Ministry of Munitions to the cabinet's new Ministry of Supply under Lloyd George, with a coalition government and, ultimately, with the replacement of Asquith as Prime Minister by Lloyd George in December 1916.[4]

Lieutenant General Sir Roger Haking of XI Corps, who had commanded the 1st Division in 1915 at Fromelles, was about to fight a similar battle in 1916 against the same experienced soldiers of the 6th Bavarian Division.[5] On 5 July 1916, Haig ordered generals Herbert Plummer of the Second Army and Charles Munro of the First Army to 'select a front on which to pierce the enemy's lines'.

In vain Munro attempted to get the Fromelles attack moved to Hill 70 at Loos (where the Germans were equally well dug in),[6] while Plummer suggested, and Munro agreed, for a joint attack at the junction of their two armies at Fromelles. Haking was ordered to prepare a plan of attack. On 13 July Munro was informed that Haig no longer wanted a breakthrough, but a 'threat' against Lille and a limited 'holding' attack.[7,8,9] The rationale for the diversionary Fromelles attack was to prevent German forces in the area from moving to the Somme to oppose the offensive that would be launched on 1 July.[10]

Haking repeated the mistakes of the previous year, revisiting his maps for another attack at Fromelles towards the Aubers Ridge, whose commanding position the Germans still occupied. The possession of the ridge was considered strategically important, with its domination of all approaches to the city of Lille. The village of Fromelles itself lay 2 miles behind the German front line.

In his training manual of 1913 Haking had written: 'There is one rule which alone will lead to success, and that is to push forward, always to attack.'[11] He

Map 7: 3rd Australian Tunnelling Company at Fromelles

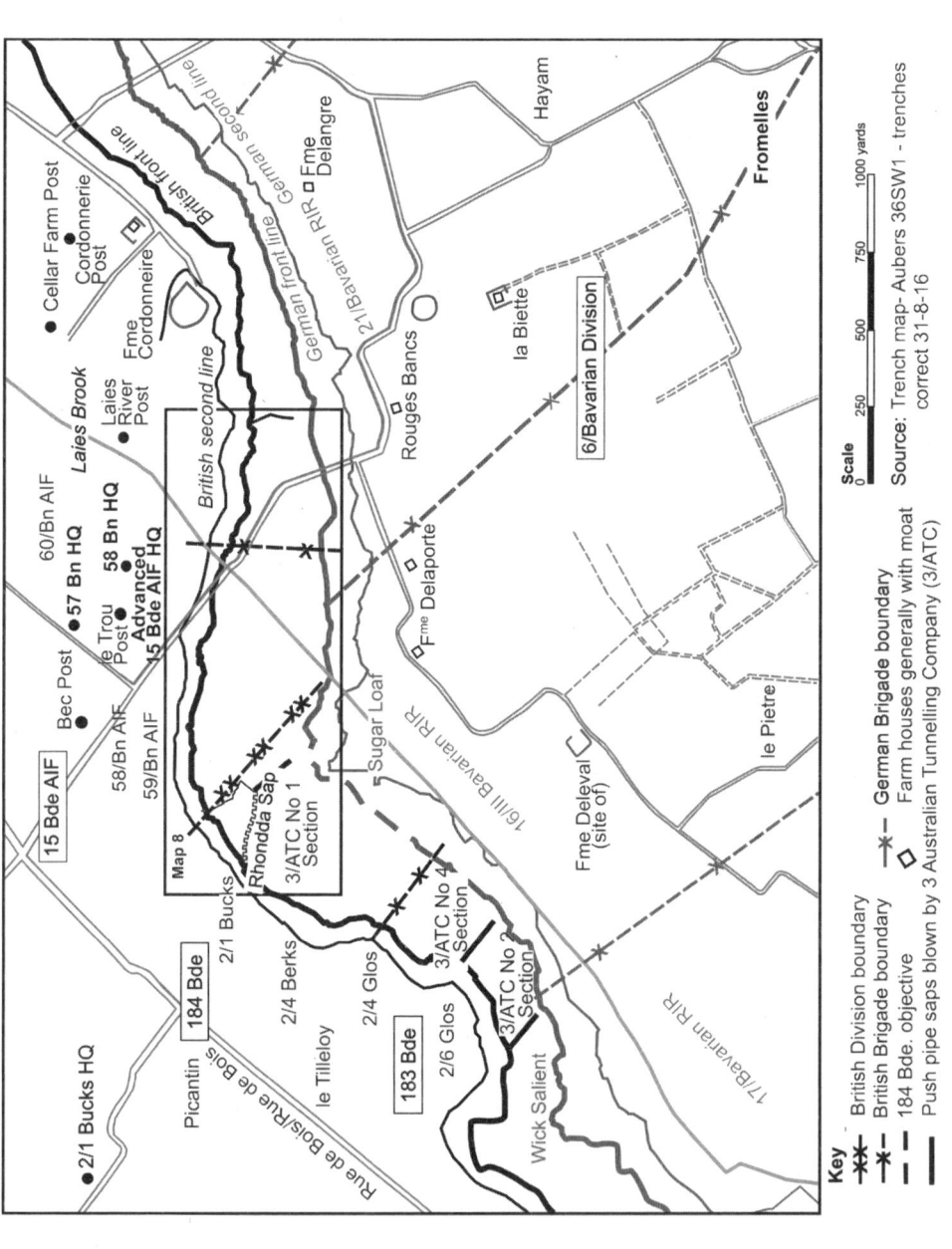

shared the strategic offensive mentality of General Nivelle, whose exhortations to boldly attack with *élan* (spirit) would lead to terrible French losses, the mutinies of 40,000 troops in 68 divisions, Nivelle's own dismissal in May 1917 and his replacement by Pétain.[12]

At a 16 July conference, Haking over-optimistically assured his divisional commanders that: 'the narrow depth of the attack should make it possible to reduce the defenders to a state of collapse before the assault.'[13]

The official British historian, Captain Wilfred Miles, a staff officer attached to the 61st Division, outlined the folly of the 19 July assault:

> The pity of it was that the action need not have been fought, since the First Army had perfect liberty to cancel it. To have delivered battle at all, after hurried preparation, with troops of all arms handicapped by their lack of experience and of training in offensive trench-warfare, betrayed a grave underestimate of the enemy's powers of resistance. The utmost endeavours of the artillery were unable to subdue the German batteries or to 'reduce the defenders to a state of collapse before the assault' so the infantry, advancing in broad daylight, paid the price. Even if…the infantry had succeeded, it would probably have proved impossible to hold the objective under the concentrated fire of the enemy's artillery, directed by excellent observation.[14]

The Fromelles attack

The short 1916 advance across the flat Flanders countryside, known to the Australian troops as 'the Fleurbaix stunt',[15] would be under the observation of the Germans on the Aubers Ridge, 500 yards behind their front lines, from where, during daylight hours, they could see all the preparations for attack. A successful advance would only bring the British under still closer enemy observation.[16] Thirty feet above the battlefield, an Observation Post (O.P.) in Fromelles Church afforded a telescope, with its Zeiss lens providing a perfect view of the allied trenches and beyond.[17] Enemy observers could watch the advanced battle headquarters of the Australian and British brigades, as well as the allied troop columns heading for the front lines, together with all the preparations being made for the forthcoming assault.[18]

In his detailed book on Fromelles, which includes meticulously translated German Munich archives, Peter Barton quotes the succinct maxim: 'Artillery conquers, infantry occupies.'[19] On 14 July, Haking learned that he could deploy the guns of only two inadequately trained artillery divisions, not three trained ones, and that the available ammunition was a third of the quantity promised.

Crucial to the success of the attacks would be accurate and precise heavy shelling. Haking could, and should, have cancelled the assault.[20]

Moreover, the Anzac artillery had been given little time to register their guns for the accurate shelling of German lines and barbed wire defences, having been moved into position only three days before the attack. Two R.F.C. squadrons were briefed to help with target spotting and registration, but the mist did not clear until mid-morning and this vital task was delayed for two days.[21]

A major error of XI Corps' Commander Haking's battle planning lay in the siting of the boundary line between the Australian 5th and the British 61st divisions, on the axis of the critical German defensive feature of the Sugar Loaf salient; a tactical position from which the Bavarians dominated No Man's Land. A brigade from one division should have been given the sole responsibility for capturing the Sugar Loaf. Coordinating troops from two armies to attack together, with all the inherent complications of communication between separate commands, proved a recipe for disaster.[22]

This was the first major A.I.F. battle on French soil for the 5th Australian Division, whose Gallipoli veterans and untrained raw recruits had arrived on the front only eight days previously.[23] The majority of the 14th and 15th Australian brigades' officers and N.C.O.s had fought at Gallipoli, although only a quarter of their men were experienced veterans of the old 1st and 2nd brigades.[24] Three inexperienced divisions would now fight side-by-side and would pay a heavy price.[25]

Inexperience was not the sole reason for defeat in a fight with little chance of success. The German front was now much stronger than in 1915.[26] By July 1916, the Germans had benefitted from ample opportunity to strengthen their breastwork defences, including many machine gun concrete emplacements, which were well-sited and concealed.[27] The German parapet had been widened to 15–20 feet and was now 6–8 feet high. With the water table 18 inches below the surface, defences were constructed upwards with earth-filled sandbags. Soil to build up the parapet was dug out and bagged up in front of the breastworks, with heavy gauge barbed wire strung along and inside the excavated ditches, creating a further barrier for assaulting troops.[28]

German defences

The 6th Bavarian Division, raised in 1914, and in the line since March 1915, consisted of the 12th and 14th reserve brigades. From south to north, over a distance of about 4.5 miles, waited 12,000 men of their four regiments: the 16th & 17th (12th Brigade) and 20th & 21st (14th Brigade) Bavarian R.I.R. (Reserve Infantry Regiment), each with three battalions. One battalion held the front line while half of the second battalion were in posts to the rear of the front line and the other half on the ridge, or in billets. The third battalion was held 3 miles back as a reserve. The 16th Bavarian R.I.R. manned the salient from Petillon to Tilleloy, including the Sugar Loaf.[29,30] The latter's name derived from the form and shape of this important defensive position, which was situated on a slightly raised area of land, perhaps on the site of a ruined old building. The salient would be a thorn in the side of the attackers given its crucial dominating tactical position.[31]

German front-line infantry was usually well protected in deep, often comfortable, reinforced defensive positions. An Australian brigade report on a dugout seized in the late sunlight of 19 July described the: 'four or five steps down to a duck-boarded floor… Heavily timbered and concreted structures, steel roofs covered with soil, drain wells, with pumps to excavate water. [Lit by] electric lights, some with passages to snug living areas, often decorated with looted paintings, and ammunition stores.'[32]

The Germans' drill was to shelter in their concrete bunkers during bombardments before rushing out to man their parapets as soon as a barrage ended (although at the Sugar Loaf it was reported that one machine gun was firing during the barrage).[33]

The 16th Bavarian R.I.R., positioned in the center of the attack front, had constructed seventy-five concrete emplacements with reinforced roofs 9–12 inches thick. The strongest were on their main fortification site of the Sugar Loaf salient, which jutted out into No Man's Land with parapets 8 feet high, with machine guns covering the entire section of the attack area and enfilading both left and right.[34] The heavily defended bunkers housed the Spandau MG08 water-cooled heavy machine guns with their crew of eight, positioned to enfilade any troops advancing to the ridge from any of three directions. These belt-fed deadly weapons, German versions of the American 1884 Maxim gun, fired at a murderous rate of 500 rounds a minute, with an effective range of 2,200 yards. (Four miles southwest of Fromelles at Neuve Chapelle in March 1915, 200 men of a Jäger Battalion, armed with one MG08, had prevented a breakthrough of 9,000 allied soldiers.)[35] The machine guns had to be carried on men's shoulders or dragged on a sled. At Fromelles they were manoeuvred out of their shelters and up onto raised wooden platforms inside their parapets. Machine gunners could fire thousands of rounds in a day. In a letter in February of 1915, Adolf Hitler, a runner behind the lines, had invoked revenge on the British for the List Regiment's losses at Ypres, writing that his comrades of R.I.R. 16 should: 'even scores with that crew, to get at them no matter what the cost.'[36]

British attacking forces

Major General C.J. Mackenzie's 61st British Division consisted of three brigades: the 182nd, 183rd and 184th. The 183rd Brigade's 2/4th & 2/6th Gloucesters and the 184th Brigade's 2/1st Buckinghamshires and 2/4th Royal Berkshires each had two of their four battalions waiting in the line, positioned at the southern flank of their First Army's junction with the Second Army. The 15th, 14th and 8th Australian brigades of the 5th Australian Division were in trenches to their north.

Flanked by the Australian 15th Brigade's 59th and 60th battalions, the British 184th Brigade would advance across No Man's Land to attack the German front line on the pivot point of the Sugar Loaf salient, opposite the British Petillon-Tilleloy section. The total attack frontage was 3,500 yards of low-lying land on the wet Flanders plain, with No Man's Land consisting of long self-sown grass, sparse crops and fields pitted with shell craters.[37]

The plan was for the attacking lines of the 184th British and 15th Australian brigades to be initially separated by a gap of 300 yards, which gradually reduced as they advanced across No Man's Land. Firing into this gap, until the advancing infantry masked their fire, would be four machine guns of the 15th Brigade and five Lewis guns of the 58th Battalion, all sweeping the parapet of Sugar Loaf.

Blowing the saps

Major Coulter, Captain Sanderson and a small party of 3 A.T.C. tunnellers were positioned with the 61st Division in the British 184th Brigade sector.

CB/AS: *The 3rd Company was sent to the front where preparations were being made for the attack by the 5th Australian Division on the Sugar Loaf Salient in front of Fromelles. No 3 Company was in a section of the 61st Division and was given the duty of boring shallow workings across No Man's Land to form communication trenches for the infantry after the attack. There were to be three or four long tubes going across No Man's Land and three or four shorter ones. The longer sap was just south of the Sugar Loaf salient near the 61st Division and the 5th Australian Division. These saps were blown a few minutes before zero hour on the afternoon on July 19th. One of them actually reached through the German wire to a point not far from the parapet. Two others reached as far as the German wire, and the other a shorter distance.*[38]

Sanderson and Coulter's push-piping was one of these three. The pipes they would explode on 19 July created both a large crater and an extension sap, which together extended 290 feet from a previously dug sap called the 'Rhondda Sap'.

The carrying of the sap detonators up to the front line was a precarious job in itself, as Sapper Fred Strode of the A.I.F. explained:

> On the morning of 19th July 1916 we left our place, about 4 miles back, to go to the trenches. In the support line Sgt. Pressious of No.1 section which I was in, call[ed] for a volunteer to take a box of detonators to the front, so I step out, and got the job. I had to keep 20 steps ahead of the others. When we had to go over the top at 6 o'clock, we was told to read a verse out of our bible, because a lot of us, won't be coming back.[39]

Red Lamp Sap

From 17 to 18 July Lieutenant 'Bertie' Priestman, from a ditch full of water at Red Lamp salient, had pushed an explosive pipe 238 feet across No Man's Land. The pipe was initially flooded and took over ten hours to insert. On the afternoon of 19 July, Priestman completely detonated the charge, making a crater 150 feet long by 5 feet deep. On the same day, Lieutenant Oscar Howie exploded a second push-pipe at Red Lamp. It had entered the earth in front of his parapet, extending forward 30 feet. When enemy shells destroyed the leads, Howie went back into No Man's Land (under 200 yards wide here), in the face of heavy shell fire.[40] Aided by Sergeant Kerby, who came with an extra charge of explosives, and Corporal McKay, Howie attached 25 lbs to the end of the push-pipe and successfully exploded it, making a crater 100 feet by 90 feet and 10 feet deep. Howie later received the M.C. for his efforts, while McKay was promoted and awarded a D.C.M.[41]

In May and June 1916, freshly dug Australian communication trenches had been reconnoitred and backfilled at night by Bavarian sappers guarded by infantry, as was – more than once – the Rhondda Sap, dug by the men of the 10th Battalion, the Welsh Regiment of the 113th Brigade.[42] The Welsh Sap had been dug in June with the intention of meeting other saps which the Australian pioneers had been digging from their sides. The sap was afterwards dug back by the Australian Pioneer Battalion.[43, 44] On 4 June the Welshmen had retaliated for the backfilling of their sap by raiding the enemy lines, after laying mats to cross the enemy's barbed wire.[45]

2/1st Buckinghamshire Battalion

Around 1,500 gas cylinders had been in the British front lines since mid-June 1916, some of which were released at Fauquissart on 15 July. 'At about 9 pm on 14 July the 61st Division discharged a gas-cloud which…floated over the

Sugar Loaf salient and drifted back into the British line, causing casualties in the incoming 60th British Brigade.'[46]

By chance, the release of this poison gas on 14 July, together with the strong resistance of the Australian 58th Battalion, had impeded a large raid on the allied trenches at Fromelles by ninety-seven German troops of the 21st Bavarian R.I.R. crossing over to the Australian lines to take prisoners and gather intelligence. The raiders did manage to capture three members of an Australian Lewis-gun team with their gun, but at a cost of ten killed and twenty-two wounded.[47, 48]

On 17 July the 2/1st Bucks had taken up their positions in the front line opposite the Sugar Loaf salient, with supplies that included preserved rations, tins of water, thousands of Mills bombs and trench mortar ammunition.

Shelling

Shelling by one's own artillery was a constant concern. On 18 July an Australian battery mistakenly dropped several H.E. (High Explosive) shells into the British front lines, with one falling on the trenches of 'A' Company 2/1st Bucks and rupturing a gas cylinder. The released gas, enfiladed by the wind, then spread down the line, instantly causing seventy to eighty casualties: 'Captain H. Church and his CSM…got a slight dose.'[49] According to Captain Knyvett, when many 'friendly' shells from another Australian division were falling among their own troops: 'Our first message…was very polite: "We prefer to be killed by the Germans, thank you."'[50]

From 15 July to daylight on 19 July, every available man in the 61st Division not detailed for the coming assault was employed in removing the poison gas cylinders from the trenches. After 470 cylinders had been shifted, the men were completely exhausted and no further cylinders could be moved before the attack.[51]

On the night of 18 /19 July 15th Brigade patrols reported that the enemy in Sugar Loaf had scouts or sentries stationed 80 yards in front of their own lines. Peter Barton's Map 10 has three HP *Horchposten*/Listening Posts in front of the apex of Sugar Loaf.[52]

Captain Ivor Stewart-Liberty of the 2/1 Bucks, one of the few of 'D' Coy who would survive the Sugar Loaf attack, later wrote:

> It was a beautiful morning…at the appointed hour our guns and trench-mortars started the bombardment…it was not many minutes before the Germans 'opened-out'… There we sat, unable to do anything, while the enemy battered our trenches and many a good man was wounded and killed… By the time the hour for the assault arrived, we were all boiling with anger and only too eager to get to grips with 'Master Bosch' and to use cold steel and bludgeons which many of us carried.[53]

The British bombardment opened up at 11:00 on the German trenches. In his book on *Pompey Elliott*, R. McMullin described the scene as it: 'continued with growing intensity for seven hours. By mid-afternoon, when all guns were blazing, the sights and sounds were awesome. Exploding monsters of destruction descended in quick succession, catapulting geysers of earth skywards, hurling metal fragments far and wide.'[54]

The allied barrage of H.E. shells was 'lifted' for a few minutes four times during the seven hours of bombardment: at 15.29 for four minutes; at 16:09 for five minutes; at 16:36 for seven minutes and at 17:31 for eleven minutes. During each lift men in the allied trenches were to show their bayonets and hold dummy figures above the parapet to deceive the Germans into thinking the assault was beginning. The rationale was that the lull in H.E. shelling would cause the enemy to rush out and man their parapets. Then, for two minutes after each lift, enemy trenches would be hit with shrapnel shells to inflict heavy casualties on the exposed infantry.[55]

The Bavarian R.I.R. 16th Regiment noted that the British shelling had caused considerable destruction and many casualties, but that sixty of their seventy-five shelters, built into their parapet, had remained intact. The Germans began shelling at midday.[56] The Battalion commander *Hauptmann* Hans Gebhardt wrote that several of his battalions' concrete-roofed artillery shelters were 'completely destroyed' by British medium-calibre artillery direct hits, killing three to five men inside. The trench garrison were lying on the floor of the trench, under the firestep or in traverse niches.[57]

The British assault, originally planned for noon, was now moved to the zero hour of 18:00, three hours before dusk.[58] The German defenders were ready:

Bavarians declared a state of alert and heightened combat readiness at 12.30pm [British Time = BT* of 11:30]…By 1.00pm [BT midday] every Bavarian soldier had received the order to: 'Stand To' and a message went to the German 14th Bde. in Fromelles advising of enemy infantry to the left opposite their wire in sub-sector IIIb; these were the British 184th Bde troops of the 2/1st Bucks and 2/4th Berks, gathering in the advanced saps opposite the Sugar Loaf.[59]

[* German continental time was one hour ahead of British time.]

The R.I.R. 16 commander *Oberstleutnant* Spatny messaged: 'At 1.00 [BT midday] Intense artillery fire, characteristic of an imminent raid on the whole of Sector III.' At 16:00 [BT 15:00] he reported that: 'Some of the sentries in IIIb [garrisoned by 11 Company] have seen English troops in No Man's Land.'[60]

The British reported in the early afternoon of 19 July that the wire in front of Sugar Loaf was undamaged. Instructions were issued to carry out an additional heavy artillery attack on the Sugar Loaf to begin at 14:35, but this note did not reach the British artillery opposite Sugar Loaf until 17:10.[61] The message in pencil read: 'Told [the artillery]. Too late.'[62]

Peter Barton's research from the Munich archives noted that at 14:35 [BT 13:35] Bavarian observers reported: '*Engländer* lying in No Man's Land in front of their own wire opposite IIIa, and the *Australierstellung* [Rhondda Sap] occupied.'[63]

Quoting Bavarian archives (*Die Bayern in Grossen Krieg*), Charles Bean writes that: 'At 3.15pm troops – no doubt some of the 3rd Australian Tunnelling Company who were trying to create a 'pipe-pusher' sap – were observed by the Germans in the saps in No Man's Land opposite the Sugar Loaf and fire was directed on the area.'[64]

The Bavarian 11 Company had been observing the Rhondda Sap since 15:00 when they saw Sanderson's company trying to explode their push-pipes. Lieutenant Plenge directed the artillery to fire on them up to the moment the Australian sap pipes were fired on the fourth attempt.[65]

3 Company of R.I.R. 16 reported (again Peter Barton's German translations) that:

At 4.20pm [BT 15:20] all telephone lines to the front line were knocked out… At around 5.00pm [BT 16:00] runners arrived from the companies… and reported that the front-line was under intense drumfire. Casualties… were heavy and the trenches were badly damaged. At 5.45pm [BT 16:45] flare signals calling for barrage fire went up all along our Regimental front, and our light and heavy artillery, which had been continuously engaged in counter-battery work… went over immediately to barrage fire… the heavy artillery had already been requested by the Commander of III/R.I.R. 16 on 18 July to concentrate especially heavy fire on the *Australierstellung*.

The Sugar Loaf was not within effective range of the Stokes mortars, but the British heavy artillery fire was increasing in intensity. Von Braun's report noted [Barton's translation]:

Hostile fire then increased to the level of a drumfire and, in…some batteries…was directed by aircraft… I gave orders at about 5.00pm [BT 16:00]) to the support battalion to move one section of the regimental reserve… At the same time a report was received from the artillery that the enemy was transferring men from the second line into his front line.

Ada Crossley, the contralto singer, underground in the Golden Horseshoe Mine, Kalgoorlie in 1904. Ada owned shares in this gold mine. On 10 January 1904 Alex Sanderson and Maudie Turner attended the concert given by Ada Crossley and the soprano Nellie Melba in Her Majesty's Theatre. (Photo G.M.M.1063. Golden Mile Museum.)

Below: Miners underground in the Oroya Brownhill Gold Mine in December 1903, when Alex Sanderson was employed as the Mine Manager re-lining a shaft. (Photo G.M.M. 1500. Golden Mile Museum in Kalgoorlie.)

Above and left: Augusta Sanderson (née Lyle).

The author's father, John Sanderson, recollected:

'In January 1926 my grandmother Augusta Sanderson came to stay with us in Calcutta. She had not had an easy life. She had been adopted as a young child and was obliged in 1860 to leave her mother, sister and her homeland of Scotland on board *Lady Elgidia* to New Zealand. Her husband William died young of diptheria in Perth, leaving Augusta with five children to support. What occupation Augusta had for the next 46 years, I don't know, but it must have been a hard struggle to bring up this large family alone. She must have worked as a dressmaker, or similar, to keep the family together. She had arrived from Perth, Western Australia on the SS *Narkunda*, a formidable lady, then 74 years old. She lived into her 90s. In 1934, aged 82 years, she had still been riding her horse in Glen Forest, Mundaring, West Australia. I encountered my grandmother only twice in my lifetime – during her visit to India, and in 1942 during the war, before I left by boat for the Indian Army. She was very aristocratic in appearance with aquiline features, white silky hair piled up on top, tall and slim. She usually wore handmade silk shirts with a tie neckline, a loose moroccan jacket and a long black skirt. Augusta had come over to England in 1939 to visit the family and was unable to return home because of the war. She was never happy here and always wished to return to West Australia. She used to sit up in bed and bang her tin cabin trunk with her stick and call out for me. Our family home was bombed during the Blitz but Augusta simply refused to come down to our shelter, even though the windows were blown out and the plaster ceilings fell down. She did manage to get in touch with her niece Agnes, Henrietta Lyle's granddaughter. On her two visits, I was impressed by her stamina, intelligence and handsome appearance, but I cannot say that I had any affection for her. In India I was frequently chased by her, wielding an umbrella like a witch's broomstick!'

Augusta's husband William Sanderson (Alex's father) as a young man in South Island New Zealand

The legendary Charles Yelverton O'Connor (1843-1902) the Irish born Engineer-in-Chief of Western Australia. (Photograph in the Sanderson Archives, treasured by his former cadet Alex for 70 years.)

Alex Sanderson (seated) with a fellow Civil Engineering Cadet of the Public Works Department, Perth under C.Y. O'Connor. (Sanderson Archives)

Below: Major A.Sanderson D.S.O., M.C. and bar, MiD. Note 'T' for 'Tunnelling' and the Company Number '3' on Alex's right shoulder.

Captain Alex Sanderson A.I.F. with three Crown 'pips' on his epaulettes.

'Queen Victoria's Head' in the Napier Range overlooking the Gibb River Road Pass, near the Lennard River.

(Author photo)

Battye Library 2160/1

The Napier Pass from Fred Brockman's map. (Battye Library)

Battye Library 2160/6

Below: Two original group photos from Alex Sanderson's expedition to the Kimberley, W.A. These early Australian explorers faced extreme conditions in a challenging, unforgiving environment of dust, heat, snakes and insects. The region had many rivers to fill their soaked canvas water bags and to water the sturdy horses. Sanderson's riders, travelling light, with slouch hats, spurs on their boots and armed with Winchester rifles, would have set off early and travelled under a blazing sun. Sanderson took longitude measurements at noon, like a sailor navigating, then consulted his compass and maps. After a shaded rest midday, the party rode until dusk when they watered, fed and hobbled out their horses, after checking the horseshoes. Barrels were filled with water from streams.

'Tarp' tents were quickly set up, with their swagbags thrown inside. Food was damper bread cooked in the camp fire with jerked beef and billy tea. Kangaroo dung could catch a spark from a flint lighter before grasses and branches took the flames. As the party surveyor, in the evening Alex would have written up his log and pored over Brockman's maps and charts, perhaps using the moon for latitude measurements. Alex's early training in navigating by the stars, using a sextant under the Southern Cross, was invaluable.

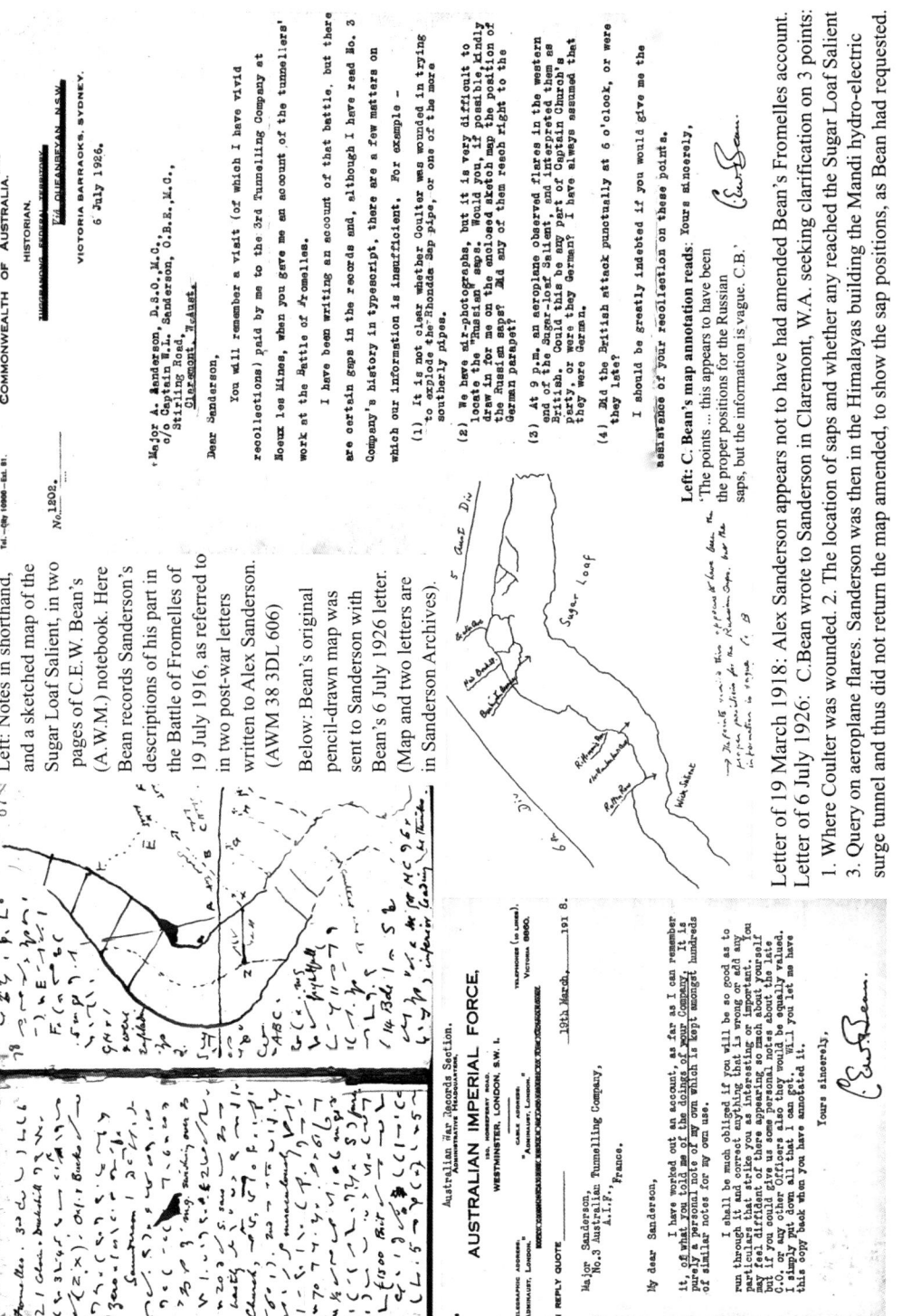

Left: Notes in shorthand, and a sketched map of the Sugar Loaf Salient, in two pages of C.E.W. Bean's (A.W.M.) notebook. Here Bean records Sanderson's descriptions of his part in the Battle of Fromelles of 19 July 1916, as referred to in two post-war letters written to Alex Sanderson. (AWM 38 3DL 606)

Below: Bean's original pencil-drawn map was sent to Sanderson with Bean's 6 July 1926 letter. (Map and two letters are in Sanderson Archives).

Australian War Records Section.

AUSTRALIAN IMPERIAL FORCE,
130, HORSEFERRY ROAD,
WESTMINSTER, LONDON, S.W. 1.

IN REPLY QUOTE _____ 19th March, 1918.

Major Sanderson,
No.3 Australian Tunnelling Company,
A.I.F.,
France.

My dear Sanderson,

I have worked out an account, as far as I can remember it, of what you told me of the doings of your Company. It is purely a personal note of my own which is kept amongst hundreds of similar notes for my own use.

I shall be much obliged if you will be so good as to run through it and correct anything that I have got wrong or did any particular that strikes you as interesting or important. You may feel diffident of there appearing so much about yourself but if you could give us some personal notes about the late C.O. or any other Officers also they would be equally valued. I simply put down all that I can get. Will you let me have this copy back when you have amended it.

Yours sincerely,

C E W Bean

COMMONWEALTH OF AUSTRALIA.
HISTORIAN.
HIGGINBOTHAM FEDERAL TERRITORY.
VICTORIA BARRACKS, SYDNEY.
6 July 1926.

No.1802.

Major A. Sanderson, D.S.O., M.C.,
o/o Captain W.L. Sanderson, O.B.E., M.C.,
Stirling Road,
Claremont, W.Aust.

Dear Sanderson,

You will remember a visit (of which I have vivid recollections) paid by me to the 3rd Tunnelling Company at Noeux les Mines, when you gave me an account of the tunnellers' work at the Battle of Fromelles.

I have been writing an account of that battle, but there are certain gaps in the records and, although I have read No. 3 Company's history in typescript, there are a few matters on which our information is insufficient. For example –

(1) It is not clear whether Coulter was wounded in trying to explode the Rhondda Sap pipe, or one of the more southerly pipes.

(2) We have air-photographs, but it is very difficult to locate the "Russian" saps. Would you, if possible, kindly draw in for me on the enclosed sketch map the position of the Russian saps? Did any of them reach right to the German parapet?

(3) At 9 p.m. an aeroplane observed flares in the western end of the Sugar-loaf Salient, and interpreted them as British. Could this be any part of Captain Church's party, or were they German? I have always assumed that they were German.

(4) Did the British attack punctually at 5 o'clock, or were they late?

I should be greatly indebted if you would give me the assistance of your recollection on these points.

Yours sincerely,

C E W Bean

Left: C. Bean's map annotation reads:
'The points ... this appears to have been the proper positions for the Russian saps, but the information is vague. C.B.'

Letter of 19 March 1918: Alex Sanderson appears not to have had amended Bean's Fromelles account.
Letter of 6 July 1926: C.Bean wrote to Sanderson in Claremont, W.A. seeking clarification on 3 points:
1. Where Coulter was wounded. 2. The location of saps and whether any reached the Sugar Loaf Salient
3. Query on aeroplane flares. Sanderson was then in the Himalayas building the Mandi hydro-electric surge tunnel and thus did not return the map amended, to show the sap positions, as Bean had requested.

Royal Engineers' greetings card sent by the Inspector of Mines. (Original in the Sanderson Archives) The cartoon caption at the bottom of the card reads:
"*Tunneller* (embarrassed by the sudden encounter) :— *Er-er-third return 'Ammersmith, please !*"

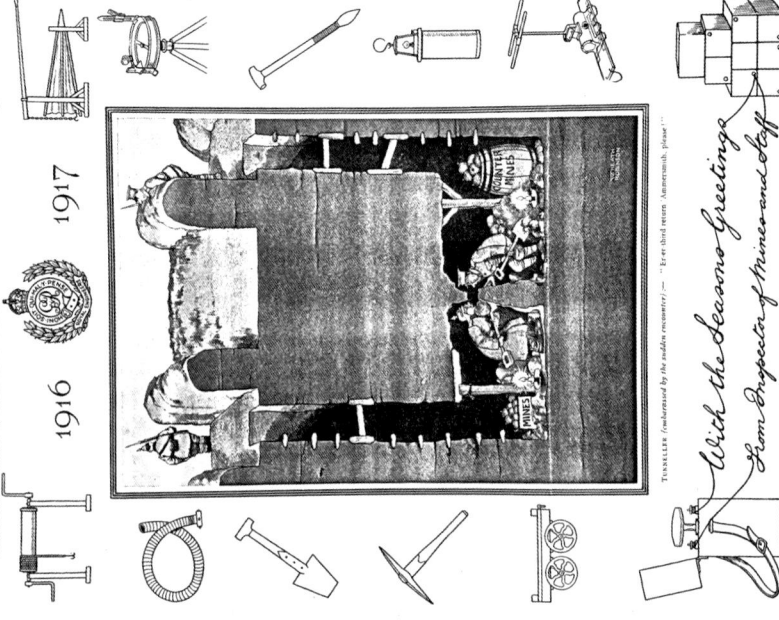

Heath Robinson Cartoon. Illustrations clockwise from top: Royal Engineer's Insignia, Bellows, Tunnel Surveyor's Instrument*, Push Pick (2'6"), Miner's Lamp, Pump, sealed petrol tins of Ammonal Explosives (wired to) a Dynamo Exploder, Gallery Truck, Miner's Pick (2'6"), Grafting Tool, Hose and a Windlass.
Beneath Flanders Fields p.84*

* The Mine Surveyor's instrument, similar to a theodolite with a compass attached, was attached to a tripod set up at the bottom of a shaft and levelled. Using the plotted mine plan, the surveyor found the required bearing on the graduated circular plate before the sights were clamped on. The centre line for the tunnel direction was then indicated by a bearing marked on the roof timber of the tunnel head, to be followed by the face worker.

Captain Alex Sanderson's sketch, with the 12 November and 5 December 1916 reports to Major Coulter on the severe flooding and foul gas in shaft No. 21. That day a German mining trolley was heard, just ahead of the face.

'Major, The gallery running S.E. from the bottom of Shaft 21 strikes the edge of broken ground at about 112 feet. The ground is very much fractured in the left side going in. At 120 feet, just as the chambering was about to be commenced, a heavy flow of water started to come in at the face. This was about half an hour before I arrived at ...2.30p.m. I sounded the ground on the left side of the face and it is very drumming, almost too much so for broken ground. It sounds as if there may be a chamber or cavity filled with water there. Probably the camouflet bulled down to form a chamber and it has since filled with water. Lt Russel has plugged the crevices as much as possible and is installing a pump to force the water into Black Watch. The Bosch will probably judge that something is wrong when he loses water from his side. If the water eases up we may be able to get a chamber in on the right side near the face. I think it would be advisable to put an augur hole that we can plug through on the left side of the face in case there may be chamber there which we could charge. The listeners reported hearing a trolley just ahead of this face a few minutes before the relief came in at 2pm today. I am stopping here tonight in case of further developments, if we can get the water out. A Sanderson Captain.'
(3 A.T.C. War Diary)   24 November 1916

(As above) A. Sanderson, with No. 1 Section, to Major Coulter:
'The incline gallery from the bottom of Shaft 21 is quite sound to the foot of the slope (about 50 feet from the top of the slope). I could not get in any further as the level position of the gallery is nearly full of water. Looking along the surface of the water the gallery appears to widen as it goes in and also the back gets higher. In plan view it would be as follows. As the space between the water and the back was full of foul gas I could not get in to make a detailed examination. I estimate there is from 15,000 to 20,000 gallons of water in the bulled gallery. This could not be got rid of in less than about ten days pumping in the same way and with the same appliances as previously used in Black Watch. If the power pump can be obtained right away we could quickly get to the end of the gallery. The line through Black Watch is being lifted and two men will be stripping the back today, more if possible. About 20 feet is being left open under the rails in the deepest part for a sump as was done at Gordon slant. The Proto men will make an examination of the 60 foot level at 21 Shaft this morning and I will probably examine them myself. A. Sanderson Captain.' 3 A.T.C. War Diary note. 5 December 1916.

Author sketch of : Proto Rescue Breathing Apparatus

'Eh bien; mon vieux, nous avons de bien mauvaises mines!'
'Well, my old friend, we have some very bad mines.'
('Mines' in French means both 'Mines' and 'Expressions.')

A cartoon drawn in 1915 by the French Poster Artist Bernard Lancy. (Author's French cartoon collection)

Weekly Mine Reports SECRET dated 26/7/1917

Hill 70 System No. 1 R1L1 from Deep Deep Lateral at N1a 45.95 at a depth of 110 feet in hard chalk (6 feet x 2 feet 6 ins inside timbers at a gallery length of 166 feet.) At 8 a.m on 24 July inst. this gallery connected with the enemy system: 774 feet of enemy galleries captured. Listening in all galleries captured. Enemy 69 (Vendin Alley). Enemy heard working near his own line at N1a 65.90 & N1a70.96 and also at H31C 65.05 also very distant picking heard from 'A' Main at Chalk Pits. (signed Alex Sanderson Major O.C. 3rd Austr. Tun. Coy 26/7/17

July 27th 1917 SECRET MINE EXPLOSION REPORT (BRITISH) At 4.58 a.m. we blew a Maximum Camouflet of 10,000 lbs of Ammonal in Hard Chalk from the end of main, to destroy enemy galleries between the chamber and the surface. Charge: 200 x 50 lb cases of ammonal. Duplicate electric leads with 2 electric detonators in guncotton. Primers on each, in 4 priming charges of 20 lbs guncotton. 1 instantaneous fuse to No. 8 detonator in G.C. Tamping: In old enemy gallery 150 feet of solid tamping (bags of chalk). In No. 1DDM 60 feet of tamping (chalk in bags), 20 feet air space, then 20 feet tamping, then 20 feet air space, then 20 feet tamping. Underground effects: About 1,000 bags of chalk debris in 1DDR1L1. Old enemy gallery at N1a 48.24 crumped to entrance and a small amount of chalk has fallen in other galleries. At 1 a.m. two enemy picks were working at about 150 feet east of the charge. Surface effects: Parapet shaken into front line trench for length of about 100 feet near camouflet. Alex Sanderson Major

'Secret Mine Mine Reports by Alex Sanderson. On 26 July the capture of enemy galleries. On 27 July an Australian camouflet of 10,000 lbs of ammonal was exploded.

Captain O.H. Woodward (M.C., two bars) 1 A.T.C. wrote that the plan was: 'to bore a hole under every trench, push in a torpedo carrying a charge of high explosive, fire the charge, hurl some hundred-weights of Huns into the air, and repeat the performance.'

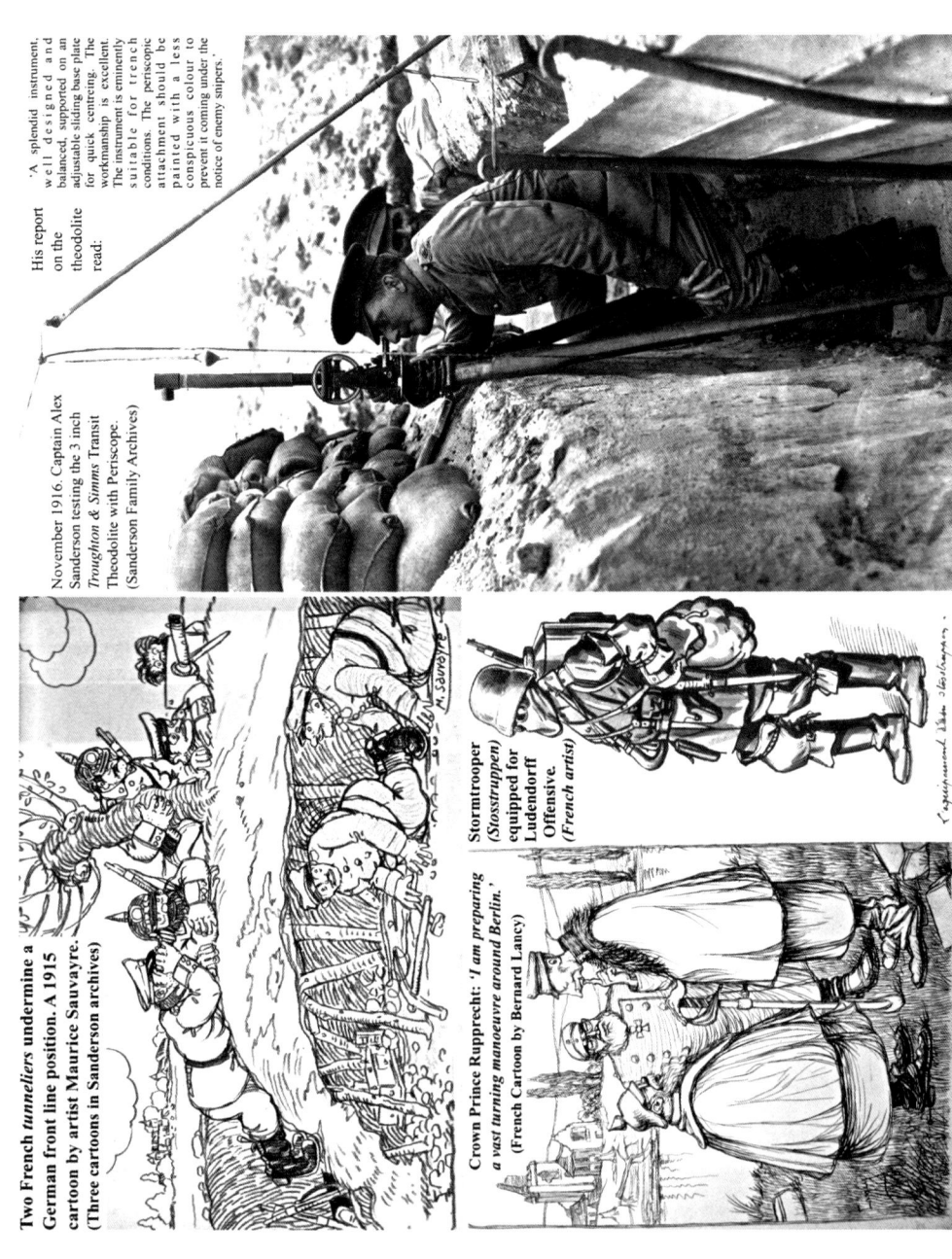

November 1916. Captain Alex Sanderson testing the 3 inch Troughton & Simms Transit Theodolite with Periscope. (Sanderson Family Archives)

His report on the theodolite read:

'A splendid instrument, well designed and balanced, supported on an adjustable sliding base plate for quick centreing. The workmanship is excellent. The instrument is eminently suitable for trench conditions. The periscopic attachment should be painted with a less conspicuous colour to prevent it coming under the notice of enemy snipers.'

Two French *tunneliers* undermine a German front line position. A 1915 cartoon by artist Maurice Sauvayre. (Three cartoons in Sanderson archives)

Stormtrooper (*Stosstruppen*) equipped for Ludendorff Offensive. (French artist)

Crown Prince Rupprecht: '*I am preparing a vast turning manoeuvre around Berlin.*' (French Cartoon by Bernard Lancy)

Heavy Trench Mortar Emplacement.

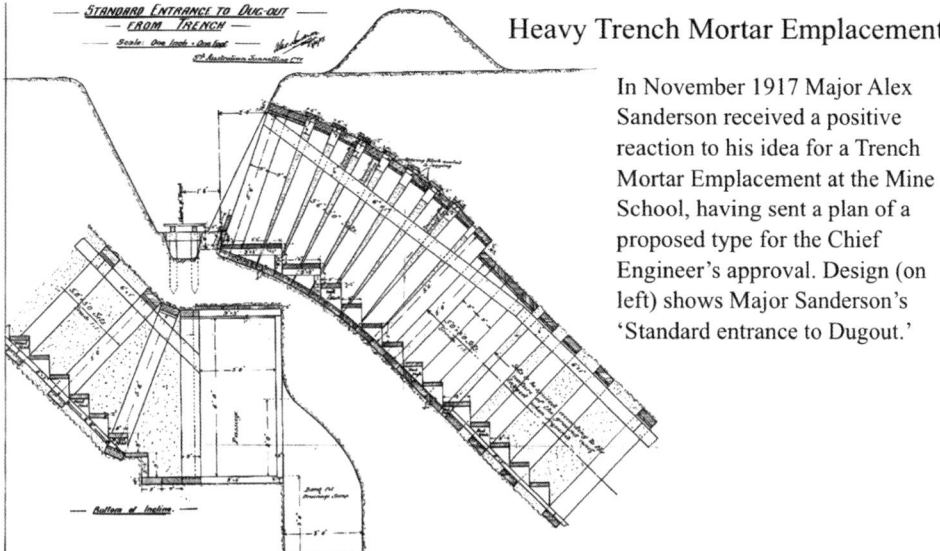

In November 1917 Major Alex Sanderson received a positive reaction to his idea for a Trench Mortar Emplacement at the Mine School, having sent a plan of a proposed type for the Chief Engineer's approval. Design (on left) shows Major Sanderson's 'Standard entrance to Dugout.'

Major Sanderson on 30 January 1918 in a heavy mortar emplacement (with camouflage netting rolled back) constructed by No. 2 Section of 3 A.T.C. close to Counter Trench at Cité St Pierre, near Lens. Alex Sanderson is standing with two British 11th Division soldiers next to a projecting heavy mortar gun barrel capable of firing a shell weighing 152 lbs every six minutes, with a range of between 660 and 2,400 yards. Timber had been salvaged from enemy dumps.   (AWM EO4600)

ML 9.45 inch (240mm) 'Flying Pig' heavy mortar had a muzzle-loaded propellant charge. A Lee-Enfield rifle's bolt mechanism was screwed into the breech and a blank cartridge loaded. When the lanyard was pulled, an igniter was fired to ignite the propellant and launch the bomb. The Mark 1's barrel was 51 inches long. Base was secured to a timber base platform, embedded into the ground. The carriage could traverse. Used for 'siege warfare' to destroy enemy dugouts and strongpoints i.e. command posts, gallery entrances and mine shafts.

Brave Men Who Live Like Burrowing Moles
British and Australian Official Photographs

Members of an Australian Tunnelling Company on the western front constructing an underground dug-out. Wonderful underground work has been achieved by the miner soldiers from Australia. Right: In the subterranean cookhouse of an Australian Tunnelling Company.

Australian machine-gun position on the western front. Right: In an Australian Tunnelling Company's rescue station. The men are provided with special respirators and have small cage-birds to give warning of impure air.

In a British underground cookhouse near the front line, fully equipped so that everything can be carried on in the deep dug-out; the prepared food is hauled to the surface for distribution. Right: Australians boring with a Wombat drill a ventilating hole for a deep dug-out.

Above: 3rd Australian Tunnelling Company sappers working underground. (Sanderson Archives)

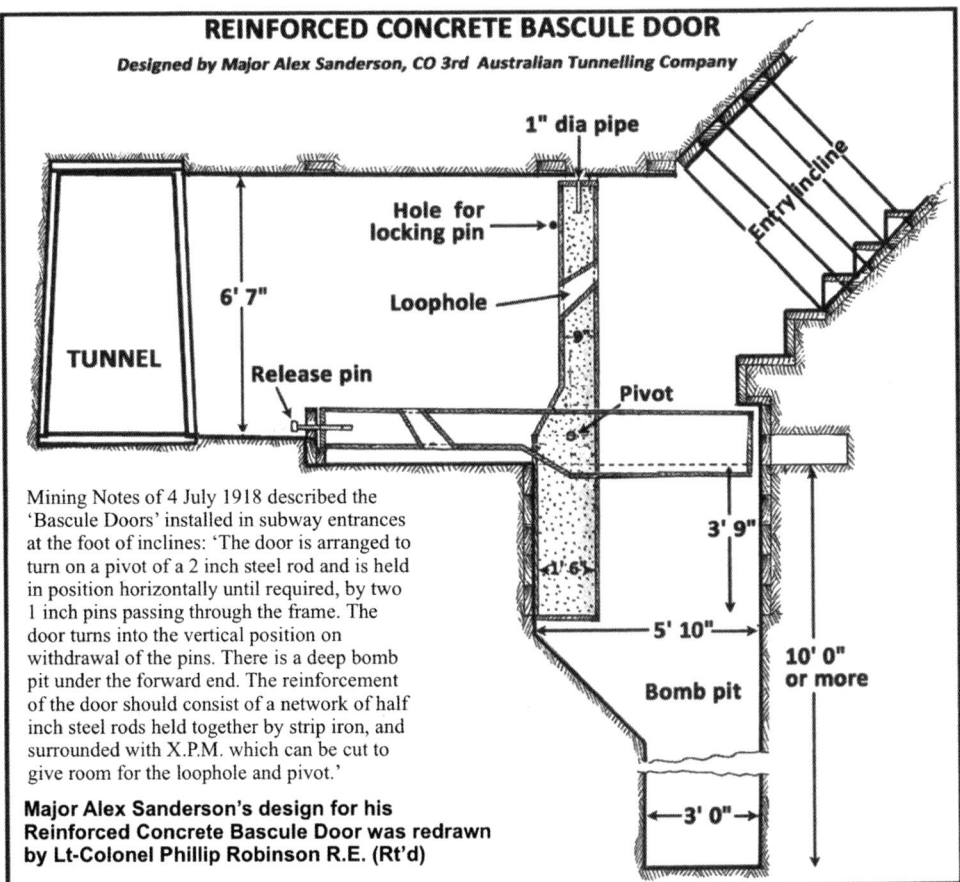

Mining Notes of 4 July 1918 described the 'Bascule Doors' installed in subway entrances at the foot of inclines: 'The door is arranged to turn on a pivot of a 2 inch steel rod and is held in position horizontally until required, by two 1 inch pins passing through the frame. The door turns into the vertical position on withdrawal of the pins. There is a deep bomb pit under the forward end. The reinforcement of the door should consist of a network of half inch steel rods held together by strip iron, and surrounded with X.P.M. which can be cut to give room for the loophole and pivot.'

Major Alex Sanderson's design for his Reinforced Concrete Bascule Door was redrawn by Lt-Colonel Phillip Robinson R.E. (Rt'd)

The Bascule Doors, as yet undiscovered by the Durand Group, are known to be installed somewhere inside the entrances of the Hythe Subway and the Hulluch Tunnel.

Captain H.R.Dixon M.C. R.E. wrote in the 1930s that:
The Hythe tunnel was constructed in early 1918 when a German offensive was expected, so elaborate defensive features were built into it. The tactics to be adopted in the event of an attack had been very carefully thought out, and the garrison, which comprised a whole brigade of infantry, had very special training in the use of the many new devices employed. At the foot of the steps leading down from each trench entrance was an ingenious trapdoor, also made of concrete, arranged on a pivot across the gallery so that, when a bolt was pulled out, the outside end turned downwards into a hole 20 feet deep, into which the pursuing enemy or his bombs could drop, while the inside part of the door rose into place and blocked the gallery. The doors were also provided with loopholes
(Robinson & Cave *The Underground War.* pp.112-3)

Captain Reginald Langdon of No.1 Section of 3 A.T.C. reported in 1918 that:
On 1 January a party of about twenty of the enemy entered our trenches under a heavy barrage, opposite the Southern Tunnel entrance. The N.C.O. in charge of the post withdrew his men to the bottom of the incline and manned the loop-hole in the traverse with his Lewis gun. The enemy was thus prevented from entering the tunnel system. After throwing down a few bombs, which did no harm, they withdrew, leaving two large unexploded mobile charges, one in the tunnel near the exit, and one on the parapet.
(3 A.T.C. War Diary)

Sapper Charles Leaver recorded the success of the tunnel defences in his diary on 2 January:
A raid last night and Old Fritz nearly got over to the tunnel but got stopped. He had some mobile charges with him and was coming over to try and blow it in. Our lads were waiting for him.
(tunnellers.net)

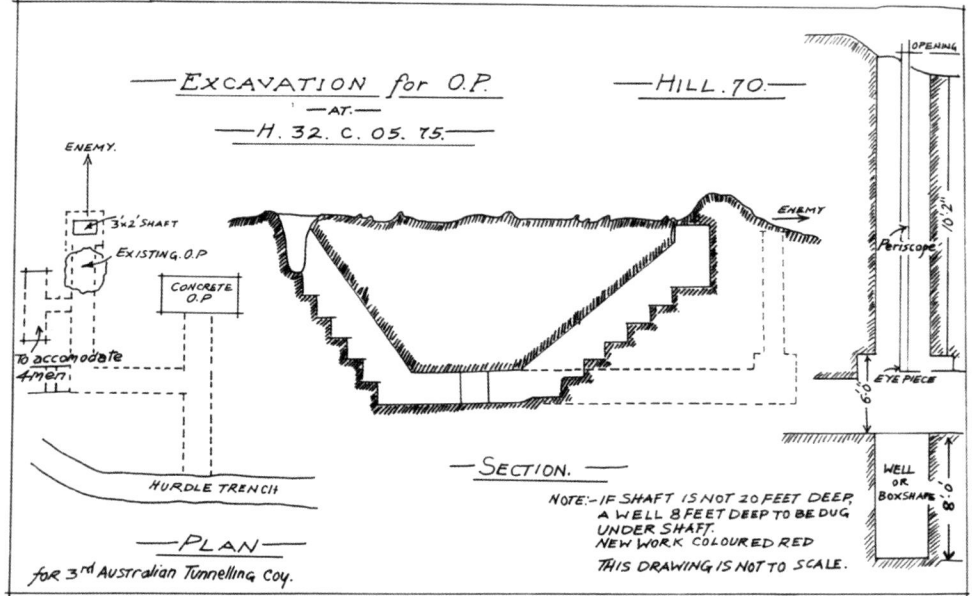

Above: 3 A.T.C. War Diary Plan of Periscope Post 'redrawn by the author, 2014.'

In September 1918 the Brigadier-General of 1st Corps requested 3 ATC to 'construct a small concrete O.P. for periscope observation, close to an existing dug-out.' A post-war memoir of Major H. R. Dixon M.C., the GHQ Assistant Inspector of Mines, wrote on a visit that: 'Away out under our own wire was a special observation chamber, from which a large periscope was arranged in among the wire, camouflaged to look like an old tree stump. This instrument was of special design, and looking into the eye piece one had the whole of the German lines in view over a wide area, and their working parties were spotted at once if they ventured to do work outside their trenches. Telephone communication with all the other parts of the system enabled swift action to be taken if the enemy were seen.' Robinson P. and Cave N. *The Underground War. Vimy Ridge to Arras.*

Below: Captain Albert C. Morris, of No. 3 Section of the 3rd Australian Tunnelling Company, standing on duck boards next to an intermediate entrance to the Hythe Tunnel, in Hythe Alley, a communication trench across the Hill 70 Ridge overlooking Loos-en-Gohelle. (Photo E01712. Australian War Museum, Canberra.)

On 22 January 1918 Lt. Hugh Russel M.C., who had organised the Special Bomb Investigation Parties and had surveyed the Hythe Tunnel, was fatally wounded by a shell explosion in Hythe Alley on Hill 70. Sapper J.Carden was killed by him. Lt. Russel died at Bracquement the next day of his wounds. Russel had been wounded on three separate occasions.

Major Alex Sanderson with a group of his officers outside their Nissen hut quarters at Bracquement near Noeux-les-Mines, 19 June 1918 **Front row, left to right**: Lt W.R. Jones (B.E.F.); Captain Albert Morris MC; Captain Arthur Hillman MC; Major Alex Sanderson DSO, MC and bar (CO); Captain Reginald Langdon MC; Lieut. Edward Horn (adjutant); Lt. James Robertson: (Quartermaster). **Back row**: Lt. James Shaw MC; Lt. D'Arcy Wentworth; Lieut. Karl Moore; Lt. Ronald Ashcroft MC; Lieut Ron DePassey; Lt. Oscar Sternberg; Lt. Colin Shaw MC. (AWM E02485)

THE TUNNELLERS' FRIENDS.

Left: A sculptured plaque tribute in the Scottish National War Memorial in Edinburgh. (Author photo)

Canaries and Mice were carried by miners to warn them of dangerous carbon monoxide gas underground: a canary's metabolic rate is faster than a human. Canaries are fifteen times more sensitive to poisonous gasses than humans. Their demise made miners aware of CO gas in their galleries. The canaries' claws were regularly trimmed so that they would fall off their perches when reacting to gas in a tunnel. (Otherwise the birds would tighten their long claws and die in three minutes, still perched upright and unremarked by tunnellers.)

The army had a big aviary in Calais where canaries were bred. On 12 September 1916 a memo arrived at 3 A.T.C.'s H.Q. from the Controller of Mines of the First Army, asking for an audit of the canaries, or foreign birds, received since 1 July, their current total and the numbers of bird casualties caused by: (a) gas in mines (b) shellfire or (c) other causes. He asked which type of bird stood up to the front line conditions best. Canaries were more sensitive to CO gas than mice, though a Mine Rescue O.C. preferred mice, keeping a tame one in his pocket when underground because he said they were more easily observed than canaries. (3 A.T.C. War Diary)

In the Hulluch Subway System near Wing's Way, at 'The Oval', carved out of the hard chalk (the right side is damaged), still legible after over a century, is a Bell Directory for the duty sentry to ring through messages. V111 Corps advice to 3 A.T.C. in case of attack: 'Sentries will be posted on all tunnel entrances day and night. The alarm will be sounded by hand and electric bells.
* 1 long ring ~ Gas.   * 2 long rings ~ Alarm S.O.S. (Attack).
* 3 long rings ~ Stand To. * 4 long rings ~ Officer wanted at post.
* 6 long rings ~ Test.' (Author photo, courtesy of Durand Group)

'After the Armistice': An impeccable A.I.F. soldier in Paris with a Scottish Highland Sergeant Major. (*Illustration* First World War) After the 1915 Battle of Loos, tunnellers named alleys and shafts (see Map 10) after five Scottish regiments who had fought there: Scots, Gordon, Cameron, Seaforth and Black Watch. Black Watch Tunnel was blown by the Germans on 27 November 1916, killing twenty of the 3 A.T.C.'s tunnellers about to blow their own mine.

(1) Steel Bridge built by 3rd Aust. Tunnelling Coy over Haute Deule Canal in 5½ days. Owing to severe bombing by enemy aeroplanes could work in day light only - 120 ft Span to carry all loads Tanks at 20 yards intervals. Width of Roadway 11 feet. Built during advance in October 1918. — "Pont Maudit" between Lens & Lille.

(2) Another view of Pont Maudit Bridge. — Actual working time of construction 65 hours.

Note the old bridge underneath which had been destroyed by the enemy two days prior to our commencing construction of the new bridge.

The Pont Maudit ('Cursed Bridge') over the Haute Deûle Canal: a steel-girdered Hopkins Bridge, erected in October 1918 by 3 A.T.C. in 65 hours.
Width: 11 feet
Span: 120 feet.
It supported 35 tons of weight: loaded lorries or tanks 20 yards apart.

AWM: CO737

Top and far right: Alex Sanderson's photograph and handwritten descriptions of the Pont Maudit. Sapper J. Hallinan described his part in its construction:

'The first thing, the infantry and artillery was following the Germans back. When it came for us tunnellers to follow the Germans back we went up to build a temporary bridge over the Canal near a place called Lens. There was a steel bridge there but, when the Germans were falling back, they dynamited the bridge and blew it up, blew it down into the canal. The British Army, who were following the Germans up, had to come in and put their pontoon bridge across the canal. They had to dismount their horses from the guns, walk the horses over the bridge, then they had to drag the guns over. Our job was to put a bridge over the canal. Well, we were jacks of all trades then, do you see, putting the steel bridge over.' (Tunnellers.net) These reusable 'flat pack' bridges used standardised span sub-assemblies and a minimum number of bolt holes, simplifying construction. Hallnan and fellow sappers next had to de-mine dangerous booby-traps near Lille.

Between 1923 and 1924 Alex Sanderson designed and constructed the first reinforced concrete bridge in India, the Dum Dum bridge in Calcutta (now named Kolkata).
(Photographs are from Alex Sanderson's 1924 personal album of the bridge's construction.)

Alex examines the reinforcing rods, as the Indian workforce looks on.

A view of the beams and supporting arches.

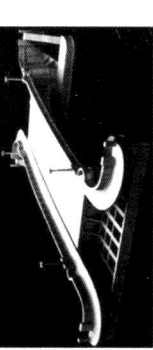

Model of Alex Sanderson's Arch Bridge, completed a century ago.

The complex structure of the new bridge takes shape.

The completed bridge.

The original Beam Bridge.

Sanderson surveys the bridge-building from a barge.

On 7 April 1924 Sanderson inspects the concrete beams, setting in their timber moulds.

I therefore ordered the regimental reserve to be brought forward… The message did not reach our front line as all direct communication with the front line…had already been interrupted. There was now a danger that the front line, weakened by losses due to enemy artillery and trench mortar fire, might be unable to withstand an attack in heavily superior numbers long enough for support to be bought up from the rear.[66]

Meanwhile, the allied troops moving from support lines to jumping-off positions were being hit by the enemy's artillery, mortars and often rifle grenades.[67] The Bavarian official account states that: 'the backbone of the British attack was broken, before it left the trenches at 5.30pm, by the 50th and 54th Reserve artillery.'[68]

Blowing the Welsh Sap

Captain Alex Sanderson's post-battle report of 20 July describes his actions on 16–19 July:

> The communication crater was blown from the end of Rhondda Valley sap at 5.11pm yesterday, during bombardment of the enemy's positions. An excavation was made at the end of the Rhondda sap after inspection by the C.O. Major Coulter and myself on the 16th July and the necessary machinery installed by midnight. 200 feet of 3-inch tubing was then pushed towards 'Sugar Loaf salient' commencing at a depth of 4 feet, on a dip of 3 degrees. The pipes were charged with cannisters of ammonal 3 lbs per foot. Owing to the muddiness of the sap, the depth of slurry being 2 feet in places, and having to do a great deal of the work in the dark, some difficulty and delay was experienced owing to grit getting into the hydraulic pump valves, but the pushing and charging of the pipes was completed and the plant returned to store by 4am on the 19th.
>
> At 3.24pm yesterday, in the presence of the O.C. Major Coulter, I connected the leads to the exploder and endeavoured to fire the charge, but could not get a circuit, the leads having been cut by shell fire which was particularly heavy at this point. I then lit the 'standby' instantaneous fuse, but this failed to fire the charge, it having also been cut by shell fire. Major Coulter and I then rushed along the sap with the intention of lighting the fuse further down the sap, but a shell bursting between us unfortunately wounded and temporarily stunned Major Coulter. I was able to proceed and light the end of the fuse at the break and then assist Major Coulter back to our firing line. As the mine did not explode, I proceeded with Corporal

Street down the sap and found the electric leads and instantaneous fuse broken in a number of places. We then disconnected the instantaneous fuse, lit the time fuse (15 feet of which had been provided) and rushed back to the firing line. This again failed to produce the desired result. At 5.03pm Corporal Street and I again proceeded to the end of the sap and discovered that a shell had burst close to the end of the tube, cutting the fuse 6 feet from the charge and burying the face. After clearing the debris from the end of the tube we cut the fuse 2 feet from the charge, ignited it, and rushed back towards the firing line. The charge successfully exploded. All this time our C.O., who was painfully wounded in the back and arms, refused to leave the firing line and the entrance to the sap until the charge was exploded.

The resulting crater was 120 feet in length by 20 feet wide and 6 feet deep with an extension of 170 feet by 3 feet wide by 18 feet deep, the pipe having twisted to the surface towards the end. The crater subsequently proved to be of great value to the Infantry advancing from Sally Port 5.

Alex Sanderson, Captain. 20.7.16.[69]

Alex Sanderson's letter of 1 August to his C.O. Major 'Jack' Coulter described the crater they exploded from the Rhondda Sap as being: 'about 140 feet long x 20 feet wide x 8 feet deep (with a tail 150 feet long x 2 feet wide x 1 foot 6 inches deep, where the end of the pipe had run over a big root of a tree and turned up and along the surface).'

In his official post-battle report, Sanderson referred to exactly the same combined length of the crater plus the sap 'tail' as 290 feet, but the crater's length he amended to 120 feet and the extension sap's length to 170 feet. With the extension being only 18 inches deep, it would have been too shallow to offer much standing protection in the attack, but the shallow sap may have proved useful for several attacking infantry to advance along by crawling, and later provided refuge for shelter and for aiding wounded casualties, both English and Australian.

Sugar Loaf attack

61st Division had only 600 men in each battalion. The infantry were still inexperienced. Both the 183rd and 184th brigades had been heavily shelled before deployment: the 184th Brigade, which formed the right-centre of the attack, had already lost 140 men.[70] Haking's plan called for the 184th to attack and seize the enemy line at the apex of the Sugar Loaf salient. Their objective instructions, given on 16 July, were 'to capture and occupy the German front and support lines this side of the River Laies'.[71] The Australian infantry would then attack the northern trenches and battle through to link up with the British.

Orders for the 2/1st Bucks and 2/4th Berks infantry stressed: 'It was vital for the success of the attack that the whole of our assaulting line is deployed in No Man's Land as close to the enemy's parapet as possible during our bombardment.'[72]

In front of 2/1st Bucks and 2/4th Berks were 459 yards of open ground to cover to the Bavarian breastworks.[73] Peter Barton's German records noted: 'At 4.00pm [BT 15:00] 11 Company sentries in the Bavarian breastwork reported: "English troops in No Man's Land". At 5.45pm [BT 16:45] more were spotted, "forming up in No Man's Land in front of IIIb [German sector opposite 2/1st Bucks and 59th Battalion]".'[74]

The 2/1st Bucks had been ready in the line since 09:00. They were taking casualties and needed hasty re-organisation at 17:00; an hour before zero hour.

Bean writes that the enemy anticipated this attack and the 61st's forward battery positions were heavily shelled. P.A. Pedersen notes that shelling caused almost 100 casualties, on top of the accidental gassing the night before. Meanwhile, the assault companies of the 2/1st Bucks were reinforced with a platoon from their reserve company.[75]

Into No Man's Land

The 61st Division was to deploy into No Man's Land out of open sally-ports at ground level through gaps made in sandbagged parapets the night before.[76] These were described by W. Miles in his *Official British History* as 'death-traps as German machine guns had registered their positions and were ready to open fire on each of them'.[77]

The historian of the 16th Bavarian Reserve Regiment, whose centre and left confronted the 183rd and 184th brigades, stated that the German infantry, machine-gun and shrapnel fire caught the British while they were still trying to 'unravel themselves' from their sally-ports.[78]

The disastrous Fromelles infantry operation began between 17:30 and 17:40 (20 minutes before zero hour) when the 61st Division troops struggled to file out of their front-line trenches into No Man's Land through their narrow sally ports.[79]

Lieutenant Colonel H. Williams, the 2/1st Bucks C.O., had recognised that the sally ports were lethal exits. When he saw that his leading troops, bunching up at the sally ports, were being checked by accurate machine gun fire, he ordered them to proceed instead up the Rhondda Sap, to afford them a sheltered approach of almost 200 yards.[80]

Captain Alex Sanderson's personal letter of 1 August to Major Coulter describes his actions on the afternoon of 19 July:

After you left I went down and examined Priestman and Howie's 'blows' which were both successful. They had left so I hurried back and went out to have a look at my crater. The actual crater was about 140 feet long x 20 feet wide x 8 feet deep with a tail 150 feet x 2 feet wide x 1 foot 6 inches deep. On coming back to the trenches I met Captain Church who was marshalling the remnants of his Coy. to advance on the 'Bosches' through the Rhondda Valley Sap. The Australians on the left and two Battalions on the right were to advance and, as the Bosch trenches had been well peppered, I arranged with Capt. Church to take three of his bombers and go over with him. We were able to marshal the 60 men he had in the crater and explained to them what to do by pointing out little landmarks ahead before the time came to charge. What happened afterwards I must not write but I don't think I will ever forget one iota of the experience. My idea was to get in and have a look at their mines and it should have come off.[81]

C.E.W. Bean describes in his Official History how, making use of the Rhondda Sap, the 2/1st Bucks managed, under heavy machine gun fire, but without heavy loss, to creep out into position in No Man's Land.[82] At the same time, P.A. Pedersen writes that: 'When the pitifully thin assault waves crawled over the lip of the Rhondda Sap and into No Man's Land at 5.40pm, shrapnel was falling heavily and the machine gunners were very busy.'[83]

The sun of a bright summer afternoon was still quite high and German guns opened up on the allied front and reserve lines. The survivors of the assaulting 'A' and 'D' companies, about 120 men, are described as filing out into No Man's Land and laying down in four waves under a hail of shrapnel.

No Man's Land itself was flat, open and waterlogged and it had been under fire from German artillery and machine guns since 17:30. The assaulting troops were instructed to go over in four waves of 100 yards distances.

The 2/1st Bucks were positioned in the centre of the line of attack, with the Australian 59th Battalion on their left. The 2/1st had to attack on a 300-yard front, between Bond Street and Picanton Avenue. At 17:45 the first wave of the Australian 59th and 60th battalions, in the adjacent Second Army sector, went over their parapets into No Man's Land. Their artillery would shell the enemy's front line for a further fifteen minutes until 18:00.[84]

2/1st Bucks' objective was the Sugar Loaf, held by 11 Company 3/16 Bavarian R.I.R. under *Leutnant* Plenge. 11 Company garrisoned sub-sector b of sector III: the apex of the salient. The Bavarians were defending against simultaneous attacks by the Australian 59th Battalion, 2/1st Bucks and 2/4th Berks.[85]

'A' and 'D' companies of 2/1st Bucks had to attack across 459 yards of open terrain.[86] They would have been sheltered, more than other companies, when they exited the Australian Tunnelling Company's 47-yard-long crater, blown at the end of the 150-yard-long Rhondda Sap. However, they still they had a further 230 yards to advance across No Man's Land until they reached the two German Observation Posts which extended 80 yards in front of the salient.

Crawling along the tunnellers' 18-inch-deep and 2-feet-wide extension sap and lying along it, all while awaiting the 18:00 attack, would have reduced 2/1st Bucks' charge across No Man's Land to 180 yards. Since this 170-feet-long extension sap – beyond the Australian tunnellers' crater – was available and empty, it is possible that under such very heavy machine gun fire, some of the infantry would have crawled over the lip of the crater (as they had done over the lip of the Rhondda Sap) and crawled along this extension sap, keeping their heads down, as far as they could, in the direction of the salient.

The British charge

Paul Cobb describes the bravery of the 2/1st Bucks when: 'At 6.00pm with a cheer the four waves leaped up and assaulted the enemy's trenches. The advance was described by an officer in the Royal Flying Corps, observing for the Artillery, as magnificent. Not a man was seen to waver.'[87]

The 2/1st Bucks' War Diary reads:

> Even before 5.40pm the enemy's machine-guns had become busy, and at 6.00pm they mowed down our advancing waves, so that only a few men actually reached the German parapet and none of these ever returned. The Germans appeared to have some six teams of machine-gunners. Even after seven hours' bombardment by our guns these six teams appeared intact, firing over the parapet at our assaulting infantry. By crowding three companies into 300 yards of front, our casualties from shellfire were more heavy.[88]

Meanwhile, Bean notes:

> The records of the 16th Bavarian R.I.R, which faced them, attributes the repulse of these Australians, and of the neighbouring British, to the determination of the regiment to sustain, in spite of the fire playing upon it, continuous observation from its front-line trenches. As soon as one of its men, killed or wounded, fell from the parapet, another took his place. This rifle and machine-gun fire was kept up.[89]

Captain Stewart-Liberty of 2/1st Battalion remembered: 'The German machine guns, until now hidden deep in the ground, swept us… Some got to the German trenches; some got only a few yards.'[90]

The landscape in front of Sugar Loaf was very flat so German machine guns used 'grazing fire' with lethal bursts, uninterrupted by any ground cover, which stayed below a man's height for hundreds of yards along No Man's Land. Enfilading grazing fire could devastate an assault's flank.[91] There were ten machine guns deployed across the R.I.R. 16's sector: two British with eight German, four of which were in the Sugar Loaf and two in the apex covering a separate quadrant.[92] The 2/1st Bucks' War Diary calls the hostile fire 'annihilating' and records: 'those who reached positions close to the enemy line went to ground and waited until dark: they were few.'

Captain Church and Sanderson's attack

No machine gun was used within a cover (of a pillbox) and all were deployed from the parapets. Bavarian machine gun crews, notes Barton, sustained numerous casualties.[93]

CB/AS: *Church's party were nearing the end of the saps when a machine gun from almost ahead of them began to fire practically along the sap itself. The party did not hesitate. Sanderson saw Church fall at his side but there was no time to wait. At 20 yards from the German parapet, he suddenly saw straight ahead of them a second German Machine Gun in the act of being placed on the parapet. It was pointing full down the sap, and what would have happened could only be guessed, but at that exact moment as they were rushing towards it, one of our shells fell right on the gun and blew it to pieces. This lucky chance probably saved Sanderson and the party now under his command entered the German trenches, captured the other Machine Gun and made its way along the German line.*[94]

Major General Colin Mackenzie G.O.C. of 61st Division reported that:

> Both companies of the (2/1st) Bucks advanced precisely at 6 p.m. from their position close to the enemy parapet. The Right Company were almost all killed and wounded at once by machine gun fire; the Left company, led by Captain Church, who was killed on the slope of the parapet, also suffered heavily, but a number got into the SUGAR LOAF, as was substantiated later by eye-witnesses of the 15th Australian Brigade on their left.[95]

The official British history records: 'On the left a party of the battalion reached the northeastern face of the salient, but there was sharp fighting on the parapet till all were killed or wounded. A third company of the battalion, bearing material for consolidation, left the British line at 6.10pm but was stopped by the fire of the machine guns.'[96]

Bean's Official History notes:

Captain H. Church, 33, was a barrister and graduate of Trinity College Oxford, where he had been a prominent Rugby football player. He was killed, leading his company, as he reached the German breastwork… As to the assault on the Sugar Loaf, reports of artillery observers seemed contradictory – at 6.23 it was stated that the 184th Brigade was 'in'; but afterwards: 'Germans holding parapet strongly all along. No sign of our people.'[97]

The 2/1st Bucks' War Diary notes that:

Reports were very contradictory. Owing to the distance between the trenches, and to the continuous bombardment and smoke, the officers who were observing found their task almost impossible to fulfill with any degree of accuracy. Our men having been actually seen on the German parapet, it was concluded that a certain number must have got in. But it is certain that very few survived the enemy's machine-gun fire, and whether they got in or not they never returned. The whole attack was unsuccessful in that the enemy's trenches, though penetrated, were not consolidated and held.[98]

Michael Senior estimates that 2/1st Bucks had to advance a further 200 yards from the Rhondda Sap to reach the enemy trenches, which proved impossible. Such was the devastation, only 100 of the 300 infantry of 2/1st Bucks would return to their lines after the assault.[99]

CB/AS: *About seventy men were in this party. Sanderson says that they were the only part of the 61st Division which reached the trenches. He was now in command of it, Church having been killed. The fire of the German Machine Guns across No Man's Land was very withering, although the whole line he thinks could have made certain of reaching the trenches. It was hopelessly impossible for a small party of 70 to attempt to return across No Man's Land as a concentrated fire would have been turned on them. Away to the left on the eastern side of the Sugar Loaf, the Australian Infantry could be seen making their way across country far inland of the trenches. Sanderson's anxiety was now largely for them. He thought that they would scarcely realise that their right flank had been cut completely off. He had been quite confident that they would get across, and was furious at the danger to which the failure of the 61st Division had exposed them. He at once decided that his best course was to take his seventy men across the open beyond the German trenches towards a point where these Australians were advancing and to warn them that their flank was unprotected,* *and if possible, to take up a position facing towards the Australian right flank so as to cover it. After about five minutes in the German trenches this course was taken. The party as it moved across the open towards the Australians came under a very heavy machine gun fire. The Machine Gun from the German line south of the salient were, Sanderson thinks, brought back by their crews, after the attack on their own front had been defeated, and were firing as it appeared to him from a position behind their own trenches straight into the flank of Australian infantry. Of the 70 men who started out with him only eleven actually reached the Australian position. The ground was cut up heavily by our artillery, whose bombardment Sanderson thinks was very destructive and unfortunately was full of shell holes. This small party ducked from one shell hole to another. Sanderson says that the swish, swish, swish of machine gun bullets was so constant and close that it was a miracle that any one of them got through. On reaching the Australians they made their way back through the German communication trenches and finally, through the saps blown by the 14th Brigade, into our line. Sanderson went straight to the British Divisional authorities and spoke his mind freely, being in a very disturbed and excited condition. He says that the Officer whom he tackled (I think it was the Divisional Commander) was just as upset as he was. Having calmed down, he made his way to where Coulter was supervising the work on one of these westernmost saps. Coulter had been once wounded lately, but the gallant chap was carrying on until he was a second time wounded and they forced him to the rear. While out, Sanderson came across a number of wounded men whom he bandaged. One poor chap's side had been so badly torn by a shell that the working of his heart could be clearly seen. The man was sitting against the parapet perfectly conscious and talking quite naturally, but Sanderson imagined that his case was quite hopeless. He bandaged him with a field dressing so that the wound was covered, and the man made not the slightest complaint and showed no signs of the pain which he must have felt.*[100]

Attack by the Australian 59th and 60th battalions

According to Barton's Map 7 (M.D. / Kriegsarchiv, Munich, 6 BRD, Bund 8) IIIa was the German defensive sub-sector of R.I.R.16 opposite the Australian 15th Brigade, specifically 60th Battalion.

Barton describes how, for almost three hours before the allied attack, mortar fire and artillery – including from two further batteries on the Aubers Ridge – were directed on the area.[101] Brigadier General H.E. 'Pompey' Elliott had recently received a circular from G.H.Q. warning that attacks could not succeed unless the 'jumping off' position was within 200 yards of the enemy's trench. Elliott's troops would have to advance 350–420 yards from their own trenches. Haking tried to meet the difficulty of the width of No Man's Land by sending out the troops before the bombardment lifted.[102]

Haking's plans called for the British infantry to exit onto No Man's Land from sally ports in their parapet. The Australians had previously experienced the difficulty of exiting sally ports when in Gallipoli and so ignored Haking's order, with Elliott warning Brigadier General Carter, commanding 184th Brigade that just one shot man could block the sally port exit. Carter replied that he would try that way first and, if it failed, he would send his men 'over the top', which is what happened.[103]

Impressed by the Australian artillery, Elliott was convinced the Australian shells would keep the Germans down in their dugouts and told his men: 'Boys, you won't find a German in the trenches when you get there.'[104]

A.D. Ellis, in his book on the 5th Australian Division, notes that: 'The men had received especially good breakfasts and dinners and were in high spirits.'[105]

Elliott and his men were unaware that the German fortifications and dugouts were much deeper, stronger, and less penetrable to shells than their British equivalents. Nor did they know that the tremendous noise of the British and Australian shellfire was more impressive than its accuracy. McMullin described the difficulties the Australian artillery faced in neutralising these defences:

> Officers in the 60th Battalion, looking across No Man's Land to the enemy fortifications…could see plenty of German wire uncut and at least three machine-gun emplacements undamaged. Afterwards a senior artillery commander complained that he had been severely handicapped by the hasty preparations that had prevented him from familiarising himself sufficiently with the battlefield and registering his batteries properly…by the near-total absence of support staff and, incredibly, the lack of a decent map.[106]

The deeply concave curvature of the line in Elliott's brigade lent itself to the installation of advanced jumping-off trenches. Some had been dug the previous year and others by the Australians themselves in the weeks before the battle, i.e. the trench that ran from the Tommy-Brücke to the southern corner of the Orchard and another from the end of the Rhondda Sap towards the western corner of the Orchard. All were interconnected and linked by communication trenches to the front line. All but the Rhondda Sap (ultimately shared by both British and Australians) fell within the Australian assaulting territory.[107]

According to the Bavarian maps, the 59th Battalion's four assaulting waves universally employed the jumping-off positions. In the 60th Battalion sector only the first wave used them: later assaults clambered over the original parapet.[108]

R.I.R. records show that *Minenwerfers* were firing: 'continuously on the attacking enemy as long as their ammunition held out…in particular where they gathered in groups.' At 17:45 R.I.R.16 reported: 'the enemy artillery fire lifted once more to the rear and the enemy infantry left their trenches, some over the parapet and others through... sally ports. The enemy advanced towards our trenches in dense waves, carrying scrambling ramps and mats.'[109] A.D. Ellis writes that: 'The assaulting troops were instructed to go over in four waves, 100 yards apart.'[110]

In some units only the Australians in the first two waves wore steel helmets, with the rest wearing Australian 'slouch' hats, the only occasion when these hats (with khaki band and left side folded up, held in place by the rising sun badge) were used by units in action on the Western Front. (Post-war, some slouch hats were found in front of Sugar Loaf and sent to the A.W.M.)[111]

15th Brigade's leading wave was deployed at 17:45, leaving the parapets at five-minute intervals.

> The 59th was scarcely over the parapet before a little desultory rifle fire was opened on it, chiefly coming from the Sugar Loaf. Before the men had gone 30 yards, this fire had grown in intensity and a machine gun added its significant voice to the rapidly increasing fusillade... the enemy fire grew hotter and hotter... the enemy front lines were seen to be thickly manned with troops.[112]

Lieutenant Knyvett, Intelligence Officer of 15 Brigade, recalled: 'The Germans swept a hail of bullets in our faces, like a veritable blizzard... The first wave went down like wheat before a reaper.'[113]

The following two waves left the parapet at 17:50 and 17:55. Plenge's 11 and 10 companies of 3/16 B.R.I.R., under Second Lieutenant Bachschneider, had destroyed the waves. The attackers were enfiladed by the Sugar Loaf on their right flank. '10 and 11 companies began a fusillade so devastating it was thought there was one man per yard on their parapet.'[114]

Lieutenant Colonel Harris of the 59th was incapacitated by a shell and suffered shell shock.[115] 'Major Layh took over charge of the dwindling lines which, finding a slight depression about 100 yards from the enemy parapet, halted in the scanty cover provided and commenced to reorganise their broken and depleted lines.'[116]

The Australian 60th Battalion War Diary noted:

> Battalion established in the Australian front-line trench by 4.20, Lewis guns excepted, a few casualties... Battalion scaled parapet and advanced in four waves, the first wave leaving at 5.45pm. Each wave advanced under very heavy artillery, machine gun and rifle fire, suffering very heavy casualties. Advance continued to within 90 yards of enemy trenches. The

attack was held up, although it is believed some few of the battalion entered enemy trenches.[117]

Barton quotes Gebhardt on the 60th Battalion's attack:

> In front of IIIa the enemy ignited several smoke pots. Our trench garrison was immediately alerted by the sentries and hurried to the breastworks. A barrage of machine-guns, small-arms and artillery fire mowed down the attacking enemy like a scythe. Only a small number reached our wire and were shot down there, while the remainder tried in vain to retire to their trenches.... The Bavarians defensive artillery was 'excellent' with their guns laying down 'an impenetrable curtain of fire in front of our trenches' while signal flares...calling for barrage fire were 'clearly seen and recognised, even in daylight'.[118]

While the front attackers of 59 Battalion were taking refuge in a shallow depression 100 yards from the German parapet, 60 Battalion was digging desperately 90 yards away. Behind them, others lay flat in the undulating soil or crouched in shell holes.[119]

At 17:55:

> The third wave went forward searching for the place where it thought the previous waves must be lying ready to make the final rush. But like the previous waves it was stopped by withering fire from the flank. But here and there a group, led by some surviving officer or N.C.O., pressed forward until it found itself alone...in front lay the enemy's parapet 150 yards distant, fringed by a line of Germans standing out shoulder high. Lts Gibbs and Carr of the 59th are said to have been killed on the German wire: and, according to one account, Captain Liddelow commanding 'A' Company of the 59th, although wounded, actually reached the German parapet with a few men, but the position there being hopeless, withdrew them into a shell hole to await support.[120]

A private soldier in 57th Battalion, an eyewitness of the 60th Battalion's (third wave) attack, later wrote:

> The 60th climbed on to the parapet, heavily laden, dragging with them scaling ladders, light bridges, picks, shovels and bags of bombs. Scores of stammering German machine-guns spluttered violently, drowning the noise of the cannonade. The air was thick with bullets, swishing in a flat lattice

of death. There were gaps in the lines of men – wide ones, small ones. The survivors spread across the front, keeping the line straight… The bullets skimmed low, from knee to groin, riddling the tumbling bodies before they touched the ground. Still the line kept on… Hundreds were mown down in the flicker of an eyelid, like great rows of teeth knocked from a comb, but still the line went on, thinning and stretching. Wounded wriggled into shell holes or were hit again. Men were cut in two by streams of bullets. And still the line went on… It was the charge of the Light Brigade once more, but more terrible, more hopeless.[121]

At 18:00 Major G. McCrae, O.C. of 60th Battalion, a Gallipoli veteran and an exceptional young officer, led out the fourth wave of the 15th Brigade; 2,000 infantry, including 60 officers. Within 80 yards McCrae was shot through the neck and killed. Before dark 'his whole staff and almost every officer and N.C.O. of his battalion were lying dead or wounded in the low fields round the Laies.' Among the casualties were McCrae's signallers. Runners would now have to carry messages back to the Australian lines.[122]

The historian R. McMullin states that: '60th Battalion was practically annihilated. This fine unit had gone into action over 900 strong, its talented leaders and well-trained "rank and file" eager to perform well. The next day only 61 men and a handful of officers were present at the roll-call.'[123]

No Man's Land was an overgrown and boggy landscape through which ran a stream and muddy ditches. Soldiers under shell fire in the smoke, haze, dust and shrapnel dropped into the foot-high summer grass, into bomb craters or sought refuge in numerous ditches where they continued to crawl. Some sheltered in the Laies Brook that ran diagonally across the battlefield. The sound and smell of explosives was overwhelming.

Within half an hour of the assault commencing, along the whole of the Australian 15th Brigade front, it was evident that the British 61st Division had failed to seize the Sugar Loaf.

Private R. Lording, a teenage soldier of Australian 30th Battalion, who received terrible wounds, wrote later: 'The gunfire merges into a continuous roar above which are heard only the sharp explosions of nearby shells. To make themselves heard in the din, men have to shout. The Boys are hugging whatever cover they can find, tensely awaiting their fate.'[124]

At 18:34 and 18:40, an observer of 114th Battery could see troops advancing in No Man's Land but only halfway across. At 20:40 Major Layh, 2 I/C of 59th, came back and reported that the battalion (forming the right of the Australian attack) could get no more than half-way across the open terrain. Layh was placed in command of the 59th.

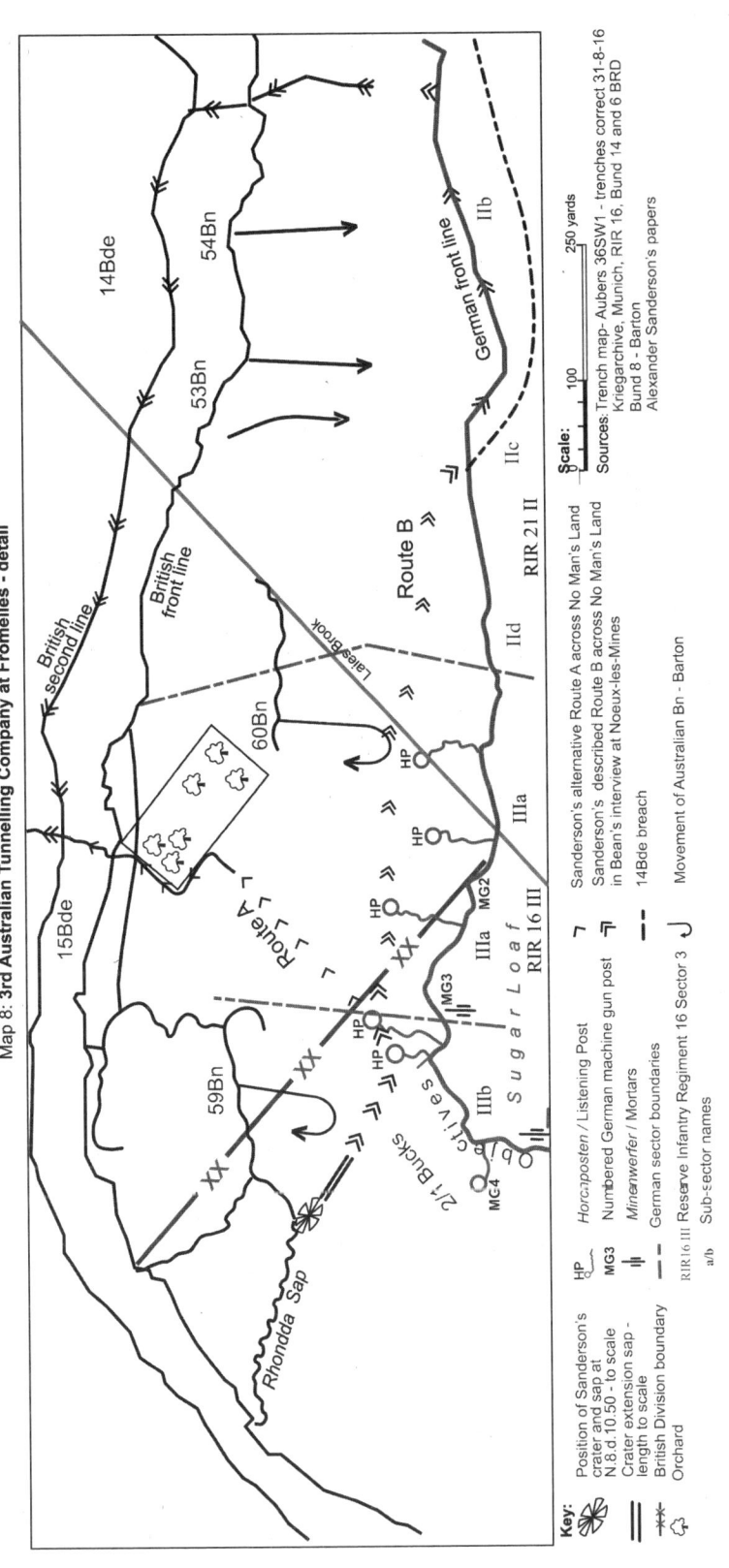

The first wave of returning wounded told the story of the attack. Halfway across, as they emerged between the grassy drains, the Sugar Loaf machine guns, now on their right front and flank, had opened up. The fragments of the first wave had sought what cover they could in shell-holes or in the channel of the Laies Brook (only 2 feet deep and 4–5 feet wide). Later waves were under heavy fire from the moment they left the parapet and on reaching the grassy undulations half way across were shattered by the same deadly machine guns. The third wave at about 17:55 crossed the parapet but could only see 'the unkempt pasture, perfectly still, with the dead scattered thickly'.[125]

The crater, blown by Coulter and Sanderson's push-pipes, offered a measure of shelter to the wounded of the attack and was used as an advanced dressing station.[126] It proved very difficult to evacuate the wounded along a narrow sap.[127]

R.I.R. 16's commander *Hauptmann* Gebhardt noted later that the deployment of large numbers of machine-guns in the front line was the main reason the attack was completely repulsed. Meanwhile, Peter Barton concludes: 'Every British and Australian account adds force to these fateful words, for at no point within and around Sugar Loaf were troops able to pierce the enemy line.'[128]

In his battle report R.I.R. *Oberstleutnant* Spatny later noted: 'Not one of the English troops entered R.I.R. 16 sector.' ('English' here meaning British and Australians), while Major General Mackenzie later noted in his 61st Division reports that: 'a number got into the Sugar Loaf', and that the action was 'substantiated later by an eyewitness of 15th Australian Brigade'. Peter Barton concludes: 'there is no evidence to support this statement', except in Sector IIId.[129]

Alex Sanderson's personal account of his actions at Fromelles, recorded in the shorthand notes of C.E.W Bean at Noeux-les-Mines in 1918, offers an alternative version of events in the British attack area.[130]

In interpreting Sanderson's account, we are left with two alternative possibilities:

First possibility: Route 'A'

What is very likely is that the 2/1st Bucks survivors with Captain Sanderson and his few tunnellers, after the destruction of the German machine gun by a shell (Sanderson's account above), had reached and entered some of the German's *Horchposten* (Listening/ O.P. posts) dug by the Bavarians in front of their Sugar Loaf parapets, to warn of British raiding parties approaching their front line at night.[131] Captain Sanderson's party would have realised that fighting their way across the German breastwork and taking the Sugar Loaf was impossible. As Sanderson reported later, Captain Church had died on the parapet. If they stayed where they were, they too would soon all be dead.

If one accepts that Bean's shorthand has mistakenly noted 'German' communication trenches instead of 'Australian', one return scenario follows the illustration showing Sanderson and his eleven survivors making their way back to the southwest corner of the Orchard and through the Australian 'jumping off' positions and allied communication trenches, back to allied lines.

Second possibility: Route 'B'

In their original orders – which Sanderson would previously have discussed with Captain Church: 'the 2/1 Bucks, once in the Sugar Loaf, were to have bombed eastwards to link up with 15th Australian Brigade on the far side of the Sugar Loaf.'

Sanderson would have observed the Australian 59th and 60th battalions of 15th Brigade on his immediate left, being strongly enfiladed by the Sugar Loaf's 'harassing' machine gun fire. It is entirely credible, and the author's view, that Sanderson would have decided to take Church's party and his handful of tunnellers east across No Man's Land to warn the attacking Australian 15th and 14th Brigade Infantry about the enfilading fire, as Sanderson described to Bean in 1918.

Peter Barton's translation of BRD Bund 8 III/ RIR 16 (Action at Fromelles 19.7.16) notes that: 'At 6.45 the…enemy infantry left their trenches in dense waves… In front of IIIa the enemy ignited several smoke pots.' This smoke and the dust from shells would have disorientated but helped Sanderson's party, now running across No Man's Land, as they 'ducked from one shell hole to another' until they reached IId. Here the Australians of 14th Brigade (and some of the Australian 60th Battalion of 15th Brigade who had veered to the left, alongside 53rd Battalion) had entered German front lines.[132] Bund 8 had noted: 'At 7.00pm the two runners who had been lying up in the rear of sub-sector "a"… reported that the English had broken into our lines near the right flank of IIIa.'

As Sanderson later explained, such was the deadly machine gun fire from the Sugar Loaf that only eleven of his party of seventy made it to the 14th Brigade Australians, who had broken into the (IId) German front-line trenches. As Sanderson told Bean: 'On reaching the Australians they made their way back through the German communication trenches and finally, through the saps blown by the 14th Brigade, into our line.'[133]

Major General McCay had ordered Brigadier General Elliott to arrange for a trench to be dug across No Man's Land to join up with 14th Brigade's position in the German front lines. Early on the morning of 20 July, the 14th Brigade engineers, under Major Bachtold, were busy constructing this new communication trench, which they successfully achieved with extra troops.

When the sap, 4 feet 6 inches deep and duck-boarded, was only halfway across the old No Man's Land, 14th Brigade soldiers began: 'to file along it back to their own lines…the survivors from the captured trenches, and those men going across, all tumbled and raced back to the accompaniment of a chorus of machine guns.'[134] The sap reached the German front line at midnight.

Peter Barton notes that there existed an Australian 'protected' communication sap across No Man's Land (at IIc from the Bavarian H.P. post No.2) back to the Australian lines.[135] This could well have been the route taken by Alex and his ten fellow survivors to cross No Man's Land back to the Australian lines, as Sanderson described in his 1918 account to Bean.

Bean could easily have made an error when transcribing certain details of his shorthand notes. However, it is difficult to believe that an experienced and highly decorated Australian officer would have given an inexact account of his role in the Fromelles battle to the Australian Official Historian only two years later: the majority of the details given are too specific. Elements of this enigma do still remain unclear and unresolved. Indeed Bean, a decade after the battle when writing to Sanderson in 1926, was still trying to piece together the full details of the battle. To be open-minded and to accurately piece together the events of a confused battlefield, one has to consider all evidence, from both sides of No Man's Land. German accounts of the 16th Bavarian R.I.R. stationed at Sugar Loaf suggest that their front line was cut off for a time: 'At 4.20pm all the telephone lines to the front lines were knocked out.'[136]

It is important to note that the numbers of sixty-seven English soldiers reported as 'Missing' in the 2/1st Bucks War Diary seem to tally exactly with the Bean/Sanderson account, where Sanderson describes his party in front of the Sugar Loaf as being seventy in number. Captain Sanderson and two O.R. tunnellers, plus the 'believed killed' of 2/1st Bucks (Lieutenant G. W. Atkinson, Second Lientenant R.B. Hudson and sixty-five O.R.s) make an exact total of seventy men.[137]

CB/AS: *For this fight Sanderson obtained through the Infantry his Military Cross. I imagine that neither he nor the one or two tunnellers who went out with him across No Man's Land had the slightest right to be there. The majority of the tunnelling party was of course sent back to the rear the moment the saps had been blown, and only the officers and two or three men remained for the actual attack.*[138]

Sanderson noted in his post-battle letter of 1 August 1916 to Major Coulter that he 'must not write' what had happened (in No Man's Land): no doubt because he had not been authorised to accompany Captain Church in the attack towards the Sugar Loaf. Sanderson's motivations for his foray were revealed in his letter to the wounded Coulter: 'One does not get much fun here except in the work and risks one has to take.'[139]

In June 1917 at Loos-en-Gohelle, on the spur of the moment, Coulter would decide to accompany the departing Sanderson on a night-time raid into German lines. Coulter had not been authorised to do this either and, subsequently, Sanderson would omit from his own report on the raid the significant fact that Coulter had joined him and had been killed in action by a German sniper.

For those who say that Sanderson and eleven of his party could not have survived their journey across No Man's Land from the Sugar Loaf to Australian lines, we have Pompey Elliott's description of the actions of Australian Private Reg Poulter, who courageously volunteered and successfully carried an important message from practically under the German parapet all the way back to the 15th Brigade's front line 'under a withering machine gun and artillery fire' and made eight trips across No Man's Land to deliver messages or rescue wounded. (Poulter was awarded both a Military Medal and a Russian Medal of St George.)[140]

The Australian attack

Below is an explanatory timeframe for the British – and Australian – leadership failures and misunderstandings on the evening of 19 July, which were directly responsible for the disastrous Australian second attack on the Sugar Loaf salient and which resulted in so many unnecessary deaths and casualties. After the Fromelles battle, Australian survivors blamed the British commanders for the chaotic attack fiasco that had cost so many of their comrades' lives, as well as for the perceived failure of the British 61st Division.[141]

18:30 Major General MacKenzie, British Commander of 61st Division, believed that 2/1st Bucks had managed to get into the Sugar Loaf and instructed his brigades to reorganise and prepare for a further attack at 21:00. In the chaos of battle, MacKenzie was receiving mixed reports of the overall situation.[142]

18:30 Brigadier General Carter, at 184th Brigade's Battle H.Q., 1.5 miles behind the lines, ordered Lieutenant Colonel Williams of 2/1st Bucks to renew the attack two hours later (at 20:30). Williams was in the trenches, close to the action, and was furious on receiving these orders: 'when every man, save a few telephone operators, orderlies and wounded, was in No Man's Land.' Williams persuaded Carter that none of his men was in the Sugar Loaf. Carter postponed a planned fresh assault until 21:00.[143] (Carter and his staff of 184th Brigade later negligently failed to inform 15th Brigade H.Q. that they were no longer needed for a renewed combined attack at 21:00.)[144]

18:30 Brigadier General Elliott reported that the Sugar Loaf attack appeared successful. Yet no definite word came back.

18:45 Elliot at 15th Brigade H.Q. messaged the divisional commander: '59th Battalion held up half way across No Man's Land. Heavy casualties. 60th Btn. and others appear to have got across.'[145]

19:18 A handful of 60th Battalion men had managed to enter enemy territory, but only by drifting left of their objective and sliding in alongside the 53rd Battalion (across some of the seven small bridges of the Laies Brook/Leik Bach). Peter Barton writes that the rest of 60th and 59th Battalion 'were either dead, pinned down in No Man's Land or back in their original line. No digger was in any part of the Sugar Loaf.'[146]

19:18 Elliott forwarded the news from the 59th to the Divisional Commander that: 'The trenches are full of the enemy. Every man who rises is shot down.'[147]

19:30 A special order was received from Haking to 'extend the hold on the Sugar Loaf' in order to help the Australians. However, this order was rescinded when it became known that the 184th Brigade had no men in the salient.

19:34 The 12th Bavarian Brigade H.Q. received the message: 'There are great masses of English dead 150 metres in front of IIIb' (the apex of Sugar Loaf).[148]

19:52 Carter sent a message, relaying MacKenzie's 21:00 attack order, to the 15th Brigade through the two divisional H.Q.s: 'Am attacking at 9pm. Can the right battalion cooperate?'[149]

19:55 Believing 2/1st Bucks 'A' Coy. had penetrated Sugar Loaf, Haking issued an order for them to bomb their way along and link with the Australians. But all were dead, missing or wounded.[150]

20:00 The 184th Brigade reported: 'they have not taken German trenches on their front… Germans still hold Sugar Loaf.'[151]

20:10 Elliott received Carter's telegram request to support a British 21:00 attack.

20:13 Elliott sent orders for the two companies of the 58th Battalion waiting in the forward lines to prepare to attack across No Man's Land. (The 15th Brigade had brought forward the 58th Battalion to make a new attempt east of the Sugar Loaf.)[152]

20:20 Haking learned of the failure to take the Sugar Loaf and issued a verbal order for the British 183rd and 184th brigades to cancel their 21:00 attack.[153,154]

20:30 Haking did not directly inform the 5th Australian Division of the 21:00 attack cancellation, with Bean saying that Haking was probably unaware that they had been asked to cooperate. On learning of the attack cancellation, at 20:30 61st Division sent a message to the 5th Australian Division stating: 'Under instructions from corps commander am withdrawing from captured enemy line after dark.'[155]

20:35 Message cancelling the attack at 21:00 was received at the 5th Australian Division's H.Q. They failed to grasp the meaning of the message or to understand the urgency in forwarding it on to Elliott.

20:55 Haking's direct message was now sent to the 61st Division, countermanding the projected 21:00 British attack, due in five minutes, and ordering all troops to withdraw from the captured trenches after dark.[156]

21:00 Unaware of the British lack of participation, the Australian 58th, with some 59th survivors, rushed into No Man's Land and attacked. To Elliott's dismay and disbelief there was no sign of any advance by the British 184th Brigade, whose battlefield support was the rationale for his half battalion's assault.[157]

21:10 Haking's direct cancellation message is received at the 5th Division's Australian H.Q.

21:25 With reckless delay, McCay forwarded this message on to Elliott at the 15th Brigade H.Q. '61st Division not attacking tonight. General Elliott may withdraw 59th Battalion… if he thinks attack is not likely to succeed.'

23:00 Haking telephoned Mackenzie and instructed that the 184th Brigade should 'attack the Sugar Loaf during the night', after ten minutes' concentrated bombardment.[158]

00:30 [20 July] A major in the 58th messaged his division's H.Q.: 'Two companies of 58th mown down when close to enemy's trench… very few came back. Men of all battalions are coming back from No Man's Land. Many are wounded, many not. Enemy flares are coming from the whole of front.' Elliott added: 'The message indicates that attack of the Brigade has completely failed.'[159]

03:00 When Carter reported that his trenches were being heavily shelled, Haking's night attack order was cancelled. Haking now advised 61st Division to prepare for an attack in the morning of 20 July.[160]

By the time 15th Brigade headquarters knew the 61st Division's attack had been cancelled, it was too late to stop their attack at 21:00, during which all of Sugar Loaf's machine gunners would be able to focus on this one thin Australian line that was attempting the impossible task of penetrating their line.

Bean described the needless tragedy: 'By then night was closing in, and in the failing twilight there had gone forward, punctually to the minute, one of the bravest and most hopeless assaults ever undertaken by the Australian Imperial Force.'

The two companies of the 58th: 'went forward with splendid dash opposite the Sugar Loaf, carrying with them a number of survivors of the 59th, until, when they were two-thirds of the way across No Man's Land, there was opened from the salient a fire of machine-guns so severe the line was shattered and the men dazed. The survivors obtained slight cover in a ditch.' Their leader, Major Hutchinson, went on alone: 'and fell riddled by bullets close to the German wire. The two companies of the 58th… were practically annihilated.'[161]

After the battle

Reports of the three or four days after the battle recount misunderstandings, sacrifice, cruelty and selflessness, as hundreds lay wounded across No Man's Land. Opposite 61st Division, the Germans: 'allowed the stretcher-bearers… to wander around No Man's Land in broad daylight, picking up the dead and wounded, without firing a shot.'[162] Looking out into No Man's Land, Australians 'could be seen everywhere raising their limbs in pain or turning hopelessly, hour after hour, from one side to the other.' Any movement was met with cruel fire from the enemy machine guns.[163] Captain Knyvett was appalled by cruel acts of the enemy: 'I have found the Bavarian even worse that the Prussian, and this day, and the next, again did they sweep No Man's Land with machine guns and shrapnel, so as to kill the wounded.'[164]

A statue in the Memorial Park at Fromelles commemorates the bravery of Sergeant Simon Fraser of 57th Battalion, who carried back wounded fellow soldiers from No Man's Land. Fraser, afterwards commissioned as a Lieutenant before being killed in May 1917, had modestly described his heroic work: 'I must say Fritz treated us very fairly, though a few were shot at the work. It was no light work getting in with a heavy weight on your back… You had to lie down and get him on your back; then rise and duck for your life with a chance of getting a bullet in you before you were safe.' He also wrote home of how: 'a man about 30 yards out sang out: "Don't forget me, cobber." I went in and got four volunteers with stretchers.'[165]

Paul Cobb, whose own great-uncle was killed at Fromelles, quotes one admirable act: 'Two gallant enemies carried a wounded Australian to our parapet, stood at the salute, then turned and walked away. They unfortunately neglected to secure a safe conduct and were shot…by someone in the next bay…who were in ignorance of their errand.'[166] 15th Brigade's War Diary recorded on 23 July that: 'Our machine guns were very active at night in the hope of killing some of the enemy snipers who came into No Man's Land during our rescue operations.'

Major General J. McCay's over-optimistic orders given to the Australian 8th, 14th and 15th brigades for the battle had been rushed and badly planned. The Australian divisional commander, following Haig's specific order about such agreements, now forbad a truce allowing each side to retrieve their wounded and thus save hundreds of British, German and Australian lives. Bean describes how an Australian major and a private had crossed to the German lines, carrying an improvised Red Cross flag and water bottles which they distributed to the wounded on the way. 'The parapets on both sides were crowded with soldiers watching… On reaching the enemy lines… an immaculately dressed lieutenant emerged.'

On listening to their proposal, the German officer left to telephone his authorities. A truce was then agreed, provided that the Australian stretcher-bearers worked in their half of No Man's Land, while the Germans cleared the wounded from their half. Hostilities had ceased until McCay prohibited this truce.[167] McCay later claimed that both Haking and Munro approved his decision. Under military law, however, McCay was officially entitled to approve a local suspension of arms without Haig's ratification.[168] Many critics would afterwards refer to McCay as 'Bloody McCay'. In January 1917 he would be made a scapegoat, relieved of his divisional command and ordered to England.[169]

Ross McMullin describes how Pompey Elliott visited the front line, consoled the wounded and witnessed the carnage of his shattered brigade among the debris of the destroyed trenches. He 'never spoke a word all the way back to advanced brigade headquarters but went straight inside, put his head in his hands, and sobbed his heart out.' More than two decades after the battle, a 58th Battalion lieutenant, recollected: 'I will always have before my eyes the picture of Pompey… the morning after Fromelles, tears streaming down his face, shaking hands with the pitiful remnant of his brigade.' Meanwhile, an officer of the 57th recalled: 'Pompey's agony was palpable; his eyes were filled with tears' as he lamented: 'Good God, Bill, what's happened to my brigade?'[170]

Elliott later described the attacks as: 'like the charge at the Nek on a tenfold scale'. He wrote to his wife:

I think over 2,000 of my own Brigade alone are killed, wounded or missing, and very, very many of these will be killed, as the Germans fired at them as they lay all night and all today… many, many must perish slowly and miserably of starvation and want of attention in that No-Man's-Land. God help us all, it is cruel indeed… The casualties will be worse I fear than even the landing at Gallipoli…We attacked in four waves and there was not the least hesitation in any one of them although they saw the preceding waves going down before the machine guns like corn before the reaper… The Anzac men who helped to build up my Brigade are all dead. I presume there was some plan at the back of the attack but it is difficult to know what it was.[171]

On 26 July Alex Sanderson was given 'Temporary Command of the 3rd Tunnelling Company during the absence of Major Coulter L.J. DSO, from 30 July 1916 to 12 September 1916'.[172] Alex was officially transferred from Mining Corps H.Q. to the 3rd Australian Tunnelling Company on 30 July 1916, the same date that his Next of Kin were advised that he had been wounded on 19 July but had remained on duty. Major Coulter, his wounds being more serious, was hospitalised. 107 years later, Alex Sanderson's daughter Janet, aged 86, would remark that her father had a long scar on his neck caused by a shell explosion. Alex must have received a significant wound at Fromelles when earning his first wound stripe, worn on the sleeve of his uniform. In June 1917, promoted to Major, Alex Sanderson would take permanent command of the company.

On 1 August 1916, Alex Sanderson was to write (see colour photo plate):

Dear Major Coulter,
We have only just discovered where you are located and are all very pleased to discover you are recovering speedily. I went down to Lillers on the afternoon that you left, only to find I was about half an hour too late. I would dearly have liked a few minutes chat to let you know how 'successful' the 'blow' was and what occurred afterwards. I expect to hear that you have been honoured with the D.S.O. when the next list comes out as I know it has been recommended and no-one realises better than I do how well it is deserved. We are all trying to keep up the reputation which the No.3 Coy. earned under your leadership. I feel proud to think that I have been posted to command the Coy. Taking them all round you could not get a finer lot of officers, N.C.O.s & men and if I can do as well with them as you did I will be happy even if I get one of those 'blightys'. We will try and keep the nest warm for you in case they do not find something better with a Lt-Col attached to it. [Note: Alex's description, written here, of the attack

on Sugar Loaf has been inserted earlier in the chapter.] The minework is going on swimmingly – Righthand Left gallery is a bit behind hand as the shaft was knocked about and had to be repaired quite a lot. I am trying to get more men on each face at that point. What bad luck it was to lose poor old Charlie [Lieutenant Charles Whyte]. He seemed to have some presentiment that he would not go back. Prospects seem brightened by the grand progress made by the Russians lately and our own chaps have done excellently. We are having a few days of quite Australian summer weather which seems to have improved everyone's feelings after the epidemic of colds which occurred lately – I have packed all your things together on one side of the hut and am occupying the other pending your return. If you want any of them sent along just let me know. Give my kindest regards to Seale and Kennedy. I hope they will get well quickly and yourself also. Have a good time old chap before you return. One does not get much fun here except in the work and risks one has to take.

Yours Sincerely, Alex Sanderson.[173]

Sanderson here makes light of the horrors and risks of war. Whereas in his interview with Bean, we are told: 'Sanderson went straight to the British Divisional authorities and spoke his mind freely, being in a very disturbed and excited condition.'[174]

The commander of the 61st Division was Major General Mackenzie. If Captain Sanderson had 'tackled' the British divisional commander, as Bean suggests, by 'speaking his mind' when he returned to the British lines, Sanderson was past caring of the consequences, having witnessed at first hand the tragedy of a disastrous assault. Sanderson had already challenged the 'Red Tabs' at Hazebrouck in May 1916 when he had rejected their instructions not to take his specialist tunnelling equipment, shipped with him from Australia, up to the front line. Australians felt less intimidated by higher ranks and Sanderson counted his ex-colleague John Monash as a friend.

On 20 July Captain Sanderson reported formally to Major Coulter O.C. 3 A.T.C. that:

I have to report the following particulars re: the communication crater blown from the end of Rhondda Valley sap at 5.11pm yesterday, during bombardment of the enemy's positions. The crater subsequently proved to be of great value to the Infantry advancing from Sally Port. After piloting the infantry through the sap to the crater, I proceeded to the points where craters were formed by Lts Priestman and Howie and found that they had satisfactorily completed the work designed. I desire to express my appreciation of the valuable services performed by Cpl Street during the carrying out of the work and of the assistance subsequently given in exploding the charge under heavy shell fire.

(signed) Alex Sanderson, Captain.[175]

As for Captain Alexander Sanderson, his commendation for his first Military Cross appeared in the London Gazette of 26 September:

Near Picantin on the night of the 18/19th July 1916, he worked under heavy shell fire in a forward sap, which gave little or no cover in pushing and exploding loaded pipes to form a communication trench. The leads for exploding were several times cut by shell fire, and it was therefore necessary to go out in front of the trenches to light the fuse. The first attempt was stopped by shell fire, which caused six casualties including the O.C. of the Company. He succeeded however in a second attempt to fire the charge, which was entirely successful. He showed great pluck and determination throughout.

R. McNicoll in *Making and Breaking* writes that in the operation to blow a communication sap across No Man's Land from the Rhondda Sap:

the commander of the 3rd Tunnelling Company and six of his men had been wounded in trying to fire the piped charges after the leads had been cut by shell fire: the three sap pipe charges were ultimately fired by parties led by Captain Sanderson, the second-in-command, and Lieutenants O.R. Howie and B.Priestman. Unsuccessful though the battle was, but there could be no doubt about the gallantry of the units that took part, and there was a long list of awards. The work of the 3rd Tunnelling Company with push-pipes was recognised by the award of the D.S.O. to Major L.J. Coulter, the M.C. to Captain A. Sanderson and the D.C.M. to Sergeant M. Kerby and 2nd Corporal Street. This may seem disproportionate but one must bear in mind that the 3rd Tunnelling Company was under the direct command of a corps. The tunnelling companies, no less than field companies, were part of the Corps of Australian Engineers. [Not a separate arm of the service, as Bean mistakenly believed.][176]

At the time of the Fromelles battle, Charles Bean was on the Somme, poised to report on the three A.I.F. divisions' involvement in the British offensive at Pozières. Hearing of the battle, Bean had hurried to Fromelles, arriving early on the afternoon of 20 July. At the 15th Brigade H.Q., he found Elliott 'dead asleep'. McCay went to wake him, and Bean later wrote: 'When Elliott came out I felt almost as if I were in the presence of a man who had just lost his wife…he could hardly speak.'[177]

In his Official History Bean noted: '5th Australian Division was crippled by the fight at Fromelles.' The Australian soldiers were: 'unwisely combined with a British division whose value for offense, in spite of the devoted gallantry of many of its members, was recognised as "doubtful" and the Australian soldiers tended to accept the judgement – often unjust – that the "Tommies" could not be relied upon to uphold a flank in a stiff fight.' A page note added: 'The fate of Captain Church, and of several other officers, whose bodies, with those of their parties, were long afterwards found lying near the German wire, proves the quality of parts of this division.'[178]

Haking stated that: 'The attack of the Australian division… was carried out in an exceptionally gallant manner… Their difficulties on the right flank were caused by the failure of the 61st Division to carry the Sugar Loaf.' Meanwhile, Bean observed: 'It is only fair to remember that the 61st Division, like the Australians, was faced with machine guns which, under Haking's plan, should have been suppressed, but which fired through the barrage.'[179] And an officer of the 2/1st Bucks concluded: 'The whole plan for the infantry depended on the effectiveness of the artillery plan. It was not fair to blame the troops for the failure of the artillery.'[180] One British survivor even called Haking's words: 'an abominable libel on a gallant division that was massacred through no fault of its own.'[181]

Haking unfairly described the Australian division as: 'not sufficiently trained to consolidate the ground gained', (in spite of his confirmation to Haig before the battle that: 'the reserves were adequate both for the preparation and the execution of the enterprise'.) Ignoring his own blundering planning, Haking, inexcusably, further declared that: 'The 61st Division was not sufficiently imbued with the offensive spirit to go in like one man at the appointed time… I think the attack, although it failed, has done both divisions a great deal of good, and I am quite sure as a result of the attack that the Germans are not likely to move troops away from this front for some time.'[182]

Whether the complete tactical failure at Fromelles achieved the strategic aim of preventing a transfer of German troops to the Somme is debatable, with intelligence reports being inconclusive. Mike Senior in his biography of Haking, in mitigation for the general, quotes an Australian soldier's statement in 1919 that German troop movements to the Somme were delayed, even if not prevented: 'A captured German, who spoke excellent English, told us that his battalion was preparing to entrain when news of our "breakthrough" reached them. Immediately the men were ordered to detrain and were turned back to help their severely pressed comrades… A couple of days delay meant these two German divisions were not on the Somme where every man was wanted.'[183]

Documents on an XI Corps' British body, a copy of Haking's order, confirmed to Kronprinz Rupprecht's Chief of Staff *Generalleutnant* Hermann Von Kuhl the limited 'holding' aims of the Fromelles 1916 attack. On 20 July, at 20:30, the O.H.L. (German High Command) ordered Kuhl to send the Guard Reserve Corps from Fromelles into reserve at Cambrai, indicating that the disastrous attack had had no effect on the transfer of German troops.[184]

Cobb quotes the German war correspondent W. Scheuermann's article of 3 August in the *North German Gazette* that: 'the English were of the opinion that we were taking troops from this part of the front for employment on the Somme… The Bavarian Division…gained the ascendancy by themselves… without needing…the reserves which were naturally ready to come up from the neighbouring sectors.'[185]

General White, on Birdwood's staff, is reported as making this realistic appraisal: 'I hate these unprepared little shows. What do they do? We may deceive the enemy for two days; and after that, he knows perfectly well that it is not a big attack… We won't get anything that does us any good – the trenches are hard to keep, and it would mean the smashing of two divisions.'[186]

As a result of the defeat, in late July several British high-ranking officers lost their commands: General Munro, the First Army Commander and the brigadier generals in charge of the 183rd and 184th brigades. The popular C.O. of 2/1st Bucks Lieutenant Colonel Williams relinquished his command at the end of July, being returned to England. Williams wrote in the 2/1 Bucks' War Diary: 'By crowding three companies into 300 yards of front our casualties from shellfire were more heavy.'[187]

Haig tried in vain to promote Haking to an Army command, though he remained in command of XI Corps until the end of the war. To add insult to injury, in the afternoon of 20 July, Haking sent the Australian divisions an insensitive farewell message: 'I wish you all still a more complete victory in your next attack and I hope I shall be somewhere near when it takes place.'[188] The response of 5th Division Australian soldiers can easily be imagined.

On 20 July, in an official communiqué which attempted to minimise the tragic losses at Fromelles, the British High Command announced: 'Yesterday evening, south of Armentières, we carried out some important raids on a front of two miles in which Australian troops took part.' Bean at once drafted a cable for the Australian press, describing Fromelles as an 'attack' rather than 'raids' and the A.I.F. casualties suffered there as 'severe'. R. McMullin in *Pompey Elliott* described Bean's angry reaction to this announcement: 'What is the use of deliberate lying like that? The Germans know it was an attack – they have numbers of wounded as prisoners.'[189]

Casualties

R.I.R. 16 survived the attack with 340 casualties, 107 of which were fatal.[190]

2/1st Bucks Btn. had lost half their men. Their survivors were relieved at 13:00 and left for billets. Their fatalities numbered 7 officers & 127 O.R.s, while casualties from the three companies numbered 244. On 17 July, 2/1st Battalion had counted 20 officers and 642 O.R.'s, but three days later, on 20 July, there numbered just 5 officers and 335 O.R.s.[191]

V.C. Corner Cemetery listed the names of 1,299 Australian dead, then with no known graves. On one day and night 5,533 officers and men in McCay's 5th Division were lost, either killed, missing, wounded or taken prisoner (496). Paul Cobb notes that the Australians incurred the highest casualties in the Great War by any division in one day, apart from the 34th Division on the first day of the Somme offensive.[192]

59th Battalion Casualties: 20 officers and 675 O.R.s
60th Battalion Casualties: 16 officers and 74 O.R.s.

The battle was a greater disaster for the Australians than the British. Casualty returns were:

61st British Division: 79 officers and 1,468 O.R.s
5th Australian Division: 178 officers and 5,355 O.R.s

Total Allied Casualties: 257 officers and 6,823 O.R.s = 7,080 men[193]

Awards for bravery at Fromelles were not a reflection of the courage of all the soldiers fighting that day since medals were almost always awarded to the survivors.

Australian Forces:
D.S.O.: 9 (incl. L.J. Coulter)
M.C.: 48 (incl. Alex Sanderson)
D.C.M.: 45
M.M.: 63
Foreign Medals: 14
MiD: 38

British Forces:
M.C.: 4
D.C.M.: 2
M.M.: 9[194]

Pheasant's Wood

In 2008 Australian and British casualties were discovered in a mass grave, with around 400 casualties believed buried in several mass burial pits. In 2009 work began to excavate the site, with the first reburial ceremony, with full military honours, held in February 2010 in the Fromelles (Pheasants Wood) Military Cemetery, which was completed on the 94th anniversary of the battle. Poignantly, discovered in the excavations was a folded – and tragically unused – railway ticket for a return journey from Fremantle to Perth.[195]

Currently 177 of the 250 soldiers interred in the new cemetery have named graves. Of this figure, 225 are Australians, of which 59 are unidentified. Two are unidentified British soldiers, and 23 are entirely unidentified Commonwealth soldiers.[196]

The Australian nameless headstones each describe: 'An Australian soldier of the Great War. Known unto God.'

C.E.W. Bean's letter to Alex Sanderson

Almost exactly a decade after the Battle of Fromelles, on 6 July 1926, Bean wrote from Victoria Barracks, Sydney to Major Sanderson at his family address in Perth. Bean enclosed a sketch map of the Fromelles battlefield and posed several questions.

> Dear Sanderson,
> You will remember a visit (of which I have vivid recollections) paid by me to the 3rd Tunnelling Company at Noeux les Mines, when you gave me an account of the tunnellers' work at the Battle of Fromelles.
> I have been writing an account of this battle, but there are certain gaps in the records and, although I have read No.3 Company's history in typescript, there are a few matters on which our information is insufficient. For example -
>
> (1) It is not clear whether Coulter was wounded in trying to explode the Rhondda Sap pipe, or one of the more southerly pipes.

(2) We have air-photographs, but it is very difficult to locate the 'Russian' saps. Would you, if possible, kindly draw in for me on the enclosed sketch map the position of the Russian saps? Did any of them reach right to the German parapet?

(3) At 9 p.m. an aeroplane observed flares in the western end of the Sugar-Loaf Salient, and interpreted them as British. Could this be any part of Captain Church's party, or were they German? I have always assumed that they were German.

(4) Did the British attack punctually at 6 o'clock, or were they late? I should be greatly indebted if you would give me the assistance of your recollections on these points.

Yours sincerely, C.E.W. Bean.[197]

In response to queries (1), (2) & (4), I can confirm that my grandfather Alex Sanderson did receive Bean's letter and pencil-drawn map. I have the originals before me now. Bean's sketch in Alex's archives, kept in a trunk all his life, has no markings of a crater and saps beyond the Rhondda Sap, and I have not seen a copy of Bean's pencil map with the crater and extension sap marked. I assume Alex did not complete Bean's task.

Almost a century later I have 'drawn in', as Bean requested, the 'blown' crater and sap extension, to the relative lengths to scale, as my grandfather detailed at the time (see Map 8). I have explained earlier how far the crater and its extension would have extended and their uses. My previous pages on Fromelles should answer Bean's questions, noting that the Fromelles saps were not 'Russian' saps (which were dug below the surface and 'broken out of' at the moment of an attack). The Fromelles saps were open.

Regarding query (3), the flares seen at 21:00 in the western end of the salient would have been German, as there were 'many flares sent up by the enemy'.[198] H. Lovejoy of 54th Battalion desperately digging in the wet German lines further north from Sugar Loaf, messaged: '9.15pm. Flare just dropped from aeroplane. Have no pistols or flares here with which to reply, neither have I any flares for use tonight.'[199]

Chapter 9

Sanderson Takes Command

August 1916

Four 3 A.T.C. tunnelling officers and 51 O.R.s were in hospital. The strength of the Australian company was now 9 officers and 277 men, with two attached B.E.F. officers and 186 O.R.s. With Major Coulter wounded, Captain Sanderson would now be signing off the Mine Reports until 19 September, when Coulter returned from hospital.[1]

On 19 August a memo from the First Army Controller of Mines (C. of M.) arrived, requesting any evidence of enemy signalling by 'knocking' and pointing out that any signalling to the enemy was strictly forbidden and regarded as disobedience. Alex Sanderson issued instructions that: 'It is particularly important that work in progress when enemy sounds are heard should not be stopped immediately after hearing the sounds. This is tantamount to a reply to the enemy and may endanger the lives of those subsequently working in the vicinity.'

Sanderson replied to the C. of M. that: 'On several occasions the listeners at Winchester, Colvin and Red Lamp reported that the enemy had sent signal knocks, presumably with the idea of drawing reply signals from us. The "Platman's knock" was the one generally heard. I have myself on two occasions distinctly heard this knock signalled by the enemy.'[2]

A 'Platman' was a miner whose signal to hoist was four knocks, a pause and then one knock. The term was well known to deep-shaft Australian goldminers thanks to this old folksong from the later period of gold-mining, when the alluvial gold had been exhausted.

1. The Miner he goes and changes his clothes
   And then makes his way to the shaft
   For each man well knows he's going below
   To put in his eight hours of graft.

2. With his calico cap and his old flannel shirt
   His pants with the strap round the knee
   His boots watertight and his candle alight
   His crib and his billy of tea.

3. The Platman to the Driver will knock four and one.
   The ropes to the windlass will strain
   As one shift comes up, another goes down
   And working commences again.

4. He works hard for his pay at six bob a day
   He toils for his missus and kids
   He gets what's left over, thinks he's in clover
   To cut off his 'baccy' in quids.

5. And thus he goes on, week in and week out
   To toil for his life's daily bread
   He's off to the mine, hail, rain or shine
   That his dear ones at home may be fed.

6. Digging holes where gold's to be found
   And most times where gold it is not
   A man's like a rabbit with this digging habit
   And like one, he ought to be shot.

On 30 August the precise listening directions, positions and distances of five enemy teams heard working underground were calculated: 25 feet S.W. of face of 2 Main, 25 feet right of 2/RH1B, 40 feet S.E. of 1A /RH2B, 20 feet to left of 1/RH1/ and 54 feet from face.[3]

Shaft-sinking was starting at Fauquissart and Tilleloy. After shell-proof head covers were installed, timbering was started for the first few feet of vertical shafts. The ground was very wet with slurry and blue clay hit at 11–12 feet. Collar sets were fixed. At Shaft 18, the first inclined shaft was put down in clay.[4]

Trench mortar shelling

A report of 29 August filed by Sanderson recommended a swift response to the enemy shelling of their shafts:

> Yesterday at 8.15 am the enemy threw a heavy *Minenwerfer* shell onto the top of the hard cover over No.10 Shaft at Chapigny, removing all the sandbag cover and bending the steelwork underneath downwards. Altogether four *Minenwerfer* shells were thrown into the vicinity, each falling within a radius of 50 yards, and making craters about 15 feet diameter x 10 feet deep. This is the second shaft head which has been dealt with by

the Germans during the past few days. Either he is particularly anxious to prevent us from mining in this locality or else it is retaliation for the work of our heavy Trench Mortar. I would recommend that we should therefore thoroughly straffe his mine shafts opposite with heavy Trench Mortars.'[5]

A hostile blow occurred at Winchester on 15 September, but no damage was inflicted on the workings there. At the beginning of October, the enemy would be forced to abandon their underground work for seventy-four hours due to the heavy British trench mortar fire. Listeners deduced this by the absence of sounds heard in the enemy galleries. Afterwards, on three occasions, work was heard in the distance, but diminishing. Alex concluded: 'Our continued trench mortar bombardment has undoubtedly helped to discourage enemy mining. No sounds of hostile mining have been heard in any other part of our front.'

The Germans, however, were soon to respond in kind by returning mortar fire and by raids to disrupt the successful Australian mining they could clearly hear through the chalk.

Geology

Meanwhile, the geologist Major Edgeworth David was busy estimating the accurate absolute seasonal variations in water levels; a vital task for advising the tunnelling companies of the water they could expect in their galleries. He wrote to the British Major O.C. 258th R.E. Tunnelling Company: 'My dear Pope, the measurements now show that there has been a fall in the chalk water-level of about 11 feet between the end of May and September.'[6]

Each German Army had their own geological staff. Deep level galleries were lost by both sides in the early days due to ignorance of the water levels. Australian geologists soon drew up tables, the first scientific ones in Europe, showing the water levels for given maximum winter rainfall; invaluable information for the tunnellers. At the end of 1916, water levels in the tunnels near Loos rose 18 feet in fifteen days, an eventuality they anticipated.[7]

258th R.E. Tunnelling Company on Hill 70, June to September 1916

The Loos mining systems levels, in substrata chalk down to 115 feet, would be accessed from the front-line trenches through six shafts into Cameron No.1, No.2, No.21 and No.4. The system could also be accessed through four inclined tunnels from behind the front line: 'Grants', 'Scots', 'Gordon' and 'Black Watch', named after famous British regiments that had fought in the 1915 Battle of Loos.[8]

A week after 258th Tunnelling Coy., whom 3 A.T.C. would replace in November, arrived at Loos in June 1916, the German tunnellers had fired a deadly camouflet opposite No.23 mine, killing seven British tunnellers. On 10 June, when the enemy pioneers were within 15 feet of No.1 Mine, the British C.O. Major Pope had blown a defensive camouflet of 2,000 lbs, forming Cameron Crater.

Next, the enemy exploded a deadly sequence of camouflets. On 12 June there were two blasts by No.22, followed by single camouflets on 13 June (by No.14); 22 July (by LG10); 25 July (by No.1); and 4 August (by No.23, killing five miners). On 17 June, 258th Coy. retaliated with three camouflets of their own: a 1,500 lbs camouflet (by No.21 & No.3); a 2,500 lbs (in No.22 Main) on 16 July; and another of 4,000 lbs (No.3 Main) on 11 August. Despite the British tunnellers' efforts, the enemy were now tunnelling well past No.3 in a 100-feet-deep gallery, heading for the British front line. The Germans were evidently working deeper than the British.

On 3 September, the enemy blew a heavy crater south of No.3, causing considerable damage and filling No.3 Mine with gas, just when 258th Coy. was preparing a mine. Pope called in the First Army Mine Rescue with Proto gas gear to charge No.3 Mine in the Cameron Crater's area, and they managed to explode their charge on 19 June. In response, the Germans destroyed No. 3 Mine's shaft with a large mine, closing three other galleries and killing twelve British miners.

Wintry conditions, October 1916

Meanwhile 3 A.T.C.'s mining was vigorously continued at Red Lamp, extending four galleries. Work on the three galleries at Tilleloy section also advanced. At Fauquissart a shaft was sunk 100 feet before work stopped. At Chapigny, where the galleries had been extended 164 feet, listening patrols continued. 3 A.T.C. took over the pumping at Winchester from 257th Coy R.E., completing the galleries in hand and continuing to listen. The new front for the company was now to be north of the First Army.[9]

From the autumn, 3 A.T.C. would be based in the chalk area of Loos, where the excavation of tunnels called for a different technique from tunnelling through clay. On 12 October Sergeant James Webster Berry, a 44-year-old married mining engineer and member of the Kalgoorlie Municipal Council, who had arrived in September, found a quiet moment to pen a letter, later published in the Kalgoorlie *Western Argus*:

We went into the firing line on September 29: 12 hours in and 36 out. We were under fire as soon as we reached the trenches, and in much heavy fighting. Arras is about 9 miles away. La Bassée 7 miles, and Lens, about 15, are held by the enemy. Our mining operations are with infantry units, but we work independently at our own particular duties. The artillery behind us are continually strafing the enemy with heavy metal and mortar bombs ('rum jars'). Stokes' mortar and rifle grenades fill the chorus with the artillery and guns of various calibre. At night the whole line is lit up with the brilliancy of star shells and parachute shells. The business of war goes on night and day.

The burial ground extends from the foot of the trenches to hundreds of feet back from the front line, and many a mother's son lies buried there. Hundreds of graves have simply a cross or a head board: English, Irish, Scottish, Welsh and Australians are recorded there in one embrace. Our position in the trench lies within the remains of a once thriving village. All that is left of the village is around us, levelled to the earth.

To the Kalgoorlie Comforts Fund: I have just received, in the trenches, a packet of cigarettes from your kind selves and the thoughtful members of your club. I am not usually a cigarette smoker, but I will certainly smoke the whole ten, and try to fondly imagine myself for the time being once again in dear old Kalgoorlie. The boys are reminded to pause and think of home and dear ones 12,000 miles away, of their duty to their country and of a resolution for the greater task ahead for them and other Australians yet to come over the seas. We have no doubt Australia will do her part.[10]

Gas poisoning was an ever-present danger for the tunnellers. That autumn, at Loos, after six days' hard digging to clear 44 feet of chalk in Seaforth Main, 3 A.T.C.'s work would be interrupted 117 feet down by pockets of gas detected in the broken ground.[11]

Beneath Flanders Field describes the threat of CO gas to sappers. Carbon monoxide was almost impossible to detect in low concentrations, being invisible and odourless. Its effects were very rapid: 1/10 of 1 percent in the air was dangerous. Double that percentage meant a man could be unconscious in twenty-five minutes, as the CO began to displace oxygen in the blood. Long term damage to the nervous system was a result. The effect of gas on the tunnellers was greater than the total number of casualties from mine explosions. Unlike methane and hydrogen gas, the deadly CO from explosions could remain trapped in broken chalk or cracks for weeks or months. After an enemy blow that gassed miners, the designated and trained Mine Rescue Staff donned their Proto gear and attempted to retrieve casualties with electric torches (candles risked secondary explosions). Their equipment gave them two hours' protection. A local rescue station was situated near every shaft or incline but kept separate. Before work could resume in effected galleries, the Proto men would have to identify them as 'free of gas'. Sometimes rescue teams needed to carry out urgent countermining or the charging and tamping of camouflets where poisonous gas was present.[12]

At Red Lamp, Shaft No.2's cover was 'much knocked about' by a succession of heavy mortar bombardments. In Shaft No.3, the miners installed rails for the trolley track and were busy re-timbering, pushing a lateral system 150 feet nearer the enemy to protect the northern end of the salient. Listening galleries were dug to protect the laterals.[13]

CB/AS: *While at Red Lamp they heard what seemed to be sounds of working in some of the enemy mines. Major Coulter took a party over in the next raid and discovered the sounds they heard were of a small German electrical power plant used for lighting the dugouts on the German side with electric light. This was destroyed before the party returned.*[14]

Small teams of the company were now working at three locations: driving faces, listening and pumping. At Fauquissart, five men were driving the face of Shaft No.24, with three listeners and pumpers and an N.C.O. At Chapigny, four men were driving the face of Shaft No.20 with three listeners and pumpers, and one N.C.O. At Winchester, eight men were driving the two faces of shafts No.8 and No.15, with twelve listeners and pumpers and an N.C.O.

Enemy raid on 3 A.T.C. at Red Lamp

During the night of 28 October, coinciding with a divisional relief of 61st Division, an enemy raiding party entered the trenches in the Red Lamp salient where 3 A.T.C. were still based. They found almost no infantry protecting this section of the salient, where forty miners were engaged in a night-shift underground. The enemy raiding party entered the trenches at around 18:00 and threw mobile explosive charges into a shaft dugout where an officer and several O.R.s were working. Three sappers were wounded and one killed. Several bombs were thrown into a shaft and onto the head cover of another shaft, both of which were slightly damaged. Lieutenant Grainger and Sapper Cassin ran out under heavy shellfire between the entrances to the dugouts, camouflaging them to prevent their destruction by the enemy, which was the aim of the raiders' incursion. The pair then went underground to lead the men out to safety. As the miners ascended ladders to the surface, however, they were bombed by the raiders and retreated underground to exit from Shaft No.3, at the southern end of the salient. Sapper Cassin was wounded by a bomb. The enemy retired to their lines following a tape laid across No Man's Land. For their selfless bravery, Lieutenant Grainger was awarded the Military Cross and Sapper Cassin the Military Medal; he died nine months later from wounds caused by an exploding shell near Hill 70.

In November the C. of M. would advise tunnelling companies that they must install alarm systems, either electrical or mechanical, throughout all galleries. Since most miners working on forward faces had distant entrances in rear lines, they were vulnerable in case of enemy attack or raids,[15] which were more frequent now that the Germans had reduced the numbers of their miners working underground and were increasing activity above ground against shaft heads, through *Minenwerfer* fire or by mobile charges left on raids.[16]

Minenwerfer shelling

The head-to-head underground conflict waged between the Australian and German tunnellers was about to enter a period of intense and relentless ferocity. Soldiers on the front line became used to the sounds of different types of ordnance heading their way and took evasive action accordingly. Captain G.I. Adcock of 2 A.T.C. described the effect of a *Minenwerfer* (mine thrower) heading your way: 'It made a distinctive pooping sound…heard clearly from the British lines… the mortar shells could be seen cart-wheeling and wobbling through the air… Even at night, their glowing fuses were easily identified and the path of the shell could be tracked in flight… As the shell began its downward trajectory, those below would quickly make a calculated guess as to its probable landing spot.' If they estimated it was heading their way, the observers rushed to get out of its destination.[17]

There were three versions of the *Minenwerfer*: those projecting mortars that could be seen in flight due to the shape and size of their mortars; the *schwerer* (heavy) with a 250mm calibre; and the *mittlerer* (medium) with a 170mm calibre. The *leichter* (light) was a *Minenwerfer* of 75.8mm.[18]

Sergeant James Berry described the psychological effects of the constant bombardments:

> On October 29 the enemy began strafing our lines and hundreds of 'Minnie Werfers' were hurled at us, not to mention 'rum jars', pineapples and rifle grenades. The 'Minnie' is a species of mortar bomb, 10 inches wide and 3 feet 6 inches long; woe to anything that comes within its reach. The nearness of death acts in various ways on our different temperaments. The crash of the gun gives you, altogether, not an unpleasant sensation. You are right in

the thick of the whole business, there is no escape and therefore everybody appears to be resigned to the conditions. You feel a certain expectation, or rather a vivid interest, in your surroundings. Some of the 'blokes' are apparently happy. One hums a tune, another a piece of lively music. You are in a tornado of death, and your senses are at a maximum alertness. A few yards away a half-dozen men are blown up. You mentally note the incident, and sorrow surges through you. However, events are passing quickly; others are falling, and your mind is alive with action, and if you are calm you can think of everything. No other tonic can so command the attention of all your faculties as the closeness of death and the immediate dead. It compels you to the most complete appreciation of life, and also of death. It flashes though your mind that death holds something just as beautiful as life, but from safety or ignorance we cannot appreciate either under ordinary conditions. A shell bursts in the cookhouse – exit cook and cookhouse. You curse the shell and the man and gun that fired it: he has jeopardised your dinner and you are very hungry. One crashes into your dugout: luckily you and your mates are outside, cogitating on the vivid life and very much alert. A 'Minnie Werfer' drops a hundred feet away, the earth quivers, you scatter and spread on the ground, and the life in you clutches desperately at its physical flesh and blood. Other events follow rapidly; the other incident passes, and life sings exultingly through your veins, expectantly again for life. The winter is now fairly upon us, and such a winter for plain frigidity has not been experienced here for 30 years.[19]

Chapter 10

3rd Australian Tunnelling Company under Hill 70

November 1916

The Battle of Loos

In the previous year, from September to October 1915, the British had carried out a series of ambitious but ultimately fruitless attacks on the German lines from the La Bassée Canal to Hill 70 at Loos-en-Gohelle, under Field Marshall Sir John French. General Joffre, who planned to attack in the Champagne region, had requested a diversionary attack. The British objective was to try to batter through the German lines and restore a war of movement. The B.B.C.'s 'Great War' documentary series described how:

> Among the slagheaps, the ruined cottages, the derelict machinery and twin mining pylons of 'Tower Bridge' of the shattered mining village of Loos, the new 'Kitchener's Army', replacing the fallen 'old sweats' of the regular army, had attacked at 5.15 am on 25 September. The wind had changed direction during the artillery bombardment, however, and blew the yellowish-white chlorine gas cloud back in the faces of the advancing troops, laden down with kit and with their sight restricted by primitive gas masks. The London and Scottish Regiments managed to storm through Loos to the enemy's second line, which they found unmanned. Frustratingly, for all their sacrifices, success could not be followed up. General French had kept his XI Corps army reserves at a distance of six hours, 16 miles behind the front line.[1]

Richard Holmes, in his biography of General Sir John French, notes that: 'The twelve attacking battalions…10,000 strong when they moved down the slope into the Loos valley, lost over 8,000 officers and men in under four hours…The enemy re-grouped and the untrained British army broke and fled, massacred by the German machine-guns.'[2]

Around 60,000 British soldiers died in the three-week Battle of Loos. D. Winter's research of the 15th German Reserve Division archives shows that the Germans were 'nauseated by the sight of the massacre of the *Leichenfeld* (field of corpses) of Loos'. When the British retired: 'no more shots were fired at them for the rest of the day, so great was the feeling of compassion and mercy after the victory.'[3]

There is some controversy about where the blame lies for this defeat, which Haig afterwards insisted was due to General French's ineptitude. The intense rivalry between these two generals following the battle was expressed in bitter accusations and recriminations, resulting in the dismissal of Field Marshall French and his replacement by General Sir Haig, then Commander of the First Army. The elevated hill, 70 metres above sea level, would be a powerful strategic asset for the Germans, dominating the village of Loos, with its commanding views over miles of the surrounding landscape. As well as their Hill 70 position, the German lines in late 1916 also overlooked the British lines from the Double Crassier, a huge mining waste pile, one of two crassiers at Loos, whose front line curved around its southern perimeter.

In 1918 Major Alex Sanderson's Hythe Tunnel, planned beneath Hill 70, would become a veritable fortress and be judged one of the finest tunnel systems of its kind on the Western Front.

3 A.T.C.'s move to Hill 70 sector

CB/AS: *On 28 October 1916 the 3rd Australian Company was ordered to leave Winchester and Red Lamp. A very difficult centre of mining had grown up at Hill 70, near Lens, where the Infantry had been badly blown. No 3 Company was sent to try to get things into a more healthy condition. They found 258th R.E. Company and worked with them for a week. When the Company was first sent to Hill 70, the British were only on the edge of the Hill.*[4]

From the autumn of 1916 this would be the main operating area for 3 A.T.C. There were then three British tunnelling companies based in the area: 258th R.E. Coy. operating in front of Hill 70; 253rd R.E. Coy. around the Hohenzollern Redoubt; and 170th R.E. Coy. from there to La Bassée.

November 1916

On 1 November orders were received for 3 A.T.C. to relieve 258th Coy. R.E. in the Hill 70 sector at Loos in the area of XI Corps First Army. On 5 November, four days before the Australians took over Hill 70, Major Pope noted: 'There is undoubtedly a small error in the survey of the connection between No.21 mine and the Black Watch slant.'[5,6]

CB/AS: *The 258th Company could give no information at all about the points where the Germans were dangerous. They seemed to have no idea of the German works, except in those points where the German had proved that he was working by blowing our men up. As this information was quite useless, No.3 Company had to start and fight the Germans in the dark. This was very dangerous, but there was no way for it. The 3rd Company knew that the Germans had probably got their defensive galleries out and finished. They could obtain no information as to where these were. They knew the German listeners were probably waiting quietly in their galleries listening to our work approaching them. The German mines might have already been charged for blowing. With three weeks of the start, the expected happened. On 25, 27 and 28 November the Germans blew into our works and no less than 22 men were lost. However, during this period, the Germans had given their own position away by their activity. When we started work after these blows, our men, by careful listening, had discovered exactly where they were and in what direction they were coming.*[7]

On 7 November 257th Coy. R.E. took over the shallower mining area at Laventie, vacated by 3 A.T.C., while the Australians marched into their Bracquement billets and new Company Headquarters at Noeux-les-Mines. Their advanced billets would be in the cellars of Loos-en-Gohelle's ruined houses, below Hill 70. By 12 November they had completed the takeover and would be based there for the next twenty-two months, until August 1918.

Captain Sanderson's surveys

So began a long period of deep mining work in hard chalk at Hill 70, and other underground locations, along a front from Loos-en-Gohelle (Loos) to La Bassée. A complete survey of the mine galleries and the adjustment of their levels was immediately undertaken by Captain Alex Sanderson.[8] The tactical advantage in mining warfare was to the man in a gallery deeper than the enemy. It was harder to hear sounds when above the enemy and it was easier to blow them from below, rather than from above.[9]

In a *Ranger* article, Phillip Robinson of the Durand Group noted that the only instrument available to the tunnellers was an ordinary 4-inch land-surveying theodolite. This required a direct bearing, distance and the difference in level between shaft head and objective, obtained from observation points within British lines or from aeroplane photographs using recognisable features to scale the distances. Magnetic bearings were accurate for the first 1,000 feet of gallery, after which a fixed bearing was taken down the shaft and carried to the face. Distances were measured along the gallery roof.[10]

Sergeant Berry's Military Cross

On 9 November, Sergeant Berry and three fellow tunnellers rescued a 258th Coy. tunneller buried when a *Minenwerfer* hit Shaft 22. While two British tunnellers worked from below, the two Australians dug from the surface, ignoring incoming mortars destroying trenches around them and, at one stage, partially burying them too. Sergeant Berry later explained:

> We had been exactly ten hours over the job. From 8 until 12 o'clock Fritz had bombed us with 'rum-jars', and one 'Minnie' every ten minutes, with rifle grenades and 'pineapples' filling the gaps. Towards dark Fritz began firing a random shot or two, with his machine guns sweeping the area. We had the rescued man carried down to the cellar at Loos, thence to the divisional hospital.

Berry's companion in the rescue later wrote:

> I was with him when he won the Military Medal. I shall never forget Sergeant Jim Berry. If ever a man won honour on the battlefield, he did that day. He worked like a tiger: calm, cool, and as a brave a man as ever it has been my lot to meet. When we got the poor buried lad out into safety he took both Jim and me in turn by the hand and said: 'God bless you, Australians. I will never forget you'.[11]

By 16 November a total of 280 feet of galleries was excavated. With water rising 3 feet in Black Watch Shaft and 30 inches in Gordon Shaft, pumping continued. At a distance of 112 feet into Shaft No.21 DDL chamber, the ground was broken up and deeply cratered. Work was needed to plug a strong flow of water from the face. With very wet conditions underground, the C. of M. ordered 200 extra thigh gum boots to be issued to each tunnelling company.

On 22 November Coulter reported evidence of a German raid the previous night in an old front-line trench and Listening Gallery (L.G.) No.50. Two bags of bombs and five mobile charges were found, three of which were piled together in the entrance to the gallery. Luckily the pulled German fuse lighter had failed to explode. Close by was evidence of fresh footprints and disturbed earth over the parapet.

In the last week of November work was delayed by the charging of two mines and the blowing of three mines, one by 3 A.T.C. and two by the enemy.

Black Watch blow

Close to No.22 Shaft R1L1, four officers working near the Black Watch mine noticed what they thought were sounds of the enemy excavating chalk with their push-picks or bayonets at a depth of 65 feet. In fact, the Germans were completing the tamping up of two deadly camouflets. Listeners in their tunnels under Shaft No.22 had also heard the noises and were noting them down. The decision was taken to blow an immediate camouflet of 6,000 lbs.

On 27 November at 12:40, however, misfortune struck the Australians a severe blow at a depth of 115 feet. Just as the miners on the night shift had finished charging their chamber with ammonal, and were themselves tamping up, the enemy blew both their charges. The desperate race to be the first to detonate was won by the Germans, who exploded two camouflets opposite the Black Watch gallery, simultaneously igniting the Australians' charge of 6,000 lbs of ammonal. The gallery was blown apart by the massive force of the two tremendous, combined explosions. The death of twenty miners on a night shift, including Sergeant Kerby who had received the D.C.M. after Fromelles, was the greatest number suffered by any one of the three Australian companies during the war. Second Lieutenant Russel and eight O.R.s were 'mine gassed'. Lieutenant Howie organised a rescue party, leading them down into the mine and saving several lives during the arduous, dangerous task of recovering the dead and wounded. Howie carried on for twenty-four hours until relieved. For his actions on this day and at Fromelles in July, Howie received the Military Cross.[12]

At 08:00 on the day after the Black Watch explosions, the enemy blew a second camouflet at a depth of 108 feet, opposite a deep gallery and below Shaft No.1. At the time Sapper Edwin Bird was working in a 70-foot gallery with three other miners. The force of the enemy blast killed Sapper Cockton and gassed the three others. Bird and a sapper managed to struggle to the shaft base, where Bird realised that Sapper Allen had been left behind. After returning through the gas-filled tunnel, Bird dragged back the unconscious Allen and assisted him up the 100-foot shaft, in spite himself suffering from shock and the gas. On reaching the shaft head, Bird collapsed. Sadly, Allen later died of gas poisoning. Bird was awarded the Military Medal for his 'conspicuous conduct in the field'.[13, 14]

December 1916

The strength of the Australian company was now 17 officers and 486 men. In the first week of December, 750 feet was driven into hard chalk at Hill 70. Fighting points were excavated and listening chambers commenced. Around 60 feet of the

Black Watch gallery, damaged by the enemy blow of 27 November, was stoically reclaimed in seven days of hard work during the first week of December. The loss of so many of their comrades only strengthened the tunnellers' resolve to push on underground and strike back at the enemy. In the Black Watch incline off the support trench, 90 feet of the gallery at 120 feet depth was cleared of debris resulting from the enemy blow of 27 November.[15]

Bean records in Appendix 3: 'The marked feature of the struggle that followed was the way in which the Australian Tunnellers, after hitting back on 29 November with a maximum camouflet in the deep workings, steadily persisted with their effort in face of these casualties.'[16]

Turning the tables

In December, four deep mine camouflet chambers were set up and charged as 'a defensive curtain', mainly in front of No.1, No.21, No.22 and Cameron shafts. A total of 35,000 lbs of ammonal was laid, with the 9,000-lbs charge with 6 lbs of guncotton blown five days before Christmas.[17]

CB/AS: *When we started work after the November blows, our men by careful listening had discovered exactly where the enemy were and in what direction they were coming. By driving certain galleries towards them, our miners practically steered the Germans into other galleries where they were waiting for them and finally blew them badly. They caught them again and again, so seriously that the German offensive mining on that front gradually ceased altogether.*

It was during these operations in December that the Germans were badly caught. Our Company knew that the German galleries were shortly to be blown and they were anxious to catch as many Germans as possible in the tunnels and gas them. They therefore arranged with the Artillery that, at the moment when the blow was to take place, the Artillery should bombard the entrances to the German tunnels, back in the German lines. (By that time the entrances were pretty well known to us.) The Artillery started over just one minute before zero hour. To keep our men clear of the gas, which follows up mine explosions, the electrical leads by which the mines were to be fired were brought out of the mouth of the shaft and into the dugout nearby. This exposed the wires for a short distance to shellfire. (There was an emergency fuse which could be fired by hand if anything went wrong.) By bad luck, the very first shell fired by the enemy exploded right on top of our own parapet, just where the shaft went down to the mine. The burst of the shell cut the electrical wire. When the contact button was pressed one minute later, the mine failed to explode.

Sanderson at once went to the place and, finding out what had happened, went down the shaft and fired the instantaneous fuse there. He could not resist taking up the listening apparatus for a moment to hear whether the Germans were still busy at their mine. The sounds showed that they were working furiously and were charging up their mine with explosives, prior to a blow. Sanderson dropped the listening instrument, cleared up the shaft and had just got five yards from the entrance when a low rumble showed that the camouflet had been blown. It was a maximum camouflet, the biggest which could be calculated upon not to break the surface, but just to crumple in the walls of the enemy's tunnels. Sometime afterwards, the Germans were driven back in the Battle of Arras and these workings came into our possession. In September 1917 we were working on certain points of the German galleries and it was decided to dig into these and see what had been the effects of our blow. Within five yards of the affected gallery, just on the limits of the explosion, there were found skulls of four Germans. The explosion had stopped them but there were undoubtedly a great many more men who were caught in this blow.[18]

The *Western Argus* of 5 December published a letter from Sergeant J. Berry M.M.:

BERRY IN FRANCE / WITH THE MINERS' CORPS / INCIDENTS OF TRENCH LIFE.

From the trenches 'Somewhere in France': Star shells light up the night. The business of dodging shrapnel and the bullets and shells from the guns keeps your mind free from boredom. A shell, a big shell drops alongside one of our dugouts, and there is a hole, as big as the open-cut mine on the Golden Dream. The boys are paralysed for a moment, but immediately begin to make practical use of the hole, and it is soon transformed into a strong, substantial dugout. The front line for hundreds of feet in breadth is a burial ground. Without any shadow of a suspicion of levity, the Tommy will hang his towel to dry upon the head boards and crosses, which abound right to the foot of the front-line trenches.[19]

The fight back

On 20 November at a depth of 130 feet, the tunnellers of 3 A.T.C. completed No.21 DDL1 chamber and charged it with 11,000 lbs of ammonal, nine cases of guncotton, with eight electrical detonators in gun-cotton primers and one No.8 detonator on an instantaneous fuse. Continuity of current was tested. Next the tamping was carried out ready for a blow. Very accurate reports from the listeners identified the Germans, between 15:00 and 22:21, in the process of charging a mine 30 feet to the west of the chamber in 1DDR1L1. A pre-emptive charge of 9,000 lbs of ammonal was exploded in this Deep Deep listening gallery to wreck the German gallery and explode their tamped charge. No damage was caused to the Australian workings. Alex Sanderson's report of 21 December described the blow:

> At 10.21 pm. on 20/12/1916 we exploded a maximum camouflet 60 feet West of Cameron Crater. The enemy had stopped chambering and was commencing to charge a mine 30 feet to the right of our charge and only 70 feet from the front line. On firing the charge the ground moved slightly, leaving a broken surface but no crater formed. No damage was done to the main workings, but a portion of Listening Gallery 14 was crushed. The enemy was heard working in his gallery seven minutes before the explosion. At least 70 feet of his gallery would be crushed. The charge consisted of 9,000 lbs of ammonal and 96 lbs of guncotton, fired at a depth of 108 feet below the surface. After the explosion the Artillery bombarded the enemy mine shafts opposite. A new gallery is being pushed out as quickly as possible at the same level as the one from which the charge was exploded, to protect our front at this point.[20]

On 21 December the chamber of Seaforth R. Main Gallery system was completed and charged with 10,000 lbs of ammonal and 160 lbs of guncotton. Haste was vital as the enemy workings were making progress towards this point. At No.1 Double Deep Main sounds of enemy mining were heard under his line south of this face. This was identified as likely to be a shaft being sunk to a deeper level. Then the enemy exploded a camouflet about 60 feet below the surface and 60 feet southwest from the charge in 21 DDL1. The blast slightly injured one Australian officer and one sapper, but practically no damage was caused to the Australian galleries. All miners except for one listening patrol were withdrawn from the galleries. 3 A.T.C. then charged No.1 Deep Main chamber with 5,000 lbs of ammonal and five cases of guncotton.[21]

A Welsh Christmas

Sapper Caradog Owen Jones, who was born in Carnarvon, Wales, was working in Boulder W.A. when he enlisted in Perth, and was assigned to 3 A.T.C. in November 1916.[22] His recollections of his December 1916 wartime tunnelling experiences appeared post-war in an American-Welsh newspaper in his native Welsh language (here translated):

> I well remember the night before Christmas Day. There were eighty of us going into the trenches. We started at eight pm. To reach the work, we

had to go down a hillock to the ruins of Loos. Opposite was Hill 70, on the slopes of which the enemy had dug in and consolidated his position. It was impossible to see even a yard ahead, and there was not a single 'Star of Bethlehem' to lead us, only a path shattered by the enemy's cannon shells beneath our feet. Suddenly, seven flashes came, as lightning penetrated the gloom in front of us; these were the enemy's cannons opening up. I counted twelve seconds before they exploded at the bottom of the hill we were upon. Then another seven shells headed towards us, but closer this time, and several machine guns opened fire upon us from the hill opposite: there was no-one happier than us to find a shell hole in which to shelter until the storm ended. Mercifully no-one was killed, but sixteen were wounded, some badly.

The following day, we all wanted Christmas pudding, though we were only four hundred yards from the enemy. With great difficulty a marvellous Christmas dinner was cooked: bully beef mashed up with potatoes and onions (called 'dry-hash'), tea, bread and butter and jam, as well as the incomparable pudding. Well, our old friend Fritz remembered us too well. As he couldn't get his share of the delicacies, he made his mind up to spoil it for us, which he did far too thoroughly by sending over a 'whizz-bang' 18 pound shell through the roof of our kitchen. Though it was Christmas, and a holiday of peace and goodwill, we did not feel peacefully towards the enemy after this. The air about us was full of the most brimstone-like language, for quite a while.

That night, two mines were set off under the enemy, and this blow, to a great extent, repaired our injured feelings at losing our Christmas dinner.[23]

The regimental history of the German 153 Infantry Regiment, celebrating Christmas in the trenches opposite Caradog Jones, recorded: 'The enemy did not pay any attention to the festive spirit either at Christmas or at New Year – but neither did we! Shells, shrapnel and mortar bombs flew backwards and forwards in abundance and even the so-called rest quarters received a generous allocation of razzers [the German name for a 'Whizz-bang': a light shell].'

Chapter 11

Underground War Intensifies

January 1917

Sergeant Berry described the appalling weather that continued into the New Year of 1917:

> All men participating in this war at the front line in France have been through the melting pot in the trial of Australian manhood – the howling gale of winter, the blinding snowstorms, the frozen earth of the bitterest winter known for over forty years – rain, hail, snow, mud and ice – facing an ever alert enemy, entrenched in almost impregnable lines.[1]

In this freezing January winter, with ice and light snow reflecting the sunshine in one of the coldest winters on record, the company was working entirely on the Hill 70 mining system, on both defensive and offensive mining. The frozen surface offered one advantage for the tunnellers: their boots would not be sinking into wet mud. Temperatures into mid-February would plunge to –8°C, with La Bassée recording –16°C.[2]

The Times reported on 30 January that: 'In London many Australian soldiers had their first experience of ice…blocks floating down the Thames. To the man from Queensland or West Australia this is particularly a new experience.'[3]

Sapper William Powell wrote home positively:

> Dear Mother, as you know I never seen snow until I came over to France but I can assure you I have seen quite enough this last three weeks, as the earth has been robed in white for near a month and talk about iced treats, you can get them here without going to the ice works. At times the bread gets frozen and it's like cutting iron to cut it. But us lads are standing it better than expected and I think the snow and frost is better than the slush and mud. What do you think of the Kaiser declaring war on the world? We expect America in with us, I hope they do join as every bit helps,
> I remain your Loving Son & Bro,
> W. Powell[4]

During January and February, 3 A.T.C. prepared a further 45,000 lbs of charges in six more chambers, while 26,000 lbs of ammonal waited, already primed, in three other chambers. In the week following 4 January, the fighting point 1DDR1L1 broke through into an enemy gallery, evidently thoroughly wrecked by the Australian 'blow' of 20 December. The location was promptly charged with 9,000 lbs of ammonal.

Sapper James J. Hallinan described his arrival at Loos and the labour that awaited him underground:

> In England we was picked out and allocated to Australian companies in France. When we landed at the end of 1916, we got the train in the dark of night in a snowstorm to a station called Béthune. Lorries took us to our final Company, which had four sections. That particular night it was snowing like hell and there was a bombardment on. We weren't used to bombardments and we didn't get a wink of sleep.
>
> Our first month of active service was in January 1917, and by Jesus it was active! Our section was taken about six to eight miles in a motor lorry, out to the line where the real war was on. Then, we left our motor lorry and we had to walk about two miles up zig-zag trenches to get to the front line where our underground headquarters was. At six o'clock in the morning, the incoming morning shift would relieve the night shift. We'd go in this underground billet and head up to where the working was to relieve the shift up there. It was underneath No Man's Land. They would then come back to the billet, have a meal and try their best to snatch a few hours' sleep to be ready to go back up to the front line again at 10 o'clock at night.
>
> Being newcomers, the first job we got up there was in an underlay, turning a winch. We were six men and worked as a team turning the winch, drawing up from underground a trolley, loaded up with chalk. It was chalk, not rock or stone, white chalk that the men down below at the face had put into sandbags. When we got them to the top, 'bag snatchers' would grab the bags, roughly the size of ordinary sugar bags, and take them along under the protection of a covered way to a stack of hundreds of bags. Then, when the night shift came on, they took those bags out into the trenches where they would be passed up and over into No Man's Land and in amongst the barbed wire. It was: No Man's Land; Barbed wire; Empty out these bags; Send them back for a refill. It might be for one, two or three hours, depending on how many bags had to be emptied out. Then we'd go back and do whatever duties remained. This was in one section of the underground workings called 'Scott's Alley'. Then my team shifted to 'Cameron's Alley'. At first, we were only at about 70 feet down but the

Germans got working underneath us, and we had to go down further, down 150 feet, down wooden ladders, to get underneath the Germans. At one stage we were working underneath the Germans, like we were working on this floor and the Germans were upstairs. The idea was that we were digging off the lateral in a straight drive.[5]

The underground war was about to intensify, but the determination of the miners was undiminished. The heroism of these tunnellers, all volunteers, working deep in the bowels of the earth was all the more laudable for the secrecy of their efforts, unwitnessed by their comrades above ground: in stark contrast to the feats and displays of bravado of the brave pilots and navigators of the R.F.C., whose combats were played out across the skies and witnessed by the men in the trenches below.

This period was also marked by endless heavy rain and enemy trench mortar bombardments. Water troubles in the galleries became acute on 3 January. The Deep Deep workings were severely flooded in Gordon Incline and at 02:00 two electric Stott pumps were installed in series, which succeeded in lowering the water level in No.2 Shaft by 18 inches in forty-seven hours. Pumps were permanently installed in this incline, as well as in the Black Watch main.

On 24 January the extremely cold temperatures froze the gallery hoses. Hand-power air pumps had to be energetically operated: the increasing length of the tunnels and their poor ventilation restricted the natural flow of fresh air through the galleries. Around No.1 Shaft the intense enemy bombardment interrupted work in the trenches. Access was only possible during the hours of darkness. No.2 Shaft was again crumped in. At Listening Gallery 15D, the fighting point was chambered and charged with 5,000 lbs of ammonal.[6]

A destructive enemy raid

German retaliation for the December blows came early in the New Year. Major Coulter, who had by now recovered from his injuries, described the chaos caused in this early morning German raid:

On 5 January the enemy raided our trenches at 5.45am. They entered our system by Seaforth Crater, destroyed No.21 Shaft with a mobile charge, leaving behind a heavy unexploded charge. They followed Seaforth Alley, turning east along the support line, while sending a party with mobile charges along Pioneer Trench towards Seaforth Slant. Disturbed by two sappers, they did not light the four heavy mobile charges placed in the shaft. The main party followed the support line, took three Proto men out

Map 9: Showing the enemy raid on 5/1/1917

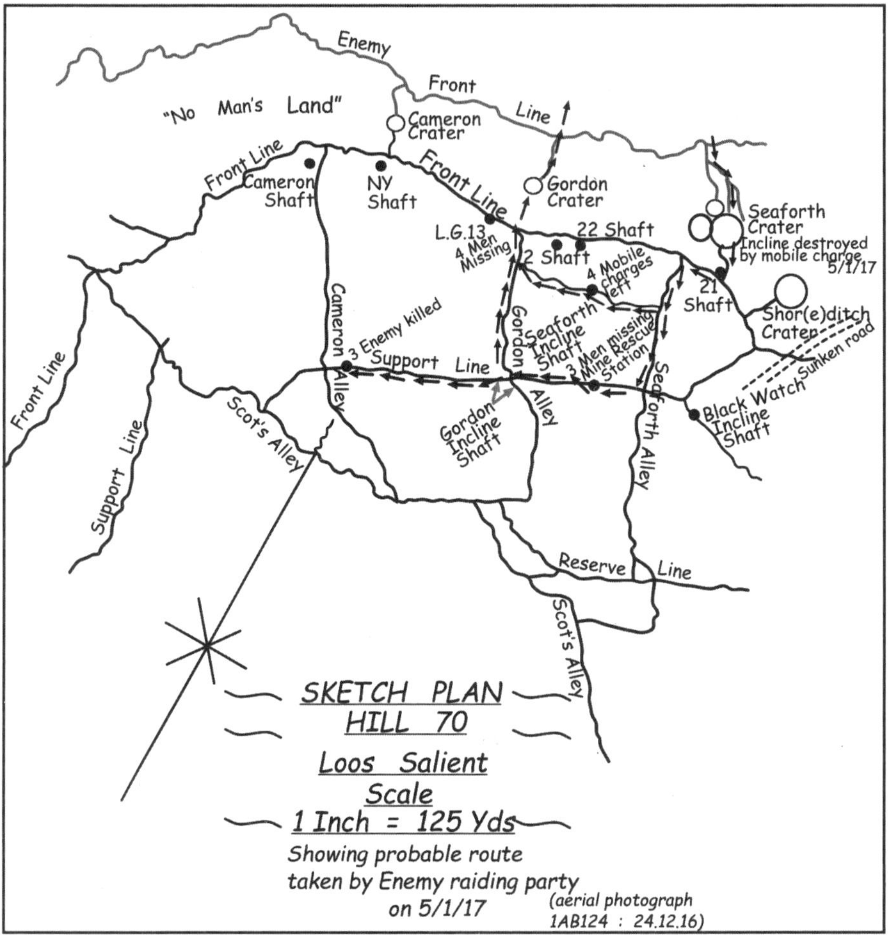

Source: Redrawn from the original 3/ATC War Diary January 1917, page 12 - AWM4 16/4/11

of the mine rescue station, and blew up the main entrance with a mobile charge, forming a small crater. They then went up Gordon Alley, bombing dugouts and Gordon Incline Shaft's main entrance. Here they called out in English for a sapper to surrender: he disappeared down into the mine. From Gordon the raiding party followed the support line into Gordon Alley, where three of the raiders were killed. They then turned back along the support line into Gordon Alley where they bombed a dugout, causing casualties. When returning to the front line, they captured four listeners heading for the billets in pairs. An N.C.O. in L.G.13 heard them going over the parapet singing at the junction of Gordon Alley. A.I.F casualties were seven missing.[7]

The German raiders' singing, as they left the British lines, was intended to identify themselves in No Man's Land and ensure that they were not shot by their compatriots returning to their own lines. As they were accompanied by a large number of prisoners in British and Australian uniforms, this could easily have occurred.

As well as the seven Australian sappers wounded in the raid, forty-six attached infantry and seven tunnellers, including George Clingin, who would later die a prisoner in Germany, were forced back across No Man's Land.

The German raid destroyed an incline, No.21 Shaft, and the entrance to the mine rescue station. The bombing of Gordon Shaft caused little damage. Repairs were completed to the damaged shafts, inclines and trenches. The tunnellers, however, felt they had been badly let down by the British infantry sentries who had been 'caught napping' and made prisoners before they could warn the tunnellers below ground. Henceforth, the Australian sappers rarely trusted the infantry to protect them in the front line and, where possible, arranged to post their own sentries.[8]

Increasing tension

The further the galleries were extended, the greater the workload became for the men hauling out the spoil in bags and the worse became the air quality, due to poor ventilation. Electric pumps and blowers made a noise. In mid-1916 less noisy electrically run fans had been installed which carried larger volumes of air through 6–9-inch diameter tin pipes, connected by rubber and canvas joints and fixed to brackets in the chalk roofs.[9]

The removal of spoil had to match the chalk dug at the face or the tunnels would get blocked. The enemy workings were now very close and, as a precautionary measure, several torpedo charges, to be inserted into drilled wombat holes, were made ready for rapid explosion from the ten in stores (where one was always at hand, fully charged and primed with a detonator). These torpedoes, measuring 8 feet long by 8–10 inches diameter, carried 100 lbs of ammonal.[10] All the cables from the exploders to charged mines were regularly tested. Instructions were issued that in galleries affected by a blow where the men were still working, a mouse or canary had to be kept nearby, as well as a trained Proto man.[11]

On 11 January 3 A.T.C. exploded a camouflet of 5,250 lbs of ammonal at a depth of 76 feet. This was blown (with a previous day's one) to destroy enemy workings close to Cameron Shaft. After 14 January, a total of 21,000 lbs of ammonal had now been placed carefully in the underground chambers of Hill 70, tamped, wired and ready for firing. 8,000 lbs of ammonal were carried into the chamber in Cameron R1L1A and charged without tamping. 22 DD Main was charged with 9,000 lbs of ammonal. Cameron DDR1L1 B was charged with 7,000 lbs of ammonal.

During January the concentrated effort and perseverance of 3 A.T.C. tunnellers resulted in a total of 1,915 feet of 6 feet x 3 feet galleries being driven in all faces through the chalk of Hill 70, an impressive average of 61 feet excavated per day. All the excavated chalk spoil had to be transported out of the galleries, with the bagged chalk being hauled up inclines or lifted up the vertical shafts using a windlass operated by two sappers.[12]

February 1917

From 9 February to 20 March, Prince Rupprecht's group executed a 'Retreat to Victory' *Operation Alberich* (the sorcerer dwarf in a medieval German epic poem), a meticulously planned retirement of 100 miles to the *Siegriedstellung*, the Hindenburg Line, a new, deep defensive line, east of the Somme battlefield constructed in the winter of 1916 to shorten the Western Front by 25 miles, thus freeing up a division. Rupprecht had protested but he was overruled by Ludendorff, who called it a 'military necessity'. Around 1,000 square miles were ceded to straighten out the salient, with 900 German trains hauling 37,100 cartloads of equipment and materials.[13]

The tunnellers never knew when their luck would run out underground. On 15 February practically no damage was caused when the enemy blew a charge between Cameron and 15D shaft. However, as Lieutenant J. Purves, on his first tour of duty in the line, was being 'shown the ropes' underground by Lieutenant R. Cavanagh, and they were making for a listening gallery in Cameron DDR1L1B, the enemy blew a camouflet only 120 feet away in their *Dora* gallery. The walls of the Australian chamber shook badly and then cracked, bringing down 2 tons of chalk which partially buried the two officers. As CO gas poured through the cracks in the chalk, the officers were carried up to the shaft in a dazed condition, luckily only slightly wounded. Lieutenant Cavanagh (from Cottesloe, W.A.) returned to duty after two weeks, while Lieutenant Purves (from Sydney), was evacuated to hospital suffering from shock and a slight injury to his back. He never returned to the unit and was later seconded for duty to the Alphabet Company.[14]

On 11 February, the O.C. Canadian 24th Division wrote to the C. of M:

> I am writing to say how much I appreciate the services rendered by the Tunnelling Companies on my front… Every precaution has been taken by them for the safety of the Infantry: not a single Infantry soldier has lost his life through underground operations since we came into the line. My

Infantry have gained absolute confidence in the men whose work it is to protect them underground.[15]

Canada paid a heavy price in the First World War, with 418,000 Canadians fighting overseas in the C.E.F. (Canadian Expeditionary Force), suffering 210,000 casualties, with 56,500 killed.[16]

March 1917

By early March, 36 tons of high explosives lay primed and ready in twelve mine chambers 100 feet below the surface, over an extent of 450 yards.

Frank Miles' diary described the constant danger the tunnellers faced:

2 Friday	Went out to trenches. On duty 2 to 10. Tommy killed with a Minnie.
6 Tuesday	Went to trenches. Saw plane burst into flames, men fall out. One of ours shot down three Fritzes. Worked 2 to10, dragging bags.
7 Wednesday	Blown in by Minnie. Had to come out. At 3.15 four mines sent up. Much damage done.
8 Thursday	Bitterly cold, howling wind and snowing. Got a tin of tobacco.
11 Sunday	On duty 6 to 12.30. Left off to send Mine 21 up. Fritz seen moving troops. Artillery broke him up.
12 Monday	Rained at night. Fritz shelled communication trench.
14 Wednesday	Went to trenches. Nearly sniped. On the winch from 6 to 2. Ordered to 'Stand To'.
15 Thursday	On duty 6 to 2 on winch. Trenches worse than ever. Came home at seven in the dark. Trenches too bad.
16 Friday	Sent up 2 mines followed by a terrific bombardment. We put the wind up Fritz.
19 Monday	On duty 12 to 8 listening. Fritz bombarded for three hours, came over and took a few Buffs, blew one of our saps and put gas down. Luckily no one hurt. On duty listening 10 to 12 and 8 to 5. Had to 'Stand To' at Garrison for 3 hours. Rained.
22 Thursday	On duty 12 to 8 removing bags for stemming charges on Shaft 21. Boring is going well. On duty 4 to 12 cutting chamber at 60 foot level of No.21. Very quiet but cold.
27 Tuesday	On duty 12 to 8 bagging, very quiet carrying bags. Sniper busy - caught and killed some Tommies. No.21 blown afternoon.

	Duty 4 to 12 and 8 to 4. Fritz shelled relief. Working from trenches. Saw a triplane.
30 Friday	Fritz shelled, killed three horses and two men. On duty 12 to 8 dragging bags. To dump for timber.* On duty 4 to 12 on winch.
31 Saturday	On duty 8 to 4 winch. Trenches knocked about a lot. 'Stand To' at 6am.
	Buffs made a raid with 104 men. Many casualties. Got one prisoner and a machine gun – Fritz sent over twice as much stuff as us, also gas shells.[17]

*There was a huge demand for timber for tunnels, dugouts ('possies' in Australian slang), duckboards and huts.

Series of Australian camouflets

The 3 A.T.C War Diary succinctly noted: 'At Deep Deep 1 Main, off the Front Line Trench, the enemy is working towards us and, while the enemy works, we do likewise.'[18]

From the beginning of 1915 until the spring of 1916, Allied tunnellers had been directed to pursue a defensive policy underground. Through their early months of defensive mining, 3 A.T.C. tunnellers had risen to the challenge of the gauntlet thrown down (*camouflet* means a 'gauntlet' in French). Now the Australians threw the glove back in the enemy's face with a vengeance with Australian 'esprit de corps' vied against German *Kameradschaft*. The Australians countered the German offensive mining, driving towards his galleries and smashing them whenever the enemy went on the offensive. Anticipating his moves through careful listening and astute tactics, the Australians outmanoeuvred and blew him on every opportunity, extending their fighting points before he could repair his crumped galleries or drive new ones.

C.E.W. Bean summarised the Australians' underground methods as: 'Working and fighting in a maze of tunnels and saps and burrows like a band of murderous trolls.'

The hour of reckoning had arrived. The careful planning and the sustained effort was about to be rewarded. On 7 March, watches were synchronised at noon at the officers' dugout. Here the officers used their galvonometers to confirm 'all correct' with the electric current continuity and resistances of the cables, leading to the charges, and with the state of the fuses.

Double Gas sentries were posted at Black Watch, Seaforth, Gordon, Cameron and No.1 shafts. The Lewis gun team on No 1 Dump were told not to return until dusk. The gas-tight cover was placed over the top of No.21 Shaft in the front-line sap. The fan in Seaforth airway, where the airflow would be 'down' the shaft, was started just prior to the mine firing and a gas tight blanket was placed between this fan and the incline to avoid ingesting impure air.

Alex prepared his binoculars: 'Captain Sanderson will endeavour to observe gas or smoke effects from the Crassier or other Observation Points up to X-2 minutes.'

All men underground were instructed to withdraw at 13:30, except the listeners who had to put down their instruments at 15:00. The 3 A.T.C. War Diary recorded in a typically understated manner that:

On 7 March at 3.15pm we exploded three Camouflet charges satisfactorily within 30 seconds in conjunction with an artillery and trench mortar bombardment in the following galleries:

* 5,000 lbs in 21 Deep Main at a depth of 80 feet
* 2,000 lbs in 22 Deep Right 1 at a depth of 80 feet
* 9,000 lbs in No 1 Double Deep Right1 Left 1 at a depth of 100 feet.

The 5,000 lbs charge detonated first, followed at two second intervals by the 2,000 lbs and 9,000 lbs charges. The Camouflets were blown in coordination with a sustained trench mortar and artillery bombardment of the enemy shaftheads. As the enemy had been heard working in their galleries in close proximity (10–25 feet) right up to the detonation of the Camouflets, they would have suffered heavy casualties. A fourth Camouflet charge of 11,000 lbs at 125 feet below the surface should have exploded at the same time as the other three charges but did not.[19]

Charles Bean recorded later that German records show these explosive charges smashed 13 feet of the enemy's *Imgard* gallery but no lives were lost. On 9 March Captain Langdon went underground to seek an explanation for the unexploded fourth charge and subsequently reported:

21 DDL1: I removed the top of the original tamping for 8 feet. From this point, with the aid of a torch, I was able to see down the drive, above the tamping, for a distance of about 30 feet. There was absolutely no sign of any movement of the timbering; leads were still hanging on nails; very little broken chalk; instantaneous fuse was not fired. In my opinion the charge was not fired.

21 D Main: As the air was very bad, I investigated from No.21 Shaft. There is no tamping from 21 DR to the shaft and no sign of movement. There is a considerable amount of broken chalk lying about. There was evidence of gas here, so we did not carry on with any untamping. Before receiving your note I had already cut the leads and rolled them up on reels.[20]

Major Coulter explained to the C. of M. why the largest charge had failed to ignite:

After the three explosions, a shock was felt, a pause of 30 seconds, then another heavy shock – thought to be the secondary explosion – which caused some damage. A candle burning in the fan chamber in Black Watch airway undoubtedly caused the second and smaller explosion. The four shocks were felt by sentries in the support line, by officers in the airway of Black Watch shaft and by another on the Crassier. The officers underground were leaving the airway to return to the surface when the secondary explosion occurred: the two officers rearmost were knocked over. The others had just got clear. No.21 Shaft was strong upcast, with thick fumes pouring out. Only three explosions were felt at Cameron shaft. Untamping and the testing of the listening apparatus leads for continuity proved that the fourth charge had not exploded. It was laid on 18 December and is under water, the greatest depth of which on 31 December 1916 was 185 feet. An attempt was made on 11 March to fire the charge but it was again unsuccessful.[21]

The 11,000 lbs charge, still partly under water, was finally detonated on 26 March as a maximum camouflet by a torpedo inserted through very hard chalk into a Wombat-driven 6½ inch hole sunk 93 feet from the higher gallery of Black Watch. This delayed explosion allowed the gallery to be safely driven. The gap in the Hill 70 underground defences was finally closed. Major Stokes noted: 'The explosion of the 11,000 lbs charge by means of a Wombat drill hole, was confirmed by heavy falls of chalk 100 feet away. In the Seaforth chamber DL1R1, they are drilling toward an estimated enemy mine, 90 feet from the charge, and may induce a blow.'

The three mines successfully exploded on 7 March were subsequently untamped. Coulter reported at midnight, after inspecting the workings with the Proto men: 'The whole of the deep levels and new levels of the mining system was free of gas by 9pm. The 6am shift will go on but, as a precaution, a Proto man will stand by.'[22]

The sections of men worked usually on six-hour shifts. The tunnelling companies on both sides were aware of their enemy's preferred times for mine firing and regulated their shift to meet the risks. A German mining officer noted: 'the most favourable time for charging a mine is from 5am because the British generally blow mines between 5pm and 9pm, and around dawn.'[23]

The Proto men returned at 5am to confirm it was safe for the morning shift to enter. All faces were working again eighteen hours after the explosions and all repairs were effected within twenty-four hours of restarting work. A charge of 2,500 lbs laid in 22 Left Deep was untamped. On 16 March two further camouflets, of 6,000 lbs and 4,600 lbs, were fired at 12:20.

Enemy raid of 18 March

The enemy reacted to the Australian camouflets by raiding Scots Alley at 02:00. Two small mobile charges of 18 lbs each were placed in Scots Shaft. One exploded at the entrance while the second, thrown 30 feet down the shaft, fortunately failed to explode.

Hearing the explosion at the mouth of Scots Shaft, the men below were collected and ordered to put on their respirators, which they wore for over an hour. Two listening galleries were 'completely smashed and no longer accessible' by the accompanying *Minenwerfer* bombardment, with another being 'wiped out' and a fourth 'poison-gassed'. The third gallery was later examined by an officer, who took a mouse with him to test the air. The mouse showed no ill-effects after twenty minutes and all damage was repaired in twenty-four hours.

Major Coulter was furious at this second German raid in two months; his frank report to the British Brigadier General was couched in strong and exasperated language:

> A hostile raiding party entered our lines at Scots Alley, without meeting the slightest opposition from the Infantry holding the line. Two mobile charges were placed in Scots Incline Shaft. Small gas cylinders were bought over and three of our listening galleries are full of gas. There were 15 miners underground at the time. At least four of the raiders penetrated our line for 300 yards and investigated our 'covered way' and the dummy trenches behind our line.
>
> On the 17th I visited Battalion HQ, and informed the C.O. of the 2nd D. L. Infantry, that an enemy raid would probably take place between Cameron and Scots Alley within a few days because we have now 'blown' the enemy three times near Cameron Shaft, in each case causing casualties (in each instance he was working right up to the actual time of firing the mine) and that he will probably raid to damage our shafts and delay our work until he could gain the ascendency under-ground.

We were accumulating a large dump of chalk well back from the shaft heads of Alley and it was likely that the enemy would come over to investigate. This is the second time since this Company has been mining in this section of the front, that the Infantry protective arrangements have utterly broken down, and it has rendered ineffective the whole of the elaborate work carried out for the past three months to disguise the actual sites of the shafts. Three months of our work has been wasted, since now the enemy knows all our arrangements of shafts and will undoubtedly raid again or at least give us a great deal of trouble with *Minenwerfer*.

At the end of March, the chamber of I DD Main was charged with 5,000 lbs of ammonal, while the enemy were heard working hard 40 feet away.[24]

The mining war ends

The War Diary recorded: 'In March ended the mining work in an offensive and defensive-offensive way. The enemy ceased mining, evidently realising, as it had been proved time and time again, that our Miners and mining methods were far superior to his own.'[25]

As Matthew Leonard of the Durand Group noted succinctly: 'The reality was somewhat less heroic…the Germans had only withdrawn as part of a wider plan to consolidate their positions, re-establishing their defences further east beneath the slopes of Hill 70. They had certainly not lost the stomach for fighting underground.'[26]

Some offensive and defensive mining, however, was carried out by 3 A.T.C. until the middle of April, with 1,123 feet of galleries being driven in hard chalk. Several days before the Arras offensive, 3 A.T.C. took over 170th Tunnelling Coy'.s mining front, including the Copse tunnel system on the southern outskirts of Loos-en-Gohelle, in front of which lay the large craters of Harrison, Mannings and Harts, bearing witness to the earlier underground conflict when 173rd Tunnelling Coy. were operating in the Copse system. It comprised three levels with listening and fighting tunnels, subways and a narrow-gauge railway. In 2011 the author accompanied the Durand Group in clearing chalk from the Copse Deep Tunnel, 850 feet in from the system's entrance, directly below the *Rocade Minière* (Mining Road), the A21 Motorway. Copse Tunnel's narrow shaft descends vertically for 72 feet to the hazardous Deep Deep section, 98 feet below the surface, untouched for a century and then pluckily explored by the specialist engineers of the Durand Group.[27]

Chapter 12

Battle of Arras

9–15 April 1917

The Inspector of Mines for the B.E.F. was Brigadier Robert N. Harvey. His assistant was Major Ralph S.G. Stokes M.C. who later, as a lieutenant colonel, became Controller of Mines of First Army. On 1 April, Major Stokes visited 3 A.T.C. on Hill 70:

> I went up to Loos by Railway Alley. The situation at Hill 70 is now very satisfactory. During the past 4 to 5 days the enemy activity has fallen right away. For one or two days, no work was heard, as opposed to a previous 12 to 16 faces. It appears, the enemy has finished his defence – and that will allow the Australians to finish theirs. All the 'Double Deeps' are clear of water, there appears to be no danger.
>
> The survey work of the Company appears to be excellent. Lines are followed more consistently and accurately than I have seen practiced in any other Company. It is an extremely good principle and indicates technical discipline.[1]

The Battle of Arras (9–15 April) began in appalling weather on Easter Day, stretching from Lens in 3 A.T.C.'s British First Army sector to 60 miles further south. Thirty-seven German divisions faced thirty-three British and Commonwealth divisions. The Canadian Corps, under General Horne, stormed the well-defended Vimy Ridge in April. The Battle of Vimy Ridge forced the Germans to give up the area in front of Lens. They swung their front line round, from its southwesterly direction, to face due south pivoting near the Loos Crassier. The British lines were now facing east and directly opposite Hill 70.

The short part of the new British line, joining the old line near No.1 Shaft (colour plate map), also swung south and crossed over old No Man's Land. Alarmingly, it now had the German mine galleries underneath, these being still accessible from their new front line.

The sudden German withdrawal by 12 April back to their third defensive line was ordered by Crown Prince Rupprecht after the German 80th Reserve Division was pushed into an unfavourable salient.[2]

Map 10: **An overview of the Loos front at the time of 3 A.T.C.**
Trenches correct 1-4 May 1917

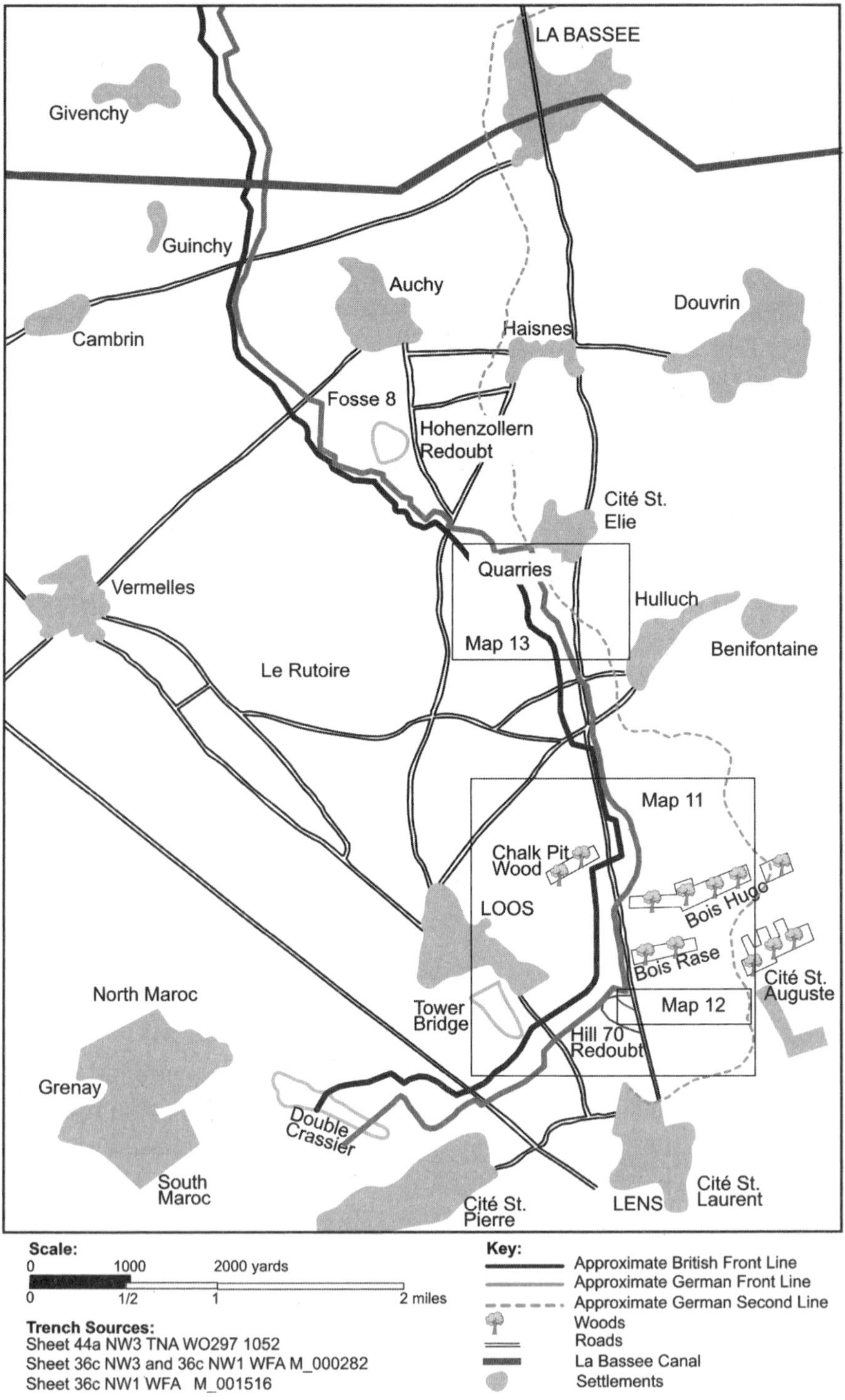

CB/AS: *On April 9th came the Battle of Arras. The Germans, attacked at Arras, decided to pivot their line on Hill 70. The British endeavoured to make them retire from Hill 70 and pivot on a point much further north, near La Bassée. Hill 70 was attacked by a British Brigade but they were seriously counter-attacked and driven off it. Sanderson put the losses as 300.* [This figure would be too small if the fighting was heavy.] *We did not take the Hill 70. However, with the advance of the battle further south, as our line south of Hill 70 swung forward across No Man's Land, the old German mine galleries were left underneath our 'switch' across No Man's Land. The British succeeded in taking Hill 65, the next height south of Hill 70. Between these two points the new British line was over the old German workings to which the German mining troops still had access. This raised a highly dangerous position, especially if we wished to make further advances. It was the opinion of the experts of the Company that, if the Germans anticipated any advance, they would perhaps charge up the old galleries with explosives to dislocate our attack and blow up our trenches at the hour of the actual advance.*[3]

On 9 April, Alex Sanderson's second cousin Private Joseph ('Toby') Sanderson, a goldminer from Gundagai, N.S.W. and a Lewis gunner with 1st Battalion, 1st Brigade, was killed in action while assaulting the Hindenburg Line. Toby had been among the earliest to enlist in August 1914. In 1915 he had been wounded in the face and arm by shellfire aboard SS *Balika* off the Dardanelles coast, before even setting foot ashore. After treatment in Alexandria, he returned to fight ashore at Gallipoli. In France, in June 1916, Toby took part in the first battle of Pozières. In July of that year, he was again admitted to hospital, this time with wounds to his knee and arm. In Birmingham for medical treatment, he met a young Scottish woman called Heather, whom he planned to marry. Once recovered, he went A.W.O.L. temporarily, before rejoining his battalion in December 1916. In February 1917 Toby was in pursuit of the retreating Germans. On Easter Monday he attacked at 04:00 and dug in with his Lewis gun crew outside Demicourt, west of Cambrai, where he was killed instantly by a shrapnel shell bursting above his 'A' Company position. His name is inscribed on the 'Missing' wall of the Villers-Bretonneux Australian Memorial. Toby was a descendant of Edmund Sanderson who had sailed to Queensland in 1855.

From 14 April 3 A.T.C. was engaged in road repairing, salvaging enemy material opposite the Copse, erecting M.G. (Machine Gun) emplacements, and repairing dugouts in their own systems and the captured part of the enemy mining system. The respite from mining gave the tunnellers a welcome opportunity to rest. The surveyors were busy surveying the enemy mining system in the part of the line that the enemy had been forced to abandon. The town water supply was connected with the mine system and used.

Map 11: **Hill 70 in detail showing some trenches - March 1917**

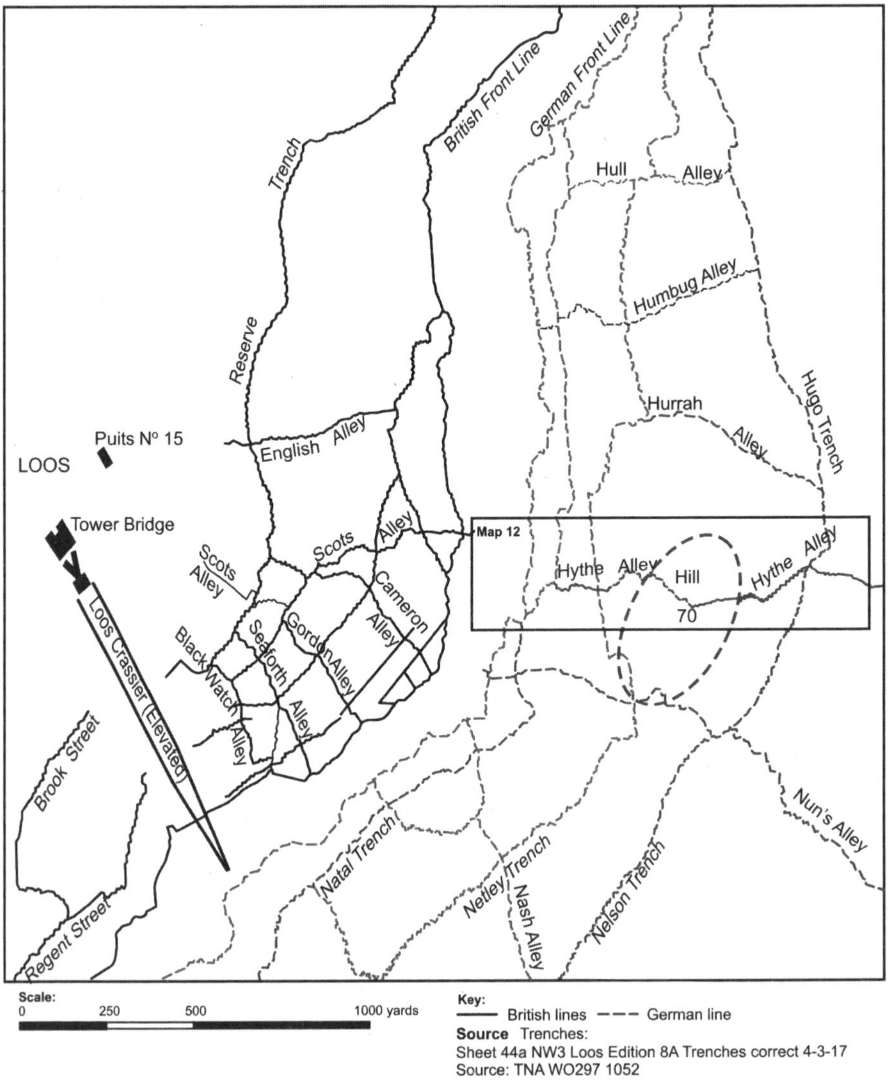

Parties advanced the Northern Road and also helped move heavy mortars and hundreds of heavy shells, through mud up to 2 feet deep, from the tramway terminus in Loos to Hill 70. The infantry were often exhausted after their days of heavy fighting. The fruit of their work was the successful operation on 21 April when a 'strong point' holding up the infantry was captured and prisoners taken.[4]

George Oxman's diary entry for 9 April noted, 'Carrying shells weighing 60 pounds up to the front line. We had to go for the officers' rations. Coming back Fritz shelled the place killing one, and wounding one of the 6 of us. We lay down on the road when we heard the guns and a shell burst 10 yards behind us. They went to work on the road.'5

Although all mining had ceased in this period, listening was carried on at the Chalk Pit, the front-line galleries and at Cameron No.1, as far as Seaforth.

Frank Miles' diary entries for the period read as follows:

APRIL

2 Monday	Got a rum. Very cold. Fritz shelled Loos and the road. Six of our chaps injured.
5 Thursday	An icy cold wind blowing all day, with a snowstorm at night.
6 Friday	Came out to trenches at night. Took over 173 Coy. workings. Went lamp lighting in two tunnels.
7 Saturday	Wet day. Bombardment all day. Had some narrow shaves. Canadians went over at Vimy. Got 10,000 prisoners and much booty. We used a shell called 'termite', a sort of liquid fire.
13 Friday	Buffs got over at Loos. Cold wind. Fritz blows all his dugouts in, except two which have helmets attached to charges.
14 Saturday	Beautiful day. Fritz driven back to his 4th line. Lens burning lit up the sky.
16 Monday	Big batch of Germans came over to surrender. They got close to the Buffs, then bombed them. Great aerial activity.
19 Thursday	Heavy shelling all night. 6 inch howitzer fired 1,000 rounds from 6pm to 6am on Lens. Byers lost his leg. Roden died of wounds. Acted as his stretcher bearer.
21 Saturday	Shelling continued all night. Big attack by the British. 1,300 prisoners taken.
28 Saturday	Three aeroplanes and a balloon were brought down. One of ours also.6

On 10 April Sergeant Berry penned his impressions of the 'Victory of Vimy Ridge':

Great events are taking place in the fortunes of the allies. The German in many places is being well and thoroughly hammered… Politics in Australia are very much disturbed. Many people in Australia do not appear to have understood what has been happening: a 'death or victory' grapple with a desperate enemy who, to his credit, lacks not courage.

I have just been watching a great battle begun on the right. Those who all winter have faced the Germans, now stand straining at the leash to charge forward toward the enemy. We are upon the edge of a great artillery storm. The whole air is filled with a continual hail of metal. The darkness is lit up by the flash of artillery and the bursting of the shells. The great battle is on the Ridge.

You know the cyclonic dust storm of Kalgoorlie. Here on the hurtling winds, slaughtering shells are bursting in the air, or in the earth. Every second is filled with the uproar of bursting shells. A huge great flame, red as blood, appears like a vast cloud of fire in the sky. We 'stand to' on the outer edge of the war storm, facing the enemy. Fritz's trench mortars are ploughing almost every foot of the ground around our trenches.

Dawn breaks and a greater event on our right occupies our attention. A great silence falls over our section, broken only by an occasional rifle shot and the rat-tat-tat of machine guns. The sun rises and a land skylark or two breaks into song, an indictment against the artificial hell of war.[7]

An intelligence summary was sent on 20 April from First Army C. of M. to the O.C. of 3 A.T.C.:

Our troops have made a further advance and captured 15 prisoners who state that instructions have been given that HILL 70 must be held at all costs. They have no knowledge of a retirement, but state that all dugouts contain explosive charges, which the pioneers have instructions to blow up if necessary. A prisoner of the 297th Pioneer (Mining) Company was taken this morning.[8]

Charles Bean noted in his Official History an inaccurate German mining report:

The German 297th Pioneer Mining Company, responsible for Hill 70 mines, attempted on April 20 to destroy the entrances to their *Regensburg-Hans* galleries – which lay at the hinge of their withdrawal from Hill 70 – by lightly charging them at points, as the British feared they would. The Germans reported that they had successfully fired them, after repairing the leads laid through the *Hans* gallery to the German second line and repeatedly cut by bombardment. (Their leads misfired.)[9]

May 1917

The Australians were unaware but in May and June, with an industrial German crisis caused by the allied blockade and a shortage of coal for industry, many of the experienced German mining officers with 50,000 miners were withdrawn to Germany, to be replaced by inexperienced attached infantry.[10]

Three officers and thirty men of 3 A.T.C. had been detailed on 30 April to be ready to move forward to search for, investigate and remove enemy mines and traps. The 3 A.T.C. War Diary noted, scornfully: 'Their officers do not go underground to the extent our officers do.'[11]

Bomb disposal

In May detachments of 3 A.T.C. were ordered to search for mines and booby traps. Green-painted traffic arrows were placed in streets that were searched and considered safe. Red-painted 'Danger' boards were placed on roads and structures where traps were suspected.

On 30 March a report was received on the many types of malevolent enemy booby traps left during the German retirement, designed to inflict troop casualties on unsuspecting souvenir hunters or careless explorers of vacated dugouts or buildings: 'Cap badges, new trench boards on fire steps which detonated when trod on, a sandbag blocking a dugout door and wired to a dozen stick bombs, lumps of coal and 7-inch shells. Hundred-pound charges were left in attractively equipped, undamaged dugouts to be set off by clockwork or delayed action charges.'

Clearly abandoned or captured enemy dugouts had to be entered extremely cautiously as the scorpions had a dangerous sting in their tail. Captain Sanderson reported on a trap found in an enemy mine shaft:

> In a stepped incline Lt J. McArdell and Lt Neil Campbell were examining the shaft. They noticed a box with the lid partially opened and found that the box was arranged on a step and disguised. It was filled with enemy rifle grenades with primers, but without detonators, except a central grenade which was detonated and raised higher than the others with the lid laying upon the striking mechanism. The detonator and its accompanying mechanism were removed from the body of the grenade.
>
> Lt McArdell examined it, and was gently unscrewing the threaded ring that secures the detonator, when it exploded on the faintest pressure from the nose-cap, wounding both officers. It was intended to explode the box-full and formed a very effective 'booby' trap.

Second Lieutenant Neil Campbell accidentally sustained wounds to his hands, face and eyes and was taken to London for treatment. He would not rejoin his unit until 25 October 1917 and would later be reported 'missing in action' on 11 April 1918. His body would never be found. Having no known grave, he is commemorated on the Villers-Bretonneux Memorial.[12]

Frank Miles' Diary

MAY

5 Saturday	Aerial activity very strong. One of our planes brought down in flames. Several air fights.
6 Sunday	Went through Fritz trenches, thousands of bombs and aerial torpedoes, some gas shells.
7 Monday	Severe air fights. Two of our planes driven down.
8 Tuesday	40 enemy shells around billets got 4 horses and 22 men and a wagon on Australian Road. Gas shells came over and caught two motor drivers.
9 Wednesday	Fritz aeroplane came over at night and made for our balloon, the men came down all right in a parachute.
10 Thursday	Fritz shelled Noeux Les Mines all last week. Hit a lot of civilians.
19 Saturday	Beautiful day. Aeroplanes very busy. One of Fritz aeroplanes brought down. Put on mending the road. Fritz shelled a 6 inch battery. Dropped two shells about 100 yards from us on the road. Killed a Tommy and wounded 2 others.[13]

June 1917

On 6 June Sergeant Berry wrote home saying:

> It is a far cry from the bloody plains of France to the rock ridges of Kalgoorlie's industry. Beautiful, terrible France, in spite of the guns of friend and foe, is now a lovely garden of flowers, blood red roses predominating and millions of crimson poppies shaking their coquettish heads above the green plains and hills. The vigour of nature and of the soil working its will, almost blinds the desolation of war. Australians are doing well in France. You will see, perhaps, where a company of our battalion had a big hand in a little job up north at Hill 60 with 450 tons of the right explosive. Many Kalgoorlie lads are in the Miners' Battalion and the Goldfield Boys, in whatever branch you find them in the trenches, stand with the pick of the earth.[14]

Messines Ridge's Magnum Opus

Three and a half million shells, including gas, were fired over eleven days at Ypres to 'soften up' the enemy, while Monash's 3rd Division raided the German lines almost nightly, going over in large numbers and taking heavy losses.[15]

On 7 June at 03:10 the heavy artillery opened up and nineteen huge mines, with almost a million pounds of explosives, detonated under the German positions (two of the twenty-one mines laid failed to explode). Captain Oliver Woodward (M.C. and two bars) of the 1st Australian Tunnelling Company set off the two mines under Hill 60, on the southern boundary of the Ypres salient. He later wrote: 'The tongues of flames shot upwards, then seemed as if they would roll towards our lines and consume their creators.'[16]

Lieutenant A.G. May, who attacked that day, described the spectacular sight:

> A terrific roar and the whole earth seemed to rock and sway. The concussion was terrible, several of the men and myself being blown down violently… Flames rose to a great height - silhouetted against the flame I saw huge blocks of earth that seemed to be as big as houses falling back to the ground. Small chunks and dirt fell all around…it was awful, a sort of inferno.[17]

Jim Henry, the son of Major James Henry O.B.E., D.S.O., Captain Woodward's O.C., told the author in 2009 that: 'My father invited your grandfather Major Sanderson to come up to Ypres to see the Hill 60 mines go up.' The two tunnelling commanders would have shared a strong whisky afterwards. Purpose-built dugouts were constructed on Kemmel Hill for Sir Douglas Haig, the Press and selected guests, including the Inspector of Mines, to safely witness the Messines Ridges explosions (codenamed Magnum Opus).[18]

Four of the mines exploded opposite Monash's 9th Brigade's positions. The Australian infantry advanced into the German lines in clouds of dust and smoke, suffering 4,000 casualties in the following action. Monash was not impressed with C.E.W. Bean's reporting of the Messines battle, describing it as: 'The apotheosis of banality. Not only is the language silly tosh, but his facts are, for the most part, quite wrong.'[19]

Hill 70 dugouts

In June 1917, 3 A.T.C. continued work on the dugouts on Hill 70; the enemy shells constantly destroying the trenches which they afterwards remade. Company Headquarters were established in an old German mine, utilising part of an existing enemy shaft which was cleared and renovated. Four old German dugouts were opened up and renovated.

On 6 June Sapper William Powell wrote home from 'Somewhere in France':

> Dear Sister, a few lines to let you know I am still well. This morning we have just come out of the trenches after six days and will be out for two days. The war is not half as bad now as its bonza weather. We are fighting

near a town called Lievin. Tons of flowers and strawberries, rhubarb, gooseberries. I don't think I will go to the next war.

I remain your loving Bro, W. Powell[20]

Two days after writing this letter, Powell was one of forty-six men gassed. He recovered, but in August would be sent to Le Touquet Hospital. In November, Powell would depart for Fremantle to rejoin his family.

On 10 June the 1 Corps Chief Engineer issued instructions for the 3 A.T.C.'s mobile section to: 'move with the advanced troops, charged with the duty of searching and rendering harmless German traps and Land Mines.'

A report by Alex Sanderson to the Controller of Mines/Advanced First Army described explosions of enemy traps left in dugouts entered off Ahead Trench: 'The enemy left this trench on 24th June. The first explosion occurred 41 hours later, completely wrecking the entrance to a dugout. Six explosions occurred in dugout entrances afterwards, at intervals up to 85 hours after the enemy had retreated.'

On 28 June, Lieutenant Russel, with a party of sappers, examined dugouts and found an explosive charge of about 60 lbs weight in the back of one entrance, behind the timbers about halfway down the stairway. The charge exploded at 10:30, one hour later, and destroyed the dugout. The charges were exploded by a time device, probably of the 'copper wire in acid bath' type. 'These dugouts are situated outside the area allotted to my Company for investigation, otherwise the examination would have been made earlier.'[21]

Chapter 13

Allied Mining Raid on Hill 70

28 June 1917

Alex Sanderson would submit a report in July to the C. of M. of First Army outlining the history of recent mining operations in the area:

> The capture of the enemy's trenches to the west of Hill 70, during the April offensive, necessitated the carrying of the new British front line across 'No Man's Land' and over the defensive mining system which the enemy had constructed below and forward of his front line. Before being driven out from that portion of his trenches, immediately behind our newly advanced positions, the enemy destroyed all entrances to his mining system. So well was the work done that an exhaustive investigation failed to discover where an entrance existed. Systematic listening, in the forward fighting points of our deep deep system had been established and it was carefully carried on, to find out whether the enemy had access to his mine galleries under our new front line. During late May, and in June, the enemy was heard working, intermittently, in the region of his old front line between Nash Alley (opposite Cameron Alley) and our new front line. Possibly the work of recovering some of the entrances, which we had destroyed, leading to his mine galleries. During the nights of June 24th to 27th, walking was heard in the enemy galleries. Permission was obtained for a party of the 3rd Australian Tunnelling Company to accompany the Infantry on the 28th in a raid on the enemy for the purpose of destroying the entrances, which were known to exist in the mining system.[1]

CB/AS: *On June 22nd instructions were received to prepare for an attack on Hill 70. The Canadians were not able to make their attack before August 15th. Work in our infantry subways etc was immediately heard by German listeners, and on June 26th our listeners noticed that the Germans, in their turn, had suddenly become very active. They probably thought that we were working on our mine. At any rate their movements showed clearly that they were charging their old galleries as was expected by us. When the mine blow is nearing completion, the usual care and secrecy have to* *be thrown overboard. The operation is always dangerous and is also carried out with the greatest possible speed. The Germans by June 26th had thrown off all secrecy and were obviously working tooth and nail in charging their mines. It became a question of how to meet this work. The tunnellers decided that the only way was to ask the Division to make a raid on the German lines opposite in order to enable a party of our tunnellers to go across to the points where they were certain the German mining shafts were and blow them up. This raid was arranged for the night of June 28th.*[2]

Nicholas Lovell describes the start of the raid, in which Second Lieutenant Frank B. Wearne of the 11th Battalion of the Essex Regiment distinguished himself through his outstanding bravery, which was later recognised by the award of a posthumous Victoria Cross, presented to his father by King George V:

> On the evening of 28 June at 19:00, over 100 men assembled in a large dugout at the junction of Scots Alley and the British Reserve Line. Just after 19:10 Parties 'A' and 'B' left their trench and rushed forwards. They were to attack, capture and hold a section of the German front line. Prisoners were to be taken, dugouts destroyed, and German mine shafts investigated and blown up. The smoke barrage was let off a minute before zero. The wind took the smoke over the area of operation, and absolutely concealed everything from view for about twenty minutes. Boiling oil was successfully projected onto an enemy strong point. The artillery barrage, which was thickened by stokes mortars protecting the flanks of the raiders, was perfect. The wire was no obstacle. Wire cutting had been carried out with 6 and 4.5-inch howitzers and torpedoes. Thirteen machine guns searched the enemy trenches in the rear of the raiding area; about 63,000 rounds were fired.[3]

CB/AS: *The raid was made by a party of fifty men of the 11th Essex and fifty of the 2nd Durham Light Infantry (D.L.I.) With these went over three parties of tunnellers, twenty in all. Captain Sanderson, who was commanding the Company in the absence on leave of Major Coulter, asked to be allowed to take the raid over but was told that he could only go over if Major Coulter was already back. Coulter arrived back from leave just in time to reach the Company at the hour of the raid, and therefore Sanderson considered he could go over in charge of this section of the raid. When he reached the German trenches he heard behind him a voice which he recognised. It was Major Coulter. He had arrived by car at the Company Headquarters, heard that the raid was in progress, had told the officer that he was going down to the line and see them off, and had gone down and followed them across.*[4]

Brigadier General Bridgford reported on the raid, describing how the 2nd D.L.I. attacked on the left, and that the enemy fought hard throughout, with a determined resistance, and were alert and very aggressive. A German barrage had been put down 25 yards in front of his own wire, but the raiders moved through this to enter the enemy trench, with orders to penetrate to the enemy second line at least, take prisoners and capture machine guns. The 2nd D. L. I. experienced no difficulty in getting through the wire. Unfortunately, they lost direction, preventing them from dealing with a German strong point and linking up with the 11th Essex. At least twenty-five Germans were killed. When some were seen running into dug-outs, two Stokes bombs were dropped into one, completely wrecking it. German reinforcements were soon brought against them over the open. A number of these were seen to fall.[5]

Nicholas Lovell's 'Hellfire Corner' account explains how the 11th Essex Regiment went over in three parties, 'A', 'B' and 'C':

Party 'A'
At the centre of the attack, one officer and 30 O.R.s, crossed No Man's Land and captured Nash Alley, a junction of the German trenches. They had to rush down the trench blowing in dugouts with Mills bombs, shooting all opposition, either coming up the trench or over the top from the German support trench. Initially meeting little opposition, they were later continually attacked, suffering heavy casualties.

Party 'B'
Twenty men, commanded by Second Lieutenant Wearne, attacked to the left of Party 'A', to capture and hold the northern front-line trench and prevent the rest of the force from being attacked by German reinforcements. In spite of stiff opposition, they held their block until withdrawal time, seizing that section of the enemy front line where the fighting was heaviest. The Germans repeatedly attacked along the trench and over the top, from their support trenches. Their defensive fire caused heavy German casualties but only one of the sixteen infantrymen holding the left flank escaped injury or death. Wearne realised that holding his flank was vital to prevent parties 'A' and 'C' being overwhelmed. He leapt up onto the trench parapet, running under a hail of machine gun and rifle fire along the top, while firing his revolver and throwing bombs down on the enemy below. His brave example encouraged his men to follow him. Their unexpected attack temporarily repulsed the Germans.

Party 'A' went to the assistance of Party 'B', bombing from behind a traverse. Despite a severe wound, Wearne refused to leave his men and stayed at his post, defending the left flank. Just before the recall whistles sounded (and searchlights flashed), Wearne suffered a second severe wound, and, as he was being dragged away, he was hit a third time and died.

Party 'C'
Seven men of the Essex Regiment rushed a strongly held position to the right (south) of Party 'A', meeting no opposition, the Germans in the trenches they entered having been driven into a dugout.

3 A.T.C. under Captain Sanderson M.C., followed Party 'C' at 19:05, under their protection, to take prisoners, and to destroy dugouts and mine shafts.[6]

Captain Sanderson's post-raid report described how:

> During the raid at HILL 70 by the 18th Infantry Brigade yesterday evening, three parties of the 3rd Australian Tunnelling Coy. each comprising one NCO and six sappers, under my command, went over the block in the old German line to examine and demolish the enemy's mine system. The parties left at zero plus 5 minutes. The following mine shafts were found and destroyed (at 5-minute intervals):
>
> - Shaft marked 'A' on map. Inclined for 49 feet from surface at 3:1. at which point it junctions with a second gallery from the communication trench. This gallery is level and was followed on a bearing of about 340 degrees for 30 feet until an incline commences on a 3:1 slope. Three German electric leads tacked on the back of the gallery, were destroyed. The infantry bombing party's bombs completely filled the shaft with smoke and the party was unable to continue the examination. A charge of 150 lbs of ammonal and 10 lbs of guncotton was fired at 7.50pm, completely wrecking the gallery.
> - Shaft marked 'B'. With the smoke from the infantry's bombs, it was found impossible to examine this shaft below the depth of about 30 feet. Here a similar charge was fired at 7.55pm, completely wrecking the shaft.
> - Shaft marked 'C' is a big shaft, on a 3:1 incline, with a gallery turning off to the right about 30 feet below the surface. This shaft was followed down for about 50 feet: due to the very dense smoke from bombs, it was impossible to further explore it. Two electrical leads, fastened along the back of the gallery, were destroyed. A charge of 130 lbs of ammonal and 10 lbs of guncotton was fired in the junction 30 feet below the surface at 8pm, destroying the shaft. The two dugouts marked 'D' and 'E' from which some of the enemy threw bombs were both destroyed at 7.18pm by mobile charges.

At 7.45pm the order went out to retire. The parties commenced to slowly withdraw at 8.05pm and reported at the rendezvous of Cameron shaft at 8.30pm.

Casualties: One Officer slightly wounded (remaining on duty), one N.C.O. severely wounded, one O.R. killed and another slightly wounded. (Signed) Alex Sanderson Captain, Acting O.C. 3 A.T.C.[7]

Death of Major Coulter

CB/AS: *The three entrances to the German mine shafts were found exactly where they expected them to be. Three charges of ammonal each, detonated by a (guncotton) charge of 10 lbs, were taken over to be exploded, one in each shaft. Germans were found in the tunnels of the shaft and bombs were thrown up. One bomb whizzed past Captain Sanderson and exploded immediately inside a shaft or dugout entrance. Coulter, seeing the position in the first shaft, flung a charge which he had with him in among the Germans near the entrance. This charge had a long fuse, and our men had to be kept back from the entrance for about two minutes before this charge exploded. It was afterwards found that the charge had blown up the Germans inside. All the fighting in the shafts was done by the tunnellers. Coulter, who had been with the infantry in the trenches, was killed. One other tunneller was hit, but otherwise the tunnellers seem to have got off well.*[8]

The 3 A.T.C. War Diary of 28 June recorded the event in further detail:

Captain Sanderson saw Germans firing at our men from a dugout; these were driven in. They refused to emerge and a mobile charge sealed the dugout. Major Coulter remained to cheer and hearten the Infantry by his fearless example fighting by their side. The enemy counter-attacked three times to try and retake the trench. During the second counter-attack, Major Coulter was shot through the mouth and spine at close quarters. At the same time Sapper Griffen was killed alongside him in the same way. The retirement was successfully carried out under cover of rifle fire by rear guard parties. Major Coulter's body was carried back by the Tunnellers. This left Sanderson in command of the Company.[9]

German snipers were often extremely accurate. Robert Graves described how in May 1915, he had poked his small rod-shaped metal trench periscope above the parapet, offering only an inch-square target: a sniper at Cuinchy placed a bullet dead centre at a range of 400 yards.[10]

A fellow officer described Coulter's death:

Coulter was using his revolver and after this ammunition gave out, he took the rifle from a dead soldier. He was taking steady aim at what appeared to be a sniper, when a bullet struck him on the corner of the mouth and came out of the back of the head. Five of the men then started to carry him back to our lines. Many times they had to crawl along dragging the body as best they could. Their escape was miraculous.

On 29 June, Sergeant Berry described, in his patriotic manner, the loss of his O.C. Major Coulter:

This evening the rain is pouring in torrents. Simultaneously with the burst of the thunderstorm, the flash of lightning and the crash of artillery, our heavy guns dropped shells on the enemy. We have lost in this action our company commander, Major Coulter, D.S.O., a bold and skilful officer. The Major knew nothing of fear, particularly when duty beckoned him to any task that was humanly surmountable. A few minutes before he was hit, a big shell burst within a few feet of where he and others were standing. The shock knocked five of them into a trench. Afterwards Major Coulter was fatally hit by a sniper. It is satisfactory to know that we at once got that sniper through the throat with a bullet, as only about 25 yards separated Fritz and our blokes. Frank 'Griffo' Griffin was killed about the same time: he was well-known in the West, and you can rank him with the best of them.[11]

The raid was considered a success, however, despite almost half of the attacking force becoming casualties. Wearne was recommended for the Victoria Cross, awarded posthumously.

Captain Sanderson wounded in action

Alex Sanderson was wounded in this action (his second wound stripe), again remaining on duty, as advised to his mother Augusta on 7 July. A sketch by Sanderson (map redrawn by author, see colour plate section) accompanied his report of 29 June, which was sent to the C. of M. First Army and to the Army Commander. Surprisingly, Alex Sanderson makes no mention of the part Major Coulter played in the raid, nor of his death in enemy lines.

The Inspector of Mines Brigadier General Harvey wrote on 5 July:

I have read with great interest and admiration the report by O.C. 3 A.T.C. on the successful raid on the enemy's trenches at Hill 70 on 28.6.17. This is one of the few instances recorded where adequate charges for wrecking enemy shafts have been employed by us, and should form a valuable precedent. It with the deepest regret that I learned of the death of Major Coulter on this occasion, though no mention is made of it in the report.[12]

CB/AS: *After the capture of Hill 70 on 15 August, when the old German mining section which had been blown up by us on June 28th was approached, it was found that the galleries ran almost exactly as they had been mapped out by our listeners.*[13]

July 1917

Company strength: A.I.F. 20 officers, 659 O.R.s. Attached B.E.F. Infantry: 11 O.R.s

CB/AS: *After the raid the Australians tunnelled vigorously forward to break through into the German workings. There immediately followed a race for the ground which had been lost to the Germans by this explosion. In two cases our tunnellers got ahead of the Germans and prevented them from reaching their own galleries. In one case, they managed to reach their old electrical leads before we broke through. The danger of this was known to us and we had warned the British to keep clear of this sector. The enemy managed on 8 July to set off on an untamped mine already laid under the British trenches. This caused no infantry casualties as no infantry was above. This finished the active mining on this part.*[14,15]

Captain Sanderson's report on this enemy explosion read:

> The (German) crater in hard chalk was 60 feet diameter x 30 feet deep. The lip of the crater covered 40 yards of the new British Front Line OG1 (Old German). It is likely that the enemy occupies other galleries between Natal Trench and our Hill 70 mining system: we have not found entrances from his old front line (OG1) to his galleries which are known to exist from our listening results.[16]

The German crater was named 'Coulter Crater' (see colour plate map) after the fallen Major Coulter. The 3 A.T.C. War Diary records that this enemy mine was exploded at 11:20, at a depth of 50 feet under Hill 70, opposite Gordon Alley. It caused minor casualties from falling chalk, one of whom was Sapper Henry McAlinden, who afterwards was repatriated. Twenty years later, Henry would attend a Perth reunion for the 1880's Kimberley goldfield diggers.

3 A.T.C.'s new activities

The company moved from active tunnelling to building dugouts, accommodation and machine-gun pits, as well as reconnoitring and building roads and bridges for the big push to the Hindenburg Line. In defeating the enemy pioneers by destroying their offensive tunnels with deadly camouflets, the Australians miners had eliminated the underground threats to Canadian troops in their trenches. Now 3 A.T.C. tunnellers laboured to protect them in ever more effective and complex dugout systems and subways.[17]

Alex Sanderson promoted and awarded second M.C.

On 16 July, a message from the Headquarters A.I.F. to Lieutenant Colonel Stokes read: 'Approval has been given for the appointment of Captain A. Sanderson 3rd Australian Tunnelling Company A.E. to command the Company vice Major L.J. Coulter, killed in action, and for Captain Sanderson to be promoted Major from 1.7.1917.'

Six days later, Captain Sanderson M.C was awarded the Bar to the M.C., and on 17 September, the *London Gazette* would record the awarding of this bar to Sanderson's Military Cross for his actions:

> During a raid carried out against enemy trench east of Loos by two Infantry Battalions on the evening of the 28th June 1917, Captain Sanderson entered the enemy trench with some men of his Company. This Officer did excellent work reconnoitring the enemy's mining system behind the point of entry, and cutting the leads. The party successfully destroyed three enemy mine shafts and blew in two dugouts.

Canon Scott commented on the decorations worn on uniforms: 'Little do people at home know by what supreme self-sacrifice and dauntless courage those strips of bright-coloured ribbon on the breasts of soldiers have been won.'[18]

Investigation parties

8 July: Classified SECRET. A party of officers and O.R.s of 3 A.T.C., 170th T.C. and 172nd T.C. were detailed as special investigation detachments to seek booby-traps or delay action mines left in enemy dugouts, under buildings, at cross-roads or in embankments and to give immediate warnings of any dangers discovered. The C. of M. issued instructions for these parties:

Officers will wear upon both sleeves a strip of red cloth, 1 inch wide, from shoulder to cuff for ready identification. Each dugout or cellar passed by a first examination as free of traps, numbered and logged (though not necessarily free of delay action mines, requiring a longer search) will be marked with a full green circle, 4 inches in diameter, under the word: EXAMINED. A Red Circle must be shown and a red warning written: MINED-DANGEROUS where a trap is found and not removed, or if delay-action mine, not actually discovered, is suspected. If, after a thorough examination, there is no reason to suspect a delay-action mine, the sign will read: CONSIDERED SAFE in green chalk or sign boards.

Sanderson's report on the enemy mining system at 'The Copse'

On 24 July, from a deep deep lateral at Hill 70, 3 A.T.C. broke through into a German mine system, capturing 774 feet of their galleries which they then surveyed and salvaged. Alex Sanderson submitted a report on the twenty German shafts in the old German front line, opposite 'The Copse'; a series of inclined listening galleries sunk from sapheads in the enemy's front line and communication trenches:

> Some reached slightly below the level of the British Deep Deep level at 'The Copse'. Most were only at deep and shallow levels. Many were very erratic in their courses and seemed to have been constructed without close regard to their objectives. The ends of the deepest were several feet below the high water level of the previous winter. Apart from Shaft 20, all the spoil from these galleries had been carried by hand from the faces and tipped over the parapets and parados of the German trenches. The German tunnellers' progress in constructing their galleries appeared slow; the fastest rate was about 3 feet in 24 hours. Ventilation: In most galleries, air was forced to the faces through 6 inch galvanised iron pipes with flexible canvas bends from hand-blowers (Keith-Backman type) placed in chambers close to the shaft entrance.

Final Australian camouflet

On 26 July 1st Canadian Infantry Brigade ordered their 1st Infantry Battalion to clear all front-line trenches: 'as the enemy are suspected to be renewing their activity in their old mining galleries under our front line and No Man's Land. To destroy these galleries the 3rd Australian Tunnelling Company will blow a camouflet.'

Ammonal explosives

On 27 July, 3 A.T.C. had set off a massive deep charge of 10,000 lbs (see colour plate map). Two weeks previously the Australians had extended Cameron No.1 Main gallery and cut out mine chambers of 8 feet x 6 feet x 6.5 feet. These were charged with ammonal and guncotton explosives connected to duplicate electrical leads, with two electrical detonators and one instantaneous fuse. Primers were in priming charges of 20 lbs. The successful blast crumped all the connecting works of the German system. With this decisive blow, the offensive mining struggle at Hill 70, and along the British-held front lines, was at an end.[19]

Death of Sergeant Berry M.M.

On 31 July, Sergeant James Berry, the author of vivid letters home and recently back from leave, was killed in action by a shell on Hill 70, together with three of his colleagues. Berry had been wounded in the eye by a shell in February and had been sent to London for treatment. The loss of this experienced, capable and brave soldier was a bitter blow to the company. Sergeant Berry would never return to the goldfields' life and adventures he yearned for:

> Many old gold hunters are members of this Company, and though we are interested to read of propositions to enable returned soldiers to grow wheat and vegetables, gold hunters at least, are not to be turned from their old love by bright painted pictures of the life rural. Do not forget this fact – when this king of all disturbances is finished – it's 'Heigh ho! for Australia and the Golden West', and many of us have picked out the particular territory we shall track for.'[20]

The Rev Taylor of Kalgoorlie, who had to 'communicate the sad intelligence' to the widow, wrote: 'The late Sergeant Berry, a machinery merchant in Boulder-road, Kalgoorlie was an enthusiastic worker in all movements for the development of the goldfields. Both as a writer in the press and a speaker on the platform he was indefatigable in his labours for the public good.'[21]

Major Sanderson, who would undoubtedly have had many conversations with Sergeant Berry about their shared experiences in the gold-mining town of Kalgoorlie, wrote to his widow with photographs of his last resting place.

Chapter 14

Canadian Assault on Hill 70

15 August 1917

The extensive and complex network of British mining systems that stretched from La Bassée Canal to Hill 70 was no longer threatened by German offensive mining and two tunnelling sections were allocated to underground work from Hill 70 to the Hulluch and St Elie mining system (situated further north of Loos).

Another tunnelling section returned to the Red Lamp salient, Fauquissart and Chapigny mine systems to assist 251st R.E. Coy., where they were at work pumping, listening and putting in a concrete mine dam.[1] A decision was soon made, however, to abandon two systems. Lieutenant Colonel Stokes, C. of M. First Army, wrote to Major Sanderson that: 'It has today been definitely decided, owing to the reduction of Tunnelling Coy. strength, to flood Red Lamp and Fauquissart.'[2]

On 15 July, the Canadians had relieved the British 1st Corps at Loos. Their infantry attack on Hill 70, strategically and critically important for the Loos-Lens sector, was intended as a diversionary stratagem for the impending 3rd Battle of Ypres in Belgium and the French attacks on the Aisne. The Hill 70 battle would successfully tie down five German divisions. The costly Ypres conflict meant that no German troops could be transferred down to Lens. The Prussian *Generalleutnant* Hermann von Kuhl, admiringly called the Canadian Corps: 'Some of the best troops the English had.'[3]

At the beginning of August, 3 A.T.C. were preparing for the planned Canadian attack on Hill 70. Shelters, mine shafts, galleries and dugouts which had fallen into partial disrepair were opened up and new cables were laid from the signallers' H.Q. to the advanced front through the old laterals and mine galleries.

The Australian Special Investigation parties were organised and trained to 'go over' with the attack. On 30 July Major Sanderson had issued more detailed 'secret' instructions for the organisation of these three parties on Hill 70, co-ordinated by Lieutenant Hugh Russel. Attached to the 2nd and 3rd Canadian Infantry Brigade areas, the tunnellers' duties would be to seek out, remove and destroy any traps or mines installed by the German Third and Fourth Army in their retreat in enemy dugouts or under buildings, roads, railways, bridges or embankments. Any trap or mine was to be moved or rendered harmless 'at the earliest possible moment, as the longer they are in action, the more dangerous they will become.'[4]

The objective of the Canadian Corps attack, delayed for two weeks by bad weather, was the reverse slope of Hill 70. While they waited, the Canadians were busy raiding the enemy and cutting their barbed wire. Their artillery was weakening and demoralising the Germans with counter-battery fire and drums of gas projected onto Lens.[5]

Australian maximum camouflet

CB/AS: *Just to the north there was another German mining section which was known to us by listening, but which was not connected with their southern section. The Germans had been heard working through from the north towards the salient which had never connected the two. It was not known, however, whether the mine in this section had been charged. It was therefore decided that a few days before the attack on Hill 70, this northern section should be blown in by the explosion of a maximum camouflet. This was done on August 10th, and all of these galleries must have been destroyed. The charge blown by us contained 10,000 lbs of ammonal. On August 15th Hill 70 was captured by the Canadians.*[6]

15 August Canadian attack

Canon Scott, the Canadian troop's padre, recalled:

> By the beginning of August, everything was ready for the 1st Canadian Division attack. It was a lovely night; the stars were shining beautifully, and the Orion constellation hung on the horizon in the eastern sky, with the pale moon above. A great silence brooded over the wide expanse of darkness. Then, at 4.25am, the guns burst forth in all their fury, and all along the German line I saw not only exploding shells, but the bursting oil drums with their pillars of liquid fire. At once the Germans sent up rockets of various colours, signalling for aid from their guns, and the artillery duel of the two great armies began. I stood on the hill with some of our men, and watched. We could see, silhouetted against the morning sky, men walking over the hilltop, and now and then jumping down into the captured trenches. In a place called the 'Chalk Pit', which afterwards became our front line, the Germans had made a determined stand. They had a wonderful dugout there, like a rabbit-warren, with many passages and

entrances, from which they were bombed out with great difficulty. Since moving to Bracquement, we had been preparing for this attack on Hill 70. Compared with the taking of Vimy Ridge, the exploit was a minor one, but it was felt to be an exceedingly dangerous task which would cost us dearly. The Germans had had time to concentrate their forces in front of us, and they knew the value of the commanding position which they held.[7]

Sapper Caradog Jones recollected:

> The thing that causes the greatest amazement is to observe the soldiers, whether at base, in the camps behind the trenches or in the firing line, and how completely unaffected they are by the prospects of injury or death. I saw division after division of the Canucks [Canadians] marching to war whilst singing the sweet rag-times and plantation songs of America. It is almost impossible to explain this disregard of death unless it is found in the old Welsh proverb 'Better Death than Shame'. But Tommy is fond of making light of nearly everything, especially those who come from the Colonies, namely Australia and Canada.[8]

Sanderson's report on tunnellers' investigations

Early on the morning of 15 August, Lieutenant Shaw moved forward at 05:05 following Lieutenant Ashcroft. They had passed through a severe enemy artillery barrage and immediately set to work examining the first objectives on Hill 70, before moving on to investigate other areas captured, particularly dugouts, noting their capacity to accommodate troops at rest, as well as machine gun posts and trench mortar emplacements.

> This was carried out under trying circumstances over four days and nights, much hampered by the presence of many wounded Canadians and Germans in the dugouts. The dugouts in the Chalk Cutting are extensive and some had been used as a Dressing Station for wounded. It had been subjected to very heavy shelling by both sides and there were still over fifty dead and wounded Germans there on the afternoon of the 17th; also a large number of machine-guns.[9]

Sapper George Oxman recorded the Canadian attack in his journal:

> 14th. Left for Loos at 8am, then walked from Loos to Hulluch. Bert and I got hit on the thigh from an aircraft shell which bounced off the side of trench. We walked about 8 miles.

15th. The bombardment opened at 4.20am. The Canadians went over about 5.30am. We followed about 6.30am. Both sides lost a lot of men. The enemy tried three times to take the hill back again but failed.[10]

The 3 A.T.C. War Diary noted that: 'Since August 10 mining on the Lens front has ceased, with a little defensive mining on both sides. Our tunnellers now have a complete apron of galleries around their works. Two Sections are now working for the Canadians at Lens where they are driving a railway tunnel through Hill 70.'

Although all objectives were taken that day, 1,056 Canadians were killed, 2,432 wounded and 43 taken prisoner. For the next three days, the Germans continued to counter-attack fiercely.

The 3 A.T.C. War Diary described the evening attacks:

At 6.40pm the enemy's artillery was shelling Hill 70 very heavily. At 7.15pm a counter-attack was launched against our newly won positions. This attack was broken up. At 8.50pm the enemy was again attacked along the whole front of the 1st and 2nd Divisions (including the Chalk Quarry) and were repulsed. Posts were established to the east of the Chalk Pit and beyond. Since the beginning of the operation we took 1,000 prisoners.[11]

At 20:15, Lieutenant Russel located the enemy mining system and their main shaft, with extensive workings towards the south and west. Russel advised that detail parties were needed to carry out surveys. A large enemy defensive mine system was discovered, with entrances from the old German front line: one gallery was found to be tamped and to contain a charge of explosives, ready to be set off.

German report on Hill 70

On 16 August Crown Prince Rupprecht's army group at General Ludendorff's Headquarters put out the following (inaccurate) wireless press release:

In Flanders the second great battle has 'burnt itself out'. In Artois, between Hulluch and Lens yesterday morning, the four Canadian Divisions delivered a violent attack on our positions. They pressed forward, after a powerful artillery preparation, and penetrated into our first line, seeking by the employment of strong reinforcements to widen and deepen the breach on both sides of Loos. The English gain is small. Renewed attacks, repeated eleven times, were delivered by the enemy in vain attempts to gain a more substantial advantage. In front of our defence the enemy attacking waves collapsed. South of Hulluch and west of Lens the enemy, who everywhere had suffered grievous losses, was driven back.

Major Sanderson, in his copy of this report, underlined the above paragraph in pencil and added in the margin, with his initials, this acerbic comment on the veracity of the report: 'A lie. All objectives were gained. A.S. Major 18 August 1917.'[12]

Brigadier General R.N. Harvey, Inspector of Mines, wrote to Major Sanderson:

I have read with great pride the generous appreciation by the G.O.C Canadian Corps of the work done by 3 A.T.C. during the recent operations near Lens. I wish to convey to you and your Company my heartiest congratulations. That you should have done well is no surprise to me, for I have watched your work develop and know it to be good, but it is a real pleasure to find it so highly commended by others.[13]

An article appeared in *The Sydney Sun* by the reporter at Anzac H.Q. Mr Keith Murdoch:

GREAT TUNNELLING EXPLOITS
It was a deadly underground warfare, with men sometimes disappearing, as though swallowed by the earth… Australian miners have made a reputation for speed, accuracy and success in mining and dugout construction on this front, on both sides of it, for their speed and skill is far superior to the slow Germans. These Australians want Australia to know how good a fellow and how fine a worker they found the British Tommy holding the line and needed for the unskilled work associated with the tunnelling.[14]

Approval was given in August for Major Alex Sanderson to have a month's leave from 3 October since: 'he has had 21 months of continuous front-line work in a responsible position and is in need of a rest. Special leave would increase this officer's efficiency for future work.'[15]

It would not be until 1918 that Alex Sanderson would take fourteen days' leave and stay at the Hotel Windsor in Monte Carlo.

September 1917

After several months, road construction and maintenance were ended. The sappers were freed up to begin reconnoitering the advanced, unconsolidated trenches at Lens and Hill 70. Major Sanderson's company was now working in the Lens/Loos/Hulluch/La Bassée sectors. In the permanent tunnels systems of Hulluch/St Elie/Vermelles, 'listening' was carried on in advance of the front-line trenches. Proposals for the Hulluch/St Elie tunnel systems were for dugouts to shelter 1,110 infantry men. (One dugout was named *Bullfinch* after the West Australian gold mine.)[16]

Infantry experience underground

In mid-September, 3 A.T.C. extended its front northwards beyond the Hulluch/St Elie mining system to the Hairpin/Border Redoubt mining sector. Unlike the tunnellers, the infantry were unaccustomed to a life underground, where the sun never shines:

> The various posts in 'Hairpin' were connected by an underground tunnel with four exits to the trench... *Rats Creek*... Along these tunnels, exits were built up to fortified shell holes, occupied by Lewis gun teams, our only supports. Down below lived Company Headquarters, the garrison, one or two tunnelling experts and the specialists, stokes mortars, machine gunners. The passages were damp and slippery, walls covered in evil-looking red and yellow spongy fungus, the roof too low to allow one to walk upright, the ventilation practically non-existent. All combined to ruin the health of those who had to live there. The main tunnel was lit with electric light. This often failed, and produced indescribable chaos. Although the tunnels had all these disadvantages, they reduced our casualties enormously.[17]

Lieutenant Russel's work acknowledged

The 1st Canadian Division H.Q. responded: 'Please thank Major Sanderson for the excellent and courageous work of the detachment, specially commending Lieuts. Russel and Shaw. Thanks to their thorough work, our people occupied the captured German dugouts with perfect confidence and they were able to have their much needed rest, without worrying.'

Lieutenant Russel was recommended for the M.C. on 30 September and Alex Sanderson granted his well-earned leave: 'Herewith pass and authority for leave of absence for five days from 15/10 to 20/10. On arrival in Paris you must report to the Commandant, British Troops at 267 Place du Marché, St Honore, near Place Vendome. Signed: A. Sanderson Major.'

Alex Sanderson's letter to Mrs Russel on 1 January 1919 explained:

During the Hill 70 operations Lieut. Russel was placed in command of the unit's investigations party of four officers and 60 O.R.s, in addition to 40 attached infantry. The work was carried out bravely and excellently and was of very great value. The whole of the main HILL 70 position was then captured. During the operation Lt. Russel personally carried out reconnaissances in the front line of the fighting, and sometimes ahead of it. This gallant work was very highly commended and he was afterwards awarded the Military Cross in recognition of his bravery and the excellent work done on that occasion.

With worsening weather, on 7 September an issue request was made by Lieutenant Colonel Stokes: 'The use of oilskins would be most desirable, especially as the Australian miners are particularly liable to get colds in severe weather. Waterproof: Hats, sou'wester x 50, Frocks, oilskin x 50 and Trousers.'

October 1917

At Hill 70 defensive works, front-line dugouts and O.P.s were constructed to consolidate this important salient. Light railway lines were carried to the forward positions of subways. The old enemy timbered galleries and emplacements were stripped of the more valuable timber. Alex Sanderson reassured the Canadian infantry that the sound of picking in old German mine systems would be the sound of his men salvaging mine timber sets. When the author accompanied the Durand Group, over a decade ago, to excavate the railway entrance to the Hill 70 Hythe Tunnel, below the Lens to La Bassée road, many shells were uncovered as a well as – particularly poignantly – a German foot and shoe, bringing home to all the tragedy of war. The main tunnel was driven under the old German Line No.1 and the main Lens-La Bassée Road, and constructed beneath Hythe Alley.

Poison Gas

In July an ominous circular had arrived about a new type of gas used by the Germans: the newly introduced German Yellow Cross shell containing the agent sulphur mustard, leading to blistering.

The Chief Engineer of 1st Corps wrote to Sanderson on 27 October with a suggestion for defending subways by driving poison gas along the tunnels. Alex Sanderson replied that it would be quite possible to install a fan near a power plant and regulating doors, at the junctions of tunnels, to direct a 5–6mph breeze along any forward subways. However, Sanderson did not think it wise to use gas for defensive purposes, noting that a system of forced draught could be installed to clear any portion of the subway gassed by local enemy shelling or bombing. On 25 November Sanderson sent a plan for the positioning of fans and regulating doors to ventilate the Border-Reboubt, St Elie and Hulluch Tunnels in case of gas attacks. There would need to be two steel-cased paddle wheel-type fans, driven by electric motors, each with a capacity of 10,000 cubic feet of air per minute, and sixty regulating doors to control the draught.[18]

Hythe Subway surveys, December 1917

The 3 A.T.C. War Diary notes that: 'In December, the preliminary seeds of a very important and extensive tunnel scheme at Hill 70 were sown by the reconnaissance, alignments and surveys carried out by a party under the command of Lieut H. Russel M.C., who marked out the inclined shafts necessary to open up the work.' This would be named the 'Hythe Tunnel' since it replaced the main communication trench on Hill 70 known as 'Hythe Alley'. On 14 December, on the railway cutting traverses on Hill 70, four doors and loopholes were installed. December saw the completion of the programme of works on the dugouts in the old German lines on Hill 70, in opening up and renovating the old German dugouts and in salvaging sets from the captured enemy galleries and crumped dugouts. All data for the Hythe Tunnel was obtained and the plans completed.[19]

A post-war memoir of Major H.R. Dixon M.C., the Assistant Inspector of Mines at G.H.Q., described the Hythe Subway at Loos, undertaken between December 1917 and March 1918, as perhaps:

> the most elaborate of all… The most interesting features of this fortress lay in the measures taken for protection against gas attacks or heavy gas shelling and the concrete work which was carried out. Every entrance to the surrounding trenches was fitted with a gas curtain, made from an army blanket, specially treated to prevent gas passing through it. These were arranged on rollers, above a sloping fame, so that the pull of a string would fasten them tightly in position over the door. To ensure that no gas or contaminated air could enter the system owing to damage or failure to close any door, a powerfully driven electric fan could in emergency provide the air for the whole system. This was drawn through an enormous box-respirator, and the pressure caused in the galleries when the fan was at work was such that air could not get in to the galleries, even at an open door.[20]

The dangers and responsibilities of front-line service had a harsh effect on the hardiest of men. The 3 A.T.C. medical officer reported to Major Sanderson on the fragile mental state of one officer (included in the officer group photograph of May 1917, on the first anniversary of the company's arrival in France): 'I have examined Lieut Crawshaw and find him to be in a most neurotic condition. So much has his condition worked upon his mind that I consider it will soon probably affect his mentality. I can find nothing physically wrong with him. 28.10.1917.'

Major Sanderson sent him off to Le Havre: 'owing to the fact that he is quite useless as an officer and it is inadvisable that he should remain with this unit any longer.'[21]

Sapper Leaver's diary

Sapper Charles Leaver, 51, a married miner with twelve children, from South Australia, who had enlisted on 9 April 1916, kept a vivid wartime diary:

16/12. Fritz is shelling the town. He sent word by aeroplane that he was going to shell Bethune and Noeux-les-Mines and warned the people to get out. So we are in for a hot Xmas.

17/12. Snowing all last night and today

18/12. This morning it was bright and clear but very cold with the ground frozen. The duck boards were like glass to walk on so we laid sandbags on them.

19/12. All the trees are loaded with frost. Old Fritz is still putting a few shells in the town.

21/12. Nine more Jerrys came over to give themselves up. They said that all of them would come up, if we would not fire on them. The weather is still freezing and a job to keep warm.

23/12. There was a lot of gas shells about last night. Some of our lads got gassed. It was mustard gas and a cruel thing, as it blinds them if they get a fair dose. If it does not kill them. All exits from the mine system were tamped up as a precaution against enemy gas.

25/12. [Christmas Day] We had a quiet day today. A splendid dinner and a ration of rum. We had roast beef, plum pudding and tinned fruit, with plum sauce and lollies, thanks to the Australian Comfort Fund. It has been snowing on and off all day and it is falling heavy tonight.

27/12. We heard the Canadians got a hundred prisoners last night. Another lot was coming over to surrender, but they drove them back as they did not want prisoners.

28/1. Still snowing, freezing and very cold. Got a double issue of rum.

29/12. Colder this morning than it has been all winter. The guns are going strong out in the line.[22]

Generous rum rations issued to the front-line tunnellers and their attached infantry were considered crucial for raising the men's spirits and beneficial for their health, as was the whisky drunk by their officers.

Chapter 15

Hythe Tunnel Fortress, Hill 70

January 1918

On New Year's Day 3 A.T.C. commenced digging five inclines off the Hythe Subway for entrances at Hill 70. On 4 January, to protect trench mortar emplacements in each tunnel against hostile attack, strong, heavy doors were fitted, which opened only from the tunnel.

Sapper Leaver noted in his journal:

1/1. At 5am Old Fritz bombarded, sending it over thick and heavy for twenty minutes. He started to come over on a raid but our lads were waiting. He only got to his wire and went back quick.

2/1. A quiet day in the billets. Not so cold today. Snowing a bit tonight. A raid last night and Old Fritz nearly got over to the tunnel but got stopped. He had some mobile charges with him and was coming over to try and blow it in. Our lads were waiting for him. Our side is getting ready for him, if he makes a big push here. They are concentrating troops on this front. So we have been in the tunnels to blow them in, if he does get them. I don't think he has much hope of this.

5/1. It had been freezing hard all night and as slippery as glass.

8/1. Things are fairly quiet but there is a fair amount of big stuff bursting on the tunnels. He can't hurt us. The shells just cut the lights when they come too close. The Staffords made a successful raid last night when Fritz was getting ready to come over. Our barrage caught them just as they got to their wire and cut them pretty bad. We got two prisoners.

9/1. At Hill 70, put in inclines and tram lines. Listening over the whole area.

10/1. Making great preparations in the tunnel for Fritz if he ever comes over, putting in mines and safety doors.

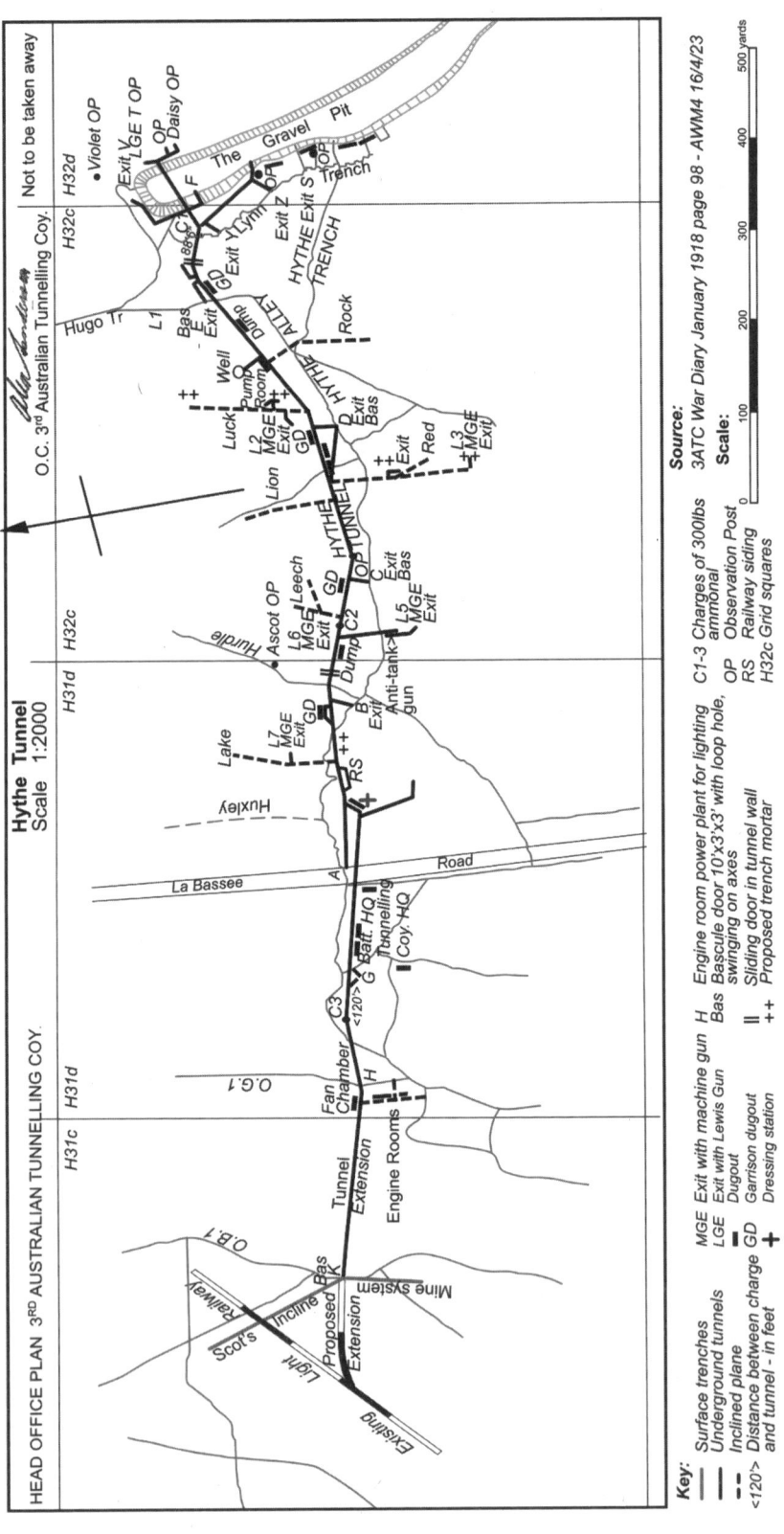

Map 12: **Hythe Tunnel and associated trenches**

15/1. We had a quiet trip out but Old Fritz started shelling the mouth of the tunnel just after we got in. He flattened the trenches all around but did not get the tunnel. It was lively while it lasted.

16/1. Things fairly quiet – a few big shells bursting overhead but we are well underground and it only shakes the timber a bit.

19/1. Going out this morning – just as we got to the line trench – we found an aeroplane that had been brought down the day before with both men killed in it. The tunnels are in a nice state! Water has come through the chalk. There are pools of water in places, nearly up to our knees.

20/1. It is cow going and coming to our work as the mud and water is all along the way.

24/1. Tunnel is in a terrible state. The thaw has set in and the water is coming through the chalk and is in the tunnel. Some places we are up to our knees and nearly all the fuses are out. We saw a great bit of aeroplane manoeuvring today.

28/1. Got the mud all out. There has been a big gang in pumping it out. Old Fritz has been over bombing tonight. It is ideal weather, for night is as bright as day.

29/1. The weather is quite like spring here this last few days, only frosty in the morning.

31/1. The guns are still going but we all wish it over. Great preparations are being made if Old Fritz does come over. There are miles of barbed wire being put out for about two miles behind the front lines, so he will get it hard.

Hughie Dodd recorded in his diary: '13/1. 170 Tunnelling Company have been getting strafed in Noeux-les-Mines. Their camp has come under some artillery fire at different times, but the climax was reached yesterday when he put seven huts out of existence and catching the rest of it on fire.'[1]

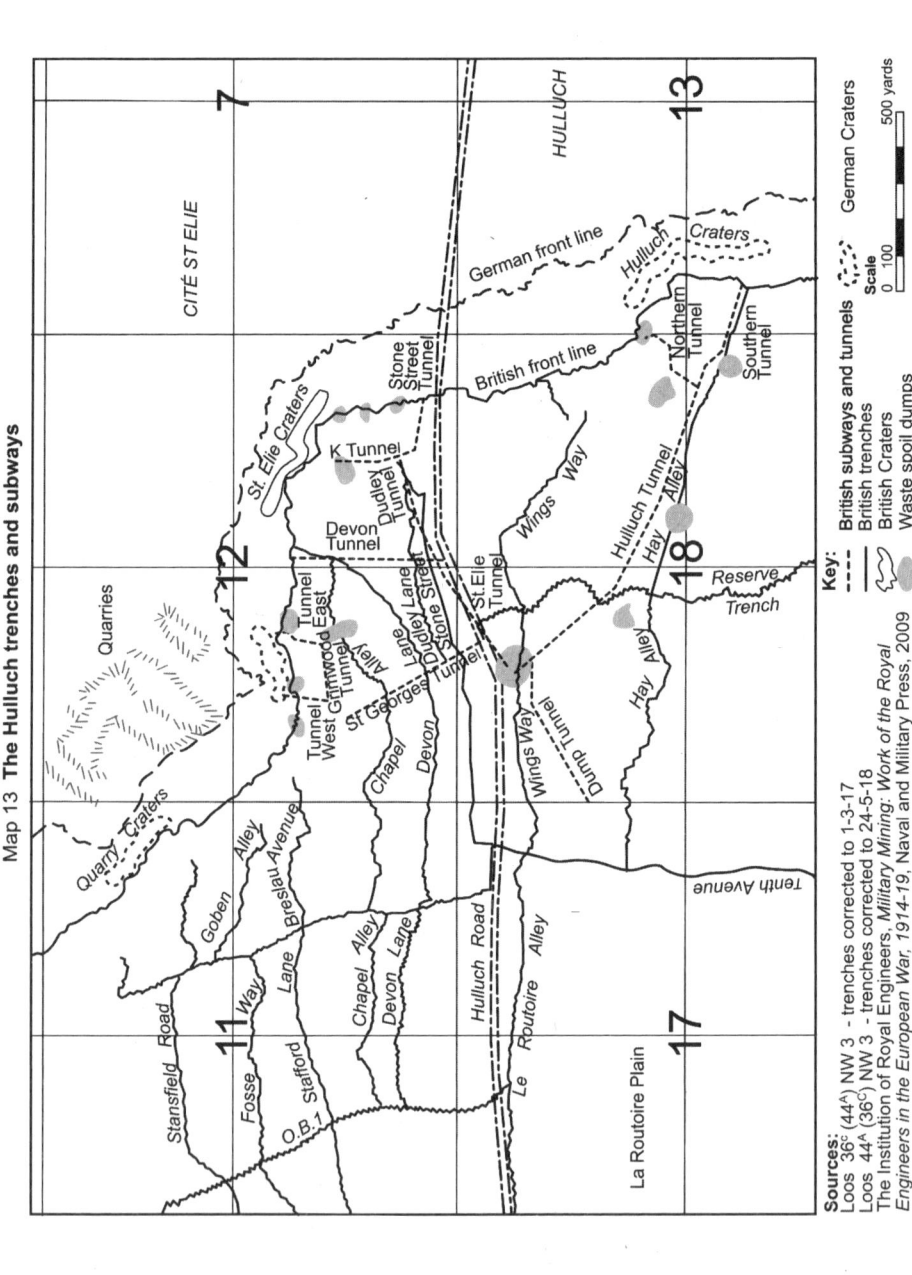

Map 13 The Hulluch trenches and subways

Death of Lieutenant Russel

On 22 January at 14:00, Lieutenant Taylor sent a note to Major Sanderson at Coy. H.Q. from the forward billets at Hill 70: 'Sir, I regret to report that Mr Russel has been badly wounded and Sapper J. Carden killed in Hythe Alley today.'

Lieutenant Hugh Russel was wounded in action by a shell explosion in Hythe Alley on Hill 70 and died at Bracquement the next day of his wounds. The death of Russel, one of the most deservedly popular officers, cast a spell of sadness over the whole company.

Sapper Leaver noted: '23/1 Poor Lieutenant Russel died last night, he was terribly wounded. His only thought was for the sapper that got killed with him. He was too badly wounded to do anything: only give him morphine to ease pain. We had a quiet time coming out.'

Alex Sanderson's letters and reports to the Controller and the Inspector of Mines, recorded in the 3rd Australian War Diaries, attest to his meticulous attention to detail and his compassionate concern for the men under his command. His informative and consoling letters, sent with photographs of the graves, to the close relatives of the fallen tunnellers of his company express his heartfelt sympathy for their loss.

Alex Sanderson wrote to Mrs Russel, offering his condolences and promising to inform her of the circumstances of her husband's death. The letter acknowledges that, for every combatant bidding farewell to a comrade, death is also looking over his own shoulders.

> Dear Mrs Russel,
> It is with very deep sympathy and regret that I have to write to tell you of the death of your gallant husband, Lieut. Hugh Russel M.C., who was severely 'Wounded in Action' in France on the 22nd inst. at 10.30am, and died in No.7 Casualty Clearing Station 14 hours later. Just before I left him, at about 11pm, he said: 'I am not feeling much pain, I expect I will pull through, although I am very badly wounded.' About an hour and a half later, he quietly passed to join many of his brave Comrades. It was a very sad day for the 3rd Australian Tunnelling Company, as he was loved by every man in the Unit. Always anxious to help in any duty, no matter how dangerous the task, he was admired by all who came in contact with him. A tower of strength to the Company. One of my most efficient officers.
> For Devotion to Duty and Conspicuous Bravery during the performance of some very important reconnaissance work in action last year, he was

awarded the Military Cross by His Majesty the King, in the New Year's Honour's List. No one ever better merited the award. He had been wounded on three previous occasions and each time so narrowly escaped death that we all thought his was a charmed life. Unfortunately, the end of the War is still a long way off and many of us will probably meet the same fate as Hugh but we are all certain of the ultimate result and, despite the loss of such fine comrades, we are not down-hearted.

I have been requested by the Officers of this Company to express to you and Miss Russel our deepest sympathy.

We grieve that you have lost such a splendid husband and we, a very brave and dear comrade, but there is some consolation in the thought that he proved himself a man, willing to die on the field of battle doing his duty sooner than be defeated by an enemy. I pray that you will be sustained in your bereavement by the Honour which the Nation will show for such a man.

Yours very Sincerely, Alex Sanderson, Major.

Exactly a year later, on 7 January 1919, Alex Sanderson would write again to Mrs Russel:

I have just received a letter from General Sir W. Birdwood K.G.B. Commanding the A.I.F. for some particulars of the service for which your husband was awarded the Military Cross. At the time Lieut. Russel was wounded he was on Hill 70 near Lens, making the preliminary survey for a tunnel which was afterwards constructed by the 3rd Austr. Tunn. Coy. through Hill 70, known as 'Hythe Tunnel'. It is a mile and a half long with numerous lateral tunnels and exits to machine gun post, accommodation for garrison, etc and in the latter stages of our defensive campaign it formed the main defence of the famous Hill 70 position. Lieut. Russel's war history is largely associated with the operations on Hill 70. A few months after he joined the unit we took over the underground protection of the front line on the Hulluch-Loos-Maroc Sector which traversed the western slope of Hill 70, the main enemy position opposite our front. The enemy was trying to force our troops further down the slope of the Hill by mining and, at the time we commenced operations against him, the enemy was actually underneath and blowing up a portion of our front line at Hill 70. We had then some very stiff mine fighting for several months during which time Lieut. Russel was wounded on three occasions, twice nearly losing his life. However, we have it to our credit that before many months we had the enemy back under his own line and by July 1917 we captured the whole of his Hill 70 mining system. This was largely due to the excellent work done by all the officers of this unit. Lieut. Russel did his share most splendidly. When the Unit's History is completed, I hope to have recorded in detail the work with which he was connected. Lieut Russel's grave is in the cemetery of Hersin, a town situated about six miles south of Béthune, Northern France. A cross has been erected over the grave. I hope to be back in Australia soon, when I hope to have the opportunity of personally telling you of the great assistance, given to me as Commanding Officer by your late gallant husband. Yours sincerely, Alex Sanderson.[2]

The conscription vote

The late Sergeant Berry had supported conscription in Australia:

Men are wanted, certainly, urgently, but why get slaves? I vote conscription, but I would not sell my soul for it. All the Anglo-Saxon world is up to the shoulders in this war, and Australia frankly boasts her independence of conscription to maintain her forces in the field. But men are wanted – yes, Brother Anzacs, free at home, it is up to you to speak. Come along, you of the bushlands, the plains, the hills and the valleys, the brown and red ridges, and your long distance pathways. Brother Anzacs, the burden is now yours, the responsibility is in your hands, and you are free men.[3]

On 31 January 1918 Sergeant Frank Angel, one of three brothers in the company, wrote to a son in Perth (from the *West Australian* newspaper):

Rain has been falling for days, making it very difficult going to and from the trenches, and it is surprising how cheerfully our Australian boys stand it. We have just recently got the results of the conscription voting in Australia and it came as a shock to every sober-thinking man on this western front. It seems hard to realise that Australia has turned down the call of the British Empire and deserted her own sons at the front. What must our enemies think of the land beneath the Southern Cross? They fear those Australian on this front, and they have good cause to. They have seen their dash, and felt their steel. They know when they start, hell cannot stop them. You may ask why so many of the soldiers here at the front voted 'No'? A very large percentage of our men are young. They take little or no interest in such matters. Amongst them are many red rag unionists.[4]

In 1916 Victoria, Tasmania and Western Australia had voted for conscription, while the other states voted 'No'. Following the failure of the Australian referenda to introduce conscription in both 1916 and 1917, the number of A.I.F. conscripts heading for the Western Front fell off.[5]

February 1918

Company strength: 27 officers and 648 O.R.s & B.E.F. attached 6 officers and 458 O.R.s.

CB/AS: *Two Sections are now working for the Canadians at Lens where they are driving a railway tunnel through Hill 70. The last four weeks has probably been a record in mining.*[6]

In the Hulluch-Vermelles sector the subsidence of the winter water-level made the tunnels more sanitary and passable. A deep well for drinking water was sunk in a gallery. Miners used lighted candles to see which way the air or gas was flowing, and the flames of the burning candles showed there was enough oxygen to breathe. Duck boarding and roofing was carried out in trenches and in posts such as *Rat Creek* and *Better 'ole*, names that reflected the infantry's dry humour.

In January Sanderson had sent a note to his officers: 'Spoil must not be dumped near entrances and should not be piled, but spread along the parapet wall back from the trench. Where the ground is under observation from enemy balloons, the spoil should be emptied and camouflaged at night time. Movement during the day in view of the enemy should be stopped.'

In February Sanderson suggested: 'Camouflaging the chalk spoils from the tunnels: I would like to experiment in spraying the spoil with some cheap form of dye: permanganate of potash and brown ochre, mixed with water and paint have been suggested as suitable materials.'[7]

Sanderson's tunnel defence scheme

On 12 February, Major Sanderson sent detailed proposals to the C. of M. for the defence of the infantry subways of Hulluch, St Elie, Hairpin, Hythe and Canteen. An inventive scheme of installing armoured trucks on rails, armed with machine guns, was also proposed for each tunnel system for counter-attacking if the enemy penetrated the forward galleries.

(a) **Defence of Exits.** A by-pass and bomb pit to be constructed in each exit. Also a loop-holed traverse with its field facing directly up the incline and through the exit.

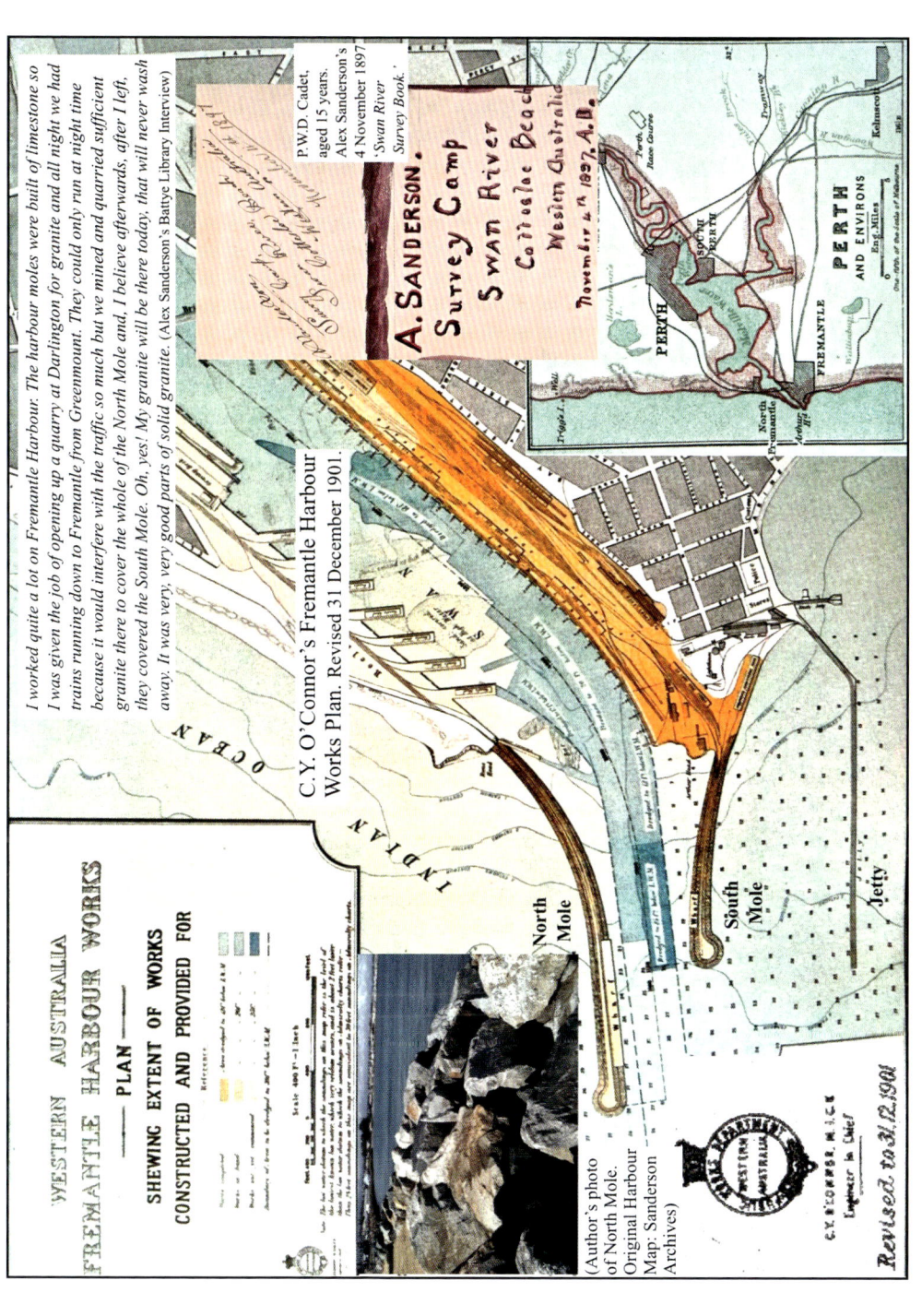

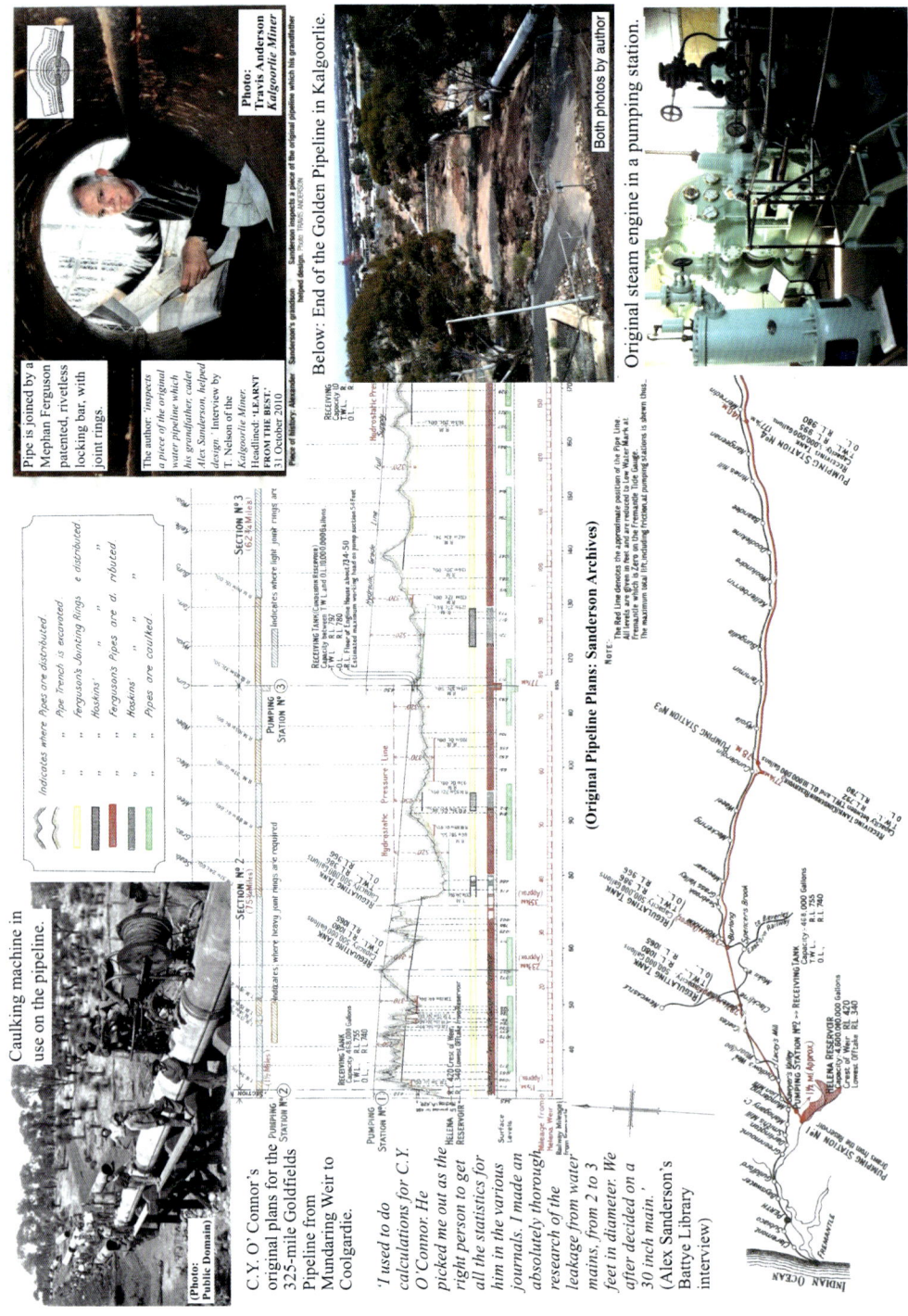

'I saw two of the finest deep water harbours in the world: Admiralty Gulf and Vansittart Bay. When I was exploring for the port, they gave me Captain Airey's government steamer: we had to take soundings. I sent a written report to the Chief of the Lands and Agricultural Department, that I did find where they could have a good deep water harbour ~ and good country behind it.'
(Alex Sanderson's Battye Library Interview)

'The Airey-Sanderson expedition will examine various inlets, for a place suitable to accommodate ships of any size, which can be reached any hour of the day and night. Captain Airey has taken a whaleboat and a dinghy, and a boat's crew and the usual paraphernalia for such expeditions.' (Perth paper)

(One of nine photos of Alex Sanderson's two Kimberley expeditions. Battye Library)

(Map courtesy of Kununurra Historical Society)

KIMBERLEY MEAT EXPORT WORKS
SKETCH PLAN
OF
NORTH EAST KIMBERLEY

Alex Sanderson's Sketch Plan of North East Kimberley. 8 October 1910.

'THE PARTY ESTABLISHING THE GOVERNMENT FREEZING WORKS ON THE SHORES OF CAMBRIDGE GULF.

Captain Airey, of the Harbour Dept., in charge of the boat party aboard the Junee, is holding a plan. The gentleman on his right is Mr A. Sanderson, Water Supply Engineer The expedition is historical, as it marks the beginning of beef export from a point nearer the equator than any similar depot in the world. The land party, under Mr Sanderson were met by the Wyndham Land party. If ever a party left Fremantle port fit to tackle anything, the Airey-Sanderson expedition can do it.'
(Unidentified, headlined Perth newspaper report)

Alex Sanderson aged 28.

Above: 'AIF Engineer Officers' Training School 'B' Squad, January 1916.' Moore Park, Sydney.
Below: 3 A.T.C. Officers on 'Anniversary of Arrival in France 5 May 1917.' (Originals Sanderson Archives)

Captain Alex Sanderson's letter (pages 1 and 3) to his wounded friend and O.C., Major Leslie J. Coulter, thirteen days after the Battle of Fromelles. He writes that: *I arranged with Captain Church to take three of his bombers and go over with him. We were able to marshall the 60 men he had in the crater and explain to them what to do by pointing out little landmarks ahead before the time came to charge. What happened afterwards I must not write but I don't think I will ever forget one iota of the experience. My idea was to get in and have a look at their Mines and it should have come off. On page 4 he writes: One does not get much fun here except in the work and risks one has to take.* (Sanderson Archive letter of 1 August 1916)

1st Aug. 1916

Dear Major Coulter,

We have only just recovered through a letter from Dow all about where you are located and see all very pleased to hear that you are recovering speedily. I would down to Killed ou la for the afternoon that you left only to find I was about half an hour too late. I would hardly have had a spare minute had I stopped to let you know how successful the show was and what occurred afterwards. I expect to hear that you have been honoured with the R.M. when the next list comes out as I know I have been recommended and no one deserves it better than you - how well it is deserved. We are all trying to keep up the reputation which No. 3 Coy earned under Donu Laster ship. I feel proud to think that I have been picked to command the Coy taking them all round. We ought not get a fair lot of officers N.C.O.s + Men

3

were to advance and so the book Temple had been well peppered I arranged with Capt Church to take three of his bombers and go over with him. We were able to marshall the 60 men he had in the Crater and explain to them what to do by pointing out little landmarks ahead before the time came to charge. What happened afterwards I must not write but I don't think I will ever forget me iota of the experience. My idea was to get in and have a look at their Mines and it should have come off. However I will tell you all about that when we meet again which I trust will be in the near future.

The reward is going on famously — R.L. is a bit behind hand as he was knocked about and had to be replaced quite a lot. I am trying to get more men on and that that Lieut Wait had

Below: Andy Prada and Chris Martin of the Durand Group stand next to a recess containing the sliding defensive brick door on rails, designed by Major A. Sanderson and installed on rails in Hulluch Tunnel.
(All colour photos taken by the author)

A junction in Copse Tunnel system. Note the 'No.5' wall sign.

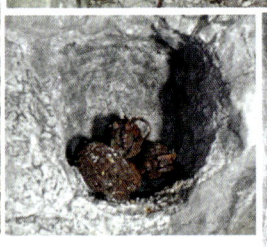

A cluster of unfused No. 5 grenades left in a wall cache in Hulluch Tunnel. Below: An original candle found in the Copse Tunnel and lit by the author, in memory of the 173rd Coy. tunnellers. Left: Copse Tunnel. Note arrow sign.

An Australian officer using a geophone and compass. (Public Domain)

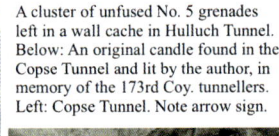

A junction in Copse Tunnel system. Note the 'No.5' wall sign.

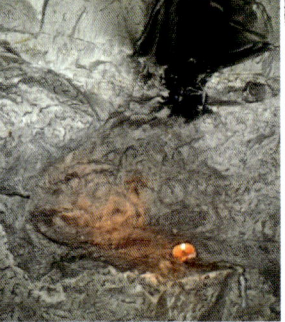

A truck with four buckets in a Copse Tunnel recess. Note the rope attached to truck and Letters/ No.s drawn on tunnel roof.

A tunneller's chalk-grafting tool found in Hulluch Tunnel.

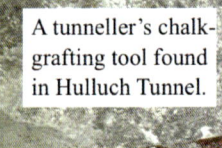

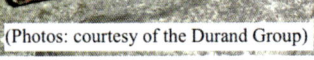

(Photos: courtesy of the Durand Group)

(Photo: A.Prada) Above: Andy Prada and the author view Sliding Wall in a Hulluch Tunnel recess.

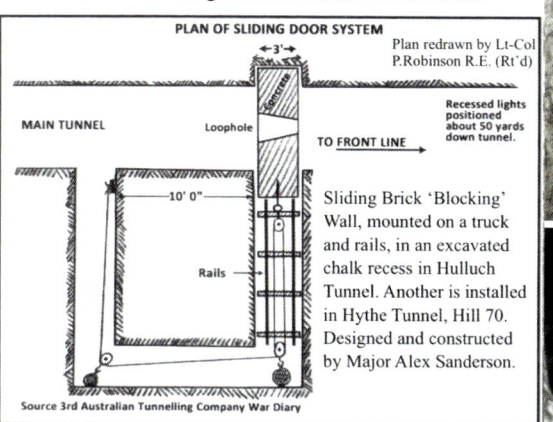

Sliding Brick 'Blocking' Wall, mounted on a truck and rails, in an excavated chalk recess in Hulluch Tunnel. Another is installed in Hythe Tunnel, Hill 70. Designed and constructed by Major Alex Sanderson.

Author's three photos, courtesy of the Durand Group

Cemented brick and wood construction with chalk infill.

Right:
Sniper's loophole, with protection of an interior pivoting iron loophole shield, made by a 3 A.T.C. blacksmith, Sergeant Leslie Forsyth M.M.

Far Right:
Defensive wall is mounted on a wheeled truck, sliding on rails.

Loophole recess.

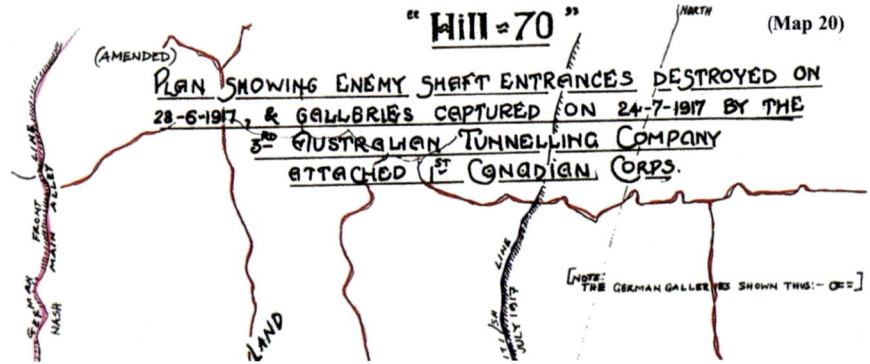

A plan of Hill 70 submitted by Major A. Sanderson to the Brigadier General 1st Canadian Brigade, showing the enemy shaft entrances destroyed in the British raid of 28 June 1917 and the galleries captured on 24 July 1917 by 3 A.T.C., attached to the 1st Canadian Corps. The German camouflets are drawn in green while the Australian camouflets are in blue. The old British front line runs west to east. In July 1917 the new British front line swung north. The overlapping camouflets and craters give a vivid impression of the deadly conflict taking place under No Man's Land from May 1916 to July 1917.

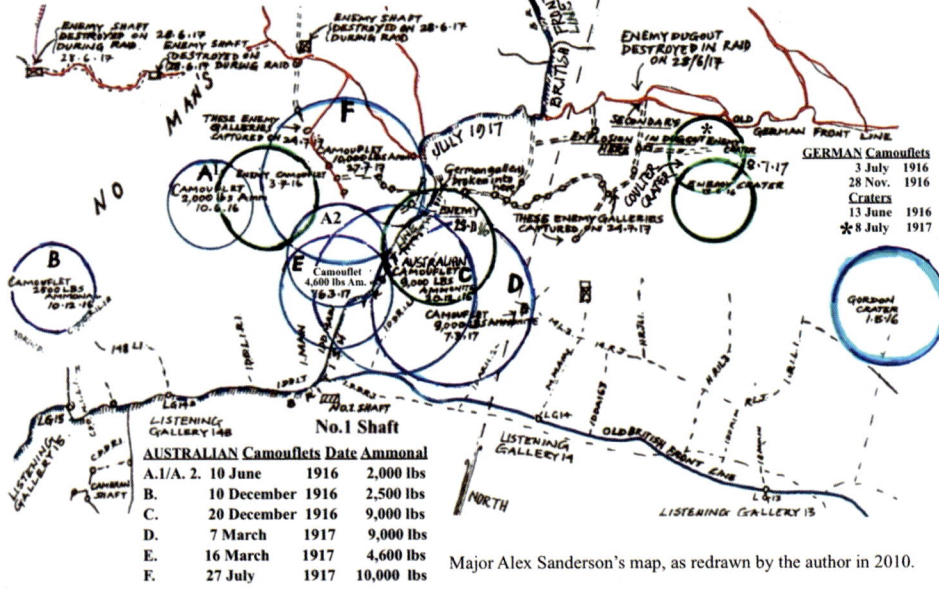

Major Alex Sanderson's map, as redrawn by the author in 2010.

Coulter Crater (* as above) blown by enemy on 8 July 1917.

HMAT "RUNIC".
Outer Harbour,
South Australia,
4-2-20.

Miss. Brown,
Ladies School,
Medindie NEAR ADELAIDE, S.A.

Dear Miss Brown,

I am sending to you, through the kindness of the Y.M.C.A., at this Port, a small present for you and the Pupils of your School from the Officers and men of the 3rd., Australian Tunnelling Company, for whose comfort while at the Front, you and your Pupils did so much. The present is a Gas Alarm Bell found at the entrance to a German Headquarter Dug-out at the time of the capture of Hill 70 near Loos, where our men did so much fighting. I hope it may be possible to make it suitable for use as a School Bell, in remembrance of the kindness and generosity of your pupils in helping to maintain our efficiency at the Front and so to beat the enemy.

Will you please convey to your pupils my thanks and best wishes and accept same yourself.

I hope you have had the pleasure of welcoming home your Brother, Captain H.W.Brown, ere now. Will you please give him my kindest regards.

Yours Sincerely,

Alex Sanderson

MAJOR.

C.O., 3rd., Australian Tunnelling Company.

Above: A letter written aboard the *Runic* by Major Alex Sanderson Officer Commanding the troopship, sailing from Liverpool back to West Australia.
Captain Harry Brown, an officer in 3 A.T.C., was the brother of Miss Margaret H. Brown, the headmistress who had established 'The Wilderness' School in 1884. A member of The Australian Institute of Mining Engineers, Harry had worked for five years in the Adelaide locomotive workshops. In September 1915 he had attended the Engineer Officers' Training School in Sydney.

On left: Photo of the German First World War Gas Bell now hanging outside the Wilderness School, Adelaide, S.A. (Photo J.Danvers)

Centre: *Schützenstand im Graben vor der Lorettohöhe* Gas Alarm/Firing Post in a frontline trench at Colline de Lorette. Watercolour painting by Max G. H. Gehlsen (born 1881). Max trained at Art School in Hamburg. A soldier in France since 1914, Gehlsen served along the Western Front. (Courtesy of Archives départementales du Pas-de-Calais.)

'Suddenly at 10.55pm on March 2 1918, when the Germans launched their fierce attack against our Fifth Army, there was a burst of artillery fire, and over our heads, our gas-cylinders sped forth. The German lines were lit with bursting shells. Up went their artillery's rockets calling for retaliation. I could hear their gas bells ringing to warn their men of the poison that was being poured upon them. It must have been a drenching rain of death.
(Scott Canon, F. *The Great War As I saw It*. Chapter 26 p. 241)

The German Gas Bell was brought back from a raid in April 1918. A 3 A.T.C. report to Major Alex Sanderson read:
'Four patrols went out during the night. One entered the enemy's front line and descended a shaft which split into two, 15 feet down. Two notice boards were brought back reading: *Galerie nach Adler* (Passage to Eagle) and *Galerie nach Gans* (Passage to Goose) ~ *Wasser* (Water). There are wooden steps, some broken. On the floor of the main shaft run a pair of wooden boards (probably rails) on which trucks have been used. The shaft appeared to be old work and not greatly used. A Gas Bell was brought back from the entrance to the shaft. As the enemy were advancing in force, the patrol withdrew, covered by a Lewis Gun which fired on the enemy: several were seen to fall. Enemy casualties are estimated as ten at least. Our patrols reached our lines, with no casualties. Bombs were thrown and shouting heard.'

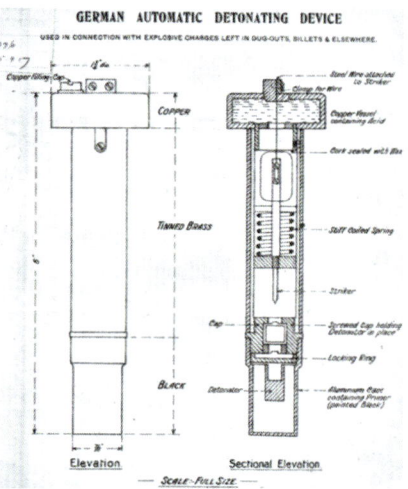

Left: First World War Magazine. 'Boche Booby-Traps.'
Above: German automatic (acid and wire activated) explosive detonator device. Hidden in dugouts etc.
Below: Original drawing of Road 'Tread' Mine.
(Major A. Sanderson's 3 A.T.C. Archives)

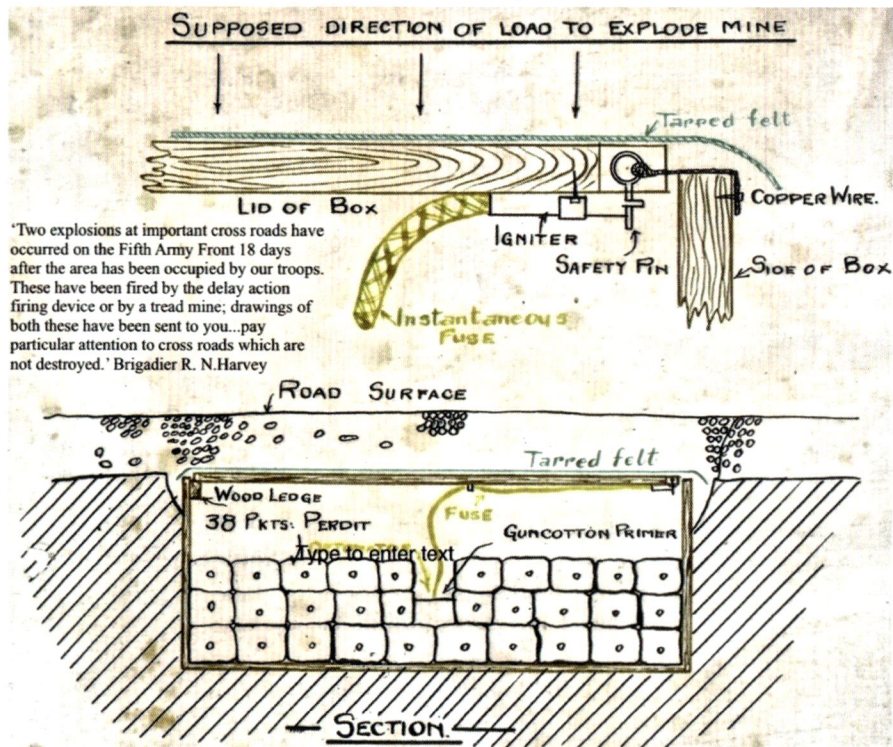

'Two explosions at important cross roads have occurred on the Fifth Army Front 18 days after the area has been occupied by our troops. These have been fired by the delay action firing device or by a tread mine; drawings of both these have been sent to you...pay particular attention to cross roads which are not destroyed.' Brigadier R. N. Harvey

'Among the surprises we'd prepared for our successors were truly malicious inventions. In some places, narrow ditches were dug across roads, and shells hidden in them: they were covered over by an oak plank, and had earth strewn over them. A nail had been driven into a plank, only just above the shell-fuse. The space was measured so that marching troops could pass over the spot safely, but the moment the first lorry or field gun rumbled up, the board would give, and the nail would touch off the shell.' Ernst Jünger. *Storm of Steel.* 1921.

Beginning and End: Lieutenant (later Major) Leslie J. Coulter with his company in 1916. 'Leaving the front line' from Christmas 1918.

Above: 3rd Coy. Miners Battalion at Casula Training Camp, Sydney.

(Photo courtesy of: Goldfields War Museum)

Left: Lt. Coulter is centre foreground Right: 3rd Aust. Tunnelling Coy's 1919 calendar. The image was drawn by Sapper George Adam McQueen.

(Source Sanderson Archives)

Coloured Photograph of Major Alex Sanderson, 1919

His medal ribbons:
Distinguished Service Order,
Military Cross with bar,
British War Medal,
Victory Medal with Mentioned in Dispatches Oak Leaves signed by Winston Churchill (see below).
Two wound stripes on sleeve.

The War of 1914–1918.

Maj. A. Sanderson, M.C., 3 Tun. Coy., A.I.F.

was mentioned in a Despatch from
Field-Marshal Sir Douglas Haig, K.T., G.C.B., G.C.V.O., K.C.I.E.
dated the 8th November 1918
for gallant and distinguished services in the Field.
I have it in command from the King to record His Majesty's high appreciation of the services rendered.

Winston Churchill
Secretary of State for War

'Lion's Head' painted in 1900 by Alex Sanderson, aged 19, in Perth, W.A.
Right: Portrait taken in London in 1919. Note two wound stripes on left sleeve, after Fromelles on 19 July 1916 and the Trench Raid of 28 June 1917.

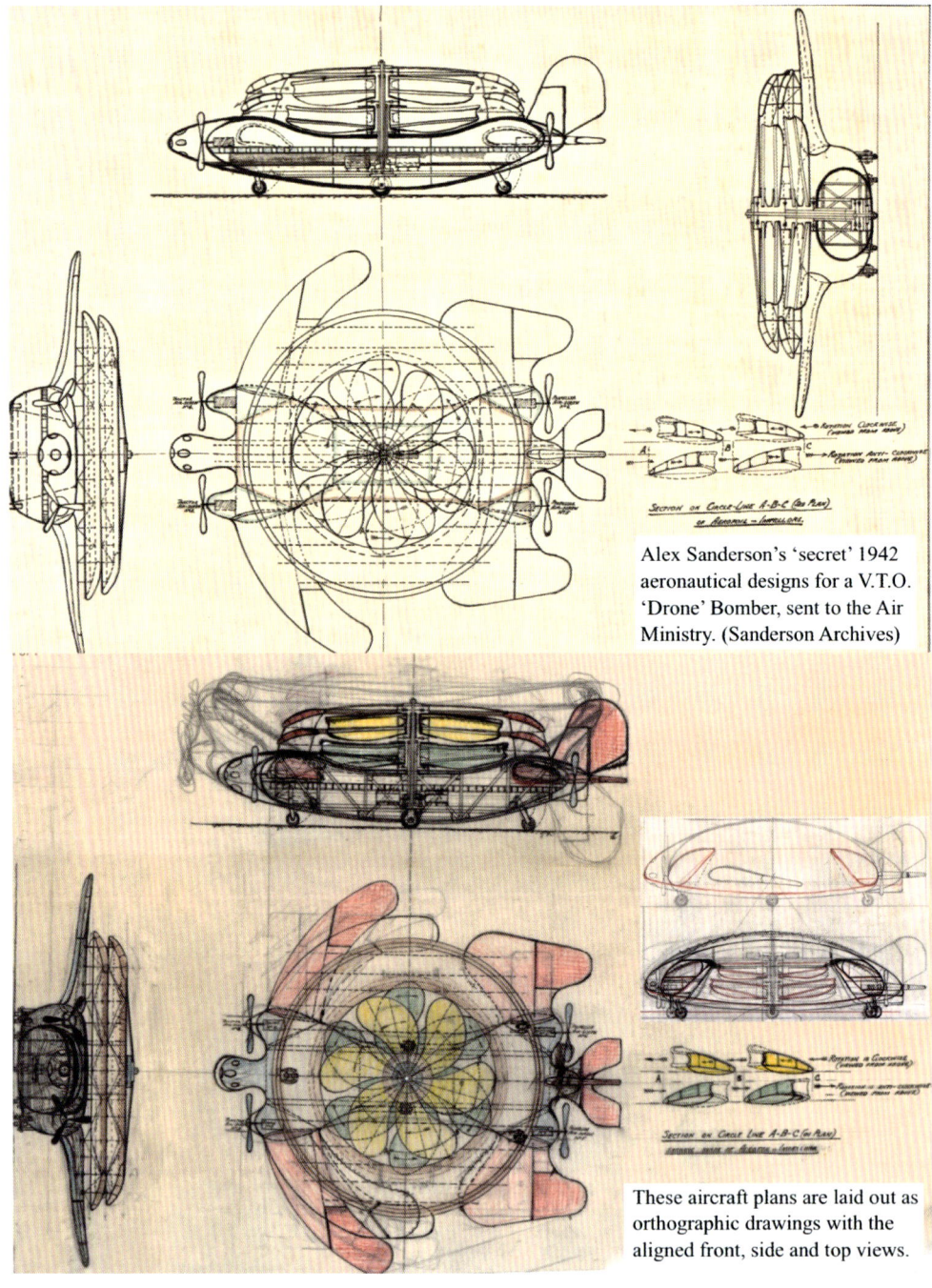

Alex Sanderson's 'secret' 1942 aeronautical designs for a V.T.O. 'Drone' Bomber, sent to the Air Ministry. (Sanderson Archives)

These aircraft plans are laid out as orthographic drawings with the aligned front, side and top views.

Alex Sanderson's 19 October 1942 'secret' designs for Tilt-Engine Bombers, as sent to the Air Ministry, together with detailed written explanations of their aeronautical properties. Tilt-engines are fitted to Bell Boeing's V-22 Osprey VTOL aircraft. Original plans for these revolutionary aeroplanes are kept in London's Science Museum Archives.

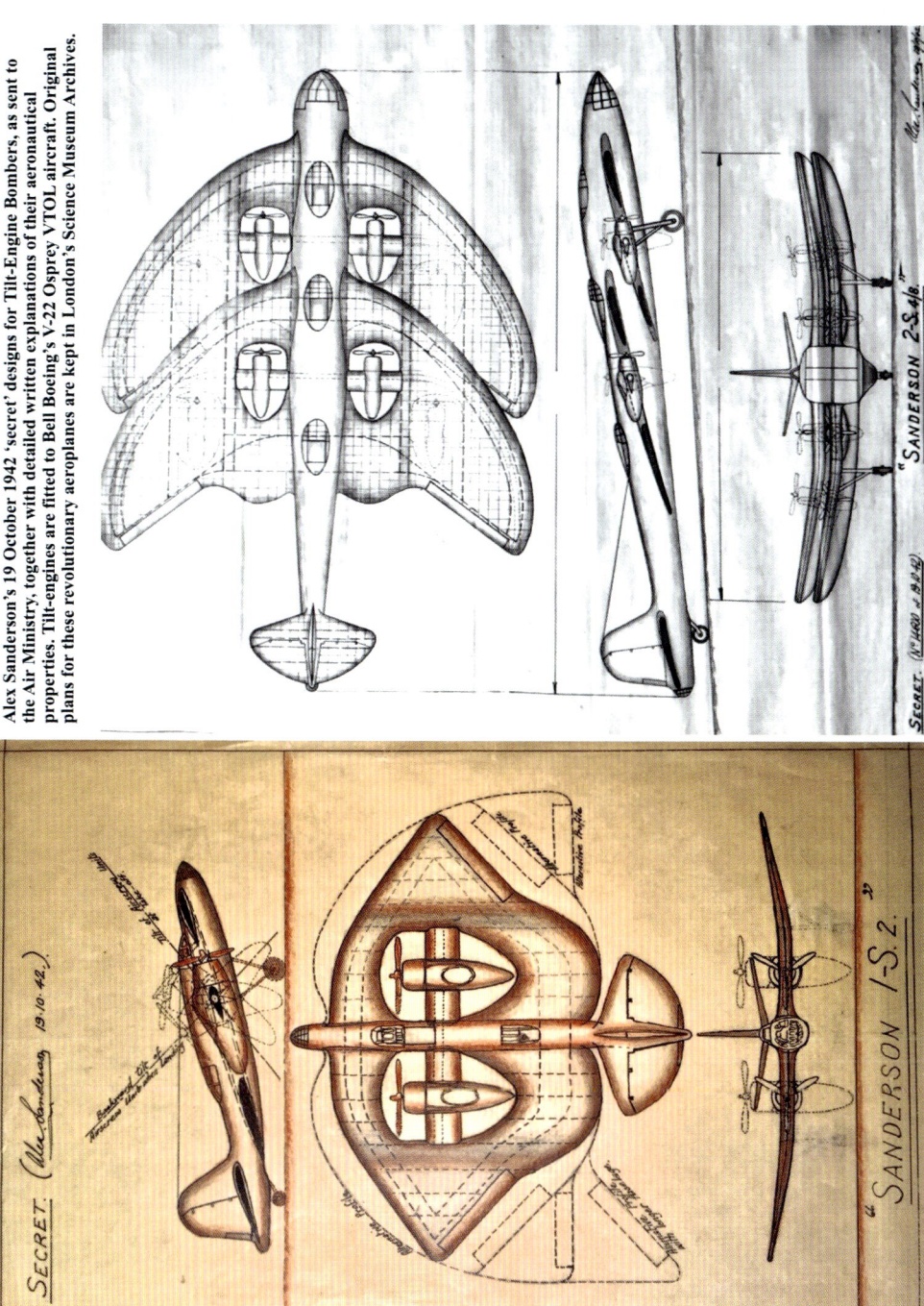

3rd Australian Tunnelling Company's fallen in the Commonwealth Engineers' Roll of Honour, a memorial book placed in Kitchener's Chapel, St Paul's Cathedral. The book's cover reads:
This Casket and Roll is Dedicated to Commemorate the Heroic Dead of the Australian Engineers who Enlisted in the A.I.F. and made the Supreme Sacrifice in the Great War A.D. 1914-1919.
(Author's photos: Courtesy of the Chapter of the Cathedral)

Map 14: Alex Sanderson's proposal for a Defence Scheme for Hulluch, St Elie and Hairpin Infantry Subway, as sent to the First Controller of Mines 23 January 1918

In order to defend all exits forward of the Reserve Line. (Infantry posts will defend those exits forward of the subways).
- Solidly tamp exits not required for ventilation etc.
- Construct bomb pits, traverses and blocks with loopholes, in all inclines, keeping these exits open.
- Install electric alarm bells in all Infantry Company and Tunnellers' Headquarters so that sentries can give immediate alarm if enemy attack.

COUNTER ATTACK. Scheme of counter attack to clear the long, straight tunnels if enemy occupy the subways:
- Use of three double-ended armoured trucks, with hinged plates opening inwards, loopholed each end and carrying a fixed machine gun, one each in the Hulluch, St Ellie and Hairpin system.
- Short lengths of straight tunnel to be captured by counter attacking party in rushes, bend by bend.
- Two O.R.'s to push each truck manned by two machine gunners, supplied with ammunitions and bombs.

At each bend loopholed traverses might be constructed thus:

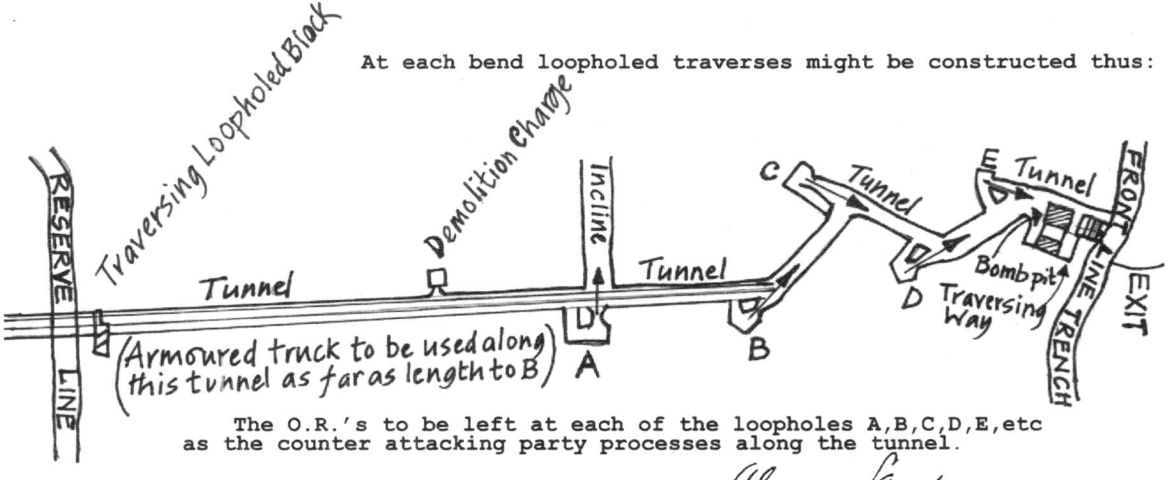

The O.R.'s to be left at each of the loopholes A,B,C,D,E, etc as the counter attacking party processes along the tunnel.

Alex. Sanderson

Source: 3/ATC War Diary January 1918 Apdx 50 (AWM 16/4/23)

(b) **Electric Alarm Cells.** To be installed in all Headquarters, with leads connecting to switches at the exits, so that an immediate alarm could be given by the sentries in case of Gas or other enemy attack. Code to be posted at each exit and near each alarm bell.

(c) **Defence of Tunnels.** Loopholes to be constructed at each end of junctions in the tunnel and a bomb-proofed sliding loop-holed door under the Reserve Line.

(d) **Garrison Dispositions.** Sentries with Lewis guns to be posted at each exit. In case of alarm all loopholes should also be immediately manned. A garrison dugout at each post to be built off the tunnel near the foot of each exit. Garrison troops to be attached to definite posts and duties such as occasional practice alarms.

(e) **Defence against Gas.** Double Gas doors, fixed in galleries leading to each exit, on alarm signal to be closed immediately. A 24 inch Sirocco type ventilating fan, driven by petrol engine, should be installed near the western end to each tunnel system so that a draught of air could be forced through the system in case of the 'Gravel Pit', or forward exits being shelled by projected gas bombs.

(f) **Defence against Fire.** Mine Rescue Station in tunnels, and men on duty, will render assistance in rescuing men and extinguishing fire. Fire precaution orders to be posted in tunnels.

(g) **Defence of Communications.** Signal and telephone wires to be carried through 1 inch diameter iron pipes buried twelve inches below the tunnel floors. Telephones in forward parts of the subway systems to be well concealed.

(h) **Lighting.** Two direct coupled 220 volt 20 Kilowatt Lighting Sets to be installed in engine room near entrance to the Hythe tunnel, with leads to tunnels, dugouts etc and lamps.

I am very strongly against the practice of laying charges in tunnels for defensive purposes. They should only be laid for demolition in the case of a voluntary retirement, when it would be advisable to do as much damage as possible to hamper the enemy. Provided that the traverses, loopholes etc., suggested above are constructed and that the surface at the rear end of the tunnel is held by our troops, there should be no difficulty in keeping the enemy out of every part of our subway system.[8]

The fortress of Hythe Tunnel, championed and conceived by Alex Sanderson at the end of 1917, and surveyed so well by Lieutenant Russel, was never tested.

Had the Germans succeeded in their *Mars* offensive, however, Lens and Loos would have been the next German objective.

Sapper Leaver's diary recorded: 21/2. A fairly lively time here this last five days. The Australians went over on Sunday night, just to the north of here and there has been heavy firing every night since. Last night it was one continual stream of fire for about four hours and the air is alive with aeroplanes all day today.'[9]

Major Sanderson was awarded his 3rd Blue Chevron for three years' active service abroad. He had left Fremantle aboard H.M.A.S. *Ulysses* on 2 February 1916.

Charles Bean's notebook of 23 February records:

Today has been one of the most interesting mornings that I have ever had on the front. I have described it in a separate note on my visit to the 3rd Australian Tunnellers and their wonderful diggings at Hulluch. A Canadian Divisional Major General A.C. MacDonnell, commanding the First Canadian Division, came with us, or rather, I was taken round with him by [Major] Sanderson who told me that the information which they had about the Germans was that they were piling up troops behind Lens and Cambrai. The troops were too far away for it to be possible to say where they were going to be used, but it was said they were being trained in open warfare, which looked as if the Germans were meditating an attempt to break through; but there was nothing to indicate where.[10]

Archibald MacDonnell's family origins, of which he was very proud, were in Glengarry in West Scotland. Major Sanderson's ancestors were of the same MacDonnell clan, descended from Norwegian settlers. (It is traditional for the Sanderson family, including the author, to be given the forename of 'Lauchlan', which is of Norwegian origin.)

On 2 September, MacDonnell would be personally congratulated by Haig for his troops' successful assault of the heavily defended Drocourt - Quéant position.

CB/AS: *Between 17 and 23 February 1918 two Sections of 3 A.T.C. cut out 544 feet of chalk, tunnelling four feet wide, and averaging 500 feet per week for the past four weeks. To the north of Lens, near Hulluch, where I went through the workings with Sanderson, the whole defence of the front appears to be underground. The infantry garrison lives underground, trench mortars and their crews and their embrasures are underground. The machine guns are underground. The men's living* *rooms are underground, and for a mile behind the front line the communication trenches are all 35 feet underground. The light railway brings the stores to an underground dump* [which are then] *distributed in lighter tramways right up to the trench mortar. The entrances to the tunnels from the trenches are defended, so that on the last occasion when the Germans raided, the sentry who was outnumbered on the top, carried his Lewis gun into a shaft and fired up the shaft at the first two Germans whom he saw. These men were about to place an explosive charge inside the shaft, but they were hit and lost their charge, and the other raiders cleared back to their own trenches. Two raids on these trenches have been defeated. No 3 Tunnelling Company originally contained a number of the Revolutionary Unionists of the Broken Hill type from Western Australia and Queensland. They showed their spirit from the first, and in the early days of the Company, there were a good number of strong battles of wills between the officers and men. But before the company had been long established, these fiery trade unionists were amongst the very finest soldiers, and the most willing, energetic, hardened workers that the Company possessed. There was a spirit among them which was of great value. Sanderson tells me that he wished the men whom he was getting nowadays were of these same old fiery soldiers.*[11]

March 1918

On 3 March peace was signed between the Central Powers and the Bolsheviks in Russia. One million Germans would soon transfer to the Western Front.

Charles Bean had recorded in his notebook for February 1918 that: 'The 3rd Australian Tunnelling Coy. at Loos also told [Captain] Wilkins that an attack with tanks is expected there. Wilkins tells me that our airmen have found 1,000 German tanks concentrated there – they can't say exactly what the tanks are like but they are there. It is said the Germans are after the Loos coalfields'.[12]

Captain George H. Wilkins M.C. and bar, the official war photographer who accompanied Bean on the Western Front, was later knighted for leading Arctic and Antarctic expeditions. Wilkins' ashes would be scattered at the North Pole by the nuclear submarine *Skate*.[13]

Anti-tank craters

In fact, Wilkins, or the R.F.C. intelligence, were wrong: the Germans possessed only a handful of tanks, relying on the 170 tanks they had captured from the allies. Their Imperial Army had recognised too late the effectiveness of battlefield tanks: their first, the A7V, had been produced only six months before. Just a fifth of the 100 ordered were produced by the end of the war. These cumbersome, heavy machines were armed with a Russian 57-mm gun and six Spandau machine guns. They required a crew of eighteen, had a limited range of 16 miles and were unable to cross trenches. The A7V's engines were operated by the Pioneers, while artillery men manned the heavy gun and infantrymen fired the six machine-guns. The La Rutoire Plain anti-tank craters described below blown by the Australian sappers in March would have proved an insurmountable barrier.[14, 15, 16]

Tank trials had been held at Bermicourt on 10 February to test craters as obstacles (see plates). Those attending included the Commander of 1 Corps, three tunnelling O.C.s and Charles E.W. Bean. It was here that Bean would have arranged with Alex Sanderson to meet for their subsequent interview at Noeux-les-Mines on 23 February.

The experience gained from the tank trials informed 3 A.T.C.'s planning of lines of craters blown on the La Rutoire plain, a flat area without the natural obstacles of rivers, woods or ridges. On 9 March, Alex Sanderson directed Captain Hillman of No.4 Section to produce two lines of craters behind the support line. (Hillman would have known Sanderson before the war as he had been a railway engineer for the W.A. Government.) 50 lbs charges were placed in sandbags and sixty bales of camouflage were used to camouflage every fifth hole. Spacings of 28 feet were marked out on 140-foot lengths of tape. Fifty feet behind the British support line, two parallel lines of anti-tank holes were bored between Posen and Hay Alley communication trenches. In one week, these were all were exploded, in spite of the technical difficulties and the rain. By 19 March all 320 craters (20–26 feet across and 7–9 feet deep) had been laid out over a distance of 1,500 yards. The tank obstacles were never needed and post-war they were all ploughed back level by the farmers.[17]

Explosive charges laid in tunnels

Sergeant Forsyth and four sappers had run 'Mine Charge Leads' from the locked chambers (at the ends of charge cables buried in the Hulluch, St Elie and St Georges tunnels) along to the Mine Rescue Station.

On 10 March a secret memo from a Canadian officer to Major Sanderson instructed:

Should certain circumstances require it, the Hulluch Tunnel will be demolished. About 100 yards east of the reserve shaft, a demolition charge has been placed, connected up with an exploder in the Fan Chamber near the Oval [intersection of Hulluch and St Elie Tunnels]. In case of enemy attack, the O.C. Tunnelling Coy. will send a picquet of one N.C.O. and ten men to man the loopholed block set in the side of the tunnel between the charge and the exploder. Picquets will be available to counter-attack if the enemy penetrate the forward parts of the tunnel. (The traverses should have a passage round them to avoid anyone being cut off by the door being shut too soon.)[18]

Chapter 16

The *Kaiserschlacht*

21 March 1918

The expected German offensive, *Michael*, suddenly erupted at 04:40 on 21 March in the low-lying thick fog, as German guns pounded the Fifth Army's front-line on the Somme with a 'shock and awe' bombardment, planned by the artillery expert Colonel Bruchmüller. It stunned the defenders and overwhelmed resistance, suppressing their ability to fight.[1] A million shells were fired in the first five hours: a barrage of high explosives, blistering mustard gas (burning skin and the respiratory system), tear-gas, chlorine, phosgene (attacking the lungs) shells and the irritant lachrymatory, which induced many defenders to remove their gas masks.[2] The biggest breaches of front-line trenches for over three years, by a series of coordinated attacks, would end the stalemate on the Western Front and finally bring the war to an end in 1918. The breakthrough that the Allies had so dearly attempted was now achieved by the German Army on several fronts, as resistance collapsed.

With troops returned from the Eastern Front and the Dolomites, before American troops could arrive and be deployed in significant numbers, Hindenburg and Ludendorff were making a final throw-of-the-dice attempt to break through allied lines and bring a peace on their own terms, before the gathering unrest in Germany forced their hand. In 1917 the Reichstag had passed a July resolution calling for peace with the Allies. The U-boat campaign to cut the jugular vein of allied merchant shipping supplies had come close to severing Britain's crucial Atlantic link but had failed, mainly through the Royal Navy's 'shepherding' convoy system. Anti-war protests were increasing at home, in spite of the iron hand of a domestic military dictatorship. The German High Command's vain hope was that, if the offensive in the west went well, Germany could retain Alsace, Lorraine and Belgium and preserve her armies and her navy, in a more favourably negotiated peace agreement.[3]

Crown Prince Rupprecht understood that the planned offensives to advance through the allied front would be fraught with difficulties. Rupprecht had been sceptical of Ludendorff's optimistic attack ambitions but was sidelined. Ludendorff considered, wrongly, that improvised strategy, on the hoof, would follow on from tactical successes. By 23 March he would decide that Amiens, the vital railway hub of the Allies, was his objective. Ludendorff would be denied this prize by the stoic defence of English and Australian forces.

The Allies had known that the Germans would strike, but not where the blow would fall. Hindenburg and Ludendorff had chosen to attack a weak 12-mile sector of the Fifth Army with incomplete and shallow defensive trench systems, occupied after the German retreat to the Hindenburg Line in 1917. The Somme Front the Germans now attacked was the weakest sector of the Western Front, but its landscape, devastated by the Somme battles, would hold up advancing forces. Strategically, it lacked the closer objectives to be found further north: the coalfields, stores and coastal ports.[4]

Ludendorff judged the Lens / Hill 70 area above Arras, where the First Army and Major Alex Sanderson's tunnellers had expected a mass tank attack, to be too well defended. The sector from Arras to the La Bassée Canal, previously the location for the British Army's 1915 attempt to break through, would lie in 'eye of the storm'. It would be the only part of the Allies' front line, along the whole Western Front from Rheims and the Marne in the south to beyond Ypres in the Belgian north, that would remain unchanged.

At 09:40 on 21 March, the German *Stoßtruppen* Stormtrooper infantry, moved forward in groups of seven to ten men, the spearhead of the main force, trained to penetrate rapidly, leaving following troops to mop up enemy isolated positions. They wore steel helmets and were armed with rifles, *stielhandgranate* (stick grenades), *Wex* portable one-man flamethrowers and equipped with special torpedoes to destroy enemy barbed wiring. The five divisions of the British V Corps (Third Army) and VII Corps (Fifth Army) in the Cambrai salient and the other 21 British divisions faced seventy-six German divisions equipped with 6,608 guns and 3,354 *Minenwerfer*. In the air, 1,070 *Schlachtstaffeln* (Battle Squadrons) aircraft outnumbered the 579 of the R.F.C. (renamed the R.A.F. in April 1918).

Within the first hour almost all British positions on the Fifth Army's forward zone were overrun, as the Germans broke through in a war of rapid movement into open countryside, after years of static, entrenched warfare. Winston Churchill was visiting a front-line headquarters when the offensive began and just managed to get away. One surrounded division fought for two days before being overrun. On this first day German artillery fired 3.2 million shells. The stronger British main 'Red' battle zone held on until noon, but was taken in the afternoon. British regiments put up heroic resistance, fighting to the last man: on Manchester Hill, a lieutenant colonel refused to surrender and was shot dead, later being awarded the Victoria Cross. By nightfall the Germans had advanced 4.5 miles on a 40-mile front. The British had suffered their first breakthrough and defeat in over three years, with losses of 7,000 killed and 21,000 taken prisoner. German losses were 10,000 killed and 29,000 wounded.[5,6,7,8]

Canon Scott at Loos:

> On the 21st March, before I had gone to the Chalk-Pit on Hill 70, I heard from a staff officer at Corps H.Q. of the German attack in the South, and that things were not going well. The Americans would not be ready for some time, and the question was how to stay the onrush of the fresh divisions which the Germans were hurling against us. An order from General Currie, couched in beautiful language, told us that there was to be no retreat for Canadians, and that, if need be, we should fall where we stood. There was no panic, only firmer resolve and activity in every department. Our Division was to be sent south to try to stem the oncoming tide.[9]

Sapper Leaver recorded:

> 21/3. We have had it lively as he has been sending gas over every day. But late this morning he sent it over and it reached our billets. Those that had to go up through Armentières had it pretty rough, as he had gassed it pretty bad and started a big fire there. They had to wear their gas bags on and all around was saturated. He has been putting it over here all day and is still going strong.

> 25/3. We have had a bit of a rough time this last few days as the gas has been coming over all the time where we are working. Nearly every day we go through it. Seven went to hospital yesterday and three today and I think there will be some more in the morning. The big push has started and from all that we hear Old Fritz is not getting it all his own way. But it must be hell where the battle is, as the latest reports is a quarter of a million casualties and we are still holding him.[10]

The crucial week

From 24 to 26 March the *Michael* offensive threatened to separate the French and the British armies, who were gradually being pushed back northwest towards the French ports.

On 25 March the Germans pushed through between the French and British armies, taking Bapaume, Noyon and re-capturing all the ground seized by the British in the 1916 Somme offensive. Amiens was now threatened and a makeshift force of 3,000 men, including U.S. engineers, was moved in to reinforce the line.

On 26 March Marshall Foch took overall command of the allied forces and the tide was turning. After a week the Fifth Army, whose leaders were initially panicked and wrong-footed by the sudden *Michael* attack, began to fight back strongly, reinforced by allied troops. German morale was lowered by the outnumbered British forces' strong esprit de corps, by their stubborn refusal to yield and their readiness to counter-attack.[11]

On 28 March General Gough was made a scapegoat and dismissed from his command for his weak defensive tactics. He was replaced by General Rawlinson, with the Fifth Army being re-named the Fourth.[12] The same day, at Arras, south of Loos, Ludendorff launched 'Operation *Mars*' to try to widen the breach achieved further south. But, crucially, General Byng's Canadian Third Army held their positions on their strongly defended position on Vimy Ridge. After the Germans suffered heavy casualties, 'Mars' was cancelled. On 30 March, with the German infantry only 11 miles from Amiens, a makeshift combined force of British, Australian and Canadian troops counter-attacked and, crucially, managed to hold back the tide. The Germans had suffered 239,800 killed and wounded, almost equal to the British and French losses of 254,739 combined.[13] The enemy's ninety divisions had lost momentum and were left depleted, demoralised and worn out.[14]

Journalist visits Hulluch tunnel defences

The tunnel system of Hulluch – St Elie-Hairpin had been visited by the War Correspondent Captain Phillip Gibbs on 6 March. Gibbs described his experiences in an article entitled: 'Australian Tunnellers: Pale Faces but Great Hearts'.

> I went into a world the other day where no shells bursting high or low, can have any effect upon our men who live there. No German barrage can 'put the wind up', because in this world there is no wind. Visibility may be good or bad, but the enemy has no observation here, though he is on top all the time. I went into No Man's Land beyond our lines, and was as safe as in the Strand at home, though only a few yards away from the enemy's outposts. For this world was deep underground. It is a place of long galleries, 60 feet below the outside earth, in which I walked for hours and hours and did not come to the end of them. My guide, who knows these tunnels blindfold, pointed to the entrance of another gallery

and said: 'That leads to another part of the front, and would take another day to explore.'

My guide is one of the officers of the Australian Tunnelling Company, which during the past two years, has done a great part of the work in boring this subterranean system below some section of our battle line. They are mostly miners from the gold fields of Western Australia: hard, tough fellows with a special code of their own as regards their ways of discipline and work, but experts at their job, and with all their pride in it, and a courage which would frighten the devils of hell if they happened to meet them in the dark. When they first came over with their plant, the Germans were mining actively under our lines and blowing up our infantry in the trenches. It was the worst terror of war, before poison gas came, and I used to pity our poor officers and men who knew, and hated to know, that the enemy was sapping his way under them, and that, at any moment, they might be buried in a crater or hurled sky-high. The enemy were beaten out of the field by British, Australian, Canadian and New Zealand miners, who fought the Germans back underground from gallery to gallery, blowing them up again and again, whenever they drew near, and racing them for the possession of the leads, whenever they tried to regain part of their destroyed systems.

But the Australian tunnellers drove in at three times his speed of working, blew in the ends of one of his galleries and then broke through his timber into the tunnel. The Australian tunnellers dashed them with rifles and revolvers. The enemy had escaped, but their system was destroyed, before they could set off their mines. The Germans know now that they are beaten underground. It is an honour of which this Australian Company is proud that, apart from their own casualties, not a single infantry soldier of ours has lost his life by hostile mining.

In each side of the galleries were rooms carved out of the chalk. They were furnished with wooden tables and benches, and the miners were playing cards. Through holes in the chalk walls I looked into caverns where men lay asleep in bunks… In a big vault was a power-house with three electric engines, providing the light of the galleries. Not far away was… a kitchen with big stoves and ovens, where meals were being cooked by sweltering men, within a few yards of the front-line trenches. In a little while, a big electric fan will blow a draught through the kitchen and take away the heat. In other rooms were field dressing stations, and we came to a subway with trolley lines, down which the wounded are brought from the battlefield up above. The roofs of the tunnels were richly coloured with a reddish fungus which hangs down like stalactites.

We went deeper down and further forward. In one room men were listening to the sounds of German life in other tunnels like these, the sounds of men walking and talking and filling sandbags and moving timber. The listeners are so expert that they can tell by the nature of the sounds exactly what the enemy is doing through a chalk wall 70 feet thick.

Presently we went into a fighting point driven out beyond the lateral galleries and my guide said, 'Here we will be quiet, because we don't want the enemy to get suspicious. We are now out in No Man's Land.' The war seemed a world away. The Australian tunnellers live below ground for most of their life. Some of them have the pale look of men who have been out of the light. In their spare times down below, they play cards and yarn of old days in the goldfields, and carve faces in the chalk. One man had carved the face of Shakespeare: 'Old Bill' he called him. These men, by their toil and courage with picks and explosives and listening instruments, have saved the lives of many hundreds of British soldiers, and long after the war is finished this underground world of ours will remain as a memorial of their splendid labour.

I had seen the working of the tunnellers up by Hill 70 and elsewhere. I had listened through a microphone, by which I heard the scuffle of German feet in German galleries a thousand yards away, the dropping of a pick or shovel, the knocking out of German pipes against charcoal stoves. It was by that listening instrument, more perfect than the enemy's, that we had beaten him, and by the grim determination of those underground men of ours, whose skin was the colour of the chalk in which they worked, who coughed in the dampness of the caves, and who packed high explosives at the shaft-heads – hundreds of tons of it – for the moment when a button should be touched far away, and an electric current would pass down a wire, and the enemy and his works would be blown to dust.[15]

The German advance falters, April 1918

On 4 April the Germans' 1,200 guns bombarded Villers-Bretonneux and launched a renewed attack, throwing fifteen divisions against seven allied divisions. The British and German troops repulsed the attackers.

The Germans were within 5 miles of Amiens. They had advanced 20 miles on a 50-mile front but had been delayed in the cratered, impassably ruined landscape of the old Somme battlefield, having passed through the wasteland the Germans themselves had created in 1917 during 'Operation *Alberich*', the retreat to the Hindenburg Line. The German Second Army, now in the British 'rest areas', had been delayed and distracted by the discovery and looting of the well-stocked allied stores of food and alcohol, with whole divisions stopping to indulge. Their own meagre supply columns and artillery were overstretched logistically and left far behind their rapid advances. The realisation that they had been lied to, and that the Allies were generously supplied, further undermined German infantry morale. On 5 April, Ludendorff called off the *Michael* Somme offensive, abandoning the attack on Amiens: 'The enemy resistance was beyond our powers.'[16] German losses were 250,000 killed and wounded, these from the elite ranks of their best trained, strongest infantry whom Ludendorff could ill afford to lose. The surviving German divisions, worn out and dispirited, were denied the long-anticipated victory that would have made all their fighting, suffering and sacrifices worthwhile. Ludendorff's various offensives were Pyrrhic victories: like King Pyrrhus' foes the Romans in 279 B.C., the Allies in the First World War could draw on a greater and increasing supply of fresh reinforcements to replenish their depleted ranks.[17] The Ludendorff offensives had taken territory that was hard to defend and strategically irrelevant. The huge salient left the German armies precariously exposed to attack.

The Allies were now better equipped and materially prepared to counter-attack as the German offensives ran out of steam. The arrival of enormous numbers of American troops would soon swing the advantage the Allies' way. New techniques of infantry attacks, supported by rolling artillery barrages from overwhelming numbers of guns and shells (which were technically better able to destroy the German barbed wire), wore down the Germans and destroyed their morale. They realised that the war could not be won and they would soon seek early ways to negotiate an armistice.

Further German offensives

Ludendorff was determined to keep on the offensive, however, and three days after *Michael* was halted, he launched the first of four more offensives, *Georgette* or 'The Battle of the Lys' (British), from Givenchy north to the Ypres salient. Haig in G.H.Q. and the General Staff across the Channel, expected up to 7 April that the next blow would fall on the First Army Lens Sector, between the La Bassée Canal and Arras, where Alex Sanderson and 3 A.T.C. were based.

Chapter 17

The Battle of Lys

9 April 1918

At 04:15 on 9 April, Ludendorff's birthday, a ferocious 4.5-hour German bombardment of the *Georgette* offensive opened up in Flanders on a 10-mile front, gassing the allied batteries, as fourteen German infantry divisions advanced in dense fog. The Portuguese 2nd Division, attacked by four German divisions, was almost entirely annihilated, or fled, failing to blow the bridges. Ludendorff's objective was the coast 60 miles beyond. That day, the Germans advanced the furthest of any army to date since the trench lines became fixed on the Western Front. A pocket was advanced 5.5 miles on a 10-mile front.[1,2]

On the same day, Lieutenant General Sir Arthur Holland, O.C. 1 Corps, issued a Special Order of the day:

> The enemy, in his endeavour to seek an immediate decision by the destruction of the British Army, is extending his battle front. The 1 Corps will soon be engaged and I feel confident… will maintain the ground which has been committed to our keeping. I trust to the fearless leading of our junior officers, and to the devoted courage of the rank and file to hold their positions, even when surrounded, fully persuaded that surrender, so long as they are physically capable of using their arms, is a disgraceful act. Such high courage invariably brings Victory and the safety of our country, for which we are fighting.[3]

Captain Hillman of No.4 Section reported to Major Sanderson on 10 April: 'Yesterday on the Le Rutoire Plain, the outgoing and incoming reliefs were caught in a very heavy enemy bombardment. Sergeant Forsyth handled his reliefs very creditably.'

Leslie Forsyth and eight sappers were overcome by mustard gas and evacuated from Philosophe. Forsyth, a 29-year-old former blacksmith by trade from Tasmania, was promoted to sergeant to replace Sergeant Reid, who had been evacuated with a gunshot wound. Leslie had arrived with the first Mining Corps

Map 15: **Battle of Lys German advances 9-13 April 1918**

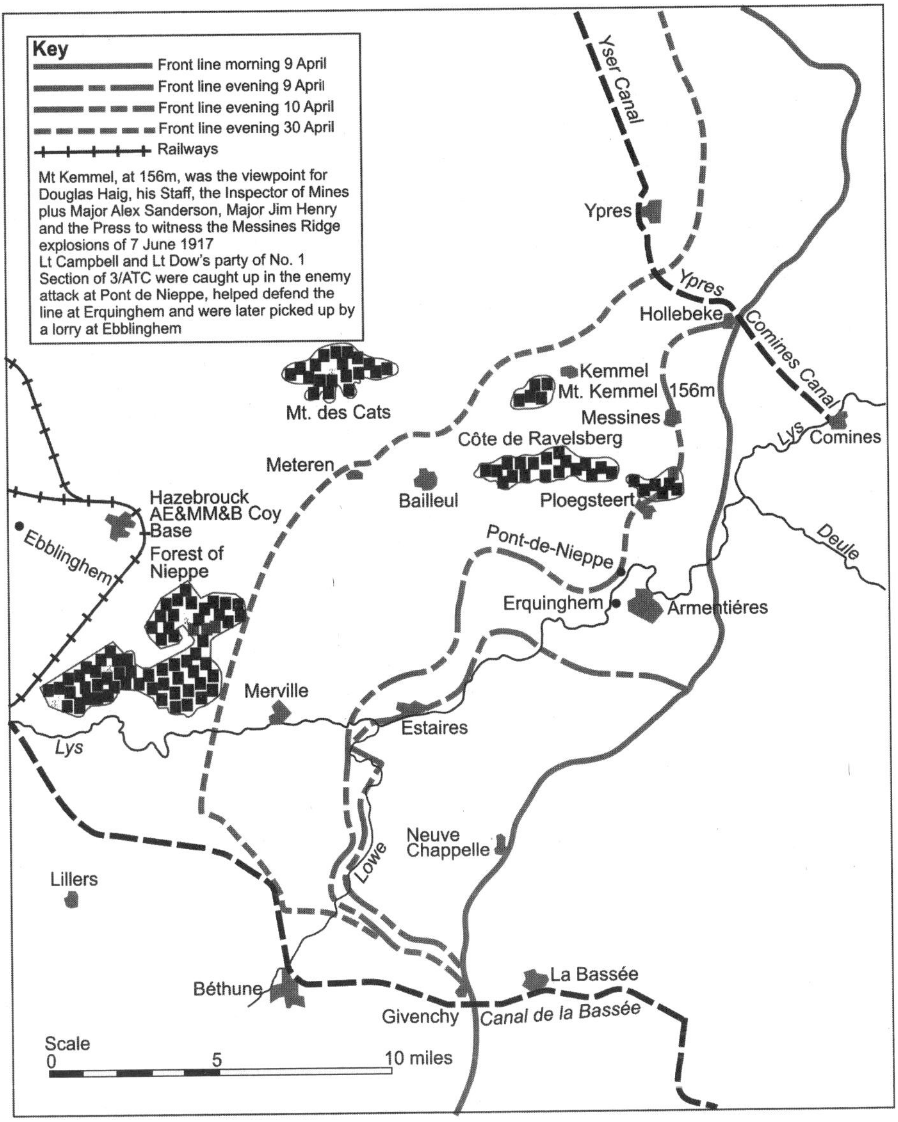

contingent and had seen consistent service with his company throughout 1916 and 1917.[4]

A detachment of 3 A.T.C., No.1 Section, were F.F.F. ('Forlorn, Famished and Far from home' in Australian vernacular)[5] and caught up in the German advance further north on the Lys. Among Lieutenant Campbell's party was Sapper Charles Leaver. On 9 April, Leaver noted in his diary at Nieppe: 'There was a rough time on the night of the 7th as Old Jerry started to put gas over at 8pm and kept it up till 10am. We went to work through it on the night with our gas helmets on. On the 9th Jerry started to advance and, after working all day, we had to "stand to" all night. After a walk of about four miles, Jerry was still coming in and we dug in at Erquinghem, just.'6

On 10 April most of Messines Ridge, where the 1st Australian Tunnelling Company had exploded their mine under Hill 60 nine months before, was re-taken by the Germans. The following day, Haig issued his famous order: 'With our backs to the wall and believing in the justice of our cause, each one of us must fight on to the end. There must be no retirement.'7 The historian A.J.P. Taylor noted: 'In England this sentence was ranked with Nelson's last message [England expects that every man will do his duty]. At the front, the prospect of staff officers fighting with their backs to the walls of their luxurious chateaux had less effect.'8

The Lys attack

A *Feuerwalze* bombardment, 2,000 tons of mustard gas, phosgene and diphenylchlorasine shells, fell on the British. By nightfall, the Germans had advanced 5.5 miles on a 10-mile front and crossed the Lys. On 10 April Armentières was abandoned[9] and on 12 April, the Passchendaele Ridge, so hard won in November 1917, was evacuated.

Lieutenant J. Dow later reported to Major Sanderson on his Section No.1's operations in the Battle of Lys from 9 to 18 April. The tunnellers were a party of three officers and thirty-eight O.R.s who acted as infantry to help defend Armentières from the south in much confused fighting.

Alarmed at their billets at Pont de Nieppe by a British battery firing directly rearwards over their heads, the tunnellers had reported to an infantry division. Then, following order and counter-order, they were marched miles backwards and forwards until, after dark, they reached their original defensive position. Early on 10 April the enemy was seen crossing their front from left to right, about 600 yards away. Their right flank was unprotected and they lengthened their line to try to close the gap, constantly under heavy enemy machine gun and rifle fire. As the enemy approached, the tunnellers opened fire at 400 yards. Then a battalion arrived on their flank: a scratch battalion of cooks, batmen and stragglers commanded by a Major Jackson, a South Australian serving in the British Army.

Sapper R. Ahearn would later state that at 19:30: 'Lieut. Campbell received a despatch. He read it and said: "This is not an order". Speaking to the men he said: "You hang on and I will go and see about it". Lieut. Campbell then left the trench for headquarters which were only a short distance away. Before he was more than 200 yards away I saw him turn around and wave for us to retire.'

He disappeared from view. A witness said that he had seen a shell burst and kill Campbell instantly. Lieutenant Dow reported later that: 'I got in a shell hole and heard one man say, "He's down", meaning Lieut. Campbell. [Then] "Oh no, he's up again."'

An English Tommy who knew him by sight later said that he had seen Lieutenant Campbell shot through the head. Asked if he had not confused him with another officer, the Tommy said that he knew Campbell, and that the officer he saw killed was wearing a patch across his eye. The 1919 Court of Inquiry on Campbell's disappearance heard from three fellow officers:

> 'He was a particularly brave man, regardless of danger. He would fight it out to a finish without any idea of surrender and would not be taken prisoner.'

> 'He had an absolute disregard of shell fire. I saw him rush out under sniper at Loos to drag (in) a wounded, sniped soldier.'

> 'He was a man absolutely devoid of fear.'[10]

During the retirement, Sapper Kelly was hit and fell, believed killed. The section then dug in and acted as a rearguard, under fire from very active machine guns and snipers. Sapper A. Hogan was sniped through the left breast. From 13–17 April the section were attached to the 1st Field Coy. of Australian Engineers, working on defences: spitlocking and digging trenches. Dow sent off a report to Major Sanderson stating their position, nominal roll and requesting orders. Under heavy shelling, they dug themselves in. At 20:00 orders were received from Major Sanderson to meet transport and to rejoin their unit. The marched to meet their lorry, picking up eight men at Ebblinghem and finally arriving back at H.Q. at dusk.[11]

On 19 April, four A7V and five captured British Mark IV tanks attacked St Quentin. On 20 April, south of Ypres, 2,000 tons of mustard gas, phosgene and diphenylchlorasine in 9 million rounds fell on the British, gassing more than 8,000.[12] However, as J. Keegan notes, by 10 April Ludendorff's three largest attacking armies had suffered casualties of one fifth: 303,450 men. *Georgette* alone had cost 120,000 men. A German Sixth Army report in mid-April advised that 'the troops will not attack, despite orders'.[13]

Hythe Tunnel

On 21 April Major Sanderson reported that fourteen days would be required to complete the Hythe Tunnel's proposed Battalion H.Q. with eighteen tunnellers, or ten days with forty tunnellers. On 23 April, Sanderson was advised of the defensive arrangements:

> In case of actual or impending attack, a counter-attack aeroplane from No.2 R.A.F. Squadron will go up as soon as possible after the start of hostile bombardment to watch for the moment the hostile infantry leave their trenches to attack. His machine will then fly to a position over the attacking infantry and fire smoke balls, followed by coloured lights. The machine will try to indicate the frontage of the attack by flying up and down the whole extent of the attack, repeating the green signal, indicating that the enemy has left his trenches. Recent experiences show that the enemy attacks with strong infantry columns after 4 to 5 hours' bombardment with Gas and H.E. shells.[14]

The Battle for Villers-Bretonneux

On 24 April, supported by thirteen A7Vs and repaired British tanks, in thick fog and facing allied troops with no anti-tank weapons, the Germans took Villers-Bretonneux, 10 miles east of Amiens, with a well-executed attack that was preceded by a murderous bombardment. Following German tanks enfiladed the British trenches. This was first tank-on-tank battle in history with thirteen German-driven tanks attacking thirteen British machines, seven of which were whippets. A determined resistance by one heavy British Mark 1 tank armed with a 6-pounder gun destroyed its adversaries and the rest retreated, closely followed by seven of the British tanks which then created deadly mayhem in the German infantry positions. On 25 April, after a twelve-hour march to the battlefield, Australian infantry retook Villers-Bretonneux in a tough night-time assault against German shock troops. Three British divisions were involved in this counter-offensive, at a cost of 9,500 casualties. The Villers-Bretonneux battle subsequently became a well-known 'Battle Honour' for the Australians, with a national memorial built on the site.[15,16,17]

On Anzac Day (25 April), a 2nd Australian Tunneller wrote that in a war-damaged village behind the lines, where defiant Australians were billeted, an Australian flag flew from a shattered window. Underneath, in charcoal on a whitewashed wall, were the words: 'Pessimists shot on sight!'[18]

On 26 April General Birdwood sent an equally stirring message to his troops from his Australian Corps Headquarters: 'Boys, the time has come when we must be prepared to "Take the strain"… I need hardly say more. Everyone fully realises what this means and I know that I can confidently appeal to every single individual in the A.I.F. to realise that it is up to him personally to "Take the strain" for the sake of his country and all he holds dear.'[19]

On the night of 29 April, after a final attempt by Ludendorff to push back the French and British with thirteen divisions was halted, he ended Operation *Georgette*. The German salients were vulnerable to counter-attack and once again they had over-extended their logistical supply lines. Ypres held, although Mount Kemmel was seized. The stiff allied resistance had slowed down the German advance. The Battle of Lys had further undermined the German morale and energy, causing heavy casualties: 86,000 were killed in the three-week offensive. The Allies also were weakened, having no idea where Ludendorff would strike next. The Germans, for the moment at least, still held the initiative.[20, 21]

May 1918

Alex Sanderson's brother, Captain William 'Lauch' Sanderson M.C., would later be recommended for the Military Cross on 24 September for his part in the defence of Villers-Bretonneux. This was later upgraded to an O.B.E.:

> For conspicuously good service and marked devotion to duty as Battery Captain, 42nd Battery, as Special Liaison Officer with the Moroccan and the 37th French Division Artillery during the strenuous and critical period at Villers Bretonneux in May 1918 and as Adjutant of the 11th Australian Artillery Brigade. His cheerful devotion to duty, consistent energy and personal resource, under very trying conditions from 25 February to 17 September, have proved of the greatest assistance and an example to all.

On 8 May Alex Sanderson sent a message to Captain Morris of No.3 Section:

> The 72nd Inf. Bde. reports that sounds have been heard in Conductor Trench which may be mining. It is unlikely that the enemy is mining in this vicinity. However, I would like the Infantry to be reassured on this point… It is important that they should receive a very definite assurance. Have you any geophones at your St Pierre Headquarters? I want you to arrange for occasional listening in the forward end of the Canteen Tunnel. A few minutes in each shift would be sufficient.[22]

Gas attacks at Loos-en-Gohelle

At Hill 70 the Allies were reciprocating with poison gas. From 22:00 on 20 May, the Canadian Special Gas Company R.E. used the Hythe Tunnel for four hours to launch gas attacks onto enemy lines. In the Vermelles area of Loos, very heavy H.E. and gas shell bombardments stopped all work for three hours and left nine sappers gassed. 'The enemy is reported to be mixing a percentage of High Explosive shells containing Triphosgene gas, with other H.E. shells not containing gas.'[23]

Blücher-Yorke offensive

On 27 May the *Blücher-Yorke* (3rd Battle of Aisne) offensive began with a *Feuerwalze* of 5,263 guns and 1,233 trench mortars firing 3 million rounds, half gas, on a 24-mile front. The Germans broke through at the Chemins des Dames, penetrating 12 miles and destroying four French divisions. Resting in a supposedly quiet area to recuperate after the *Georgette* offensive, four British divisions were abruptly thrown into heavy fighting. Between Soissons and Rheims, the attacking Germans succeeded in forcing their way through eight allied divisions, reaching the Aisne in six hours and taking Soissons on 29 May.[24, 25]

June 1918

Arguments had been put forward in 1917 by (among others) Charles Bean, the journalist Murdoch and 'Billy' Hughes the Australian P.M., that since the Australians had suffered at Fromelles and Bullecourt from the failure of British divisions on their flanks, the Australian divisions should no longer be interchangeable with British divisions but rather led by an Australian commander. Bean favoured General Sir C. White for this role: he did not see eye-to-eye with John Monash, writing in his diary that the man was 'bluff and humbug and insincerity'. Haig and Birdwood, however, favoured Monash, and on 1 June 1918 Monash was promoted to lieutenant general: an Australian (albeit of German origins) now in charge of the Australian Corps, the only volunteer army, with 166,000 infantry, five major generals and twenty-five brigadier generals under his command. Birdwood was put in charge of the Fifth Army.[26]

On June 1 the Germans were only 40 miles from Paris. The Americans, however, were on their way. The U.S. had previously agreed to put 170,000 troops into the front line in June and a further 140,000 in July. When the American 3rd Division arrived on the Marne, their engineers blew up a crucial bridge and halted the German advance. The A.E.F. (American Expeditionary Force) moved through Meaux to reinforce the defensive line. With panic spreading in Paris, the U.S. presence proved vital in restoring plummeting French morale. To French cries of 'La guerre est finie!' the Americans responded: 'We're here.'[27]

On 3 June the *Blücher-Yorke* offensive was called off. The Germans had carried out yet another brilliant tactical attack but, strategically, Ludendorff had failed. His demoralised, depleted and exhausted armies found themselves over-extended in another exposed salient.[28] To make matters worse, the first influenza epidemic, which would debilitate half a million undernourished German soldiers, was spreading.

Gneisenau offensive

On 9 June, Ludendorff ordered his fourth offensive, the *Gneisenau* on the River Matz. The French had been warned of the attack by signals intelligence and German deserters. After a horrendous bombardment of 15,000 tons of gas shells that incapacitated 4,000 French infantry, the Germans' eighteen divisions advanced 9 miles on a 23-mile front along the Matz River, in spite of strong allied resistance. Six of the eight German A7Vs were put out of action. The bridges over the Oise were blown up and the German advance was halted at Compiègne on the second day of the offensive by a well-executed night-time French counter-attack of four divisions, supported by two American divisions and 163 tanks. On 12 June *Gneisenau* was called off. The French had been forewarned of a further offensive called 'Hammer Blow' and it was checked on the first day.[29]

Explosive charges in tunnels

On 14 June the Chief Engineer of 18th Corps requested Alex Sanderson to: 'prepare a scheme for destroying the Hythe and Canteen Tunnels in the event of evacuation.'

Explosive charges had already been placed in the Hulluch, St Elie and St Georges tunnels with instructions for their use. Major Sanderson replied eight days later that:

> It would be impracticable to destroy the tunnels completely unless elaborate preparations were made, not without danger during our occupation. I would suggest three charges be placed in each tunnel and connected by electrical leads buried in the floors of the tunnels to points from which they could be fired, if necessary, in case of evacuation. In Hythe Tunnel three charges with the leads connected to a point in the old mine system at the rear of the tunnel. The firing of the charges would be from blocks in the tunnels. Any person in the tunnel at the time of firing would be killed. If the necessary cells can be obtained, the charges might be set to go off at a definite time up to 12 hours after evacuation.[30]

Chapter 18

The Allied Counter-Offensive

July 1918

Foch planned a succession of attacks, understanding the need to coordinate allied armies.¹ By the beginning of July, a million American military had arrived in France, although more would die of influenza than in combat. The spearhead of allied offensives were the 'shock armies'; the B.E.F., the C.E.F., (Canadian Expeditionary Corps) who had seized the Vimy Ridge in April 1917 in 200 minutes, the A.E.F. (American Expeditionary Force) and the A.I.F. (Australian Imperial Force) who took Le Hamel in 93 minutes. Monash devoted over four hours to briefing his commanders on battle tactics for Hamel, and on 4 July he put into operation his original new offensive tactics, devised by the B.E.F. since Messines to avoid the casualties of massed infantry assaults by combining the firepower of artillery, tanks, machine-guns and aircraft to neutralise enemy defences before the infantry moved in to finish the attack.²

General John Monash had been a civil engineer pre-war when he joined the North Melbourne Militia and, with Sir Arthur Currie, understood the importance of firepower and logistics. Like General Montgomery at El Alamein, their modus operandi were methodical preparation and patience.

Significantly for the allied fightback, German aircraft were being deprived of sufficient fuel, restricting their air sorties and ending their air superiority. The heavily armed British Sopwith Camel, in action since 1917, and powered by a light, powerful rotary engine, now proved as deadly, fast and agile as the German biplanes. On 14 July Fighter Ace Hermann Goering took over command of the Richthofen Squadron. The ace pilots of the air duels like Albert Ball V.C. M.C. and Richthofen were now dead. The legendary leader 'Red Baron' Manfred had been killed in action on 21 April, in his red Fokker DR.1.³

Final German offensive

At midnight on 14 July, Ludendorff launched his final offensive of the *Friedenstrum* (Peace Offensive), the 'Second Battle of the Marne', throwing in his last fifty-two divisions along a 65-mile front in an attempt to capture

Rheims. The French had again been forewarned, preparing a defence in depth, with sparsely manned front lines, and pre-empting the German shelling by bombarding their crowded jumping-off trenches. The German advance was limited to the French second line, as they struggled to break through. In one sector the French knocked out every one of the twenty attacking German tanks.[4]

Allies on the offensive

With the 'mouse trap' set at Rheims, the Allies responded in force, attacking the west of the German salient with four full American divisions, backed up by fourteen French divisions. On the east of the salient, they attacked with two French corps. On 18 July the allied counter-attack began with a cacophony of 2,000 guns bombarding a 27-mile front, followed up by a 200-tank assault. The Allies broke through and advanced 4 miles, capturing 20,000 prisoners and seizing 400 heavy guns. By nightfall, 30,000 German attackers had been killed and Paris was no longer threatened. The German High Command were in shock. They were now fighting a defensive war.[5]

On 20 July the German retreat from the Marne began. Around 25,000 German soldiers and 600 officers, 600 guns, 3,300 machine guns and 221 *Minenwerfen* were seized by the allies. Germany and her armies were starving, with deserters looting supply train and stores seeking food. The effective Allied naval blockade had deprived Germany of food and raw materials.[4] Meanwhile, the influenza pandemic meant some German companies could only field sixty men; 135,000 German soldiers had contracted influenza in June while, in July 1918, 375,000 fell ill in an army that had suffered 800,000 casualties in the last six months. The second influenza strain later in the year was worse.[6]

The Allies were astounded by the low morale of their adversaries, as the enemy surrendered in their thousands, disillusioned by their failed offensives. On 22 July the Allies advanced 5 miles, followed up the next day with a 2-mile advance on the Somme, taking 3,000 prisoners. The allied advances continued until 6 August, and from then on, the Germans would be on the back foot. Ludendorff's answer to setbacks was always another offensive, and he would retreat only reluctantly. His ambitious offensives had taken territory that was difficult to defend and strategically irrelevant. The huge salient had left German armies precariously exposed to attack. The *Friedensturm* offensive had failed to deliver the decisive 'Peace Victory' promised by Ludendorff.[7]

Hill 70 defences

On 24 July Lieutenant General A. Hunter-Weston, Commanding VIII Corps advised:

I have read General Collins' proposals for the defence of the Hythe Tunnel with interest. I should like to meet him on this matter on Friday 26th after luncheon. Please arrange for Major Sanderson to be present at this interview. In case Hill 70 should be taken temporarily by the Boche, my plan is to bring down a very heavy artillery concentration on Hill 70 to kill all the enemy there. If our line is penetrated, communication trenches will be used to bring flanking fire on the advancing enemy.

The Australian tunnellers were relaxing before the expected storm. On 25 July, an evening Australian Rules football match was held between the 'The Dingoes' and the 'Wallabies'. It was a close-fought match, won by the Dingoes 38–36.

August 1918

Company Strength: 20 officers and 870 O.R.s, including attached infantry.

A commemoration service

On 4 August the First Army 'Commemorative Church Service and March Past' was held in Ranchicourt Chateau grounds to 'Commemorate those who have died for their King and Country and to ask God for inspiration and strength to win the Victory'.

The company's War Diary describes the tunnellers' part in the service, representing Australia:

> The 3 A.T.C. contingent of 100 men in Church Parade Order Dress, with firearms and carrying water-proof sheets, embussed on motor lorries at Bracquement at 9am. The Commanding Officer Major A. Sanderson with five officers (carrying Webley service revolvers) and 100 O.R.s comprised the quota from the unit. They were picked men, being the only Engineers and Australians present on this day. The troops were seated, until called to 'Attention!' by the arrival of the Army Commander General Sir Henry Horne.

After the order was given to 'Stand at Ease', General Horne delivered his address:

> Today is the Fourth Anniversary of the Declaration of War by the British Empire. August 1918 is marked by the successful counter-offensive on the Marne, resulting for the second time in a defeat of the Germans. When one reflects on the situation as it appeared in the early days of 1918, when the

The Allied Counter-Offensive 203

Map 16: **Locating 3 A.T.C.'s headquarters at Bracquement**

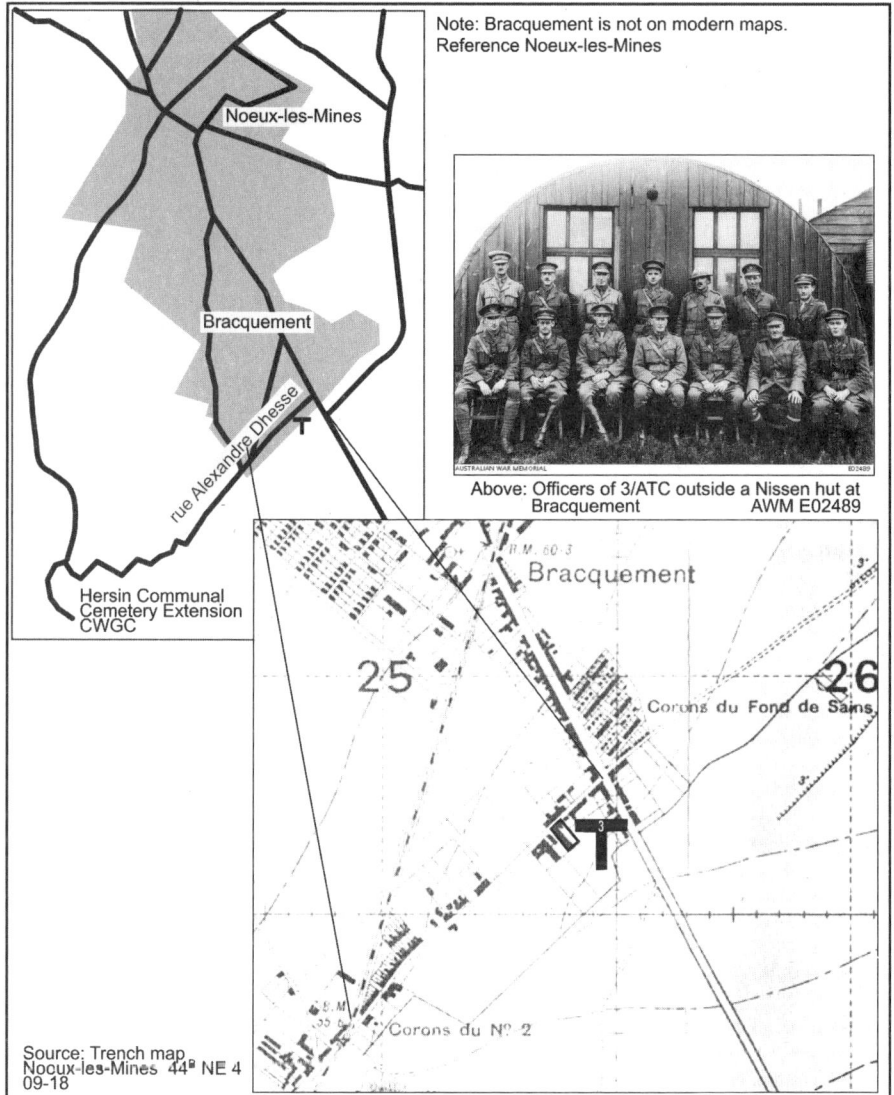

Above: Officers of 3/ATC outside a Nissen hut at Bracquement   AWM E02489

collapse of Russia had placed the Germans in a position of great numerical superiority on the Western front, who would have ventured to forecast that by August 1918 the initiative would have passed again to the Allies! The months of March, April, May, June and early July have been periods of anxiety and difficulty.

Fixity of purpose, strong determination, loyal co-operation and energetic action by governments, coupled with dogged determination, rigid tenacity, and entire devotion displayed by the troops have enable us to pass through those dark days. Here on parade stand troops from all parts of the British Empire, Great Britain, Canada, Australia, New Zealand, South Africa, India, and with us soldiers of France, of the United States of America, and of Portugal. We commemorate August 4th 1914, the day when the British Empire, true to her traditions and to herself, drew the sword once again in defence of Liberty, Justice and Honour.

A hymn was sung:

O God our help in ages past / Our hope for years to come
Our shelter from the stormy blast / And our eternal home.

General Horne then called upon the troops to give three cheers for His Majesty, the King.[8]

Battle of Amiens, 8 August

By 7 August the Allies had 1,904 aircraft, with new Spads, Sopwith Camels and Bristol fighters against the 300 aircraft of the *Luftstreitkräfte* (Air Combat Forces). They used them to bomb German airfields, to patrol and engage enemy aircraft in the air and for ground support for infantry, including dropping smoke.[9]

On 8 August at 04:00, the morning of the great Battle of Amiens, Canon Scott noted: 'The sky was growing lighter, and the constellation of the Pleiades was beginning to fade in the sky above the outline of the distant trees. Later on I met wounded men walking back and many German prisoners. In the fields in different directions I could see rifles stuck, bayonet downwards in the ground, which showed that there lay wounded men.'[10]

At 04:20 the Battle of Amiens counter-attack began with a 2,000 gun bombardment. Artillery was the key to breaking open enemy defences: the British had 6,000 guns, one third heavy. The French had more guns: the effective soixante-quinze (75-mm), 18-inch, 12-inch and 15-inch howitzers. Artillery firing became more sophisticated, taking into account the wind, air temperature, and type of guns, fuses and shells which resulted in greater accuracy. The new 106 type shell exploded on impact and destroyed barbed wire. Two thirds of the artillery would be engaged on counter-battery shelling.[11]

Around 430 tanks started the Amiens battle on 8 August. The noise of deployment of six battalions of tanks was masked by allied aircraft flying constantly up and down the front. To retain the element of surprise, troops were ordered to stay quiet and were forbidden to shout, whistle, or flash electric lights. Smoking was forbidden, except by tank commanders who would walk in front of their tanks, guiding them by the glow of their cigarettes.[12]

Eight British, Canadian and Australian divisions moved forward, with three French divisions to the south. Tanks advanced in darkness following compass bearings. Enemy machine gun fire only bounced off the tanks.[13] Creeping 4.5-inch barrages fired smoke initially, then shells for three minutes, 200 yards ahead of the infantry, lifting up to forty times and covering the infantry. The 18-pounders hit vital positions beyond up to 4,500 yards into German lines. The Australian infantry, on reaching their objectives, dug in under a protective barrier until leapfrogged by the next wave of troops. The heavy artillery covered the infantry during the second advance stage with tanks.[14]

Many Mark Vs were destroyed by German 77-mm field guns, firing over open sights and piercing the tanks' half inch plate armour (as the deadly 88-mm Wehrmacht guns would destroy Sherman tanks in Normandy in 1944). Yet the powerful allied offensive carried on, overwhelming the German Second Army's defensive lines as the Allies advanced up to 8 miles.[15]

In the three following days the advance slowed for logistical reasons: the troops were ahead of their directing headquarters, their reinforcements and vital supplies. Petrol for the tanks and motor vehicles had to come in 2-gallon cans from Calais and the rear depots. The first day had challenged the endurance of the tank crews and their machines. The Germans began to use mustard gas and their defences were stiffening in the old battlefield of the Somme. On 11 August, German armies sent eleven divisions to the Amiens sector. The allied offensive was called off while other tactics and strategies were considered. Haig had learned from Ludendorff's errors, understanding the dangers of defending a vulnerable salient and the wisdom of alternating attack sectors.[16]

The German Supreme Command (O.H.L.) was, ironically, based in the *Hotel Britannique* in Spa, Belgium. Here, Ludendorff had a nervous collapse, calling the allies' Amiens offensive of 8 August his 'black day of the German Army'.[17] The Kaiser told Ludendorff the same day that: 'We have reached the limits of our capacity, the war must be ended.'[18]

Report on allied advances

An encouraging summary by the 55th Divisional H.Q., outlining allied operations from 29 July to 28 August over the whole front, was received by Major Sanderson at his 3 A.T.C. Headquarters. It showed that the tides of war were changing dramatically.[19]

On 23 August Sir Douglas Haig notified his commanders: 'SECRET. Operations are now being carried out under changed conditions which necessitate the utmost boldness and resolution ... After very severe defeats and continuous attacks, the enemy has not the means to deliver counter-attacks on an extended scale.'

By the end of August, the Allies had advanced up to the *Siegfriedstellung*. On 31 August 500 soldiers of Monash's Australian Corps captured Mont Saint-Quentin, one of the toughest positions on the Western Front and defended by 1,800 men of the Kaiser Alexander Regiment.[20]

Hythe Tunnel connected

In the Hill 70 area, by cleaning out Scot's Incline, Black Watch, Gordon and Cameron inclines, plus other disused tunnels, the Hythe Tunnel was extended and connected up with the mining system at Loos. Drives were stripped out and improved for the infantry to pass. At Hulluch, the company dug a new incline, a fan chamber and a degassing chamber.

A light railway (the line linking and entering the south end of the Hythe Tunnel) had, from 1917, loaded rations, ammunition and stores onto trucks at 'Kingsbridge Station'. These trucks had run on a railway called 'the Northern Line' and were pulled by a tractor.

Alex Sanderson described the rope haulage system installed by the Alphabet Company that could lift 500+ bags of chalk an hour from fifteen working faces underground. One to two bags were hooked up and hauled 60 feet up an incline of 15° to 30° using a winding, geared electric bollard and a double-ended hemp rope with two hooks. The empty bags were then returned down the side of the incline on a narrow, shallow trough slide.[21,22]

On 11 August hostile aircraft were very active over Bracquement where bombs and sixty-four shells were dropped on three consecutive nights. While Major Sanderson was holding his usual weekly company conference, four bombs were dropped on their billets at 3 A.T.C.s Headquarters at Bracquement, killing five sappers and wounding seven.

On 12 August Rutoire Alley received hostile artillery shelling, including Blue Cross shells. Noeux-les-Mines was again shelled on 14 and 16 August, with several 15-cm yellow cross gas shells falling into the town.

On the morning of 24 August, two officers of No.1 Section of the 3 A.T.C. took part in the raid on the enemy on the Givenchy Front. The tunnellers' role in this offensive operation was to examine dugouts and mine entrances to mark them 'safe' or 'dangerous', to search for and render harmless any mines or booby traps found, to cut all enemy electric leads, to destroy any T.M.s (Trench Mortars) and to collect information such as documents, plans, or particulars of accommodation available for troops. The raid was successful. The British

55th Division attacked and captured the enemy forward positions on a front of 17,000 yards, including the whole of the Givenchy craters which they held against weak counter-attacks to its east and north. The enemy lost the valuable observation he had held from the north craters; the eastern lips of the craters had not been occupied by British troops since October 1914.[23]

Sapper John Punton, one of three brothers to serve in the A.I.F., was a tunneller in the Givenchy raid. They were descendants of Yarramundi, Aboriginal 'Chief of the Richmond Tribes' and his father Gomebeeree, a lineage dating back to the 1740s. Punton family folklore has it that: 'After a particularly heavy bombardment of their position in the trench sap, John Punton and others set up an ammo box for a table in a large shell crater and started playing cards. During the game the shelling started again and a large shell landed in the crater but didn't explode. One of the men was heard to say: "lucky we were in the bloody crater!"'[24]

Alex Sanderson awarded D.S.O.

On 28 September, the Royal Engineers' Controller of Mines, First Army, recommended Alexander Sanderson for a D.S.O. (Distinguished Service Order): 'This Officer has done consistent good work in mine fighting and subway construction under trying conditions during the past two years on the Loos – Hill 70 front. He has commanded the 3rd Australian Tunnelling Company since 1.7.17 with exceptional ability and has always inspired his officers and men by his gallantry and coolness when under heavy shell fire'.

September 1918

On 2 September Sir Arthur Currie's Canadian Corps was the spearhead of the British First Army that broke through the Drocourt-Quéant Line, with its hundreds of dugouts and reinforced trenches held in depth by seven German divisions. For six days Canadian artillery had bombarded the line with 10,000 tons of shells. The German Fourth and Sixth armies around the Lys were ordered to retreat, giving up all the land taken in the spring. The Germans in retreat fired mustard gas as an area denial, causing yellow clouds which saturated the ground and persisted, often for weeks. Mustard gas penetrated cotton and wool. The only hope was to put on a gas mask and to rapidly evacuate the area, but even then the goggles would cloud up. Tear gas (blue cross gas) symptoms were sneezing, choking and coughing, causing men to remove their masks, leaving them vulnerable to a second attack of more deadly gases like phosgene or mustard gas. It could take years to recover from exposure to mustard gas, if at all.[25]

Sapper Oxman records in his journal: '4/9. Went to work at 8pm. Lay in a shell hole for two hours, as Fritz putting gas shells over all the time. Gas very thick. One of Fritz planes hit by anti-aircraft gunshell. It went right through it.'[26]

Since 25 August, when the Germans retreated along their front, all 3 A.T.C. hands were put onto the construction of roads, repairs of bridges and causeways and to the making safe for occupation the old German dugouts in the captured area. The investigation parties followed the infantry advance. No 3. section completed their work on the Hythe Tunnel defensive system and handed over to the 176th Tunnelling Coy. R.E., after which they moved out to the Béthune District to carry on the construction of roads.[27]

The British, Australian and French engineers hurried to keep up the advances of the last four months of the war by erecting bridges, vital to maintain momentum. Lorries had to deliver the tons of steel girders, while the wood from the wreckage of the destroyed bridges was re-used from the old bridges on the river beds. The bridges themselves had to take the weight of laden lorries and tanks.[28]

The Americans, with their overwhelming A.E.F. force, attacked on 12 September, rapidly taking the German salient of Saint-Mihiel before moving on to the Meuse-Argonne. German troops had been issued with more machine-guns and the new 9-mm 32-round MP18 machine-pistols, the first sub-machine gun.[29] Their manpower, however, was reduced by casualties, disease, desertion and lack of adequate nourishment. In August and September, the German Army lost a total of 230,000 men.[30]

Chapter 19

Defusing Traps and Mines
1918

In spite of the dangerous nature of their bomb disposal work, casualties among the wary tunnellers were remarkably light due to their acute instincts for locating hidden explosives, while the French Army often made their German prisoners remove their delayed-action mines. Over the ruins of Péronne the retreating Germans had erected a large mocking sign: *Nicht argern, nur wundern.* (Don't be angry; just marvel!)[1] Ernst Jünger wrote in *Storm of Steel* of his disapproval of the booby traps being installed by some of his countrymen: 'Among the surprises we'd prepared for our successors were truly malicious inventions. Very fine wires, almost invisible, were stretched across the entrances of buildings and shelters, which set off explosive charges at the faintest touch.'[2]

British reports warned of examples of German inventiveness: boots with grenades attached; piano keys wired to explosives; poisoned food and drink; loosened staircase steps with bombs underneath. Delay action mines had been found under railway tracks, hidden in small shafts. Two graves were discovered, marked: 'To an Unknown Soldier', which, on investigation, proved to contain fuses and explosives.[3]

Sapper James Hallinan later described that:

Prior to the Armistice, things were gettin' quiet. The powers-that-be knew the war was gettin' to its end because the Germans, with their 'supposed-to be' infallible or impregnable Hindenburg line, was gettin' blown to smithereens. Instead of marching on, and making progress to Paris, they were falling back onto the Hindenburg line for protection. They were also falling back up from where we were towards the Rhine to get back home. For us, as far as the underground work was concerned, it was finished. When the war was on, some of us was picked to go to a gas training school and others to train in a booby-trapping school. I was selected to learn the tricks of the trade of booby-trapping. We were all sent to the tailor shop and had a red ribbon (sewn) down both arms. On our collars some had 'C.I.B.' Commonwealth Investigation Branch, or Corps Investigation

Battalion. The final stages then was that a team of us was picked out, after the Lens bridge job, to go booby-trappin'. Well, we had to go into houses and shops, buildings and all, to make them safe before the civilian people could come back into their homes, farms and shops.

These booby traps were set by the Germans and likely to go off any time. We lost a couple of friends near Lille through carelessness when they came to a place and opened a door. As they were going down the stairs, they put their weight on the stairs where was a booby trap. Of course, the result was: up went the stairs and these fellows! They were blown down below. The booby-trapping lasted about three or four months.[4]

On 9 December Major Sanderson would report to the Controller of Mines Fifth Army that his company had made safe 504 tons of enemy explosives: 'The total number of German mine and traps removed totalled 2,926 (weighing 613,895 lbs) comprising: 1,142 Land Mines* (211,700 lbs, including 53 under roads), 56 Delay Action Traps (9,280 lbs), 21 Other traps (900 lbs), and 1,707 Demolition Charges (392,015 lbs).'

* [Many were set under barbed-wired mine fields for defence against tanks. These were generally easily detectable, as were those laid transversely across roads.][5]

Alex Sanderson would note in a November report to the C. of M. regarding the location of hidden mines that: 'In country inhabited by civilians, valuable information can often be obtained, especially from the small boys who seem to know everything.'[6]

The British, French, Belgian and American armies attacked on 26 September with 123 divisions (fifty-seven were kept in reserve) against 197 German divisions, of which only fifty-one were effective in the field.[7] Marshall Foch's second offensive began on 27 September, as he pushed forward to Cambrai. On 28 September the attack by General Plumer's Second British Army succeeded in breaking out of the Ypres salient through German lines. At Spa in Belgium, as resistance in Flanders crumbled, Ludendorff underwent a nervous breakdown and finally accepted the inevitable. He told *Generalfeldmarschall* von Hindenburg that an Armistice must be arranged.[8]

The Hindenburg Line

This line was actually a series of four defensive positions 5–9 miles deep stretching from Armentières in Flanders down to the Moselle: a system of reinforced concrete defensive positions with many layers of barbed wire, anti-tank ditches and artillery sited on the reverse side of slopes. It incorporated the unfinished Canal du Nord, west of Cambrai, and the St Quentin Canal, a deep water-filed ravine with tunnels where the canal met high ground.

Currie organised a brilliant attack and crossing of the difficult Canal du Nord. His First Army Canadian troops advanced nearly 5 miles on a 9-mile front. Byng's Third Army gained ground against the Hindenburg Line but did not break through. The hardest obstacle to breach was the deep, well-defended St Quentin Canal with its series of tunnels. The biggest tunnel was 6,000 yards long at Bellicourt and was taken by the British on 29 September. Between 26 and 29 September, 750,000 shells and 30,000 rounds of mustard gas were fired into German lines at the Saint Quentin Canal and the Hindenburg Line was finally pierced. The Fourth Army had captured a set of maps at Amiens on 8 August that detailed all the Hindenburg Line defences.[9]

Further advances, October 1918

On 1 October two 3 A.T.C. teams were trained for a musketry and bayonet fighting competition, with energetic interest by Lieutenant J.B. Shaw M.C. and Sergeant Forsyth, who underwent training in locating and dismantling 'Delayed action Mines and Traps' and was promoted to Company Quarter Master Sergeant of 'C' Section.

On 19 October 3 A.T.C. left their headquarters at Bracquement, their base since November 1916, and began to move forward with the advance of I Corps. They were to facilitate the smooth running of road and canal transport to provide water supplies for the following troops and to defuse German traps and mines left by the retreating, yet still organised, German army. In the final months of the war the company advanced 50 miles.

New headquarters and billets were set up near *Le Pont Maudit* over the Haute Deûle Canal. Those involved in the erection of a steel bridge here were Major Sanderson, Captain A. Hillman and 60 percent of 'B', 'C' and 'D' sections, numbering 220 O.R.s and fifty-four attached infantry. Work commenced on 19 October, clearing away the wreckage of old abutments and building new abutments, often under heavy shell fire. Erection of the bridge steelwork began on 23 October (Major Sanderson's photos and descriptions can be seen in the plates). A second bridge was erected over the Haute Deûle Canal at Meurchin. This was a timber construction strong enough to carry 5.5-ton axle loads, and wood was collected from various enemy dumps abandoned by the enemy. Major Sanderson and Captain R. Langdon oversaw the sixty-two O.Rs of Section 'A' in building the bridge. The Hopkins bridge was launched on 28 October and the next afternoon was carrying traffic, including tanks at 20-yard intervals.

Two days later, it was officially 'opened' by General Holland G.O.C. 1st Corps, Fifth Army.[10]

Fighting continued in October as the weather worsened with rainstorms, leading to mud underfoot. The First Army, who suffered 15,000 casualties in October, captured 10,000 prisoners, 100 guns and 1,500 machine guns. The 3rd Canadian Division took Cambrai on 9 October. In the second week of October, with the Hindenburg Line crossed, Rupprecht, von Boehn and the Crown Prince's armies pulled back to the barely fortified Hermann Line running from the North Sea along the River Escaut and the Scarpe to Tournai and down to the River Aisne above Verdun. On 13 October, the 29-year-old Adolf Hitler was mustard gassed at Comines. His sight was affected, although not seriously. Then, on 17 October, the Germans abandoned Lille and Doaui. Within two days large areas of western Belgium had been liberated from Bruges to Courtrai.[11]

Sapper Oxman writes: '18/10. We came through two or three small towns. We took 24 big shells out of the road that Fritz didn't explode. The people are singing and crying for joy at seeing the British troops marching along. They gave us hot coffee as we dug out the shells. We wore a red strip down both arms so the Tommys would know if they found any traps to send for the 12 of us.'[12]

On 26 October, General Ludendorff resigned.

Chapter 20

The Armistice and Repatriation

11 November 1918
France, Belgium

Company Strength: A.I.F : 26 officers 635 O.R.s in Fifth Army 1 Corps Area

Sanderson 'Mentioned in Despatches'

Alex Sanderson was 'Mentioned in Despatches' of the Commander-in-Chief Sir Douglas Haig's Despatch of 8 November 1918, the award appearing in the *London Gazette* of 27 December 1918. On 1 November the 3 A.T. C. War Diary noted that Major T.W. Edgeworth David was promoted to lieutenant colonel.

Frêsne Farm Headquarters

On 2 November the company's headquarters moved to Frêsne Farm, near Bersée. Major Sanderson and his officers set up in the old barns, built in 1898, for eight days. In 2018, Sergeant Forsyth's descendant Richard Crompton and the author visited the farm and met the owner, an 84-year-old farmer, whose father Pierre Macron was 18 years old when the Australian tunnellers arrived, a century previously. Old Mr Macron remembered his father telling him about the Australian soldiers arriving 'dans la Grande Guerre'. The old farmer also remembered 1940, when British troops were billeted in the farm before their retreat to Dunkirk. In 1944, he said, the Germans and the British had been shelling each other again nearby. Mr Macron described the S.S. withdrawing and the French resistance arriving with pistols to search the farm buildings for Germans.

Back in 1918, on 4 November, a week before the Armistice, General Rawlinson's Fourth Army crossed the Sambre-Oise along a 15-mile front. Wilfred Owen was killed that day leading his men across the canal north of Ors, a week before the Armistice.[1] Captain W. 'Lauch' Sanderson (Croix de Guerre avec étoile) served as a Liaison Officer with the French Artillery during

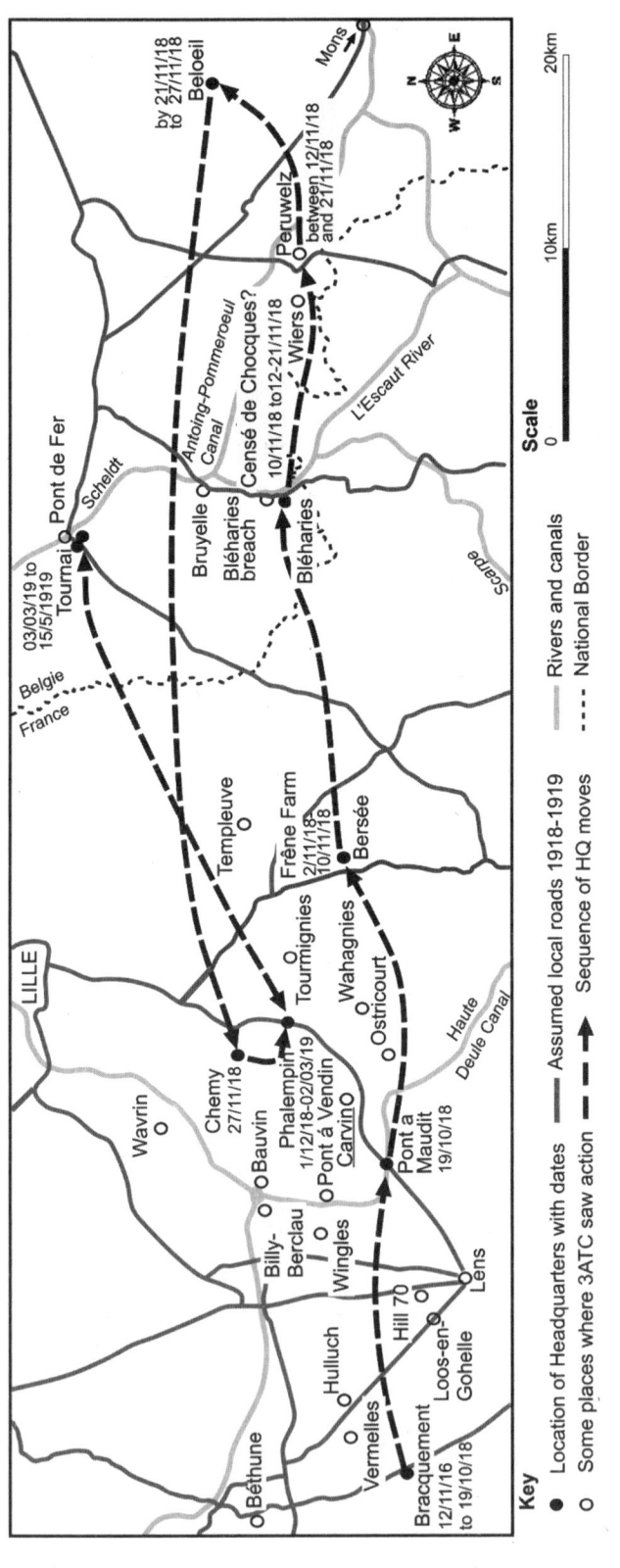

Map 17: Headquarters movements and work locations of 3 A.T.C. October 1918 to March 1919

this final set-piece battle of the war which finally broke the Germans' will to resist. He was subsequently awarded the Military Cross for directing artillery during the forcing of the canal. After the infantry assault, the 1st Australian Tunnelling Company constructed a heavy vehicle bridge at Lock No.1, despite the area being under constant, heavy shellfire while they were installing their girders. Four headstones in Ors cemetery bear witness to the sappers' sacrifice. They were among the last six A.I.F. combatants killed in the war.[2] On the same day the German sailors mutinied at Kiel.

From 7 to 8 November a German delegation crossed over the front lines and headed for Marshall Foch's advanced Headquarters at Senlis.[3] On 9 November Major Sanderson wrote to the C. of M. Fifth Army praising two 3 A.T.C. sappers who were investigating for enemy mines and traps in Rongy, Belgium when the enemy began shelling the town very heavily. They bravely carried four wounded Belgian and British soldiers through the shelling to a place of safety.[4]

That same day Kaiser Wilhelm II abdicated and a republic was declared in Germany and Austria. Meanwhile, the German armies in retreat were still destroying bridges, blowing up wells, firing gas shells and booby-trapping towns.[5]

On the last day of the war, Company Headquarters moved to Bléharies where in January the iron wreck of the old bridge here would be removed from the freezing water, piece by slippery piece, using a crane and winch, much to the reluctant sappers' displeasure.[6]

Armistice signed

At 05:00 on 11 November, the 1,568th day of the war, the Allies and Germans signed the Armistice in Marshall Foch's personal train at Rethondes in the Compiègne Forest.[7]

Sapper Oxman noted in his diary: '11/11. People very pleased over the news of war being finished. Took 8 more shells from the roads. The people stuffed a fritz with straw and hung it up and set it on fire.'[8] The 3 A.T.C. War Diary notes more succinctly: 'On the 11th the Armistice was signed by the enemy.'[9]

On Armistice Day Major Sanderson submitted a report on the reconnaissance which his company had completed on the River Escaut through the First Corps area, with estimates of possible repair work and man hours required.

- Removal of a coffer earth, and pile, dam 30 feet thick: 10 men with 250 lbs of explosives required for 2 days.
- Removal of 30 feet of earth blocking a Sluice: 4 men for 8 hours.
- Unblocking of Sluice. Removal of wrecked Sluice construction: 4 men for 16 hours.

- Repair to a breach in West Bank of River Escaut. Required: 45 feet of 9 x 2 inch timber; 18 feet of 16 x 4 inch timber; 6 wheelbarrows.
- 100 feet wide breach in Canal wall, with large volume of water flowing into the Escaut. (Locks lower down need to be opened to estimate repairs.)
- Walls and gates of a lock badly destroyed.
- Steel lifting bridge carrying a railway line and a Steel swinging bridge at Antoing Lock both completely destroyed.
- Brick Road bridge at Peruwelz over a branch canal blown.[10]

Assessing and organising these war damage repairs would prove invaluable experience for Major Sanderson during the Second World War when he was appointed the civil engineer in charge of repairing damage caused by Luftwaffe bombs and V-rockets to the London Underground system of bridges, depots and tunnels.

On 12 November General Sir W.R. Birdwood, Commander of Fifth Army, wrote:

> to express his appreciation of the work done by the 3rd Australian, 170th, 250th, 251st and 257th Tunnelling Companies in removing enemy traps and mines. The courage and determination they displayed is beyond all praise and the Army acknowledges its debt of gratitude to the devotion shown by all ranks of the Companies. The measure of success is recorded by the small number of mines and traps which have escaped detection.[11]

On 13 November the company entered Belgium for the first time and set to work on the repairs which Major Sanderson's reconnaissance had identified. Five days later, when the headquarters reached Beloeil in Belgium, Sanderson issued orders aimed at keeping his men occupied and disciplined, now that the peace had been won:

> On each day a definite task will always be allotted by the Officer… Definite orders will be given to the senior N.C.O. stating the task to be completed before ceasing work to include a) Time for starting work, b) Earliest time for finishing work, if completed, c) The task. Officers should be very careful that the tasks they set are not so great as to unduly fatigue the men in carrying them out in the proper time. An officer may vary the task but usually he should not do so except in emergencies, or for very special reasons.[12]

December 1918

On 27 November Company Headquarters had moved back into France to Chemy, between Lens and Lille. On 1 December the headquarters moved down to Phalempin where it would stay until March 1919. The Tunnelling Company Headquarters was now preparing to start repatriations. First on the list under the quota system were the longest serving and the married men.[13]

On 22 December, company orders noted that Captain R. Langdon, Captain J. McArdell, Lieutenant R. Cavanagh and Lieutenant C. Shaw were awarded the Military Cross.[10] A week later, on 29 December, the C. of M. First Army notified the commanding officers of tunnelling companies (eight British, three A.T.C and the N.Z. Company) that 'a certain number of R.E. Officers are required for employment with the Allied Control of Siberian Railways.' One can easily imagine the reaction to this proposal by the Australian officers. They had suffered enough of the freezing, cold weather.[14]

Demobilisation and repatriation

Lieutenant General Sir John Monash persuaded the Australian P.M. William M. Hughes that the soldiers' wishes of 'first come, first go home' should be respected. The demobilisation was carried out in a disciplined way, with the men being classified in quotas of 1,000 troops. Of the 155,000 troops in England, only 10,000 would remain in September 1919.[1]

Sapper James Hallinan had sad news:

> When the booby-trapping work finished, we gradually came back into camps closer to the ships. Of course, they couldn't bring us all back from France because there was hundreds of thousands of soldiers coming back. According to the time you enlisted, they were regularly bringing us back to Le Havre and Calais and those places but the first many thousands of soldiers to come back from France was the hospital cases and the sick and the wounded.

George Oxman noted:

> 27/1. The men 45 years and over left for home, about 80 of them. There is about 3 inches of snow on ground and plenty of snowballing going on.

> 6/2. The civilians and us had a bit of snowballing, we missed a bloke and put it through a window so had to pay for a new one. Went to Seclin for a walk, every corner a pack of kids used to snowball us – great fun for them.[2]

BELGIUM

On 12 February eighty sappers, including Oxman, set off from Company Headquarters at Phalempin to repair the *Pont de Fer* in Tournai. Oxman had been one of the unwilling workers tasked with removing the destroyed bridge from the river at Bléharies in January. When they arrived, fifty of the men immediately went on strike in the mistaken belief they were the only sappers in the company still working. The situation was resolved, however, when Major Sanderson arrived and persuaded the men to go back to work. The local tram company offered a carrot of 200 francs if the bridge was finished by the end of March. It was completed on 28 March, by which time Oxman had left for England and his repatriation 'on the long, long trail that leads to Home', in the apt words of the 3rd Australian Tunnelling Company 1919 calendar (See plates).[3]

March to May 1919

On 3 March the Company Headquarters and the remaining contingent moved to Tournai; the 630 sappers present in January now numbering 394. The eighteen officers remaining on 1 March would reduce to 8 on 1 April, with 175 sappers. On 9 May there remained only three officers and twenty sappers. The company folded on 26 May, with its adjutant Lieutenant C. Shaw inscribing in the War Diary: 'The 3rd Australian Tunnelling Company ceased to function.'[4]

Australia, with a population of less than 5 million, had suffered 60,000 dead and 152,000 wounded. The per capita basis of 65 percent of the A.I.F., Australia's combined wartime casualties were higher than any other country's: New Zealand had 59 percent casualties, Britain 51 percent and Canada 50 percent.[5]

Part Four

Post First World War and the Second World War

Chapter 21

To England and Marriage

England, Australia, India

Major Alex Sanderson left France on 14 March 1919 and returned to England, together with his brother, Captain W.L. Sanderson. In London, Alex was granted leave with pay and subsistence from 2 April to 30 November to pursue non-military employment (N.M.E.) in an engineering firm in London.

The brothers were welcomed to Britain and managed to lead quite a rumbustious and fun time in London, being free at last to enjoy themselves, after their stressful wartime duties on the Western Front. They were entertained by London society, able to go to the theatre and generally relax. Alex was advised that if he was to return to Australia, he should think of choosing a wife. The vicar with whom he lodged in Kent advised Alex that he had just a suitable person in mind, the young and beautiful daughter of the churchwarden of the next village, Gladys Burden living in Otford. As Alex only had three months remaining of his leave, a meeting was arranged. Happily, in their short courtship, Alex and Gladys developed a deep love for one another. Her parents, John and Alice Burden, were delighted at the thought of having such a distinguished and handsome officer as a son-in-law. The engagement took place and photographs were taken. The wedding was to be held in Otford Village Church. A train was laid on to bring guests down from London and almost the whole village were invited to join in the joyous celebrations.

Mrs Gladys Sanderson's diaries describe how she met Alex:

In 1917 when I was sixteen, we moved to the 'Brambles'. The air raids were really bad at Leytonstone. Aircraft flew right down our road to shoot at the Zeppelins. One night Dad opened the doors and said, 'Come inside, a Zeppelin is throwing out fire bombs!' But it was the Zeppelin that was on fire, standing upright and burning…

The war ended in 1918 – when I was seventeen. The milkman told us that an Armistice had been signed at 11 o'clock that morning. You can imagine the jubilations and thankfulness this brought to everyone, after four years of war and terrible losses of life.

A famous judge and his very kind Australian wife used to invite Australian officers down to stay [for] the weekends from Australia House in London. They owned a beautiful home in Shoreham, the next village to Otford. Here an Australian Officer called Alex Sanderson from Perth, Western Australia was staying the weekend.

After a church service, Alex met the Rev. Sommerville and asked him if he knew of any people who could give him accommodation, saying he would be in London on official business for some months and would like to stay in the country. The Vicar invited Alex to stay with them. One Sunday the Vicar said to Alex before the morning service: 'It's early, I will take you up to introduce you to the Burden family', which he did. We all went to the morning service together. Major Sanderson, Alex, would often come up and play tennis with us. He used to go up by train every day to London for his war office duties. Sometimes, he and I would go for walks together in the countryside where beautiful fox gloves grew at the top of the hill.

One day Alex asked Mother and Father if he could take me to Henley Regatta and lunch in the Guards' Tent.

Once, after we had played a set of tennis at home and were sitting on the seat by the lawn, Alex said to me: 'We will get married'. A great honour but as I was young – only just 18 – I said: 'I do not want to leave home and go away'.

The following Sunday I didn't go to church and Alex did. Before the sermon, however, he left the church, came to see me and said: 'If you will not marry me, I must go'.

So, of course, I did not want him to do that, and I said I would marry him, as I loved him so much. When Dad and Mum came home from church, there was great excitement. Alex asked Dad if I could marry him and that we would have to sail at the end of December.

It was a very busy time having my trousseau made and arranging the wedding for the 18th November 1919. We had a beautiful wedding – the church was full of friends and Alex looked splendid in his uniform. He was honoured that he had his brother Lauch, a Light Horse Officer, as his best man.

We had the reception in the village hall and Dad had arranged a band to play. A wonderful, happy day. Alex was granted leave for two weeks in December. We went to Scotland for our honeymoon. Alex had a great affection for Edinburgh as his mother Augusta was born there. Her father died when she was about 5 years. Her mother had a trying time until the father's will was approved. Some friends, who were emigrating to New

Zealand, said they would take Augusta for three years. They adopted her and she only came home to England to us when she was 85 years.

After our happy honeymoon I went back home to stay with my parents, until I could join Alex on the troopship. As Commanding Officer he was very particular that everything on the ship was in first class order before she sailed. Then my parents took me up to Liverpool, to the troopship to join Alex. Although I have always loved Alex dearly, it was a great wrench to leave England and my family. However, I have never regretted it. Alex gave me a wonderful married life and we would celebrate our Golden Wedding.

Voyage to Australia

Major Sanderson and his new bride Gladys left Liverpool on 23 December aboard their troopship. It was a challenging journey for an 18-year-old bride to undertake, married to the officer in charge of the ship: 'With Alex as Commanding Officer of the Troopship *Runic*, it was big position for me to hold as a C.O's wife as I was not yet 19 years old!' The ship's troops had to await the couple's arrival before they could sit down at dinner.

On Christmas Day, Alex wrote to his fellow Australians soldiers:

From MAJOR A. SANDERSON DSO M.C. bar O.C. TROOPS HMAT 'RUNIC'.
25th December, 1919 XMAS DAY:
Dear Comrades,
Today there is being issued to each one of you a personal letter from His Majesty the King, in which our most gracious sovereign expresses the wishes and feelings towards you, not only of himself, but of all his loyal subjects. We may indeed be proud of what we have helped to do to maintain the glorious tradition of the British Empire and of having made our own beloved country, Australia, one of the most famous nations of the world. Recently, His Royal Highness the Prince of Wales, who will visit us next year, said at a dinner given to our G.O.C. General Sir W.R. Birdwood that the A.I.F. was probably the most brilliant and efficient fighting force that had taken the field during the course of the Great War. Such is the high renown which we have won in the fighting line. We are now returning home, many of us, with our wives and families, all zealous of the fair fame of our country and all, I hope imbued with the intention of maintaining the same high standard of efficiency in civil lives that we have reached as a military force. But for the moment our thoughts turn to home and those near and dear to us.

We are here spending Christmas on a transport far out in the Atlantic Ocean but speeding on our course to the land we all love. Our great consideration should be to disembark the whole ship's company, men, women and children, in the best of health and happiness. Let us all combine to do our best to that end and in doing so let us this Christmas Season, while making merry, think of the teachings of the Great Master whose birthday we celebrate, particularly our duties to one another. Let us throughout our long journey be one happy family always merry and bright and ready to help each other whenever possible. My heartiest wishes go out to you and yours for a very merry Christmas and may you always enjoy health, happiness and prosperity in dear old Australia.

(signed) Alex Sanderson, Major.[1]

The *Runic* docked in Melbourne on 21 February 1920 and Alex was granted leave in the city for two months while he stayed at the Menzies Hotel. The appointment of Major Alexander Sanderson D.S.O. M.C.+ Bar MiD was terminated on 21 April 1920 in the 3rd Military District (Victoria).

INDIA

With the end of the war, the Raj beckoned, as it had for Alex's grandfather Alexander. Alex accepted an offer from the Indian government for a three-year appointment with the Military Works Department and was posted as Garrison Engineer Major to Allahabad in the central provinces. In 1923 he designed and constructed the first reinforced concrete bridge in India: the Dum-Dum bridge in Calcutta.

Later Alex's son, Lieutenant Colonel John Sanderson would describe how:

My parents moved to Dehra Dun, north of Delhi, where there was a problem with snakes in the long high grass after the monsoon. My father Alex was walking with me when he was struck on the leg. Fortunately, he was wearing riding boots and the snake's head became embedded in his leather boot. Father simply drew out a knife, and cut the snake from his boot. He was used to dealing with the desert death adders in the Australian outback.[2]

In 1924 Alex was appointed Chief Engineer of a hydroelectric scheme in the Himalayas at Jogindar Nagar, in Mandi State, at an elevation of 6,000 feet above sea level. This technically challenging project included the design and construction of a surge shaft 400 feet deep and a 3-mile concrete-lined tunnel through a high mountain spur. Enormous quantities of water collected in the mountains would flow through this tunnel and down to the turbines, situated in the Indian foothills. In December 1929, he resigned his post to return to England; his family was growing, with six children to support, numbering four boys and two girls. When the Great Depression put an end to his company producing reinforced concrete pipes in London and his ambitions to exploit his reinforced concrete patents, Alex started work with London Transport, carrying out major reconstruction works, such as those at Aldgate East Station.

Meanwhile, his mother Augusta Sanderson, who had left Scotland aged 8 aboard the *Lady Egidia* for New Zealand, would finally return to Britain in 1937, three quarters of a century after she had sailed away.

ENGLAND

London Underground bomb repair work during the Second World War

AS: *Somehow I think my most interesting time in my life was after I left London Transport. During the last war, I had charge of war damage repairs on the London*

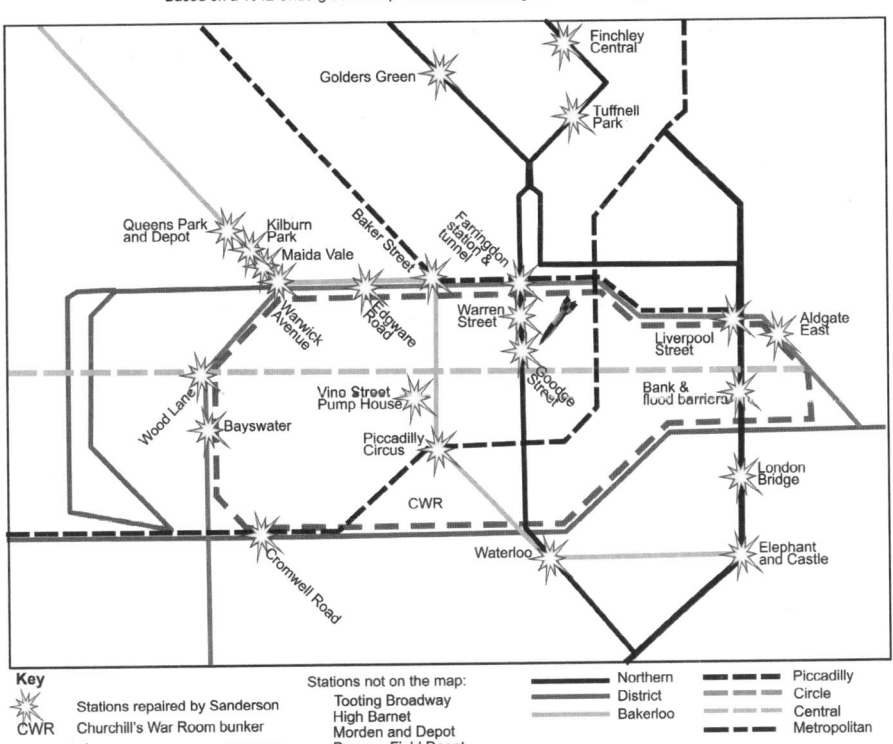

Map 18: **Some of Sanderson's repairs to Underground stations (1940-1945)**
Based on a 1942 Underground map - location of Underground stations approximated

Underground. We were bombed very, very heavily and they went for the lines, they knew where the lines were, you see, and they bombed us and I spent some millions of pounds doing repairs and I never had the lines held up for more than six weeks.[3]

Gladys wrote in her diary on 13 January 1941:

> We had a heavy raid on London on Saturday. Alex was called to go into the office as one of the Tubes had been hit and many killed. He did not get home until 3.30 a.m. on Monday. Such a terrible bomb had fallen through to the Underground station. It made a huge crater outside the Bank of England. The crater is so big that they will have to build a temporary bridge over it to allow traffic to proceed. Hundreds of soldiers are working clearing the debris. At one time everything stopped to see if they could hear any sounds of anyone trapped.

Revolutionary aeronautical designs for aircraft

When the Luftwaffe bombed the R.A.F.'s fighter airfields, Alex's thinking turned to designing aircraft that could take off and land in smaller scattered airfields, as the V-8 Harrier Jump Jet would one day land in smaller airfields and on makeshift landing strips in fields. Ahead of his time, in 1942 Sanderson sent 'secret' revolutionary aeronautical plans to the Air Ministry for 'Short Take-Off and Vertical Landing' (S.T.O.V.L.) Tilt-Engine aircraft, as well as 'Drone' bombers. Alex's drawings included plans for underground sheltered bunkers to protect these aircraft. The versatile designer would live to see man land on the moon, but not to see his plans turned into reality with the vertical flight of the Bell Boeing V-22 Osprey Tilt-Engine plane or the deadly drones, now used as bombers in war zones.

Alex was further consulted on the structural reinforcement of Winston Churchill's Cabinet War Rooms. He described how he sat on the edge of Churchill's bed in his underground bunker and would smoke Churchill's cigars while they discussed their First World War experiences.

Used to constructing solid wartime bunkers, Alex had reinforced the cellar of his Victorian house in Beckenham as an air-raid shelter by shoring up the walls and ceiling with heavy wooden railway sleepers and fitting bunks for all the family.

Alex's daughter Janet, now in her late eighties, described her father instructing her as a child to go up to their Victorian house's south-facing veranda and telling her to blow her police whistle to warn the family if she spotted an approaching V-1 rocket, which she did on several occasions. She said the V-1s either flew on into London or dropped suddenly and silently in the vicinity. Then the family would run down to the large cellar. If Janet and her sister Patricia did not get to the cellar in time, they would hide underneath their large billiard table. Janet also recollected that the family had an ivory-handled silver pistol, inlaid with jewels, which Alex's ancestor Susan had used to protect herself with during the Indian Mutiny. Reluctantly, they were obliged to hand it in to a police station.

Alex's son Peter, on A.R.P. duties, also recalled the rocket attacks:

> The house opposite us was destroyed by a V-1. All the windows of our house were shattered but the building still stood. Our cellar had an exit through the coal chute and the A.R.P. wardens shouted down: 'Are you alright down there?' I peered into the cellar and found my family safe, but looking like ghosts. The bomb's blast had caused the white limewash on the walls and ceiling to fall and cover everybody.

Alex's heroic traditions were carried on by his son John. In June 1944 Alex wrote to his oldest son in India, where he had just volunteered to join 152 Battalion of 50th Indian Parachute Regiment with the rank of major. Dispatched for jungle training in March, both under-equipped and poorly armed, their small force suddenly found themselves locked in a ferocious battle with an invading Japanese army bent on invading India. Their tenacious resistance during an intense six-day battle at Sangshak, on a small surrounded volcanic hilltop on the Indian-Burmese border, gave the Kohima and Imphal defenders the precious time needed to prepare their defences to stop the Japanese invaders in their tracks and to turn the tide of war:

> My dear John,
> We were so pleased to get your letter telling us about you joining the Parachute Regiment. What you wanted to do that for I don't understand and yet I suppose I would have done the same myself under the circumstances. It must have been a thrilling experience. If I were not so old, I would like to go through it myself. The principal training will not be the actual jumping but the methods adapted for quick cooperation on landing in enemy territory. Plenty of speed and pluck provide the best means of dealing with the enemy. I have been busy filling out estimates for about a million pounds war damage repairs still to be done to the London Underground, that is if the Government will allow us to make a start. Your loving father.[4]

Alex continued working well into his seventies. He was widely respected for his knowledge of tunnelling and explosives, as well as his role as Chief Engineer

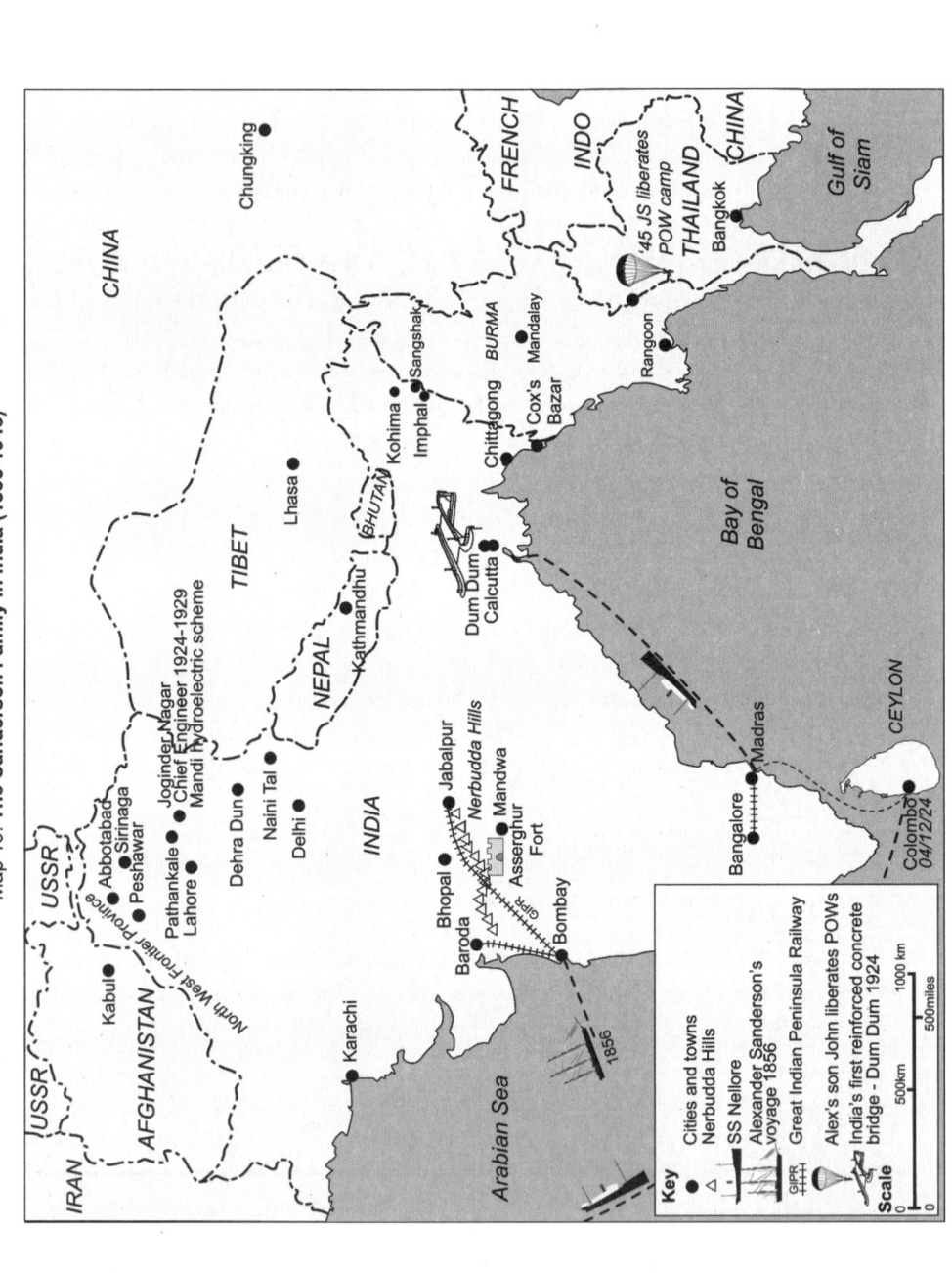

Map 19: The Sanderson Family in India (1856-1945)

of the Himalayan Mandi hydro surge tunnel. In 1953, aged 72, a century after his mother Augusta sailed from Glasgow to New Zealand, Alex left Barrow-in-Furness, where he was advising on the construction of a power station, and moved to Kilmacolm, west of Glasgow, to accept a final challenge; working as an engineering consultant for the Cruachan hydro-electric scheme, situated 19 miles east of Oban, on the shores of Loch Awe.

The Cuachan project, conceived in the 1930s and designed in 1950, had been approved by parliament in 1947 and would become the first reversible pumped storage hydro system of its size in the world. By day, the mountain water of Ben Cruachan would flow down from the dammed high reservoir through pipes in the excavated 'Hollow Mountain' to drive huge generator turbines. Power would be carried 5 miles east through a 275,000V transmission cable to Dalmally substation and then on to Windhill, north of Glasgow. At night, when electricity was cheaper, the water would be pumped back up to the reservoir. The mining and civil engineering contractors were Thyssen (GB) Ltd, a German company made public in 1953. The tunnelling excavations were carried out by a workforce of 1,300 men known as the 'Tunnel Tigers' and lasted for six years. Hand-held air drills were used to bore 8-feet holes in the solid granite rock, which were subsequently packed with gelignite and blasted out. The Loch Awe project set a world tunnelling record in the Ianachain Tunnel, with the face only 8 feet 6 inches x 7 feet, with 560 feet being driven by miners working around the clock in 8-hour shifts for seven days. Evidently, Alex Sanderson played his part in motivating these 'Tiger' tunnellers. The power station was officially opened by Queen Elizabeth II in 1965.[5]

Alex's daughter Janet recently shared her thoughts on her father's character:

God gave him many talents. He had an energetic personality, with a lively sense of humour. He was a very good leader with great common sense, always fair and well respected by his men. My father rarely lost his temper and he never shouted, always speaking in a controlled voice, choosing his words carefully and precisely, with breaks for reflection. He rarely showed his emotions, except when talking of the early death of his father, whom he much admired. In in his old age he enjoyed, with his evening glass of whisky, the occasional Havana cigar from the box Winston Churchill had given him. He knew life had been good to him and that his best luck had been in marrying my mother. They celebrated a Golden Wedding anniversary in 1969. Apart from his interview with Miss Lukis, my father never discussed his war on the Western Front, preferring to put these experiences behind him and 'getting on' with living a full, eventful life. However, my father did always refuse to have mains gas connected up to our house, recollecting the dangerous wartime effects of poison gas on his men.'

Assault and battery on the Underground

Ironically, in his eighties, and having survived uninjured in wartime tunnels, while he was in London to lodge an invention with the Patent Office, Alex was knocked down in an underground station passageway by criminals who ran off with his papers and wallet. London Transport reimbursed the stolen money, but Alex was badly shaken by the attack, and by his inability to resist the robbers.

Alex Sanderson died peacefully on 9 August 1971 in Beckenham, Kent, aged 89. His ashes were interred with unknown others in an unmarked grave at St Bartholomew's Church in Sydenham, London. Alex and his tunnelling compatriots, both British and Australian, are remembered in the French countryside at a 'Diggers' memorial site, inaugurated in July 2024 and 'guarded' at each corner by figures of A.I.F. soldiers. The site was funded and built by grateful local villagers at Haisnes close to the fields under which the tunnellers fought, and where many died, in their ultimately successful underground war.

Commonwealth Engineer Units' Honour Rolls

St Paul's was an icon of the London Blitz, with Londoners maintaining that as long as St Paul's survived, so would London. In the author's view, St Paul's was not destroyed by the Luftwaffe as, like the large Cunard building in Liverpool, it served as location reference landmark for German aircraft. It is fitting that the former commander of an Australian tunnelling company, Major Alex Sanderson, should be involved in organising repairs to the bombed London Underground system.

A total of 382 Australian tunnellers died in service of those who enlisted with the original Mining Corps or served with an Australian tunnelling company or in the AEMMBC during the First World War. Below are listed the names, inscribed in this engineer's book, of the fallen of one of these Mining Corps companies: the 3rd Australian Tunnelling Company. St Paul's records 335 names of those men who were serving with a tunnelling company at the time of their death. Ninety-four of those names are of 3 A.T.C. members, as well as the three names of members of its feeder unit, 6 A.T.C.

Sincere thanks are due to the Dean and Chapter of St Paul's Cathedral for allowing the reproduction of the Rolls, with gratitude to the Vergers and Caretakers who have kept the Rolls safe so diligently through the decades. Thanks are also due for the biographical snapshots provided by Donna Baldey of www.tunnellers.net (where fuller profiles of individual tunnellers can be accessed), who fortuitously discovered the articles below while researching the history of an Australian tunneller. This information led the author to view and photograph the relevant Rolls. The Engineer's Honour Book was funded by public subscription in Great Britain, Australia, Canada and New Zealand. At least two public advertisements for financial contributions appeared in Australian newspapers.

ENGINEERS' ROLL OF HONOUR

The Royal Engineer War Memorial Committee are arranging to deposit a roll of honour of all the ranks of the Royal Engineers whose names were officially published as killed in action or died of wounds or disease in the war in the chapel of St Paul's Cathedral, and the Engineer corps of the dominions, colonial and Indian armies have been invited to deposit similar rolls of honour in St Paul's, to be attached to that of the Royal Engineers. This invitation has been accepted in Australia. The roll will be inscribed on vellum and enclosed in a casket of Australian timber to rest on a slab of Australian marble. To defray the cost subscriptions of one shilling, restricted to members of the A.I.F. Engineers, A.M.F. Engineer units, and relatives and friends of those members of the A.I.F. Engineer units including Signals, A.E.M+M. and B. Companies, and Tunnelling Corps who fell in the war, are to be received by the president of the committee, Major J.E. Fraser D.S.O. ... The amount to be raised in this State is £70. Competitive designs for the roll and the casket are to be invited, and particulars may be obtained from the Brigade-Major of Engineers, Victoria Barracks.

The Sydney Morning Herald – Saturday, 23 July 1921

ENGINEERS' WAR MEMORIAL: THE TASMANIAN QUOTA

A fund was opened in Hobart some time ago to obtain the quota of Tasmania towards the cost of the Engineers' War Memorial and the amount was exceeded. Subscriptions obtained: Major R.V. Morse £1 (+31 others) ...Total £25 3s 9d. Debits: advertising £5 2s; stamps for circulars 6s 9d.; balance for memorial fund, £19 14s 9d.

The Mercury – Saturday, 18 March 1922

Twenty of the fallen (marked *) were killed by two fatal enemy camouflets that struck the Black Watch gallery (214 feet long) at 12:40 on 27 November 1916. They exploded the Australian's huge mine charge, which was being prepared. These tunnellers are buried in Hersin Communal Cemetery in fourteen adjacent graves. Nine men, whose bodies were not recovered, were commemorated in one grave, their names being inscribed on two adjoining headstones.

Four of the fallen (marked **) were killed during a hostile air raid on billets at Bracquement when four bombs were dropped on Headquarters' yard.

Five of the fallen (marked ***) were killed on 11 August 1918 when a *Minenwerfer* shell made a direct hit on No.25 Shafthead Cover. The men are buried in Pont-du-Hem Military Cemetery, La Gorgue, France.

C.C.S. = Casualty Clearing Station.

Sapper **Charles H. Abbott,** a single miner from Kalgoorlie, born in Adelaide S.A., was wounded in action by an enemy shell and died later that day, leaving a notebook and a testament as his only worldly possessions. In May 1919 photographs of his Hersin grave were forwarded to his mother by Major Alex Sanderson. William Powell wrote home about Abbot's death: 'Dear Mother and Sister, Charlie Abbot was killed last week and seven wounded. It's bad luck but "thy will be done".'

Sergeant **Joseph Allen,** 43, a married miner from Perth, of Irish birth, was killed by poison gas after an enemy explosion at Hill 70, the day after the Black Watch blow. Buried at Hersin and commemorated in Honour Avenue, Kings Park, Perth with a tree planted by his wife.

Sapper **Peter Baird,** 23, born Scotland, a single miner from Lithgow, N.S.W. Suffered gas poisoning on 28 October with five other sappers, succumbing to the effects of the gas and bronco-pneumonia a week later. Buried in Terlincthun British Cemetery, Wimille, France.

Sapper **Charles V. Barker,*** 35, born Gawler, S.A., a single miner from Mt Lyall, Tas.

Second Corporal **Albert E.B. Barlow,**** born Victoria, a single motor mechanic from Perth, W.A. Commemorated in Honour Ave, Kings Park, Perth with a tree planted by his wife. Buried at Hersin.

Sapper **Thomas Barnes,** 32, born Castlemaine, Vic., a single labourer from Blackboy Hill, W.A. Killed by a shell at Givenchy. Buried in Hersin.

Sapper **William H. Batson,*** 24, born St George's, East London, a single miner from Ross, Tas.

Corporal **Frederick Benson,** 36, born Coburg, Vic., a married platelayer from Kalgoorlie, W.A. Buried in Philosophe British Cemetery, Mazingarbe, Belgium.

Sergeant **James W. Berry M.M.** A married mining engineer, born Bendigo, Vic., who worked in Kalgoorlie. Awarded M.M. for his successful rescue of a British sapper, buried alive by a *Minenwerfer* explosion at Shaft 99, Hill 70, Loos in November 1916. Berry was killed on Hill 70, eight months later. A friend's tribute: 'He died like the hero he was. It was dangerous work, but he always went to it with his men. He would never send another man where he would not go himself. His death cast quite a gloom over all, both men and officers. The loss is felt by all. All respected him - a man of few words, easily understood, no nonsense, and determined, a quiet, unassuming man. He won the Military Medal, but never had the pleasure of wearing it.' Buried at Hersin.

Sapper **John Bray**,*** 30, born N.S.W., a single miner by trade who was born, and worked, in Cobar, N.S.W. Buried at Pont Du Hem Cemetery. Major Sanderson sent photos of his grave to his sister Effie, who later received a package of his personal effects: ID disc, his two 3 'T' shoulder numerals, etc. Other photos of his grave were sent by Sanderson in October 1918. Bray's name is located at panel 26 in the Commemorative Area of the A.W.M.

Sapper **James Brennan**, 44, born Richmond, Vic., a single labourer from Adelaide, S.A. When his group was ordered into a funk hole, he went up to retrieve his steel helmet but was hit by an enemy shell that wounded seven of his unit. Buried in Hersin.

Sapper **John R. Brockley**,* 47, a widowed ironworker who was born and worked in Bendigo, Vic.

Sapper **David R. Brodie**, 25, born Annandale. A single pipelayer who worked in Leichhardt, N.S.W. Wounded by a gas shell, he died within a week from effects of gas and bronco-pneumonia at 2nd Australian G.H., Wilmereux. Buried in Terlincthun Cemetery.

Sapper **Charles E. Burley**, 27, born Ballarat, Vic., a married miner from Perth. Killed in action by a machine gun bullet at Hill 70, Loos. Buried in Hersin. His family paid this tribute: 'He is not dead; The brave can never die. His eyes are closed in sleep, His soul enshrined on high. He sleeps not in his native land but under foreign skies. Far away from those who loved him. In a hero's grave he lies.'

Sapper **Monty E. Button**, 30, born Auguston, S.A., a single miner from Mt Carbine, Qld. Died of a gunshot wound received in his legs at Hill 70. Buried in Hersin.

Lieutenant **Neil Campbell**, 32, born Adelaide S.A., a married mining engineer from Meekatharra, W.A. A lieutenant in the Boer War with the 5th S.A. Imperial Bushmen. Killed defending Armentières with a detachment of his company, having been put in charge of a scratch battalion. No known grave. Commemorated on the Villers-Bretonneux Memorial.

Sapper **Joseph Carden**, 33, born in Wales, a married miner from Kurrawang, W.A. Carden was with Lieutenant Russel, surveying in Hythe Alley on Hill 70, when a shell burst a few feet away, killing him and severely wounding Russel, who died fourteen hours later. Buried in Hersin.

Sapper **Walter F. Cassin**, 37, born Wagga Wagga, N.S.W., a single miner from Perth. Awarded the Military Medal for conspicuous gallantry during an enemy raid in the Red Lamp Salient. Killed by an exploding shell near Hill 70 and buried in Mazingarbe, Belgium.

Sapper **Petter M. Christiansen,*** 29, born Aalborg, Sweden, a single miner from Geraldton, W.A.

Sapper **George Clingin**, 41, born Hillsborough, Vic., a single miner from Southern Cross, W.A. His brother Albert was in his 'T' Company. One of seven tunnellers captured during an enemy raid at Loos on 5 January 1917. Clingin died of pneumonia at Chemnitz, eleven days before the Armistice. Buried in Berlin Southwestern Cemetery, Stahndorf, Germany.

Sapper **Harold Cockton**, 29, born in England, a married carpenter from Perth. Killed instantly in a deep gallery explosion by an enemy blow in a deep gallery at 108 feet. Buried in Hersin.

Lance Corporal **Daniel F. Corkery**, 19, born Ringaromma, Tas., a single miner from Linda Valley, Tas. When engaged in forward area work with Sergeant Forsyth, was shot at close range in the stomach by a sniper's bullet, nine days before the Armistice. He insisted Forsyth left him, knowing that he was beyond help. The enemy removed his badges and paybook. Buried in St Maur Churchyard, Tournai.

Major **Leslie Jack Coulter** D.S.O. MiD x2, 26, Commanding Officer of 3rd Australian Tunnelling Company. A single mining engineer from Ballarat, Vic., where he was born. Sapper Griffin and he were killed by a sniper while assisting infantry, protecting the men of the company who were involved in a raid to destroy enemy shafts. Buried in Hersin. Two of Coulter's five brothers also died in war.

Sapper **David Coulton,*** 27, born Bunbury, W.A., a single miner from Kalgoorlie.

Sapper **John B. Cox**, 44, born Mt Torrens, S.A., a single miner from Norseman, W.A. (So named after a horse's hoof turned up a gold nugget). Slightly wounded at Hill 70 on 8 July 1917 when 'Coulter Crater' was blown. Died of bronchitis in Boulogne. Buried in Terlincthun Cemetery.

Sapper **Ernest. A. Crawford** M.M., 42, born Dadenong, Vic. and a single miner from Burnie, Tas. At Red Lamp he took a prominent part in a raiding party of 1/5 Gloucester Regt and seven fellow sappers to locate enemy shafts. He succeeded in placing stakes in the parapet over entrances, while the enemy were in their mine. Awarded the Military Medal for gallantry and devotion to duty. Died of pneumonia. Buried in Aire Communal Cemetery.

Sapper **Edward J. Crowley**, 40, born Melbourne, Vic., a single miner of Rokewood, Vic. Killed by a booby-trap on Lens-La Bassée Road when five comrades were wounded. Buried in Hersin.

Sapper **Bartholomew J. Curran**, 37, born Ireland, a single bootmaker from Kalgoorlie. Admitted to Hersin C.C.S. with pneumonia, dying nine days later. Buried in Hersin.

Sapper **Richard Daniels**,* 22, born Peckham, London, a single miner of Linda Valley, Tas.

Sapper **John Donnelly**, 43, born Ireland, a single miner from Merridin, W.A. Killed in action by a shell at Hill 70. Buried in Hersin.

Sapper **Peter Dunn** (Alias: Hermann Dunehy), 22, born Ross, Tas., a single miner from Huon, Tas. Dunn and his mate Sapper Moran had crawled a considerable distance to investigate buildings recently occupied by the enemy. When returning, Dunn was so badly wounded by a sniper's bullet that he could not crawl. Moran M.M. would not leave him and carried Dunn back under sniper and heavy machine gun fire. Dunn died at the 1st C.C.S. Buried in Fretin Communal Cemetery, Lille. Moran was awarded a D.C.M. for his act of particular bravery under sniper fire.

Sapper **Lewis B. Edwards**,* 29, born South Wales, a single labourer from Kiama, N.S.W.

Sapper **Anton M. Eliassen**, 43, born Tromso, Norway, a single miner from Perth. Died of broncho-pneumonia at West Riding C.C.S. Buried in Lillers Communal Cemetery.

Sapper **Thomas Finch**, 58 (not the 44 years stated on enlistment), born St Helens, Lancashire, and a single gold mine (Maratoa) manager from Norsemen, W.A. This 'old goldfielder' regarded by his officers as one of the most practical and reliable men in the Mining Corps. Died of disease in England on leave. Buried in Melcombe Regis Cemetery, Weymouth.

Sapper **Henry F. Francis**,* 29, a single miner who was born, and worked, in Bulumwaal, Vic. Henry's two A.I.F. brothers were killed in action in 1917. Their father John mourned his three sons.

Sapper **John Freckleton**, 45, born Scotland, a single prospector from Subiaco, W.A. Died of tubercular peritonitis, a month after his return to Australia. Buried in Fremantle War Cemetery.

Sapper **Frederick J. Fulcher**, 29, born London, a married fireman from Adelaide, S.A. Killed in action by a shell at Loos, a month after joining the company. Buried in Hersin.

Sapper **Edward C. Green**, 43, born Brighton, Tas., a single miner from Glenorchy, Tas. Died of broncho-pneumonia at 1st C.C.S. at Choques. Buried in Hersin.

Sapper **Frank Griffin**, 31, born Dublin, a single labourer from Sydney, N.S.W. Killed with Major Coulter on raid into enemy lines. No known grave. Commemorated on the Menin Gate Memorial.

Sapper **Colin Higgins**, 29, born Sydney, a single boilermaker from Balmain, N.S.W. Died at the C.C.S. of gas poisoning received three days before. His war medals were issued to his father in Scotland. Buried in Pernes British Cemetery.

Sapper **Benjamin Horrocks**, 42, born Manchester, England, a married railway worker from Boulder, W.A. Attached to 1st Canadian Tunnelling Coy. Oct-Dec 1916. Killed in action at Hill 70 by a shell. Buried in Hersin.

Sapper **William F. Horton**,* 26, born Devon, England, a single blacksmith from Kalgoorlie.

Sapper **David Humphreys**, 42, born Scotland, a single driver from Sydney. Died at the 33rd C.C.S. of multiple gunshot wounds, received the previous day at Hill 70. Buried in Hersin.

Sapper **Eugene Kelly**, 46, born Manoora, S.A., a single miner from Perth. Reported missing, believed killed, at Erquinghem during the Battle of Lys. During the retirement Kelly was hit and fell. Red Cross report: 'Kelly was also one of my party. I did not see him hit, but remember an Australian soldier lying dead near our position, shot through the head. We were the only Australians on the sector and poor Kelly was the only one missing from my party whom we could not account for.' No known grave. Commemorated on Villers-Bretonneux memorial.

Sapper **Michael Kelly**, 19, a single shearer who was born and worked in Geraldton, W.A. In action for only five weeks when he was killed at Messines Ridge, the unit's first battle casualty. 'Struck by a "whizz-bang" (rifle grenade) and lived a few minutes, being barely conscious.' Left a photo locket, two pencils, a rosary and a religious book. His comrades erected his Memorial Cross at Pont Du Hem Cemetery.

Sapper **Patrick J. Kelly**, 28, born and worked as a single labourer in Richmond, Tas. Killed by a shell at night near Hulluch Tunnel, while waiting for lorry transport. A local family he had befriended placed flowers and tended his grave in Hersin.

Sapper **William C. Kemp**, 31, born Lord Clyde, Vic., a married father, a timber cutter/miner from Kalgoorlie. Wounded in head but recovered. Later was working with his brother-in-law in a dugout when he was shot in the head by a sniper and died instantly. His relation carried his body back to their base at Noeux-les-Mines and later helped bury him in Hersin Cemetery.

Sergeant **Macklam J. M. Kerby** D.C.M.,* 30, born Ballarat, Vic. and worked in Richmond, Vic.

Sapper **James F. Kersey**, 40, born Melbourne, a married timberman from Broken Hill, N.S.W. Died of head injuries received when knocked down by an Australian Motor Ambulance while awaiting repatriation. Buried with full military honours in Tidworth Military Cemetery, England with six comrades as pallbearers.

Sapper **Albert Ladd**,* 29, born Maryborough, Vic., a married miner from Bendigo.

Sapper **William J. Lavars**,*** 41, born Creswick, Vic., a married miner from Kalgoorlie. His wife of twenty years, Mary, was left a widow back in South Boulder W.A. with their four children: a girl of 15 and three sons, two of whom would serve in France.

Sapper **Michael Lyons**,* 21, born Beaconsfield, Tas., a single labourer from Queenstown, Vic.

Sapper **William Mahoney**, 47, born Huntley, Vic., a single miner from Kalgoorlie. Fell ill in June and transferred to Etaples General Hospital on 2 July 1917, where he died of tuberculosis a month later. Buried in Etaples Military Cemetery.

Corporal **William C. Mayne**, 45, born Christchurch, New Zealand and a married miner from Belmont, W.A. Received a penetrating sniper gunshot wound to the abdomen. Treated at 48 Field Ambulance before transfer to 33rd C.C.S., where he died the same day at 10:30. Mayne had a premonition of his death and wrote to his wife: 'If I should get killed, bring the girls up to teach, the boys at what you deem best…If I should go under, I shall wait for you in another place.' Buried in Hersin.

Sapper **Hector McLean**,* 31, born Stawell, Vic., a married labourer from Perth. One of nine men listed in the same grave in Hersin Cemetery. The *West Australian* published an 'In Memoriam': 'On Nov. 28 1916, killed in action, Sapper Hector McLean, dearly beloved husband of Ettie and father of Daphne.' Inserted by his wife: 'Some will remember and miss him. Only a sapper, that's all.' In October 1918 Major Sanderson wrote to Mrs McLean, enclosing photos of Hector's grave.

Sapper **Walter R. Menzies**, 27, born New Norfolk, Tas., a married miner from Kalgoorlie. Accidentally suffered a broken arm in August 1918. Admitted to hospital where he contracted influenza, dying of broncho-pneumonia. In 1949 his sister wrote to the Army seeking information, unaware Walter had died in 1918. Buried in St Marie Cemetery, Le Havre.

Sapper **Isaac Moles**, 21, born Latrobe, Tas., a single miner from Smithton, Tas. Killed by a shell at Hill 70, exactly a month after Black Watch explosion. Buried in Hersin.

Sapper **William J. Moore**,* 41, born Kadina, W.A., a married toolsmith from Perth.

Driver **Albert Morris**,** 41, born Auckland, New Zealand, a married horse driver from Kalgoorlie. Buried in Hersin.

Lance Corporal **Oliver Morris**,** 24, born Sydney, a married motor mechanic from Perth. Buried in Pernes British Cemetery.

Sapper **John T. Munster**, 41, born Auckland New Zealand, a married miner from Mt. Magnet, W.A. Hospitalised in May 1916 with pleurisy, a week after arriving in France. Qualified in mine rescue. In June 1917 he was hospitalised with Varix. On 18 August he ingested poison gas, dying at 18th C.C.S. six days later. Buried at Lapugnoy Military Cemetery.

Sapper **Edward Mytton**, 25, born Scotland, a single miner from Meekatharra W.A. Gassed in April 1918 when his outgoing relief was caught in a very heavy enemy bombardment on Le Rutoire Plain. Evacuated to England and returned to France in November before the Armistice. June 1919 returned to England. Taken to hospital in September, where he died of double pneumonia. At his funeral he was honoured with a firing party and a bugler. Buried in Sutton Veny (St John's) Churchyard, Wiltshire.

Sapper **William Nightingale**,* 37, born in Victoria, a single blacksmith from Blackboy Hill.

Corporal **James Pember**,* 24, born England, a single pipelayer, from Perth.

Sapper **William Perry**, 38, born Plymouth, Devon, a single miner from Kalgoorlie. Died of bayonet wounds received accidentally from a British soldier. Buried in Pont-du-Hem Military Cemetery.

Lance Corporal **Benjamin Phillips**, 34, born Fishguard in Wales, a single miner from Blair Athol, Qld. Witness reported he was shot by a sniper 'right through his tin hat'. Died two hours later at Cité St Pierre. Buried in Hersin.

Sapper **John Plunkett**, 33, born Landsborough, Vic., a single miner from Kalgoorlie. Gassed 30 April and died of wounds 7 May 1917. Buried in Fosse No.10 Cemetery Extension, Sains-en-Gohelle.

Sapper **Arthur A. Pountney** (misspelled on Roll as 'Poultney'),*** born Mile End in England, a single tinsmith from Leichhardt, N.S.W. Buried Pont-du-Hem.

Sapper **William Praed,*** 27, born Eaglehawk Vic., a married grocery traveller from Kalgoorlie. His Methodist family had emigrated from Cornwall. Praed had married Ruby Ethel before he embarked from Fremantle on 1 June 1916 with his brother. Statement by Sapper Blizzard (Red Cross files): 'Praed was one of 20 men buried in a sap and killed by an explosion of a German mine, on November 27th 1916. He must have been killed by concussion: he only had a small mark on the back of the head and another on the left hand. I helped to carry him out. I saw Praed and Spr. Harry F. Francis buried. Some of the other bodies were never recovered, although the names are on a memorial in Hersin cemetery.' Praed is commemorated on the Perth Kings Park Great War Memorial. Ruby remarried. She died in 1951, still treasuring Praed's two medals, received in 1923.

Sapper **Richard J. Price**, 24, a single shunter born and working in Brisbane, Qld. Killed by bullet while walking down the road to billets after dinner, accompanied by his friend Sid who was uninjured. Buried in Hersin.

Sapper **Thomas Prosser,*** 39, born Myrtleford, Vic., a single pipelayer from Boulder, W.A.

Sapper **John Reid,*** 32, born Kadina, S.A., a single miner from Kalgoorlie.

Sapper **Joseph H. Roden**, 45, born Cardiff, Wales, a single miner from Penjarrah, W.A. Suffered a penetrating gunshot wound to chest and died the same day in 33rd C.C.S. Buried in Hersin.

Lieutenant **Hugh Russel** M.C. (misspelled on Roll as '**Russell**'), 44, born Highgate, London, a married surveyor and mine manager from Perth. Killed with Sapper Carden. His daughter planted a tree in Honour Avenue, Perth. Buried in Hersin.

Sapper **Oswald J.S. Russell,*** 23, born Brisbane and a single labourer, from Northam, W.A.

Sapper **Herbert W. Scholes**, 40, born Launceston, Tas., a married miner from Queenstown, Tas. Wounded on 8 Sept 1917. Sustained multiple wounds on 16 March 1918, dying two days later at 1st C.C.S. Buried in Hersin. His grave reads: 'Nothing in my hand I bring, Simply to the Cross I cling.' Major Sanderson forwarded a photo of his grave to his widow in October 1918.

Sapper **Patrick Sheehan**, 44, born Cork, Ireland (R.C.), a single clerk from Perth. Shell gassed at Vermelles. Died at sea during the return voyage to Australia. 'Consigned to the deep' in Indian Ocean at Latitude 50 7' North: Longitude 80 39' East. Name on panel 27 of A.W.M. Commemorative area. His will was discovered in his paybook, requesting property be divided between his brothers and sisters.

Sapper **Sydney J. Sullivan,** *** 28, a single labourer born, and working, in Oatlands, Tas. Killed by a shell while on guard duty. Buried in Hersin.

Sapper **Leslie Thompson,** 25, born Bendigo, Vic., a single miner from Boulder, W.A. Killed by a shell in billets at Loos on 3 February 1917. Buried in Hersin.

Sapper **William G. Toombs,** 23, a single labourer, born and lived in St Mary's, Tas. Died of bronco-pneumonia in Camiers Hospital. Buried in Etaples Military Cemetery.

Sapper **J. Treganowan,** 21, born Bendigo, Vic., a single trucker from Boulder, W.A. Died of shell wounds to chest and hips while standing at the head of a mine shaft at Pont-du-Hem, where he is buried. Chaplain Winter wrote to his father: 'I buried him in a sweet little graveyard that has been made from an orchard. His commanding officer, several officers, and a large number of the boys were present to do him honour, as we laid his remains to rest. I am sure you have the deepest sympathy of all his comrades. Your dear boy has given his best, not only for the dear old motherland, but for all that we hold best, and no man can die better than when he is bravely doing his duty.' In April 1917 Alex Sanderson would write: 'Sending a photograph of the last resting place of your late son, who gave his life so faithfully for his country. I trust that the photographs may be some comfort to you.' In Memoriam: 'In sad memory of our only dear son and brother, who died of his wounds somewhere in France: Midst the battle's awful din / With firm resolve to die or win / A credit to his uniform / Our hero fell, and so we mourn / Greater love hath no man than this.'

Lan Corporal **Horace P. Truman,** 27, born Grunthal, S.A., a married labourer from Perth. Gassed on 16 January 1917, remaining on duty. Gassed a second time on 18 August. Died of wounds at 18th C.C.S. Buried at Lapugnoy Military Cemetery.

Sapper **Arthur Tucker,** 24, born Hereford, England, a single miner from Kalgoorlie. Died of pneumonia. Buried in Lille Southern Cemetery.

Sgt **Alfred N. Uren,** *** M.S.M. (Meritorious Service Medal), 47, born Kapunda, S.A., a married mine carpenter from Perth. Buried at Pernes.

Sapper **Alexander Welch,** 41, born Fife Scotland, a single ship's builder from York, W.A. Died of pneumonia at 83rd Dublin Hospital, Boulogne. Buried in Terlincthun Cemetery.

Sapper **John T. Wentworth,** 32 a single labourer born, and lived, in Kerrisdale, Vic. Died of wounds when accidentally shot by fellow sapper in billets. Buried in Hersin.

Sapper **Percy J. Whiting**, 29, born Petersham N.S.W., a single farmer from Canterbury, N.S.W. Leg amputated after wounding by a shell on Hill 70. Died two weeks later in hospital. Buried in St Omer Souvenir Cemetery.

Lieutenant **Charles W. Whyte**, 34, a married mining engineer (Ballarat School of Mines), who was born, attended university and worked in Melbourne. O.C. of No.3 Section. First officer casualty for 3rd T. Coy. when cranium struck by shrapnel from a shell which landed in front of his car and exploded. Buried Bailleul Cemetery. Alex Sanderson sent photographs of his grave to his N.Z. wife Mary.

Sapper **George E. C. Williams**, 23, born Broken Hill, N.S.W., a married gold amalgamator from Noreseman, W.A. Batman to Lieutenant Bennett. He remained in a collapsed dugout for sixteen hours before his body was recovered and buried at Pont-du-Hem. Returned to his parents were a French language book and Church of England Prayer Book. *Kalgooorlie Argus*: 'Sacred to the memory of our dearly beloved brother and uncle…Though one year has gone by dear George / How our hearts with grief bow down / As our memory on you dwells / Far, far away in sunny France / In a soldier's honoured grave / With many more Australia's best / You by loving comrades laid.'

Sapper **Henry Williams**, 36, born and trained as a miner in Wales. A single miner in Kalgoorlie. Went A.W.O.L. (Absent without leave) for three days after arrival in Britain. Descendants say: 'Henry would have caught a train to Llannrwst in Wales to see the family he had not seen for four years – and been the 'talk of the town', this bronzed Welsh-Australian, the gold miner from Kalgoorlie, dressed as a sapper, with a slouch hat.' Fought in Battle of Lys April 1918. Received penetrating gunshot wound to abdomen on 1 July 1918, dying next day. Buried in Hersin.

Sapper **Robert E. Willoughby**, 43, born Eaglehawk, Vic., a married miner from Kalgoorlie. Died of bronchitis and influenza. Buried St Pol British Cemetery.

Sapper **John Wilson**, 38, born Maryborough, Vic., a married miner from Darken, W.A. His wife, the mother of his two children, met him off the hospital ship in Albany. However, four days after returning to Australia, he died of pneumonia in quarantine. Buried in Albany Old Cemetery, W.A.

Sapper **John A.F. Wotherspoon**, 26, born Newcastle England, a single groom from Narrogin, W.A. Killed by a shell on Hill 70. Buried in Hersin.

In 3 A.T.C. not listed on St Paul's Roll:

Sapper **Vincent O'Sullivan,***** 38, born Ireland, single miner from Laverton, W.A. Buried in Hersin.

Postscript

Donna Baldey and John Reading's in-depth research for their website www.tunnellers.net outlines the life of the following Australians after the war:

Sergeant James Berry M.M. KIA: 'After the job is finished, men of all nations will return home to their respective countries, wiser men, educated by the miseries and cruelties of war, educated to a sense of what is just and what is wrong. These men will be terribly in earnest; they will never again possess that feeling in the ordinary sense, because it has been rooted out of them by their experiences. Every nation should prepare well for peace, for the future carries sterner problems even than war.'

Captain **Harry W. Brown** attended non-military training with a UK iron and steel company. Harry resumed his mining career in Broken Hill, Kalgoorlie and North Queensland, before practising as a consulting mechanical engineer in Collins Street, Melbourne. Harry died in 1948, aged 72.

Sapper **Clarence Bulmer** was returned to Australia in March 1918, diagnosed with dyspnoea, then discharged with a pension. Sadly, he did not draw his pension for long, dying aged 38 in January 1919. The *Cairns Post* reported: 'Sapper Bulmer had no relatives in Australia: friends and returned soldiers assembled in strength at his graveside as a last token of respect to their dead comrade's memory. Bulmer was severely gassed in France and suffered frequently from the effects of the gas poisoning. He passed away quietly, fortified with the last rites of the Catholic Church. Just before he died, he imagined that he was back on the battlefield, speaking of the cruelty of the German officers. He breathed his last, singing: *When the Boys Come Marching Home*.'

Lieutenant John Dow remained with his unit after the Armistice in the army of occupation, clearing roads and bridges of delay-action bombs and booby traps. In 1925 the Tunnellers' Old Comrades Association publication listed Dow as living in Kalgoorlie and working at the Golden Horseshoe Mine, Boulder. In 1951 the War Service Homes in Adelaide wrote to Base Records, asking if Dow had been honourably discharged. The extraordinarily understated comment came back that: 'His service was satisfactory'. Dow died in 1954, aged 72.

Sergeant **Leslie Forsyth** received the Military Medal in February 1919 for 'bravery in the field', probably in recognition of his sustained work dealing with German booby-traps and concealed mines during the 1918 advance in the wake of the German withdrawal. This medal was the last Alex Sanderson recommended for men in his unit and his letter of congratulation was his last written to a man under his command. In September 1919 Forsyth returned safely to Melbourne on board the *Euripides* as the ship's R.Q.M.S. In 1940 he would again enlist for military service and was a Lieutenant of Engineers restricted to Victoria State because of his 10 percent gas disability. 'Les' lived to the age of 77, passing away in 1966.

Sapper **James Hallinan**: 'Well us fellows, we were all mainly kept back until the last. I arrived back in Australia in September 1919.'

Sapper **Caradog Owen Jones** was wounded in October 1918 by a booby-trapped shell on the Lens-Béthune Road but remained on duty. In June 1919 Caradog would embark from London for his return to Queensland.

Sapper **Charles Leaver** would return safely to Fremantle, Australia in March 1919 aboard the *Khyber*. Both his sons who fought in France would survive the war. Leaver would die in 1957 aged 91 and is buried in the Karrakatta Cemetery in Perth.

Sapper **George Oxman** left the 3rd Tunnelling Company for demobilisation in March 1919. George returned to work in the mines. He would live for another half century, dying aged 84.

Captain **William L. Sanderson**, Alex's brother, was later a founding member of the Flying Doctor Service in Australia. In August 1940 he enlisted for service again and was appointed a lieutenant colonel with the 16th Battalion. He was discharged in July 1945.

Australian War Museum Exhibits

On 15 June 1918 Alex Sanderson sent off a case of 'Relics' to the Museum Officer of the National Collection at the Australian War Museum:

> Herewith particulars of exhibits sent by this unit. The duckboards were found in Hythe Alley, Hill 70. The *Minenwerfer* guns in enemy emplacements on Hill 70.
>
> Re: item 21: 'Enemy Mobile Charge Case': there is some doubt as to whether this charge case was completely unloaded of explosive or only the detonator and priming charge removed. Will you please have it examined, and, if not already been done, the explosive should be removed?

The case held thirty-one enemy exhibits:

* L.T.M. bomb, * German Electric Listening Set for detecting Mine Work, found in captured enemy mine gallery at Hill 70, * Light Trench Mortar Shell Case, * Rifle Grenade, * Stick Bomb, * T.M. Shell, * Heavy Shell nosecap, * Aerial Torpedo dropped by enemy aeroplane near No.1 Section billets in May '17, * Whizz-bang shell, * French M.G. Ammunition Belt, * Portion of Miner's Safety Lamp found on Hill 70, * Enemy Shell found on Red Lamp Salient June 1916, * Anti-Gas Mask, * Rum-Jar Shell, * German Electrical Listening Instrument found in captured enemy mine at Hill 70, * Wirecutters, *Mess Tin, * Mine Rescue Apparatus, * Mobile Charge Case, * Electric Storage Cells, * Rifle, * Fuse Lighter, * Chemicals & Field Dressing, * Enemy Balloon for spreading Propaganda, * Stick grenade, * Trench Waddy.

Author's Note

The photograph on the rear cover of a gallery in the Copse system is by the author, through 'The Courtesy of the Durand Group', as is much of the history of this book. Gratitude is due for the warm welcome which the Group have extended to the author and his sons, as well as for the frequent access the group permitted into the galleries through which Major Alex Sanderson and his company once trod. The two other colour photographs of the 'Tunnellers' 'T' and the 'Royal Australian Engineers' Motto' (from the Commonwealth Royal Engineers' Honour Book) are 'Courtesy of the Dean and Chapter of St Paul's Cathedral.'

Notes

Poem: The Colonel and the Tunneller
1. AWM4, Series 16/4, Roll 386, War Diary of the 3rd Australian Tunnelling Company.

Introduction
1. Barnard, Marjorie, *A History of Australia*, Angus & Robertson, 1986. p. 219.

Chapter 1: Engineers, Surveyors and Tunnellers
1. Dow, George, *Great Central: The Progenitors 1813–63*, Vol. 1 Locomotive Publishing Ltd., pp. 3–7.
2. Ibid., p. 7.
3. Ibid., pp. 16–17.
4. Ibid., p. 17.
5. Sanderson, Henry (Senior), *A Plan for an Effectual General System of Sewage for the Cities of London and Westminster*, John Williams and Co., 1847.
6. James, Lawrence, *The Making of British India*, Abacus Books, 1979, p. 174.
7. Tauman, Merab, *The Chief, C. Y. O'Connor*, University of W.A. Press, 1978, pp. 36–7, 39.

Chapter 2: A New Life in West Australia
1. Evans, A.G., *C.Y. O'Connor: His Life and Legacy*, University of W.A. Press, 2001, p. 165.
2. Tauman, *The Chief*, p. 97.
3. Le Page, John S.H., *Building a State: The Story of the Public Works Department of Western Australia 1829–1985*, Water Authority of W.A., 1926, p. 175.
4. Le Page, *Building a State*, p. 177.
5. Tauman, *The Chief*, p. 141.
6. Ralph, Gilbert M., *Bullfinch and the Yilgarn Goldfield*, Hisperian Press, 2007, p. 1.
7. Le Page, *Building a State*, p. 178.
8. Tauman, *The Chief*, pp. 80–2.
9. Crowley, F.K. 'Forrest, Sir John (1847–1918)', *Australian Dictionary of Biography*, National Centre of Biography, Australian National University 8 (1981).
10. Ibid.
11. Tauman, *The Chief*, pp. 50–1.
12. Evans, *C.Y. O'Connor*, pp. 53–8.
13. Le Page, *Building a State*, p. 180.
14. Tauman, *The Chief*, p. 33.
15. Ibid., pp. 42–3.
16. Sanderson, Alex, Major, *Interview with Battye Library* (By Miss Molly F.L. Lukis), 1967 (copyright R. Sanderson).
17. Tauman, *The Chief*, pp. 32, 248.
18. Evans, *C.Y. O'Connor*, p. 88.

19. Tauman, *The Chief*, pp. 51–2.
20. Evans, *C.Y. O'Connor*, p. 118.
21. Le Page, *Building a State*, pp. 213–14.
22. Ibid., p. 259.
23. Bolton, G. 'Forest, Alexander (1849–1901)' *Australian Dictionary of Biography*, National Centre of Biography, Australian National University 8, 1981.
24. Le Page, *Building a State*, pp. 314–16.
25. Sanderson, Alex, *Battye Interview*.
26. Tauman, *The Chief*, p. 81.
27. Quekett, M., *West Australian*, 5 October 1999.
28. Le Page, *Building a State*, p.190.
29. Tauman, *The Chief*, pp. 69, 72.
30. Ibid., p. 73.
31. Evans, *C.Y. O'Connor*, pp. 141–2.
32. Tauman, *The Chief*, p. 127.
33. Ibid., pp. 76–7, 90, 99.
34. Ibid., p. 80.
35. Ibid., p. 85.
36. Sanderson, Alex, *Battye Interview*.
37. Tauman, *The Chief*, pp. 100–101.
38. Ibid., pp. 118, 144–5.
39. Ibid., pp. 142–3.
40. Evans, *C.Y. O'Connor*, p. 156.
41. Ibid., p. 157.
42. Tauman, *The Chief*, pp. 147–9.
43. Sanderson, Alex, *Battye Interview*.
44. Tauman, *The Chief*, p. 149.
45. Evans, *C.Y. O'Connor*, p. 159.
46. Tauman, *The Chief*, pp. 171–2.
47. Ibid., p. 150.
48. Tauman, *The Chief*, pp. 156–7.
49. Ibid., p.157.
50. Ibid.
51. Ibid., p.190.
52. Ibid., p. 169.
53. Ibid., pp. 180–1, 184–5, 187.
54. Ibid., p. 189.
55. Ibid., pp 192, 197, 227.
56. Evans, *C.Y. O'Connor*, pp. 158–9, re. PWD 8575/96, SROWA.
57. Sanderson, Alex, *Battye Interview*.
58. Tauman, *The Chief*, pp. 191, 197.
59. Ibid., pp. 192–3, 196.

Chapter 3: Success and Tragedy
1. Tauman, *The Chief*, pp. 199–200, 203–205.
2. Ibid., pp. 206, 226.
3. Ibid., p. 208.
4. Ibid., p. 214.

5. Ibid., p. 226 and interview with Lady L. Steere and Murtagh O'Connor.
6. Ibid., pp. 226–8.
7. Ibid., pp. 229–30.
8. Goldfields History, *A Brief History of C.Y. O'Connor*, Souvenir Guide.
9. Sanderson, Alex, *Battye Interview*.
10. Tauman, *The Chief*, pp. 9–10.
11. Sanderson, Alex, *Battye Interview*.
12. Evans, *C.Y. O'Connor*, p. 225.
13. Sanderson, Alex, *Battye Interview*.
14. Ibid.

Chapter 4: Student to Mining Engineer

1. Sanderson, Alex, *Battye Interview*.
2. Evans, *C.Y. O'Connor*, pp. 196, 204.
3. Nash, George H. and Clements, Kendrick A., *The Life of Herbert Hoover*, 1st ed. W.W. Norton, 1983.
4. Mouat, Jeremy, and Ian Phimister, 'The Engineering of Herbert Hoover', *Pacific Historical Review*, 77, no. 4 (1 November 2008).
5. Sanderson, Alex, *Battye Interview*.
6. Serle, Geoffrey, *John Monash: a Biography*, Melbourne University Press, 1982 pp. 131–4, 138–9.
7. Sanderson, Alex, *Battye Interview*.
8. Serle, *John Monash*, pp. 163–5.
9. Sanderson, Alex, *Battye Interview*.
10. Ralph, *Bullfinch*, pp. 2, 13–15.
11. Ibid.
12. Ibid., p. 4.
13. Sanderson, Alex, *Battye Interview*.
14. Bean, Charles. E.W., *Interview with Major Sanderson at Noeux-les-Mines*. CB/AS 1918 (Sanderson Archives as original copy sent by Bean, 19 March 1918 with covering letter).
15. Perkins, Rachel, *The Australian Wars*, Documentary: BBC/First Wars Productions 2024.
16. Sanderson, Alex, *Battye Interview*.
17. Sir William Vestey and his younger brother established the Vestey (Meat) Empire in 1897. After running a corned beef canning business they became pioneers of refrigeration, shipping frozen meat worldwide from ranches in South America, New Zealand and Australia. In 1914 he also acquired a 1,200 square mile cattle station in the Northern Territory (*William Vestey and Cattle Stations*).
18. Sanderson, Alex, *Battye Interview*.
19. Barker, H.M., *Camels and the Outback*, W.A. Hesperian Press, 1995, pp. 4, 11, 53, 153, 175.

Chapter 5: Enlistment in Mining Corps

1. Tennyson, Lord Alfred, *Ulysses*, www.poetry foundation.org.
2. Churchill, Sir Winston, *The World Crisis 1911–1918*, Penguin, 2005.
3. Serle, *John Monash*, p. 201.
4. War Diary of 3 A.T.C.
5. McNicoll, Ronald Ramsay, *The Royal Australian Engineers 2: 1902 to 1919, Making and Breaking*, Griffin Press, 1979 p. 56, quoting Commonwealth Archives, Commonwealth Record Series MP 133/2, Files W 230/1/5 & 1/9.

6. Ibid., pp. 56, 58.
7. Branagan, David F., and Cliff, Paul. *T.W. Edgeworth David: A Life: Geologist, Adventurer, Soldier and 'Knight in the Old Brown Hat'*, N.L.A., 2005, pp. 258, 262.
8. Baldey, D. & Reading, J.
9. Bean, Charles E.W., Letter to Major A. Sanderson, 9 March 1918, Sanderson Family Archives.
10. Bean, C.E.W, Interview with Major A. Sanderson.
11. McNicoll, R.R., *Making and Breaking,* pp. 56–7.
12. Sanderson, Alex, *Battye Interview.*
13. War Diary of 3 A.T.C.
14. Sanderson, Alex, *Battye Interview.*
15. Article in *Sunday Times,* Perth, W.A., 26 March 1916.
16. War Diary of 3 A.T.C.
17. Sanderson, Alex, *Battye Interview.*
18. Finlayson, Damien, *Crumps and Camouflets,* Big Sky Publishing, 2010, p. 419.
19. Finlayson, Damien, *Supporting Tunnelling Operations in the Great War: The Alphabet Company,* Pen & Sword, 2018, pp. 48, 303.
20. Sanderson, Alex, *Battye Interview.*
21. Finlayson, *Supporting Tunnelling Operations,* p. 48.
22. War Diary of 3 A.T.C.

Chapter 6: Arrival: Mining Corps
1. Sanderson, Alex, *Battye Interview.*
2. War Diary of 3 A.T.C.
3. Finlayson, *Supporting Tunnelling Operations,* pp. 5, 49.
4. Sanderson, Alex, *Battye Interview.*
5. War Diary of 3 A.T.C.
6. Sanderson, Alex, *Battye Interview.*
7. Bean, Interview with Major A. Sanderson.
8. Finlayson, *Supporting Tunnelling Operations,* pp. 59, 73.
9. Baldey, D. & Reading, J.
10. Ibid.
11. Ibid (NLA: National Library. A.I.F. Sapper profile).
12. War Diary of 3 A.T.C.
13. McNicoll, *Making and Breaking,* pp. 62–3.
14. Barton, Peter; Doyle, Peter and Vandewalle, Johan, *Beneath Flanders Fields: The Tunnellers' War, 1914–1918,* Spellmount, 2007, p. 74.
15. Bean, Interview with Major A. Sanderson
16. War Diary of 3 A.T.C.
17. Barton, *Beneath Flanders Fields,* pp. 52, 70, 72.
18. North Queensland Register, 28.8.1916 (A.I. Military Slang).
19. Baldey, D. & Reading, J.
20. Ibid.
21. Ibid (Walton Family Source).
22. Jones, Simon, *Underground Warfare 1914–18,* Pen & Sword, 2011, p. 113, and Finlayson, *Supporting Tunnelling Operations,* pp. 3–4.
23. Grant, Grieve and Newman B., *Tunnellers,* Herbert Jenkins, 1936, pp. 110–11.

Chapter 7: Into, and Under, the Front Lines
1. Bean, Interview with Major A. Sanderson.
2. War Diary of 3 A.T.C.
3. Bean, Interview with Major A. Sanderson.
4. War Diary of 3 A.T.C., Mine Explosion Report by Major L. J. Coulter to C. of M.
5. Graves, Robert, *Goodbye to All That*, Penguin Classics, 1960, p. 116.
6. *The Work of the Royal Engineers in the European War, 1914–19*, Military Mining, Sandhurst: Naval & Military Press Ltd., 2004, pp. 113–14, and McNicoll, *Making and Breaking*, p. 195.
7. War Diary of 3 A.T.C.
8. Woodward, O. H., *The War Story of Oliver Holmes Woodward, Captain 1st Australian Tunnelling Company*, Australian Imperial Force, O.H. Woodward, 1932, p. 34.
9. Barton, *Beneath Flanders Fields*, p. 87.
10. Military Mining, p. 123.
11. Barton, *Beneath Flanders Fields*, p. 101.
12. *Military Mining*, pp. 122–3.
13. Barton, *Beneath Flanders Fields*, p. 108.
14. Ibid., pp. 75–6.
15. War Diary of 3 A.T.C.
16. Bean, Interview with Major A. Sanderson.
17. War Diary of 3 A.T.C.
18. Ibid (Secret Weekly Mine reports).
19. McNicoll, *Making and Breaking*, p. 63.
20. War Diary of 3 A.T.C.
21. Pedersen, P. A., *Fromelles* Leo Cooper, 2004, p. 36.
22. War Diary of 3 A.T.C.
23. Ibid.
24. Finlayson, *Crumps and Camouflets*, p. 95.
25. War Diary of 3 A.T.C.
26. Knyvett, Captain R. Hugh, *Over there with the Australians*, Hodder & Stoughton, 1918.
27. War Diary of 3 A.T.C.
28. Bean, Interview with Major A. Sanderson.

Chapter 8: Battle of Fromelles
1. C.E.W. Bean's Diary, AWM38 3DRL 606.
2. Strachan Sir Hew, *The First World War*, Simon & Schuster, 2003, pp. 180–5.
3. Miles, Captain Wilfred, *Official History of the Great War, Military Operations France & Belgium Vol 2*, IWM / Naval & Military Press, p. 122.
4. *Battle of Aubers*, Wikipedia.
5. Miles, *Official History*, pp. 124–5.
6. Senior, Michael, *Haking: A Dutiful Soldier*, Pen & Sword, 2012, p. 126.
7. Senior, Michael, *Fromelles 1916: No Finer Courage: The Loss of an English Village*, Pen & Sword, 2011, pp. 124–5.
8. Bean, C.E.W., *Official History of Australia in the War of 1914–191, Vol. III: 1916*, Angus & Robertson Ltd., 1940, Naval & Military Press reprint, p. 332.
9. Ellis, Capt. A.D. (M.C.), *Story of the 5th Australian Division*, Hodder & Stoughton, 1920, p. 82.
10. *2/1st Bucks Light Infantry War Diary*, NTA, WO 95/3066.

11. Company training 1913, as quoted in: Pedersen, P. A., *Fromelles*, Leo Cooper, 2004, p. 35.
12. Strachen, *The First World War*, pp. 237–40.
13. Miles, *Official History*, pp. 123–4.
14. Ibid., p.134.
15. McNicoll, *Making and Breaking*, p. 64.
16. Miles, *Official History*, p. 121.
17. Cobb, Paul, *Fromelles 1916*, Tempus, 2007, p. 23.
18. Miles, *Official History*, p. 121.
19. Barton, *The Lost Legions of Fromelles*, p. 85.
20. Pedersen, *Fromelles*, p. 38.
21. Ellis, *The 5th Australian Division*, pp. 83, 85–6.
22. Lee, Roger, *The Battle of Fromelles*, Army History Unit, 2010, pp. 12, 169.
23. Finlayson, *Crumps and Camouflets*, p. 97.
24. Bean, *Official History*, p. 353.
25. Cobb, *Fromelles 1916*, p. 43.
26. Pedersen, *Fromelles*, p. 7.
27. Miles, *Official History*, p. 121.
28. Pedersen, *Fromelles*, p. 18.
29. Miles, *Official History*, p. 122 note 2.
30. Cobb, *Fromelles 1916*, pp. 26–7.
31. Ellis, *The 5th Australian Division*, p. 89.
32. Cobb, *Fromelles 1916*, p. 56 (WO95 3611).
33. Ibid., p. 34.
34. Miles, *Official History*, p. 126 note 2.
35. *The Great War*, BBC documentary series 1964.
36. Weber, Thomas, *Hitler's First War*, Oxford University Press, 2010, p. 81 (in Maser, *Letters* p. 89).
37. Bean, *Official History*, pp. 336, 353.
38. Bean, Interview with Major A. Sanderson.
39. McNicoll, *Making and Breaking*, p. 65.
40. Finlayson, *Crumps and Camouflets*, p. 101.
41. War Diary of 3 A.T.C.
42. Cobb, *Fromelles 1916*, pp. 26, 224.
43. Bean, *Official History*, p. 360.
44. Finlayson, *Crumps and Camouflets*, p. 100.
45. Baber, Glen, *The Rhondda Pals*, Pamphlet 1995.
46. Senior, *Fromelles 1916*, pp. 142–3.
47. Bean, *Official History*, p. 344–5.
48. History of the 21st Bavarian RIR, p. 49.
49. Senior, M., *Fromelles 1916*, p. 143 re: Christie-Miller Lt. Col G. *The Second Bucks Battalion 1918. An unofficial Record*, 2 Vols. p. 184.
50. Knyvett, *Over there with the Australians*.
51. Miles, *Official History*, p. 124 note 1.
52. Barton, *The Lost Legions of Fromelles*, Map 10.
53. Senior, *Fromelles 1916*, p. 145, re: *The Lee Magazine*, October 1916.
54. McMullin, Ross, *Pompey Elliott*, Scribe Publication, 2002, p. 216.
55. Ellis, *The 5th Australian Division*, p. 92.

56. Miles, *Official History*, p. 126.
57. Barton, *The Lost Legions of Fromelles*, p. 219.
58. Bean, *Official History*, p. 350.
59. Barton, *The Lost Legions of Fromelles*, pp. 187–8.
60. Ibid., p. 211.
61. Senior, *Fromelles 1916*, p. 141.
62. Bean, *Official History*, p. 355 note 38 (AWM Library).
63. Barton, *The Lost Legions of Fromelles*, p. 213.
64. Bean, *Official History*, p 356, re: *Die Bayern in Grossen Kriege 1914–19*, p. 290.
65. Pedersen, *Fromelles*, pp. 59–60, and Bean, *Official History*, p. 361 note 55.
66. Barton, *The Lost Legions of Fromelles*, pp. 213,188.
67. Ibid. pp. 213–14.
68. Miles, *Official History*, p. 134 note 2.
69. War Diary of 3 A.T.C.
70. Bean, *Official History*, pp. 359–60.
71. Senior, *Fromelles 1916*, p. 142, re: NTA WO 95/3066.
72. Barton, *The Lost Legions of Fromelles*, p. 212.
73. Ibid., p. 83.
74. Ibid., p. 213.
75. Pedersen, *Fromelles*. p. 59.
76. Senior, *Fromelles 1916*, p. 146.
77. Miles, *Official History*, p.127.
78. Ibid., p. 128 note 2.
79. Bean, *Official History*, p. 357.
80. Pedersen, *Fromelles*, p. 59.
81. Letter from Captain A. Sanderson to Major L.J. Coulter of 3.A.T.C., 20 July 1916 (A.W.M.).
82. Bean, *Official History*, pp. 360–1.
83. Pedersen, *Fromelles*, p. 60.
84. Bean, *Official History*, p. 362.
85. Pedersen, *Fromelles*, pp. 59, 67.
86. Ibid., p. 59.
87. Cobb, *Fromelles 1916*, p. 47 re: 2/1st Bucks Light Infantry War Diary.
88. 2/1st Bucks Light Infantry War Diary.
89. Bean, *Official History*, p. 365 re: *Die Bayern in Grossen Kriege*, p. 290.
90. Senior, *Fromelles 1916*, p.150 re: Stewart-Liberty, Letters, 1916 DX 780.
91. Pedersen, *Fromelles*, p. 70.
92. Burness, Peter, *Fromelles and the Somme: Australians on the Western Front 1916*, Dept. of Victoria, 2006, pp. 217, 219.
93. Barton, *The Lost Legions of Fromelles*, pp. 217–18.
94. Bean, Interview with Major A. Sanderson.
95. N.T.A. WO 95/165 First Army Gen. Staff XC13039 p. 13.
96. Miles, *Official History*, p. 129.
97. Bean, *Official History*, p. 361.
98. 2/1st Bucks Light Infantry War Diary.
99. Senior, *Haking*, p. 123.
100. Bean, Interview with Major A. Sanderson.
101. Barton, *The Lost Legions of Fromelles*. p. 213.

102. Bean, *Official History* p. 443 note 139.
103. Pedersen, *Fromelles*, p. 44.
104. Bean, *Official History*, p. 362.
105. Ellis, *The 5th Australian Division*, p. 95.
106. McMullin, *Pompey Elliott*, pp. 216–7.
107. Barton, *The Lost Legions of Fromelles*, pp. 223–4.
108. Ibid., p. 224.
109. Ibid., pp. 218–19.
110. Ellis, *The 5th Australian Division*, p. 94.
111. Bean, *Official History*, p. 355 note 39.
112. Ellis, *The 5th Australian Division*, p. 96.
113. Knyvett, *Over there with the Australians*, pp. 153–4.
114. Pedersen, *Fromelles*, pp. 66–7.
115. McMullin, *Pompey Elliott*, p. 218.
116. Ellis, *The 5th Australian Division*, p. 96.
117. Burness, *Fromelles and the Somme*.
118. Barton, *The Lost Legions of Fromelles*, pp. 219–20.
119. Pedersen, *Fromelles*, p. 71.
120. Bean, *Official History*, pp. 365–6.
121. Downing, Walter H., *To The Last Ridge*, Melbourne, 1920.
122. Bean, *Official History*, pp. 363–4.
123. McMullin, *Pompey Elliott*, p. 221.
124. Burness, *Fromelles and the Somme*.
125. Bean, *Official History*, pp. 363–5.
126. Finlayson, *Crumps and Camouflets*, p.102.
127. Cobb, *Fromelles 1916*, p. 107.
128. Barton, *The Lost Legions of Fromelles*, p. 217.
129. Ibid., p. 220.
130. Bean, Interview with Major A. Sanderson.
131. Barton, *The Lost Legions of Fromelles*, p. 128.
132. Ibid., p. 209.
133. Bean, Interview with Major A. Sanderson.
134. Cobb, *Fromelles 1916*, pp. 74, 81–3 re: Bishop, Bert, *Soldier Solomon*, and McNicoll, *Making and Breaking*, pp. 65–6.
135. Barton, *The Lost Legions of Fromelles*, Map 19, Kriegsarchiv, Munich, RIR 21, Bund 12.
136. Ibid., p. 213.
137. Pedersen, *Fromelles*, pp. 60–2 and 2/1st *Bucks Light Infantry War Diary*.
138. Bean, Interview with Major A. Sanderson.
139. Letter from Captain A. Sanderson to Major L.J. Coulter of 3.A.T.C., 20 July 1916 (A.W.M.).
140. McMullin, *Pompey Elliott*, p. 231.
141. Bean, Interview with Major A. Sanderson.
142. Senior, *Fromelles 1916*, p. 160.
143. Pedersen, *Fromelles*, pp. 61–2.
144. McMullin, *Pompey Elliott*, p. 233.
145. Barton, *The Lost Legions of Fromelles*, p. 215.
146. Ibid., pp. 209, 225.
147. Bean, *Official History*, p. 364.

148. Barton, *The Lost Legions of Fromelles*, p. 220.
149. Bean, *Official History*, p. 392.
150. Ibid., p. 391.
151. 2/1st Bucks Light Infantry War Diary.
152. Bean, *Official History*, p. 392.
153. Ibid., p. 393.
154. Ellis, *The 5th Australian Division*, p.100.
155. Bean, *Official History*, p. 394.
156. Ellis, *The 5th Australian Division*, p.100.
157. McMullin, *Pompey Elliott*, p. 219.
158. Miles, *Official History*, p. 129.
159. Bean, *Official History*, pp. 397–8.
160. Miles, *Official History*, p. 130.
161. Bean, *Official History*, pp. 394–5.
162. Cobb, *Fromelles 1916*, p. 99.
163. McMullin, *Pompey Elliott*, p. 223.
164. Knyvett, *Over there with the Australians*.
165. Bean, *Official History*, pp. 440–1.
166. Cobb, *Fromelles 1916*, p. 102 quoted in Downing W.H., *To the Last Ridge*.
167. Bean, *Official History*, pp. 438–9.
168. McMullin, *Pompey Elliott*, p. 225.
169. Senior, *Fromelles 1916*, p. 165.
170. McMullin, *Pompey Elliott*, p. 224.
171. Ibid., pp. 229–30.
172. War Diary of 3 A.T.C.
173. Letter from Captain A. Sanderson to Major L.J. Coulter of 3.A.T.C., 20 July 1916 (A.W.M.).
174. Bean, Interview with Major A. Sanderson.
175. War Diary of 3 A.T.C. (AWM).
176. McNicoll, *Making and Breaking*, pp. 57, 65–7.
177. McMullin, *Pompey Elliott*, p. 226.
178. Bean, *Official History*, p. 447 note 146.
179. Ibid., p. 445 note 141.
180. 2/1st Bucks Light Infantry War Diary.
181. McMullin, *Pompey Elliott*, p. 228.
182. Bean, *Official History*, p. 444–5 note 141.
183. Senior, *Fromelles 1916*, p. 132 re: *Sydney Morning Herald*, 2 August 1919 'Fleurbaix'.
184. Miles, *Official History*, notes on pp.134–5 re: 'O.H.L. and Fromelles'.
185. Cobb, *Fromelles 1916*, p. 161.
186. Bean, *Official History*, p. 443.
187. Senior, *Fromelles 1916*, pp. 169, 172–3.
188. McMullin, *Pompey Elliott*, p. 228.
189. Ibid., p 226.
190. Weber, T., *Hitler's First War*, p.146.
191. Senior, *Fromelles 1916*, p. 162–3 re: 2/1st *Bucks Light Infantry War Diary* (NTA WO. 95/3066).
192. Cobb, *Fromelles 1916*, pp. 112, 116–17.
193. Miles, *Official History*, p. 133.

194. Senior, *Fromelles 1916*, p. 176.
195. Summers, Julie, *Remembering Fromelles,* C.W.G.C. Publishing, 2010 p. 50.
196. www.cwgc.org
197. Letter from C.E.W. Bean to Major Alex Sanderson, 6 July 1926 (Sanderson Archives).
198. Cobb, *Fromelles 1916*, p. 87.
199. Barton, *The Lost Legions of Fromelles*, pp. 230–1.

Chapter 9: Sanderson Takes Command
1. War Diary of 3 A.T.C.
2. Ibid.
3. Ibid.
4. Ibid.
5. Ibid.
6. Ibid.
7. Military Mining, p. 6–7.
8. Finlayson, *Crumps and Camouflets,* p. 145.
9. War Diary of 3 A.T.C.
10. Baldey, D. and Reading, J., Newspaper transcriptions, *Western Argus.*
11. War Diary of 3 A.T.C.
12. Barton, *Beneath Flanders Fields*, pp. 128–9.
13. War Diary of 3 A.T.C.
14. Bean, Interview with Major A. Sanderson.
15. War Diary of 3 A.T.C.
16. Military Mining, p. 15.
17. Finlayson, *Crumps and Camouflets,* p. 150.
18. Lee, *The Battle of Fromelles*, p. 154.
19. Baldey, D. & Reading, J.

Chapter 10: 3rd Australian Tunnelling Company under Hill 70
1. *The Great War,* BBC documentary series, 1964.
2. Holmes, Richard, *The Little Field Marshall,* Weidenfield & Nicolson, 2004, p. 305.
3. Winter, D., *Haig's Command: A Reassessment,* Pen & Sword, 2004, p. 41.
4. Bean, Interview with Major A. Sanderson
5. 258th Tunnelling Company War Diary.
6. Grieve, Captain W. Grant and Newman, Bernard, *Tunnellers,* Herbert Jenkins, 1936, Reprint Naval & Military Press, pp. 136–8.
7. Bean, Interview with Major A. Sanderson.
8. War Diary of 3 A.T.C.
9. *Military Mining,* pp. 102–103, 105.
10. Robinson, Lt-Col. Phillip., Article in *Journal of Defence Surveyor's Association, Ranger Magazine,* Summer 2011, Vol 3., No. 2.
11. Baldey, D., and Reading, J.
12. War Diary of 3 A.T.C.
13. Ibid.
14. Finlayson, *Crumps and Camouflets,* pp. 151–2.
15. War Diary of 3 A.T.C.
16. Bean, *Official History* Vol. IV., p. 965.
17. Finlayson, *Crumps and Camouflets,* p. 167.

18. Bean, Interview with Major A. Sanderson.
19. Baldey, D. & Reading, J. *Western Argus*, 5 December 1916.
20. War Diary of 3 A.T.C.
21. Ibid.
22. Baldey, D. & Reading, J.
23. Great War Forum: Sapper Caradog O. Jones, article translated from the original Welsh in a Welsh-American newspaper.

Chapter 11: Underground War Intensifies
1. Baldey, D. & Reading, J.
2. Finlayson, *Crumps and Camouflets*, p. 157.
3. *The Times*, 30 January 1916.
4. Baldey, D. & Reading, J. (Letters in Powell family archives).
5. Ibid.. (National Library of Australia: Interview with Sapper James Hallinan).
6. War Diary of 3 A.T.C.
7. Ibid.
8. Ibid.
9. *Military Mining*, pp. 112–13.
10. Barton, *Beneath Flanders Fields*, pp. 114–15.
11. War Diary of 3 A.T.C.
12. Ibid.
13. Herwig, Holger H., *The First World War : Germany and Austria-Hungary 1914–18*, Bloomsbury, 2014, p. 251.
14. War Diary of 3 A.T.C.
15. Ibid.
16. Crowley, F.K., 'Forrest, Sir John (1847–1918)', *Australian Dictionary of Biography*, National Centre of Biography, Australian National University 8 (1981).
17. Baldey, D. & Reading, J., re: F. Miles' wartime diary (F. Miles' son donated Profile).
18. War Diary of 3 A.T.C.
19. Ibid.
20. Ibid.
21. Ibid.
22. Ibid.
23. Military Mining, p. 32.
24. War Diary of 3 A.T.C.
25. Ibid.
26. Leonard, Matthew, *Beneath the Killing Fields: Exploring the Subterranean Landscapes of the Western Front*, Pen & Sword, 2016, p. 84.
27. Ibid. pp. 86–7.

Chapter 12: Battle of Arras
1. Major Stokes' Inspection Reports, TNA WO 158/138.
2. Finlayson, *Crumps and Camouflets*, p. 179.
3. Bean, Interview with Major A. Sanderson.
4. War Diary of 3 A.T.C.
5. Baldey, D. & Reading, J. (War Diary of George Oxman. 1 November 1918 (AWM371 96/0316; Private Record PR00712).
6. Ibid.

7. Ibid.
8. Intelligence Summary (3 A.T.C. War Diary, Original Document Sanderson archives).
9. Bean, *Official History, Vol. IV* 1917, Appendix 3.
10. Military Mining, p. 15.
11. War Diary of 3 A.T.C.
12. Ibid.
13. Baldey, D. & Reading, J. (Frank Miles' Diary).
14. Baldey, D. & Reading, J. (Sgt. Berry's letter home).
15. Serle, *John Monash,*. p. 290.
16. Woodward, *The War Story.*
17. Brown, Malcolm, *The IWM Book of the Western Front,* Pan Macmillan, 2001, p. 240.
18. Barton, *Beneath Flanders Fields,* pp. 184, 190–1.
19. Serle, *John Monash,*. pp. 291–2.
20. Baldey, D. & Reading, J. (Sapper W. Powell's private letters, donated by great-nephew).
21. War Diary of 3 A.T.C.

Chapter 13: Allied Mining Raid on Hill 70

1. War Diary of 3 A.T.C.
2. Bean, Interview with Major A. Sanderson.
3. Lovell, Nicholas, 'V.C.s of Bromsgrove School', article appears on Tom Morgan's 'Hellfire Corner' website).
4. Bean, *Interview with Major A. Sanderson.*
5. War Diary of 3 A.T.C.
6. Lovell, 'V.C.s of Bromsgrove School'.
7. War Diary of 3 A.T.C.
8. Bean, *Interview with Major A. Sanderson.*
9. War Diary of 3 A.T.C.
10. Graves, *Goodbye to All That,* p. 110.
11. Baldey, D. & Reading, J.
12. War Diary of 3 A.T.C.
13. Bean, Interview with Major A. Sanderson.
14. Ibid.
15. Bean, *Official History Vol IV,* Appendix 3.
16. War Diary of 3 A.T.C.
17. Ibid.
18. Scott, Frederick G., *The Great War as I Saw It,* Project Gutenburg, 1917, p. 20.
19. War Diary of 3 A.T.C.
20. Baldey, D. & Reading, J. (re: Sgt. Berry).
21. Ibid. (re: Sgt. Berry).

Chapter 14: Canadian Assault on Hill 70

1. Finlayson, *Crumps and Camouflets,* p. 232.
2. War Diary of 3 A.T.C.
3. Bean, *Official History Vol. IV,* p. 728.
4. War Diary of 3 A.T.C.
5. Finlayson, *Crumps and Camouflets,* p. 234.
6. Bean, Interview with Major A. Sanderson.
7. Scott, *The Great War,* pp. 199–200.

8. Great War Forum: Sapper Caradog O. Jones article.
9. War Diary of 3 A.T.C., Appendix 1/17.
10. Baldey, D. & Reading, J. (re: George Oxman's Diary).
11. War Diary of 3 A.T.C.
12. Ibid. Prince Rupprecht's report and Sanderson's response.
13. Ibid.
14. Baldey, D. & Reading, J., article *The Sydney Sun* 31 August 1917, by Keith Murdoch.
15. War Diary of 3 A.T.C.
16. Ibid.
17. Hills, The Fifth Leicestershires, pp. 260–1: in Finlayson, *Crumps and Camouflets*.
18. War Diary of 3 A.T.C.
19. Ibid.
20. Robinson, P. and Cave, N., *The Underground War & Vimy Ridge to Arras*, Pen & Sword, 2011, pp. 110–12.
21. War Diary of 3 A.T.C.
22. Baldey, D. & Reading, J. (Sapper C. Leaver's diary extracts from relative Bill Leaver).

Chapter 15: Hythe Tunnel Fortress, Hill 70

1. Baldey, D. & Reading, J. (Sapper C. Leaver and H. Dodd's diaries).
2. War Diary of 3 A.T.C.
3. Baldey, D. & Reading, J. (Sgt Berry).
4. Ibid., re: *West Australian* article 31 January 1918 (Sgt. Frank Angel).
5. Clarke, Francis G., *Australia in a Nutshell: A Narrative History*, Rosenberg, 2003, pp. 191–2.
6. Bean, Interview with Major A. Sanderson.
7. War Diary of 3 A.T.C.
8. Ibid.
9. Baldey, D. & Reading, J. (Sapper C. Leaver's Diary).
10. Bean, C.E.W., AWM3 DRL606/101 & 2 /1.
11. Bean, Interview with Major A. Sanderson.
12. Bean, AWM3 DRL606/101 & 2 /1.
13. Wikipedia Re: Capt. G.H. Wilkins M.C.
14. Stevenson, David, *With our Backs to the Wall*, Allen Lane, 2011, p. 221.
15. Perrett, B., *Why the Germans Lost*, Pen & Sword, 2013, p.167.
16. Keegan, John, *The First World War*, Pimlico, 1999, p. 439.
17. War Diary of 3 A.T.C.
18. Ibid.

Chapter 16: The Kaiserschlacht

1. Strachen, *The First World War* p. 287.
2. Keegan, *The First World War*, p. 427.
3. Strachen, *The First World War* pp. 280, 282–3.
4. Ibid., pp. 288–9.
5. Ibid., pp. 287–8.
6. Keegan, *The First World War*, pp. 427–30.
7. Gilbert, Martin, *The First World War*, Henry Holt, 1994, p. 407.
8. Perrett, B., *Why the Germans Lost*, Pen & Sword, 2013, p. 69.
9. Scott, F. G., *The Great War*, Chapter XXVI

10. Baldey, D. & Reading, J. (Sapper C. Leaver's Diary).
11. Gilbert, *The First World War*, pp. 408–10.
12. Brown, Malcolm, *1918 Year of Victory*, Sidgwick & Jackson, 1998, p. 71.
13. Stevenson, *With our Backs*, p. 68.
14. Keegan, *The First World War*, pp. 432, 434.
15. Gibbs, Sir. Philip A.H., 'Underground War: Life below No Man's Land, *Daily Telegraph*, 1918.
16. Gilbert, *The First World War*, p. 412.
17. Keegan, *The First World War*, p. 435.

Chapter 17: The Battle of Lys
1. Gilbert, *The First World War*, pp. 412–13.
2. Stevenson, *With our Backs*, p. 72.
3. War Diary of 3 A.T.C.
4. Ibid.
5. Slang: North Queensland Register 28 August 1916.
6. Baldey, D. & Reading, J. (Sapper C. Leaver's Diary).
7. Stevenson, *With our Backs*, p. 73.
8. Taylor, A.J.P., *English History 1914–1945*, p. 102.
9. Gilbert, *The First World War*, p. 413.
10. War Diary of 3 A.T.C.
11. Ibid.
12. Gilbert, *The First World War*, p. 415.
13. Keegan, *The First World War*, p. 435 quoting Herwig, H., *First World War*, p. 404.
14. War Diary of 3 A.T.C.
15. Finlayson, *Crumps and Camouflets*, p. 430 note 11.
16. Gilbert, *The First World War*, p. 418.
17. Brown, *1918 Year of Victory*, pp. 104–105.
18. *Sydney Herald,* 24 December 1918, article by 'Willie Wombat'.
19. War Diary of 3 A.T.C.
20. Gilbert, *The First World War*, p. 418.
21. Stevenson, *With our Backs*, pp. 77–8.
22. War Diary of 3 A.T.C. Appendix. XI.
23. Ibid.
24. Stevenson, *With our Backs*, pp. 82–4.
25. Gilbert, *The First World War*, p. 425.
26. Serle, *John Monash*, pp. 298–301, 320.
27. Gilbert, *The First World War*, pp. 425–8.
28. Stevenson, *With our Backs* p. 88.
29. Ibid., pp. 88–91.
30. War Diary of 3 A.T.C.

Chapter 18: The Allied Counter-Offensive
1. Lloyd, Nick, *Hundred Days: The End of the Great War*, Viking, 2013, pp. 22, 25.
2. Serle, *John Monash*. pp. 333, 335.
3. Stevenson, *With our Backs* p. 197.
4. Lloyd, *Hundred Days*, pp. 1–2.
5. Ibid., pp. 2,6.

6. Ibid., pp 9–10.
7. Gilbert, *The First World War* p. 444.
8. War Diary of 3 A.T.C.
9. Lloyd, *Hundred Days,* p. 36.
10. Scott, *The Great War,* p. 279.
11. Stevenson, *With our Backs,* pp. 33–5.
12. Brown, *1918 Year of Victory,* pp. 198–9.
13. Lloyd, *Hundred Days,* pp. 44, 52.
14. Bean, *Official History Vol. VI* pp. 499–500.
15. Lloyd, *Hundred Days,* pp. 52, 54.
16. Ibid., pp. 55–61 and Taylor, A.J.P., *English History,* p. 109.
17. Stevenson, *With our Backs,* p.124.
18. Gilbert, *The First World War,* p. 450.
19. War Diary of 3 A.T.C.
20. Lloyd, *Hundred Days,* pp. 85–7.
21. War Diary of 3 A.T.C. Appendix
22. *Military Mining,* p. 108.
23. War Diary of 3 A.T.C.
24. Baldey, D. & Reading, J. (Sapper John Punton's family history).
25. Lloyd, *Hundred Days,* pp. 99, 102–106.
26. Baldey, D. & Reading, J. (Re: Oxman diary).
27. War Diary of 3 A.T.C.
28. Lloyd, *Hundred Days,* pp. 107–108.
29. Jünger, Ernst, *Storm of Steel,* Penguin, 2004, p. 131.
30. Lloyd, *Hundred Days,* p. 146.

Chapter 19: Defusing Traps and Mines
1. Grant, Grieve and Newman, *Tunnellers,* p. 145.
2. Jünger, *Storm of Steel.*
3. War Diary of 3 A.T.C.
4. Baldey, D. & Reading, J. (re: Sapper J. Hallinan).
5. War Diary of 3 A.T.C. Appendix 37.
6. Ibid. Appendix 112.
7. Keegan, *The First World War,* p. 441.
8. Lloyd, *Hundred Days,* pp. 176–7.
9. Ibid., pp. 144, 181.
10. War Diary of 3 A.T.C.
11. Lloyd, *Hundred Days,* pp. 202, 208, 213–14, 220.
12. War Diary of 3 A.T.C.

Chapter 20: The Armistice
1. Lloyd, *Hundred Days,* pp. 247–9.
2. Finlayson, *Crumps and Camouflets,* p. 380–3.
3. Brown, *1918 Year of Victory,* pp. 281, 285.
4. War Diary of 3 A.T.C.
5. Lloyd, *Hundred Days,* p. 263.
6. War Diary of 3 A.T.C.
7. Brown, *1918 Year of Victory,* p. 285.
8. Baldey, D. & Reading, J. (re: Sapper G. Oxman).

9. War Diary of 3 A.T.C.
10. Ibid.
11. Finlayson, *Crumps and Camouflets*, p. 397.
12. War Diary of 3 A.T.C.
13. Ibid.
14. Ibid.

Chapter 21: Peace and Repatriation
1. Brown, *1918 Year of Victory*, p. 330.
2. Baldey, D & Reading, J. (re: Sappers J. Hallinan & G. Oxman).
3. Finlayson, *Crumps and Camouflets* pp. 401–402.
4. War Diary of 3 A.T.C.
5. Clarke, Francis G. *Australia in a Nutshell* : *A Narrative History*, Rosenberg, 2003, pp. 193–4.

Chapter 22: To England and Marriage
1. Original Runic Address to Troops (Sanderson Family Archives).
2. Lt-Col J.B. Sanderson and Sanderson, Myles, *Secret Service in the Cold War*, Pen & Sword 2019.
3. Sanderson, Alex, *Battye Interview*.
4. Sanderson Lt. Col. John, *Secret Service in the Cold War*, pp. 87–8.
5. www.visitcruachan.co.uk/history.

Commonwealth Engineer Units' Honour Rolls
Commonwealth Royal Engineers' Honour Rolls Book, Kitchener's Chapel, St Paul's Cathedral.
Profiles of 3rd Australian Tunnelling Company, Donna Baldey and John Reading.
The 'A.W.M. Exhibits List' by Major Sanderson is from the 3 A.T.C. War Diary (Appendix).

Bibliography and Sources

Interviews
Bean, Charles E.W., Interview with Major Sanderson at Noeux-les-Mines. CB/AS 1918 (Sanderson Archives as original copy sent by Bean, 19 March 1918, with covering letter).
Interview with Lady L. Steere and Murtagh O'Connor, Australia.
Sanderson, Major Alex, Interview with Battye Library (by Miss Molly F.L. Lukis), 1967 (Copyright R. Sanderson).
Sanderson, Robin Myles, Interview with Tim Dunn, *Secrets of the London Underground*, Series 3 Episode 2, 'South Kensington Underground Station', ITV, 2024.

Articles
Gibbs, Sir Philip A.H., 'Underground War: Life below No Man's Land', *Daily Telegraph*, 6 March 1918.
Jones, Sapper Caradog O., article translated from the original Welsh (publication unknown, Welsh American newspaper) www.greatwarforum.org.
Lovell, Nicholas, 'V.C.s of Bromsgrove School', Tom Morgan's www.helfirecorner.co.uk.
Robinson, Lieutenant Colonel Phillip, *Journal of Defence Surveyor's Association, Ranger Magazine*, Summer 2011, Vol 3., No. 2.
Sydney Herald, 24 December 1918, article by 'Willie Wombat'.
Sydney Morning Herald, 2 August 1919, 'Fleurbaix'.
Western Argus, Kalgoorlie, W.A., 5 December 1916.
West Australian articles, Perth, W.A.; March 1894; 30 May 1916, 1917–18; Quekett, M., 5 October 1919.

Websites
www.poetry foundation.org.
www.tunnellers.net.
www.visitcruachan.co.uk/history.

Miscellaneous
Baber, Glen, *The Rhondda Pals*, Pamphlet 1995.
Christie-Miller, Lieutenant Colonel G., *The Second Bucks Battalion 1918: An Unofficial Record*, 2 Vols.
Commonwealth Engineer Units' Honour Rolls, Kitchener's Chapel, St Paul's Cathedral.
Goldfields History, *A Brief History of C.Y. O'Connor*, Souvenir Guide.
North Queensland Register, 28.8.1916 (A.I. Military Slang).
Public Works Department (Perth W.A.), PWD 8575/96, SROWA.
The Lee Magazine, October 1916.

Documentaries
Perkins, Rachel, *The Australian Wars*, BBC/First Wars Productions, 2024.
The Great War, BBC documentary series, 1964.

Archives

AWM (Australian War Museum)
AWM3 DRL606/101 & 2 /1.
AWM4, Series 16/4, Roll 386, War Diary of the 3rd Australian Tunnelling Company.
Bean, Charles E.W., Letter to Major A. Sanderson, 9 March 1918, Sanderson Family Archives, and AWM.
Bean, Charles. E.W., C.E.W. Bean's Diary, AWM38 3DRL 606.
Letter from Captain A. Sanderson to Major L.J. Coulter of 3.A.T.C., 20 July 1916 (A.W.M.).

Stadtarchiv München (Munich City Archives)
Die Bayern in Grossen Kriege 1914–18.
History of the 21st Bavarian RIR.
TNA (The National Archives)
Major Stokes' Inspection Reports, TNA WO 158/138.
First Army Gen. Staff XC13039, TNA WO 95/165.
2/1st Bucks Light Infantry War Diary, TNA WO 95/3066.

Books

Barker, H.M., *Camels and the Outback*, W.A. Hesperian Press, 1995.
Barnard, Marjorie, *A History of Australia*, Angus & Robertson, 1986.
Barton, Peter, *The Lost Legions of Fromelles*, Constable & Robinson, 2014.
Barton, Peter; Doyle, Peter and Vandewalle, Johan, *Beneath Flanders Fields: The Tunnellers' War, 1914–1918*, Spellmount, 2007.
Bean, C.E.W., *Official History of Australia in the War of 1914–191, Vol. III: 1916*, Angus & Robertson Ltd., 1940.
Bolton, G., 'Forest, Alexander (1849–1901)' *Australian Dictionary of Biography*, National Centre of Biography, Australian National University 8, 1981.
Branagan, David F., and Cliff, Paul, *T.W. Edgeworth David: A Life: Geologist, Adventurer, Soldier and 'Knight in the Old Brown Hat'*, N.L.A., 2005.
Brown, Malcolm, *1918 Year of Victory*, Sidgwick & Jackson, 1998.
Burness, Peter, *Fromelles and the Somme: Australians on the Western Front 1916*, Dept. of Victoria, 2006.
Churchill, Sir Winston, *The World Crisis 1911–1918*, Penguin, 2005.
Clark, Francis G., *Australia in a Nutshell: A Narrative History*, Rosenberg, 2003.
Cobb, Paul, *Fromelles 1916*, Tempus, 2007.
Crowley, F.K. 'Forrest, Sir John (1847–1918)', *Australian Dictionary of Biography*, National Centre of Biography, Australian National University 8, 1981.
Dow, George, *Great Central: The Progenitors 1813–1863*, Vol.1 Locomotive Publishing Ltd., 1959.
Downing, Walter H., *To The Last Ridge*, Melbourne, 1920.
Ellis, Capt. A.D. (M.C.), *Story of the 5th Australian Division*, Hodder & Stoughton, 1920.
Evans, A.G., *C.Y. O'Connor: His Life and Legacy*, University of W.A. Press, 2001.
Finlayson, Damien, *Crumps and Camouflets*, Big Sky Publishing, 2010.
Finlayson, Damien, *Supporting Tunnelling Operations in the Great War: The Alphabet Company*, Pen & Sword, 2018.
Gilbert, Martin, *The First World War*, Henry Holt, 1994.
Grant, Grieve and Newman B., *Tunnellers*, Herbert Jenkins, 1936.

Bibliography and Sources 265

Graves, Robert, *Goodbye to All That*, Penguin Classics, 1960.
Herwig, Holger H., *The First World War: Germany and Austria-Hungary 1914–18*, Bloomsbury, 2014.
Hills, J.D., *The Fifth Leicestershire: A record of the 1/5th Battalion*, Echo Press, 1919.
Holmes, Richard, *The Little Field Marshall*, Weidenfield & Nicolson, 2004.
James, Lawrence, *The Making of British India*, Abacus Books, 1979.
Jones, Simon, *Underground Warfare 1914–18*, Pen & Sword, 2011.
Jünger, Ernst, *Storm of Steel*, Penguin, 2004.
Keegan, John, *The First World War*, Pimlico, 1999.
Knyvett, Captain R. Hugh, *Over there with the Australians*, Hodder & Stoughton, 1918.
Le Page, John S.H., *Building a State: The Story of the Public Works Department of Western Australia 1829–198*, Water Authority of W.A., 1926.
Lee, Roger, *The Battle of Fromelles*, Army History Unit, 2010.
Leonard, Matthew, *Beneath the Killing Fields: Exploring the Subterranean Landscapes of the Western Front*, Pen & Sword, 2016.
McMullin, Ross, *Pompey Elliott*, Scribe Publication, 2002.
McNicoll, Ronald Ramsay, *The Royal Australian Engineers 2: 1902 to 1919, Making and Breaking*, Griffin Press, 1979.
Miles, Captain Wilfred, *Official History of the Great War, Military Operations France & Belgium Vol 2*, IWM / Naval Military Press.
Mouat, Jeremy, and Ian Phimister, 'The Engineering of Herbert Hoover', *Pacific Historical Review*, 77, no. 4 (1 November 2008).
Nash, George H. and Clements, Kendrick A., *The Life of Herbert Hoover*, 1st ed. W.W. Norton, 1983.
Pedersen, Peter. A., *Fromelles*, Leo Cooper, 2004.
Perrett, B., *Why the Germans Lost*, Pen & Sword, 2013.
Ralph, Gilbert M., *Bullfinch and the Yilgarn Goldfield*, Hisperian Press, 2007.
Robinson, P. and Cave, N., *The Underground War & Vimy Ridge to Arras*, Pen & Sword, 2011.
Sanderson, Lieutenant Colonel John Burden, and Sanderson, Myles, *Secret Service in the Cold War*, Pen & Sword 2019.
Sanderson, Henry (Senior), *A Plan for an Effectual General System of Sewage for the Cities of London and Westminster*, John Williams and Co., 1847.
Scott, Frederick G., *The Great War as I Saw It*, Project Gutenberg, 1917.
Senior, Michael, *Fromelles 1916: No Finer Courage, The Loss of an English Village*, Pen & Sword, 2011.
Senior, Michael, Haking, *A Dutiful Soldier*, Pen & Sword, 2012.
Serle, Geoffrey, *John Monash: a Biography*, Melbourne University Press, 1982.
Stevenson, David, *With our Backs to the Wall*, Allen Lane, 2011.
Strachen Sir Hew, *The First World War*, Simon & Schuster, 2003.
Summers, Julie, *Remembering Fromelles*, C.W.G.C. Publishing, 2010.
Taylor, A.J.P., *English History 1914–1945*, Oxford University Press, 1967.
Tauman, Merab, *The Chief, C. Y. O'Connor*, University of W.A. Press. 1978.
The Work of the Royal Engineers in the European War, 1914–19, Military Mining, Sandhurst/ Naval & Military Press Ltd., 2004.
Weber, Thomas, *Hitler's First War*, Oxford University Press, 2010.
Winter, D., *Haig's Command: A Reassessment*, Pen & Sword, 2004.
Woodward, O. H., *The War Story of Oliver Holmes Woodward, Captain 1st Australian Tunnelling Company, Australian Imperial Force*, O.H. Woodward, 1932.

Index

Acts:
  Government of India (1858), 6
  Goldfields Water Supply Coolgardie
    Bill W.A, 15
  Military Services Act (G.B.) 1916, 57
Aircraft: Tilt-Engine (S.T.O.V.L.) &
  'Drone' (V.T.O.), 226
Armistice, ix, 191, 209-10, 213, 215, 217,
  221, 234. 238, 242
Arthur's Pass, N.Z., 15
Asquith, Lord Herbert H., 74
Asserghur Fortress, India, 6
Australian Federation 1901, 19
Australian Imperial Force:
  Armies: 5th, 185
  Divisions: 3rd, 148; 5th, 76, 77
  Brigades: 8th, 78; 9th, 150; 11th
    Artillery, 197; 14th, 78; 15th, 78
  Regiments: 10th Light Horse Regiment,
    7; Signallers' Militia, 57
  Battalions: 58th, 78; 59th, 78, 87, 91-4,
    96, 98, 100-2,109;
    60th, 78, 80, 87, 91-4, 96, 98, 100,109
  Mining Corps, x
Australian States:
  New South Wales, 46;
  Queensland, 46-7;
  South Australia, 46;
  Tasmania, 47, 177;
  Victoria 14, 33, 46, 57, 60, 177-8;
  Western Australia, 47, 177
Australian War Museum, x

Babington, Charlie, 29
Bachtold, Major R.A.E., 9
Ball, Captain Albert R.F.C., 200
Barracks: Victoria, 110, 231; Noeux-les-
  Mines, ix, 46, 46, 122, 169, 174, 183,
  206, 236

Battles:
  Aubers Ridge (1915), 59, 62, 73-5
  Pozières (1916), 143
  Somme (1916), 64, 69, 73, 107, 108, 109,
    134, 185-7, 190-1, 201, 205
  Fromelles (1916), ix, xi, 59, 61-2, 67, 69,
    71-111, 124,198
  Arras (1917), 141-15
  Vimy Ridge (1917), 61, 141-2, 145,
    163-4, 188, 200
  Ypres 3rd (1917), 161
  Lys (1918), 192-9, 197
  Aisne 3rd (1918), 198
  Amiens (1918), 204-5
  Marne 2nd (1918), 200-1
Battye Library, Perth W.A., ix
Bazalgette, Joseph, 3
Bean, Charles Edwin Woodrow, ix, xiii,
  82, 86-7, 96-98, 101-103, 106-109, 125,
  136-7, 146, 149, 181-3, 198
  Bean's interview with Alex Sanderson:
    38, 46-7, 55-6, 59, 62, 67, 71, 78, 88-
    90, 98, 105, 117, 121-2, 125-6, 143,
    151-2, 155, 157, 162, 178, 181-2, 248
  C.E.W. Bean's letters to Alex
    Sanderson: ix, 47, 105, 110-111
Bewick Moreing, 30
Bibbulmun nation W.A., 20
Birdwood, General Sir William R., 176,
  196, 216, 223
Bridgford, Brigadier General, 153
British Army:
  Armies: 1st and 2nd Army, 62, 156
  Corps:
    1 Corps, 161, 192, 215
    V Corps, 186
    V11 Corps, 186
    VIII Corps, 201
    XVIII Corps, 199
    XI Corps, 74;

Index   267

Divisions:
   1st, 73
   55th, 207
   61st (2nd South Midland), 62, 76, 78
Brigades:
   72nd Infantry, 197
   113th, 79
   183rd, 78
   184th, 78
Regiments:
   2/1st Buckinghamshire, 79
   2/4th and 2/6th Gloucester, 79
   2/4th Royal Berkshire, 79
   10th Battalion Royal Welsh, 79
   11th Essex, 152
   Durham Light Infantry, 139, 152
   Royal Sussex (Pals), 69
Brockman Fred, W.A., 38
Brunel, Isambard Kingdom., 4
Brunel, Marc, 25
Burden, John, Alice and Gladys, 221
Byng, General Sir Julian, 188

Cabinet War Rooms, 226
Camps:
  Broadmeadows, Melbourne Vic., 49
  Casula, Liverpool N.S.W., 48
  Helena Vale, Blackboy Hill W.A., 48
  Midland W.A., 50
Canadian Army, 141:
  Divisions:
    1st, 164
    2nd, 164, 166
    3rd, 212
  Brigades:
    1st Infantry, 159
    2nd and 3rd Infantry, 161;
  Battalion: 1st Infantry, 159
Candy, Kathleen, Duchess of
   Newcastle, 17-8
Carbon Monoxide, 116
Carter, Brigadier General C., 91
Cattle Stations, W.A.:
  Lissadell, 40
  Malden River, 37
  Mallina, 13
Church, Captain H., 80, 86, 88-9, 96-8, 107, 111

Churchill, Sir Winston, 45, 186, 226, 229, 248, 263
Claremont Water Supply, 31
Conscription (Australia), 56, 177
Controller of Mines, x, 112, 142, 150, 175, 207, 210, 175
Corrigan, R.S.M., S., 6
Crompton, Richard, 213
Crossley, Ada, 32
Currie, Lieutenant General Sir Arthur, 200, 207

David, Lt-Colonel T. W. Edgeworth, 45-7, 58, 114, 213
Diseases: Diphtheria, 17; Typhoid, 17
Durand Group, 140

East India Company, 6
Elliott, Brigadier General Harold (Pompey), 81, 90
Exhibition, Mining and Industrial W.A. (1899), 24
Expeditionary Forces, Allied:
  A.E.F., xiii, 198, 200
  B.E.F., xiii 56, 200
  C.E.F., xiii, 200
Explorers and pastoralists
  Brockman, Fred, W.A., 38
  Elder, Sir Thomas, 40
  Laurie, Tom, 38
  Macleod, Don, 40
  Martin, Louis, 38
  Ross, Charlie, 37
  Smith, 'Wally', 37
  Vestey, Sir William, 40

Falkenhayn, General Erich von, 72
Ferdinand, Archduke Francis, 43
Fitzwilliam, Earl, 3
Foch, Field Marshall Ferdinand, 188, 210
Forrest, Alexander, 18, 33
Forrest, Sir John, 11, 14, 18-19, 21, 23-5, 26, 33
Forest, Lady Margaret E., 21
Fowke, Brigadier General George Henry, 59
Fraser, Sergeant Simon, 102-3
French Army: 37th Division Artillery, 197

French, Field Marshall Sir John, 121
French, (Manager Bank of N.S.W. Sydney), 38

Gallipoli, 46, 48, 76, 104
Gebhardt, *Hauptmann* Hans, 81, 93
German Army:
  Armies:
    3rd, 162
    4th, 162
    6th, 195
  Divisions:
    6th Bavarian, 74
  Brigades:
    12th, 76
    14th, 76
  Regiments:
    16th R.I.R., 76
    17th R.I.R., 76
    20th R.I.R., 76
    21st R.I.R., 76
    153 R.I.R., 128
  Companies:
    Kaiser Alexander, 206
    11 Company 3/16 R.I.R., 82
  German Mining Corps:
    Pionier-Mineur-Kompagnien, 59
    297 Pionier 146
Georgius Agricola, *De Re Metallica*, 1556, 31
Gibb, Captain Phillip, 188
Goering, Hermann, 200
Gold Mines:
  Associated Northern, 35
  Barrambic Ranges, 35
  Bullfinch, 33, 34
  Blackfinch, 35
  Chaffinch, 35
  Greenfinch, 35
  Redfinch, 35
  Yellowfinch, 35
  Fraser's Mine, 13
  Golden Horseshoe, 31
  Great Boulder Perseverance, 31
  Oroya Brown Hill, 24, 31
  Sons of Gwalia, 31
Gold prospectors:
  Bayley and Ford, 14

Cohn, 14
Doolette, Dorrie L., 33-5
Doolette, Sir George, 34-5
Hannan 'Paddy', 14
Jones, Charlie, 33-4
Lefroy, Henry, 18
Goldfields, Australia:
  Eastern W.A., 21
  Halls Creek, 13
  Murchison, 13
  Pilbarra, 13
  Southern Cross, 13
  Yilgarn, 13
Goode, Sir John, 16
Gough, General Sir Hubert, 188

Haig, Field Marshall Sir Douglas, 72, 121, 149, 194, 205, 213
Haking, Lieutenant General Sir Richard, 59, 73, 75, 85, 90-91, 100-103, 107-8,
Hales, 'Smiler' W.A., 30
Harbours:
  Admiralty Gulf W.A., 37
  Albany, W.A., 11
  Bunbury W.A., 16
  Fremantle, Perth W.A., 6
  Lyttelton, N.Z., 6
  Marseilles, France 52
  Port Chalmers, N.Z., 8
  Portland, Weymouth G.B., 5
  Sydney Harbour, 33
  Timaru, N.Z., 16
  Vansittard Bay W.A., 37
Harper, Charles 'Nat', 23
Harvey, Brigadier General Robert Napier 'Ducky', 56, 141, 156, 165
Hazebrouck, ix, 53, 55-6, 105
Hindenburg Line (*Siegriedstellung*), 134, 158, 210-1
Hindenburg, *Generalfeldmarschall* Paul von, 185
Hitler, Adolf, 212
Hodgson, T.C., 23
Holland, Lieutenant Sir Arthur, 192, 212
Hoover, Herbert Clark, 30-31
Horne, General Henry S., 141, 202-4
Hudson, Lieutenant R.B., 98
Hughes, Morris 'Billy', 198

Hunter-Weston, Lieutenant General A., 201
Hutchinson, Major A.J.S., 102
Hydro-Electric Power Schemes:
    Cruachen, Scotland, 228-9
    Hawera N.Z. 32
    Joginda Nagar, Mandi, India, 224

Inspector of Mines, x, 55-6, 66, 142, 150, 175
Institute of Civil Engineers, 5

Jackson, Major, 194
Joffre, General Joseph J.C., 72

Kaiserschlacht Offensives:
    Blücher-Yorke (Aisne), 198
    Friedenstrum, 200-1
    Georgette (Lys), 191, 197
    Gneisenau, 199
    Mars, 180, 188
    Michael, 16
    Operation *Alberich*, 134, 190
Kimberley District, ix, 1-4, 18, 37-40, 158
Kitchener, Lord Horatio H., xi, 73, 120,
Knyvett, Lt Hugh, 92, 102

Lloyd George, David, 74
London Transport, x, 225
Lovejoy, Lieutenant Harold R., 111
Ludendorff, General Eric von, 164, 212, 185, 188, 197
Luftwaffe, 226
Lukis, Miss, Molly F.L. (Archivist), ix

MacDonnell Clan, 3, 181
MacDonnell, Major General A.C., 181
Machines:
    Barrett hydraulic jack, 68
    Hand-blowers (Keith Blackman), 159
    Pipe caulking, W.A., 26
    Sirocco Ventilation fan, 180
    Wombat boring, 56
Mackenzie, Major General Sir Colin, 77
Macleod, Don, 40
Maphan Ferguson, Engineers, Vic., 24
May, Captain A.G., 149
McCay, Major General J.W., 97

Memorials, Australian:
    Diggers' Tunnelling Memorial, xi, 229
    Villers Brettoneux, 143, 147
Methuen, Lord, 52
Miles, Captain Wilfred, 75
Monash, General Sir John:
    Engineering: 32-3
    Military: 45, 149-50, 198, 200, 206, 217
Mundaring Dam, 19, 24, 27-9
Munro, General Sir Charles, 74, 108
Murdoch, Keith, 165

Naanup, Noel, Nyoongar tribe W.A., 20
Nivelle, General Robert G., 72, 75

O'Connor, Bridget, 27
O'Connor, Charles Yelverton (C.Y., 'The Chief'), ix, x, xii, 14, 20
    Early life in Ireland, 28
    Fremantle Harbour x, 9, 20-22
    Arrival in Australia, 11, 13, 17
    Recruitment by Forrest 15-16
    Relationship with cadet Sanderson, 19, 28
    Railways, 22
    Goldfields Water Pipeline, 22-29, 33
    Press attacks, 30
    Suicide, 28
Owen, Wilfred E.S., 213

Palmer, C.S.R., 29
Pearce, Senator George F., 45-6
Pheasant's Wood Cemetery, 110
Platman's knock, 112-3
Plenge, *Leutnant*, 86
Plumer, General Sir Hubert, 75, 210
Pope, Major A.W., 121
Portuguese Army: 2nd Division
Poulter, Private Reg., 99
Prada, Andy, xi
Pressious, Sergeant, A.I.F., 79
Prince of Wales, 223
Public Works Department, Perth, 5, 18-19, 21, 26, 31

Quarries, W.A.: Darlington, 22; Rocky Bay, 21
Queen Victoria, ix, 21,

Railways:
  Adelaide Electric Tramways, W.A., 31
  B.B. & C.I.R., India xiii, 6
  Doncaster to York, G.B., 3
  Eastern Goldfields, W.A., 17, 31
  G.I.P.R., India, xiii, 6
  G.T. Railway, N.Z., 32
  Great Western G.B., 5
  Liverpool and Manchester G.B., 3
  London to Brighton G.B., 3
  Southern Cross Transcontinental Perth W.A. to Adelaide S.A., 21
Ranges:
  W.A., Barrambic, 35
  Darling, 23
  King Leopard, W.A., 18
  Parkers, 34
Rawlinson, General Henry, 188
Reichstag, 185
Richthofen, Manfred von, 200
Rivers:
  Brisbane, Merton Bay Qld., 5
  Charnley W.A., 3
  Escaut, France, 215
  King Edward W.A., 38
  Lennard W.A., 13
  Margaret W.A., 18
  Ord W.A., 18
  Prince Regent W.A., 38
  Swan W.A., 19
Roads, Arthur's Pass, N.Z., 15
Rockets, V-1 and V-2, 227
Royal Flying Corps, 76, 87, 131, 182, 186 (R.A.F. No 2. Squadron, 196)
Rupprecht, *Kronprinz von Bayern*, 108, 134, 141, 164

Salients:
  Boar's Head, 59
  Mauquissait, 62, 67
  Sugar Loaf, 59, 69, 76-89, 92, 94-102, 105, 107, 111
  Verdun, 72-3, 213
  Wick, 68
Sanderson family:
  Alexander (1826-1860), 5-6
  Augusta (née Henderson 1852-1946), 7, 17, 225, 48, 157, 222-3, 225, 228
  Charles, (b.1832), 4-5
  Edmund (1825-85), 5
  Henry Junior (b.1821), 5
  Henry Senior (1798-1849), 3-4
  Janet (b.1936, Mrs Matthews), 104, 226-7
  Mary Sanderson (d.1830), 3
  Murchison (1891-3), 17
  Patricia (b.1927-2014) 227
  Peter (1926-1991), 227
  Susan (1830-1904), 6
  Victor (1883-6), 17
  William (1756-1805), 3
  William J.A. (1859-1893), 6, 8, 11, 17
Sanderson, Major Alexander 'Alex' (1881-1971):
  Pre-war: New Zealand childhood, 8
  Move to Perth W.A., 11
  Opinion of C.Y. O'Connor, 16
  Death of father, 17
  Cadetship under C.Y, 18-19
  Cadetship work on Fremantle Harbour, 22
  Pipeline calculations for C.Y., 25
  Relationship with C.Y.: 28
  Graduation of P.W.D. cadetship: 29
  Surveying Southern Cross and Kalgoorlie Railways, 29
  Working with H.C. Hoover, 30-31
  Mine Managing with Bewick Moeing; 31
  P.W.D. engineer on Eastern Goldfields, 31
  Qualification as Licensed Surveyor, 3
  Attendance at School of Mines, Kalgoorlie, 31
  Adelaide Electric Tramways, S.A., 31
  Surveys in N.Z., 32
  Manager of Oroya Brown Hill Gold Mine, 32
  Engineering with John Monash, 32-3
  Supervision of Sydney Harbour quays and sewerage system, 33
  Investment in Bullfinch Mine, 34
  Manager Barrambic Ranges Gold Mining Coy, 35
  Underground Manager Associated N. Gold Mine, Kalgoorlie, 35

Surveying Nornalup Inlet, 37
Explorations of Kimberley coast, 47
Horseback expedition across
  Kimberley, 37
Encounters with indigenous
  peoples, 38-9
First World War:
  Enlistment in Mining Corps, 47
  Instructing at Military Engineers'
    Training School, Sydney, 48
  Aboard the *Ulysses* troopship as
    Technical Expert, 49
  Repairing the *Ulysses*, 49-50
  Journey to Europe, 51-2
  Arrival in France: 53
  Unloading equipment at
    Hazebrouck, 54-5
  Joining 3 A.T.C., 59
  Defensive Mining, 62, 67-8, 70-71
  Blowing saps at Fromelles and
    wounded, 78, 83-84
  Attacking Sugar Loaf, 85-90, 96-99
  Appointed temporary O.C. 3
    A.T.C., 104
  Letter to Coulter, 104-5
  Awarded M.C., 106
  Letters from C.E.W. Bean, 110-111
  To Hill 70,
  Replacing 258th Coy R.E., 114-6
  Directing underground war and
    surveying at Hill 70, 121-2
  Mining Raid June 1917, wounded,
    bar to M.C., 152-6
  Promoted Major and permanent
    Command, 158
  Hythe subway planning, 168, 206
  Letters to Lt. Russel's wife, 175-7
  Commemorative Service, 1918;
    Award of D.S.O., 207
  Erection of Pont Maudit, 211;
Post-war:
  Return to England and
    marriage, 221-2
  Return to Australia aboard *Runic*, 223
  Indian appointment with Military
    Works Dept., 224
  Himalayan surge tunnel work, 224-5
  London Transport engineer, 225
Second World War:
  Supervising bomb repairs to London
    Underground system, 226
  Invention of tilt-engine and V.T.O.
    aircraft, 226
  Consultant for Cabinet War Rooms,
    226
Post-war:
  Engineer on Barrow-in-Furness
    power station and Cruachan
    tunnels, 229
  Golden wedding, 229
  Died aged 89 years, 229
Sanderson John Burden, Lt-Colonel
  (1921-2001), 43, (Battle of Sangshak
  1944, 227)
Sanderson, Captain William Lauchlan
  (1890-1957), 197, 213, 222
Sanderson Joseph Private 'Toby', 143
Sarajevo, 43
Schlieffen, Count Von, 45
Schools, civilian:
  Perth High School, W.A., 11
  School of Mines, Kalgoorlie W.A., 31
  Waitiki High School N.Z., 8
Schools, military:
  First Army School, Houchin, France,
    56
  Military Engineers' Training School,
    Sydney, 48
  2nd Army Mine Rescue and Listening
    School, 58, 66
Scott, Canon, 158, 162-3
Sewer systems:
  London (Victorian), 4
  Perth W.A., 19
  Sydney N.S.W., 33
Ships civil:
  Captain Cook, 6
  Karakatta, 38
  Lady Egidia, 8, 225
Somerville, Reverend, 222
Spatny, *Oberstleutnant*, 81
Special Gas Company R.E, 197
St Paul's Cathedral, xi, 230, 231, 245
Stephenson, George, 3, 4
Stephenson, Robert, 3
Stewart-Liberty, Captain Ivor, 80, 87

Stokes, Major R., Assistant Inspector of Mines, 66, 138, 141,16, 167
Strode, Sapper Fred, A.I.F., 79
Suez Canal, 50

Tanks: 182, 183, 195-6, 204-5
Thomson Lieutenant I., 45
Troopships:
   Ansonia, H.M.A.T. 81, 51
   Balika S.S., 143
   City of Edinburgh, S.S., 60
   Indara, S.S., 48
   Runic, H.M.A.T. A54, xii, 223
   Ulysses, A-38, 49
   Warilda, H.M.A.T., 60
Tunnelling Companies, Royal Australian Engineers:
   1st Australian Tunnelling Company, xi, 150, 194, 216, 149, 194
   Officers: Henry, Major J. D., xi; Woodward, Captain Oliver, 64, 149
   2nd Australian Tunnelling Company, xi :
   Officers: Mulligan, Major E. N., xi; Cook, Lieutenant G.A. C, 58
   3rd Australian Tunnelling Company, 62:
   Officers:
     Ashcroft, Lieutenant Ronald G.B., 163
     Brown, Captain Harry W., 242
     Campbell, Lieutenant Neil, 147, 193-5
     Cavanagh, Lieutenant Righton J., 134, 217
     Coulter, Major Leslie Jack, x, 47, 59, 64, 68-70, 78, 83-5, 90, 96, 99, 104-6, 109-10, 112, 117, 123, 131-9, 152, 155-8
     Crawshaw, Lieutenant G.J.,169
     Dow, Lieutenant John, 194-5, 242
     Grainger, Lieutenant William W., 117-8
     Hillman, Arthur J., 183, 192
     Homan, Lieutenant C.S., 58
     Howie, Lieutenant Oscar, 79,106, 124
     Kennedy, Lieutenant, 70
     Langdon, Captain Reginald J., 137
     McArdell, Captain John, 147, 217
     Morris, Captain Albert, 197

Priestman, Lieutenant 'Bertie', 79, 106
Purves, Lieutenant Allan John, 134
Russel, Lieutenant Hugh, 124, 150, 161, 164, 166-7, 175-7, 180
Seale, Lieutenant Harry, 70
Shaw, Lieutenant Colin C., 163, 211, 21-87
Taylor, Lieutenant, 173
Whyte, Lieutenant Charles, 105
N.C.O.s:
   Angel, Sergeant Frank, 177
   Berry, Sergeant James W., 115, 118, 123, 126, 129, 145, 148, 157, 160,177, 232, 242
   Dodd, Sergeant Edward 'Hughie', 173
   Forsyth, Sergeant Leslie, 183, 192, 211, 214, 234, 243
   Kerby, Sergeant M.J.M., 106, 124, 237
   Mason, Corporal, 70
   McKay, Corporal William, 79
   Reid, Sergeant, 192
   Street, Corporal Leslie, 83, 106
Sappers:
   Ahearn, R, 194
   Bird, Edwin, 12
   Bulmer, Clarence, 242
   Carden, Joseph, 175
   Cassin, Walter, 117-8
   Clingin, George, 133
   Cockton, Harold, 124
   Griffin, Frank 'Griffo', 155-6
   Hallinan, James Joseph, 57, 130, 209, 217, 243
   Hogan, Arthur, 195
   Jones, Caradog Owen, 127, 243
   Kelly, Eugene, 195
   Leaver, Charles, 169, 171, 175, 180, 187, 193, 243
   Miles, Frank, 135-6, 148
   Murray, Herbert 'Bert' H., 163
   Oxman, George, 144-5, 163-4, 208, 212, 215, 217-8, 243
   Powell, William, 46,129, 149-50
   Punton, John, 207
   Roden, Joseph H., 145, 239; Walton, 'Bobby', 60

Watson, William, 56
4th, 5th, 6th Australian Tunnelling Reinforcement Companies, 60-1
Tunnelling Companies, Royal Engineers:
   170th-185th Tunnelling Companies, 61
   170th Tunnelling Company, 121, 140, 158, 173
   171st Tunnelling Company, 65
   172nd Tunnelling Company, 158
   173rd Tunnelling Company, 145
   176th Tunnelling Company, 208
   251st to 258th Tunnelling Companies, 61
   251st Tunnelling Company, 59, 161
   253rd Tunnelling Company, 121
   254th Tunnelling Company, 59
   255th Tunnelling Company, 59, 62, 63
   257th Tunnelling Company, 68, 115, 122
   258th Tunnelling Company, 114-5, 121
Tunnelling Company of Portugal, 61
Tunnelling Company of New Zealand, 61
Tunnels on Western Front:
   (Allied)
      Border Redoubt, 168
      Canteen, 197, 199
      Copse, 159
      Hulluch, 168
      Hythe (Hill 70), xi, 121, 171-84, 199, 206
      St Elie, 168
      Winchester, 62
   (German):
      Dora, 134
      Imgard, 137
      Regensburg-Hans, 146
Tunnels, G.B:
   Hathersage, 4
   Huddersfield Canal, 4
   London Underground
   Rotherhithe, London, 25
Turner, Maudie and Minnie, 32
Tzar Nicholas II, 43

U-boats, 51, 185

Venn H., 23
Verdun, 72-3, 213
Vestey, Sir William, 40
Victoria Cross, xiv, 152, 156, 186
Von Kuhl, *Generalleutnant* Herman, 108, 161

Warships: *Emden* S.M.S. (German), 50; *Sydney*, H.M.A.S., 50
Wearne, 2nd Lt, Frank B., 152
Weld Club Perth W.A., 33, 50
Wentworth Woodhouse, 3
White, General C.B., 108, 198
Wilhelm II, Kaiser, 213
Wilkins, Captain George H., 182
Williams, Colonel H., 85, 108

Zeppelins, 221

Dear Reader,

We hope you have enjoyed this book, but why not share your views on social media? You can also follow our pages to see more about our other products: facebook.com/penandswordbooks or follow us on X @penswordbooks

You can also view our products at www.pen-and-sword.co.uk (UK and ROW) or www.penandswordbooks.com (North America).

To keep up to date with our latest releases and online catalogues, please sign up to our newsletter at: www.pen-and-sword.co.uk/newsletter

If you would like a printed catalogue with our latest books, then please email: enquiries@pen-and-sword.co.uk or telephone: 01226 734555 (UK and ROW) or email: uspen-and-sword@casematepublishers.com or telephone: (610) 853-9131 (North America).

We respect your privacy and we will only use personal information to send you information about our products.

Thank you!